Child and Adolescent Mental Health

Child and Adolescent Mental Health

EDITED BY
Usha S. Nayar

Los Angeles | London | New Delhi
Singapore | Washington DC | Melbourne

Copyright © Usha S. Nayar, 2012

All rights reserved. No part of this book may be reproduced or utilized in any form or by any means, electronic or mechanical, including photocopying, recording, or by any information storage or retrieval system, without permission in writing from the publisher.

First published in 2012 by

SAGE Publications India Pvt Ltd
B1/I-1 Mohan Cooperative Industrial Area
Mathura Road, New Delhi 110 044, India
www.sagepub.in

SAGE Publications Inc
2455 Teller Road
Thousand Oaks, California 91320, USA

SAGE Publications Ltd
1 Oliver's Yard, 55 City Road
London EC1Y 1SP, United Kingdom

SAGE Publications Asia-Pacific Pte Ltd
3 Church Street
#10-04 Samsung Hub
Singapore 049483

Published by Vivek Mehra for SAGE Publications India Pvt Ltd, typeset in 11/14pt Adobe Garamond Pro by Diligent Typesetter, Delhi.

Library of Congress Cataloging-in-Publication Data Available

ISBN: 978-93-532-8731-3 (PB)

The SAGE Team: Shambhu Sahu, Puja Narula Nagpal, Rajib Chatterjee, and Dally Verghese

*This book is dedicated to my students around the world
who have inspired me to think deeply about the emotional richness
in young people's lives and to my daughter Priya through whom I could learn
and live the joys of being young.*

Thank you for choosing a SAGE product!
If you have any comment, observation or feedback,
I would like to personally hear from you.

Please write to me at **contactceo@sagepub.in**

Vivek Mehra, Managing Director and CEO, SAGE India.

Bulk Sales

SAGE India offers special discounts
for purchase of books in bulk.
We also make available special imprints
and excerpts from our books on demand.

For orders and enquiries, write to us at

Marketing Department
SAGE Publications India Pvt Ltd
B1/I-1, Mohan Cooperative Industrial Area
Mathura Road, Post Bag 7
New Delhi 110044, India

E-mail us at **marketing@sagepub.in**

Subscribe to our mailing list
Write to **marketing@sagepub.in**

This book is also available as an e-book.

Contents

List of Tables — xi
List of Illustrations — xiii
List of Abbreviations — xv
Foreword by Marta Santos Pais — xvii
Preface — xix
Acknowledgments — xxv

SECTION 1: ECONOMICS — 1

1. Responding to Scarcity: Understanding Costs and Cost-effectiveness — 3
   Martin Knapp and David McDaid

SECTION 2: CLINICAL CASE STUDIES — 19

2. Childhood and Adolescent Depression — 21
   Raman Deep Pattanayak and Manju Mehta

3. Suicidality among Children and Adolescents: Complexities and Challenges — 39
   Latha Nrugham and Vandana Varma Prakash

SECTION 3: SPECIAL CONTEXTS — 55

4. Impact of HIV/AIDS on the Mental Health of Children and Adolescents in India — 57
   Shankar Das, Ashima Das, and George Leibowitz

5. Youngsters, Antisociality, and Violence: The Case of Norway — 75
   Ragnhild Bjørnebekk

6. Mental Health for the Media Generation: Balancing Coping and Riskiness — 96
   Usha S. Nayar, Ingunn Hagen, Priya Nayar, and Dan Y. Jacobsen

SECTION 4: SCHOOLS AND SCHOOL CLIMATE — 113

7. Are Schools Injurious to Health? The Implicit Curriculum and Its Relation to Mental Health — 115
   Matthijs Cornelissen

8. Mental Health of Urban School-going Children in India — 130
   Neharika Vohra and Esha Patnaik

9. Resilience and Resourcefulness of Disadvantaged Children: Lotus in the Mud — 142
   Ajit K. Dalal

SECTION 5: CHILD WELFARE — 157

10. Family Group Conferencing: Engaging the Family Culture for Improved Children's Mental Health Outcomes — 159
    Jeanette Schmid

11. Behavioral Parent Training with Abusive Parents — 174
    Patricia L. Kohl

12. From Institutionalization to Family Settings: Rethinking Practices for Children and Youth with Mental Disabilities in Brazil — 188
    Irene Rizzini and Neli de Almeida

13. Child Welfare and Children's Mental Health Needs in the Context of Development: An Integrated (South African) Approach — 200
    Jeanette Schmid

SECTION 6: INTERVENTIONS AND INNOVATIVE PRACTICES — 217

14. Effect of Yoga on Mental Health in Children — 219
    Shirley Telles

15. Raga Therapy: Power of Music to Alleviate Academic Stress in Adolescents — 227
    Vandana Sharma and Mamta Sharma

16. Cultivating the Capacity to Care in Children and Youth: Implications from EI Theory, EI Self, and BEVI — 240
    Craig N. Shealy, Devi Bhuyan, and Lee G. Sternberger

17. Research on Child Poverty and Development from a Cognitive Neuroscience Perspective: Examples of Studies in Argentina — 256
    Sebastián Javier Lipina, María Soledad Segretin, María Julia Hermida, and Jorge Augusto Colombo

18. Countering the Rush to Medication: Psychodynamic, Intergenerational, and Cultural Considerations in Understanding Children's Psychic Distress ... 275
Michael O'Loughlin

SECTION 7: COUNTRY FOCUS—STATUS, POLICIES, AND CHILDREN'S VOICES ... **289**

19. Family Structure in Ireland and Child Emotional and Behavioral Outcomes ... 291
Maeve Thornton

20. Child and Adolescent Mental Health in Chile and Latin America ... 308
Helia Molina, Paula Bedregal, and Maria Paz Guzman

21. Children's Voices in the Psychologist's Office: Contributions about Mental Health from Peru ... 325
Beatriz Oré and Martín Benavides

22. Mental Health of Children and Adolescents in Contemporary India ... 337
Usha S. Nayar and Shankar Das

About the Editor and Contributors ... 351
Index ... 354

List of Tables

2.1	Prevalence of Depressive Disorders	23
2.2	Depressive Symptoms at Different Developmental Stages	27
2.3	Summary of Interventions for Childhood and Adolescent Depression	34
4.1	HIV/AIDS Statistics: India	59
4.2	Impact of AIDS on Children	61
12.1	Number of Shelters that Reported Caring for Children With or Without Disability, and Vacancies by Region in the State of Rio de Janeiro, 2006/2007	191
12.2	Children with Disabilities in Specialized Shelters According to Most Frequently Registered Diagnosis 2007 (n = 10)	193
15.1	Learning Expectations at Different Grade Levels	229
15.2	Pre- and Post-scores on Subscales of Frequency Dimension of the Academic Stress Scale	236
15.3	Pre- and Post-scores on Subscales of Quantity Dimension of the Academic Stress Scale	236
17.1	Description of Programs 1 and 2	263
17.2	Cognitive Battery Administered at Stages 1 and 3 in Program 1	264
17.3	Cognitive Battery Administered at Stages 1 and 3 in Program 2	267
19.1	Effects of Family Type, Socioeconomic Factors, and Family Environment on Emotional and Behavioral Outcomes in Families with a Female Primary Caregiver	299
19.2	Effects of Family Type and Socioeconomic Factors and Family Environment on Emotional and Behavioral Outcomes in Families Headed by Two Parents	300
20.1	Determinants of Health in Selected Latin-American Countries	312

List of Illustrations

2.1	An Eight-year-old Girl's Drawing Depicting Herself in a DAP Test	33
4.1	Problems among Children and Families Affected by HIV/AIDS	64
4.2	Intervention for Infected and Affected Children and Adolescents	69
6.1	Roles of Media Mediators for Children's Media Use	100
6.2	A Framework to Guide the Media Generation	106
7.1	Neatly Ordered Desks with Each Child Behind a Desk and the Teacher in Front of the Classroom	117
7.2	All Children in the Teacher's Line of Vision	117
9.1	Educational Resourcefulness Model	149
16.1	The EI Self	245
22.1	Steps for Developing an effective National Child and Adolescent Mental Health Policy	345
22.2	Elements for a Mental Health Policy for Children and Adolescents in India	347

List of Abbreviations

ACTH	Adrenocorticotrophic Hormone
ADD	Attention Deficit Disorder
ADHD	Attention Deficit Hyperactivity Disorder
ADR	Alternative Dispute Resolution
ASQ	Ages and Stages Questionnaire
BEVI	Beliefs, Events, and Values Inventory
BPC	*Benefício de Prestação Continuada*
BPT	Behavioral Parent Training
CAPA	Child and Adolescent Psychiatric Assessment
CAPI	Computer Assisted Personal Interview
CAT	Children's Apperception Test
CBO	Community Based Organizations
CBT	Cognitive Behavior Therapy
CDRS	Childhood Depression Rating Scale
CEA	Cost-Effectiveness Analysis
CES-D	Center for Epidemiological Studies Depression Scale
CGAS	Children's Global Assessment Scale
CIDI-A	Composite International Diagnostic Interview-Automated
CRH	Corticotrophin-Releasing Hormone
CSO	Central Statistics Office
CUA	Cost-utility Analysis
DALY	Disability Adjusted Life Year
DAP	Draw-a-Person
DAS	Dyadic Adjustment Scale
DAWBA	Development and Well-Being Assessment
DBT	Dialectical Behavior Therapy
DICA	Diagnostic Interview for Children and Adolescents
DISC	Diagnostic Interview Schedule for Children

DSM	Diagnostic and Statistical Manual of Mental Disorders
DSW	Developmental Social Welfare
EFA	Exploratory Factor Analysis
EI	Equilintegration
ERP	Event Related Potential
FGC	Family Group Conferencing
HAART	Highly Active Antiretroviral Therapy
HDI	Human Development Index
IBGE	Instituto Brasileiro de Geografia e Estatistica
IDCW	Integrated Developmental Child Welfare
IIT	Indian Institute of Technology
IPT	Interpersonal Therapy
JUNAEB	Junta Nacional de Auxilio Escolar y Becas
K-SADS-PL	Kiddie Schedule of Affective Disorders and Schizophrenia for School-Age Children—Present and Lifetime
MBCT	Mindfulness Based Cognitive Therapy
MTCT	Mother-to-Child Transmission
NACO	National AIDS Control Organization
NICE	National Institute for Health and Clinical Excellence
NIMH	National Institute of Mental Health
NIMHANS	National Institute of Mental Health and Neurosciences
ODD	Oppositional Defiant Disorder
PAPA	Preschool Age Psychiatric Assessment
PCIT	Parent–Child Interaction Therapy
PLHA	People Living with HIV/AIDS
PMTCT	Prevention of Mother-to-Child Transmission
PTE	Peer Treatment Education
PTSD	Post-traumatic Stress Disorder
QALY	Quality Adjusted Life Year
RAD	Reactive Attachment Disorder
rTMS	Repetitive Transcranial Magnetic Stimulation
SDQ	Strengths and Difficulties Questionnaire
SFL	Skills for Life
SSRI	Selective Serotonin Reuptake Inhibitor
STEP	Systematic Training for Effective Parenting
UBN	Unsatisfied Basic Needs
WHO	World Health Organization

Foreword

This important publication presents a thoughtful and most informative collection of insightful essays and research articles on the mental health and well-being of children and adolescents. The study helps to gain a deeper understanding of the changing landscape of this critical dimension of children's rights, providing a multifaceted perspective across disciplines; socioeconomic, political, and cultural environments; and recognizing young people's crucial role in leading productive and confident lives.

Placing the child at the center of its concerns, the study addresses the evolving notion of childhood and its complexities, vulnerable to tension, stress, fear, stigma, anxiety, and violence; and at the same time also deeply resourceful, resilient, and creative in overcoming difficulties and influencing action as an agent of change.

The study emphasizes the critical role of the family, of care-givers, and of professional services in the prevention and treatment of children's mental health problems. But it also reminds us of the risks of pressure, stress, violence, and abuse these institutions may provoke, and the opportunity of empowering and supporting parents and other relevant actors in the promotion of positive and reassuring child-rearing practices.

The protection of children from violence—including physical, emotional, or psychological—is a fundamental right that the international community has solemnly committed to safeguard, for all children, everywhere and at all times. The Convention on the Rights of the Child, the most widely ratified human rights treaty, remains a decisive reference in this regard. Yet, in contrast with this strong ethical and normative foundation, violence remains a harsh reality for millions of children around the world, and children's mental health needs an often neglected area of concern.

Violence jeopardizes a child's development, learning abilities, and school performance; it inhibits positive relationships, provokes low self-esteem, emotional distress, anxiety, and depression; and at times it leads to risk taking, self-harm, and aggressive behavior, including suicide. Although of epidemic proportions, and with lifelong consequences on children's health and development, and on nations' human capital and social progress, violence against children remains hidden and socially condoned; it is largely perceived as a social taboo and a legitimate form of discipline; and it is seldom reported with official statistics hardly capturing its magnitude and incidence.

Psychosocial support in a child-sensitive and culturally sensitive way is critical to assist children in their healing and recovery, and in promoting a supportive environment that fosters their self-respect and dignity. This is, however, an area where many challenges and gaps persist. This publication on the mental health concerns of children and adolescents is a critical step to fill this important knowledge gap.

Sound research and relevant, objective, and disaggregated child-related data are indispensable to understand the environment within which children grow and develop, and to promote children's personality, talents and abilities to their fullest. Sound evidence enables governments to take the right decisions at the right time, and it is indispensable for the transparent and accurate assessment of progress in the protection of children's rights. This explains why the UN Study on Violence against Children presented significant recommendations in this area; and also why the consolidation of research and evidence constitutes a priority for my mandate as Special Representative of the Secretary-General on Violence against Children.

I am confident that this important publication will help consolidate and bring together knowledge and good practice, and will bolster public awareness and commitment to the prevention and elimination of violence and to addressing the mental health needs of children and adolescents. With strong commitment and empowered with knowledge and renewed understanding, we can build a world free from violence, a world where all children, wherever they may live, can truly develop to their fullest potential.

Marta Santos Pais
Special Representative of the United Nations Secretary-General
on Violence against Children

Preface

After almost a century of trying to place childhood as different from adulthood, child development specialists have finally reached a plateau where the differences are highlighted and remain exclusive. Children and adolescents have evolving capacities. They have competencies and perceptions different from adults when faced with the same situations or are placed in the same context. Moreover, like adults, children and adolescents are not homogeneous. There are some children and adolescents more vulnerable than other. Children growing up with poor infrastructures, material deprivations, and related poverty conditions; children infected and affected by HIV/AIDS and living with specific mental disabilities; and children living with abusive families; children going to schools where they face mistreatment and discriminatory practices are at extra risk of physical, mental, and emotional stress. If vulnerable children do not have supportive, stable families and access to creative and communicative schools with child-friendly curricula, teachers, staff, and peers, the risk of experiencing multiple levels of emotional burdens increases.

This book is a personal and professional journey of understanding mental health concerns of children and adolescents. I have had the privilege of visiting schools in various countries and of meeting and interacting with young people from disadvantaged as well as privileged backgrounds. In sharing their experiences of growing up with me, they have given me the opportunity to understand both their pleasant and unpleasant painful experiences. The latter are often due to their inability to meet expectations of families and school systems. I can say with conviction that everywhere, all that children seek is a nurturing environment to develop themselves, their self-confidence, and identity.

In my long innings of teaching courses like International Perspectives on Child Development, International Social Policy, Human Development and Human Diversity I have had intriguing discussions on the situation of children and adolescents with the students, which has motivated me to work on this pressing theme. In the course of my academic career, I have examined policies of different countries and worked with governmental agencies and not-for-profit organizations to give the voices of our young people a space, a strong push to make change happen. By focusing excessively and sometimes exclusively on their physical needs, we forget—regretfully—that to lead productive and creative lives in today's competitive world, their mental energy and emotional stability are of paramount importance.

To me, the study of children and adolescent development requires the dissolution of steadfast disciplinary boundaries to encourage creative thinking among professionals, policy planners, and practitioners. In the following pages, psychologists, psychoanalysts, medical professionals, educationists, social work professionals, sociologists, economists, media specialists, and child activists weave their knowledge around the development of children in contemporary society. They highlight the necessary conversations that schools, families, communities, individuals, and nation-states need to have, and most importantly the responsibility for everyone to develop an understanding of the mental health needs of our new generation. It is important to understand the sources of tensions, stresses, fears, and anxieties among the new generation as well as find solutions which are child-centered and rights-based.

There are many questions raised here—some for which solutions are possible, others that need further investigation. Are our current service institutions like health and education adding to the stresses of children and adolescents? In what way do changing family structures challenge children to face the stresses both inside and outside the family? What are the missing links for effective communication between school and family for the best mental health of children and adolescents? Is it possible to train parents toward best practices in parenting and child-rearing to facilitate the holistic development of children? Is it possible to persuade countries about the economic advantage of investing in proactive mental services for children and adolescents than leaving the next generation without or inadequate support when they are growing up in today's challenging diverse environments?

In this book, experts and scholars from different parts of the world, affiliated to well-known academic, policy and practice institutions and sometimes competing point of views share their cutting edge knowledge and insights on mental health of children and adolescents. They analyze complex and changing socioeconomic, political, and cultural environments within which children and adolescents live and try to deconstruct the impact it may have on their mental health and well-being. The book takes into account that the everyday experiences and challenges of the current generation of children and adolescents are not just different, but at times even contrary to those of their parents and grandparents. Social interactions and negotiations of children and adolescents with members of their families, peers, neighborhood, teachers, and society are unique in this 21st century—a consequence of inhabiting a multicultural society, being active participants in an information and communication technology revolution, and entitled to age-appropriate rights as per the United Nations Convention on the Rights of the Child.

The 22 chapters in this book are presented in seven sections. What follows is an overview of the chapters, which by no means is an exhaustive summary of what to expect.

Section 1 relevantly begins with discussion on cost and cost-effectiveness. **Martin Knapp** and **David McDaid** describe how arguments and empirical techniques developed by economists can be applied to inform and assist decisions about the allocation of resources to and within child and adolescent mental health systems. The authors bring out some of the economic consequences of mental health problems both in childhood and later in life to demonstrate the breadth of impact. They introduce two key criteria in resource allocation—efficiency and equity—and thereafter describe how economists examine for such an analysis and comment on work undertaken to date in the child and adolescent mental health field.

Section 2 presents clinical case studies that relate to depression and suicide that form a very serious phenomenon among young people. **Raman Deep Pattanayak** and **Manju Mehta** reiterate that depression in childhood and adolescence is yet to be recognized as a concern in countries like India. They emphasize the need for early diagnosis and focus on early interventions by using integrative methods of relaxation, yoga, behavior modification, and involvement of significant others in the family. **Latha Nrugham** and **Vandana Prakash** further explore the mental health dimensions relating to children and adolescent suicides and particularly the solutions and policy-oriented approaches with reference to "suicidality." Case vignettes from India reveal that although cultural contexts differ from the Western nations, certain identifiable and manageable psychosocial constructs related to suicidality remain the same. Guidelines for the clinical assessment of suicide risk among adolescents and adults exist on the foundations of research findings of statistically significant risk factors. Further, the authors emphasize that assessing risk of suicide is one of the most complex and intricate tasks within mental health and a part of emergency care.

Section 3 includes special contexts relating to physical health and violence and risk behaviors. **Shankar Das**, **Ashima Das**, and **George Leibowitz** address the serious issue of vulnerability of children with HIV/AIDS. The chapter discusses micro- and macro-level interventions. The authors also recommend further research to reduce the stigma and discrimination of children and adolescents infected and affected by HIV endemic. **Ragnhild Bjørnebekk** provides an interesting account to view antisociality among youngsters where there are safe communities and supportive family structures and where state's social policies are also proactive to bring up children and adolescents in what may be considered a healthy manner. The analysis of the situation and the programs developed to help the children and youth in dealing with their mental health issues is a useful document to understand and disseminate. **Usha S. Nayar**, **Ingunn Hagen**, and **Priya Nayar**, and **Dan Y. Jacobsen** highlight the massive presence of media and media use. The time spent using media technologies by children are clear indicators that there is a shift in the lifestyles and priorities for the new generation. We emphasize that although the importance may vary depending on social class, culture, and geographical regions, new media are so integrated in young people's lives that they ought to be considered as a valuable resource to promote mental health. This chapter examines healthy media use during childhood and adolescence and the potential parameters that may help define the boundaries better.

Section 4 brings our attention to schools and school climate that account for a substantial part of children's every day. **Matthijs Cornelissen** discusses the impact of the school environment on the mental health of children and adolescents. The implicit curriculum of schools and the way it is transacted breeds anxiety and other unhealthy effects on children. **Neharika Vohra** and **Esha Patnaik** further indicate that the pressure on students toward higher achievement goals comes from their parents as well as the school system at large; the increasing number of cases of depression and attempt to suicide are often a result of this dual pressure. **Ajit K. Dalal** highlights the resilience and resourcefulness of children from marginalized communities and the potential of using the resources they have, effectively, for optimum mental health. However, the resourcefulness approach demands a shift in educational policies that tend to favor deficiency and perpetuate the notion of vulnerability, and support for remedial interventions that develop strength.

Section 5 focuses on child welfare at home and issues relating to caregiving. **Jeanette Schmid** details family group conferencing as a culturally sensitive approach. In this method of intervention family networks are key to decision-making processes and privileges. **Patricia L. Kohl** highlights the parent-mediated interventions that clearly establish the reduction of child behavior problems. She outlines a plan to increase availability of such interventions within the system of care for children in the US. **Irene Rizzini** and **Neli de Almeida** argue that children and youth with mental disabilities are even more vulnerable in institutional settings. Besides citing numerous laws and policies, Rizzini and Almeida describe the actual problems that occur in institutional settings and convincingly put forward their case in choosing more caring settings of family and communities as the first critical step for shaping a right-based public policy. **Jeanette Schmidt** in her chapter writes that the model focusing exclusively on child development has created difficulties in responding to the needs of vulnerable children in South Africa. She further brings out that this is not only true to South Africa but this model also poses difficulties to apply in contexts where mass poverty, AIDS, and significant violence affect families. The author proposes an alternative model called Integrated Developmental Child Welfare Model (IDCWM). The goal in this model is to build naturally occurring helping systems to strengthen the families and communities to face adversity and challenges of structural inequalities.

Section 6 is an emphasis on action and innovative practices. **Shirley Telles** indicates that specific faculties such as spatial memory in delayed recall task, and performance in tasks involving strategic planning and selective and sustained attention, improve with yoga. There was also better performance in tasks for perception and motor skills. Yoga also has beneficial effects in the management of anxiety, eating disorders, attention deficit, and hyperactivity disorder and post-traumatic stress disorder (PTSD). However, there are challenges in researching the direct effects of yoga practice in children. **Vandana Sharma** and **Mamta Sharma** write about their experiments and the power of music to alleviate academic stress amongst adolescents. These writings bring to the fore approaches hitherto viewed as "alternative" and may be considered as mainstream solutions and interventions in addressing mental health concerns. The primacy of pharmaceutical solutions is challenged by these approaches. **Craig N. Shealy**, **Devi Bhuyan**, and **Lee G. Sternberger** start the discussion by asking two pertinent questions:

- First, how do we inculcate in our children not only a set of attributes that are associated with mental health, but the associated capacity to experience a sense of caring for oneself, others and the larger world?
- Second, what are the implications of the empirically demonstrable fact that our capacity for caring and our concomitant beliefs about the "other" are highly correlated with how we ourselves were cared for and experienced by others during our own developmental process?

Lipina, **Segretin**, **Hermida**, and **Colombo** in their chapter explain the contributions of neuroscience research through two multi-modular intervention designed programs which were carried out with samples of healthy 3–5 year-olds from low-income homes in two different districts in Argentina. It was revealed that development of the cognitive systems related to control, numeracy, and literacy competencies show plasticity during brain organization and the insights stemming from neuro-restorative strategies were applicable to the optimization of cognitive, emotional, and learning skills in both biologically and socially vulnerable populations. **Michael O'Loughlin** offers significant illustrations of the power of psychoanalysis as a means of treatment through social analysis, taking a particular case in point the enhancement of the psychic wellness of children. He emphasizes the limitations of following the Western psychiatric model of understanding distress among children from a biological basis and consequently the medicalization of mental disorders.

Finally **Section 7** looks at specific countries that highlight child-centric policies, status, and/or children's perspectives. The discourse on mental health issues in a local environment and their solutions provide learning lessons for others that may share partial contexts. For me this signifies the idea of shared critical differences across national boundaries when it comes to understanding and resolving mental health concerns of our new generation. A case in point is **Maeve Thornton's** chapter in which data from the first phase of *Growing Up in Ireland—The National Longitudinal Study of Children* is presented. The chapter has demonstrated that some of the main family-related factors associated with psychological difficulties in children include family type (living in reconstituted family after divorce of parents), mother's education, social class, and welfare assistance. **Helia Molina**, **Paula Bedregal**, and **Maria Paz Guzman** present specific child and adolescent mental health issues in Chile and Latin America. Evidences that promote early child mental health for children below 4 years of age and Skills for Life (SFL) Program for the ages 4–9 have resulted in a valuable contribution to mental health of children. **Beatriz Oré** and **Martín Benavides** highlight the association of poverty and poor mental health of children in Peru. The project in the district of Lima brings forth the value of listening to children in identifying as well as suggesting solutions to their mental health issues. **Usha S. Nayar** and **Shankar Das** bring out various levels of mental health programs and policies for children and adolescents in a diverse country like India. Since the mental health policy in India is currently being revised, I believe this is a timely analysis for inputs to improvise keeping the young populations' mental health concerns in focus and on priority.

As we understand from the above discussions, children and adolescents are growing up in a very complex world. Not only are there many violations of child rights and human rights but our children also face poverty, lack of educational opportunity, harmful schooling, abusive parenting, change in family structures, unsafe neighborhoods, violence, discriminations due to caste, class, gender, disability, HIV/AIDS, race, nationality, language, religion, and so on. At the same time, they are also experiencing the revolution of information and communication technology that gives them access to social networking sites with their peers and others globally. Internet and related powerful tools of communication have provided them a different kind of solidarity with their peers and has changed their perception of power and impact on their lives. It is a hard act to balance emotional stresses, competitions, confusions, and conflicts with rising democracy, freedom, wonders of world with new technology and extraordinary opportunities and choices to realize their dreams. In my opinion these new perspectives serve as a platform for further discussions and study; they also serve as a point to understand that the practices required for dealing with mental health concerns of children and adolescents indicate that any single discipline is likely to be meager and may fall short in terms of really helping the whole child. Any promising, real and tangible solutions can only emerge from the kind of multiple efforts that this book embodies.

The book is an attempt to outline the shift in perspective for mental health of children and adolescents. It clearly brings out that the landscape of mental health of children and adolescents is changing. First, in the manner in which children and adolescents are viewed by society as well as experts due to child rights perspective. The voices of children are important. Children do experience and respond differently from adults when they are in similar challenging situations. Children are constantly evolving and therefore are to be understood in local and global contexts. Second, any one discipline is too narrow to understand the mental health needs of children and adolescents and their consequences. For approaches to be most relevant for this group they have to emerge across disciplines and contexts. This book offers a range of perspectives and possibilities that can shape the well-being of children and adolescents—holistically and harmoniously.

Acknowledgments

I would like to express my sincere thanks to each and every contributor—this journey with you all has been truly synergistic and enriching. I am thankful to reviewers for their creative feedback. My deep gratitude to Marta Santos Pais, Special Representative of the United Nations Secretary-General on Violence against Children, who was able to find time in her many travels around the world to write the Foreword. My special thanks to Professor S. Parasuraman, Director, Tata Institute of Social Sciences, Mumbai, for providing vital support for the preparation of this book and to the members of the Research Council for its facilitation. Librarian K. Muttayya and the staff of the Sir Dorabji Tata Memorial Library of the Institute have given me willing assistance whenever I needed it—I am thankful to them. My heartfelt thanks to Beena Choksi, par excellence copy editor and now a trusted friend. I appreciate the encouragement I received from Michael A. Cohen, Director and Professor, Graduate Program in International Affairs, The New School University, New York, USA. I am grateful to SAGE Publications for their constant cooperation, especially, Rekha Natarajan, Payal Kumar, and their teams!

Thank you, thank you, thank you all!

Usha S. Nayar
Editor

SECTION 1

Economics

1

Responding to Scarcity: Understanding Costs and Cost-effectiveness

Martin Knapp
David McDaid

Introduction

No matter what society's good intentions may be to promote the mental health of children and adolescents, one incontrovertible fact of life is the pervasive scarcity of resources. There never will be enough resources to meet all needs or to satisfy all preferences. Consequently, difficult choices have to be taken about how to use the resources that are available. For example, if there are more children and adolescents needing to see specialist staff than there are treatment sessions available, who should get priority? Which treatment type should be offered to a child and family with a particular set of needs and circumstances? What proportion of a mental health budget should be diverted away from treating identified needs in order to uncover previously unrecognized needs? What should be the balance between prevention and "cure?" How should available resources be allocated between different medical specialties, or between (say) the health, education and housing systems?

In this chapter we describe how arguments and empirical techniques developed by economists can be applied to inform and assist decisions about the allocation of resources to and within child and adolescent mental health systems. We describe some of the economic consequences of mental health problems, both in childhood and later in life, to demonstrate the breadth of impact. We introduce two key criteria in resource allocation—efficiency and equity—and thereafter describe how economists examine these through *cost-effectiveness analysis* (CEA). We set out the main ingredients for such an analysis and comment on work undertaken to date in the child and adolescent mental health field. We then illustrate some of the ways in which economic evaluative evidence is being used in health and related systems today to inform efficiency-based decision making. Subsequently, we look at barriers to such utilization and draw some broad conclusions.

Costs

Childhood Economic Implications

Child and adolescent mental health problems have economic implications whether or not they are recognized and treated. When treatment is offered, there would be costs associated with health, education, social work or other service utilization, and in well-developed mental health systems this multiplicity of contacts is a common, indeed welcome, feature (Glied & Cuellar, 2003). On the other hand, if mental health needs are not recognized or treated appropriately, there could still be economic implications, since young people might have problems with educational engagement and attainment, or—as adults—might have difficulties with employment and income later. There could also be substantial detrimental effects of untreated morbidity on families.

One study in London illustrates the immediate (short-term) economic implications of mental health problems in childhood. Romeo, Knapp, and Scott (2006) looked at 80 children aged three to eight with severe antisocial behavior referred to child and adolescent mental health services. Although recently referred, these children and their families were using several services as a result of their antisocial behavior (in the health, education, and social care sectors), but the non-service costs to families (principally from lost income because parents had to cut back their employment) were larger.

The extent to which the economic consequences of childhood or adolescent mental health problems fall outside the health sector, or fall to families, would vary from country to country, depending on availability of treatments, how the boundaries between service systems are configured, and cultural contexts. A general point to emphasize, however, is that many young people with mental health problems have needs in multiple life domains, and each of these needs could have economic ramifications. Too often, unfortunately, decisions about treatment and care are taken in system-specific "silos" with little attempt to gain an overarching strategic view or to coordinate action (Glied & Cuellar, 2003). Professional rivalry, myopic budget protection, performance assessment regimes or simply slow bureaucratic processes are among the barriers. Yet coordinated action can pay off. Foster and Connor (2005) found that delivering child and adolescent mental health services as part of a system-of-care approach, while more expensive than standard services, reduced expenditure in other sectors (juvenile justice, child welfare, special education, inpatient services).

Adulthood Economic Implications

Mental health problems experienced in childhood or adolescence can have long-term adverse effects on psychosocial outcomes such as relationships, crime and substance misuse, and on quality of life. Some of these later effects have economic consequences. Studies that have explored the connections between childhood disorders and adulthood economic consequences point to unusually high utilization rates of health and other services in adulthood, links between behavioral problems and later criminal activities, and often very marked impacts related to employment (such as not being employed, or being frequently absent, or earning lower wages). For example, Scott, Knapp, Henderson, and Maughan (2001) described how conduct disorder at age 10 years (which was found for the most antisocial 3 percent of the London sample studied) and conduct problems (found for the next 9 percent) led to greatly elevated costs in adulthood (at around age 28) for a number of agencies, and especially for the criminal justice system.

Another English study looked at a large cohort of people born in one week in 1970, examining links between antisocial conduct, attention deficit and anxiety at age 10, and some employment-related consequences at age 30 (Knapp, King, Healey, & Thomas, 2011a). The effects of antisocial conduct on adult labor market outcomes were complex. Males with antisocial conduct at age 10 showed a higher probability of being unemployed at age 30 (after adjustment for other children and family factors), which was expected, but they also had *higher* earnings than those without such behavior. Attention deficit problems at age 10 were associated with lower employment rates, worse jobs, lower earnings if employed, and lower expected earnings overall at age 30 (for both males and females). Anxiety problems were associated with lower earnings.

The fact that childhood mental health problems are strongly linked to higher service utilization and costs in adolescence, at least into early adulthood, and also to adverse employment-related experiences 20 years later, should encourage more effort to be made to explore earlier detection and intervention to head off these negative outcomes for children, their families and wider society.

Efficiency and Equity

Scarcity of resources means that hard decisions always have to be taken about what to fund, what to deliver, to whom, over what time period, and so on. A number of objectives might underpin such difficult decisions, such as trying to maximize the impact of therapeutic services, integrating more children with behavioral problems into mainstream education, broadening access to evidence-based medications or parenting programs, improving fairness in what financial contributions families are required to pay for treatment, improving the targeting of services on assessed needs, and preventing needs emerging in the first place.

None of these is first and foremost an economic question, but each stems from the scarcity of resources relative to needs and wants. And each, therefore, generates questions about what resources get used and with what impacts (e.g., what needs are prevented, identified, treated or met), and those latter questions certainly are economic in nature. They concern the relationship between the resources used, the services or support arrangements provided, and the outcomes achieved for individuals, families, and society.

Consequently, decision makers—from those who control national or regional health or other budgets to those professionals who actually deliver the services to children and families—face difficult choices. They need to be clear about the basis upon which they choose one option over another. Two broad resource-related criteria often considered are efficiency and equity.

Efficiency

It means achieving the maximum impact from a given level of resources, or minimizing the resources needed to achieve a particular level of impact. In the child and adolescent mental health context, efficiency would most usefully be defined in terms of child and family outcomes achieved (such as needs met or quality of life improved) from a specified volume of resources (such as an available budget). Most mental health systems are inefficient. One reason is because key decision makers have little or no understanding of the relative costs and effectiveness of treatment options. This is where cost-effectiveness analyses can contribute so valuably.

Equity

This relates to the distribution of outcomes, access to services and payment for them. Most mental health systems are inequitable because they do not distribute these benefits and burdens fairly, but instead—wittingly or unwittingly—allow social, economic or underlying demographic characteristics to have an influence (or because they do not act to counter the negative consequences of random events). Hence, access to, payment for, or impact of evidence-based treatment might be unfairly distributed according to gender, ethnicity, age, language, religion, socioeconomic group, place of residence, or ability to pay.

Economic Evaluations

Defining Cost-Effectiveness

When considering whether to recommend, license, purchase or use a particular mental health intervention, decision makers are looking for answers to two questions. The first is what we can call the *effectiveness question*: Does it work? That is, is the intervention effective in alleviating behavioral, emotional or other symptoms, and more generally is it able to improve quality of life? If the answer to this effectiveness question is "yes," then there is a second question: Is it worth it? That is, does the intervention achieve the improved outcomes at a cost worth paying? This latter is the *cost-effectiveness question*. The meaning of the word "worth" in the *cost-effectiveness question* is not necessarily straightforward. One reason is because the question must be set in context. Decision makers need to ask whether the intervention is worth it—not in some absolute sense—but in comparison with what other options there might be. We discuss the meaning of worth in more detail later.

These two questions define an economic evaluation. The main ingredients when thinking about cost-effectiveness, and particularly when conducting a formal analysis, are:

- Two or more treatments or interventions or policies that are being compared, including the option of doing nothing;
- Outcomes of each of them, measured in terms of (say) changes in symptoms and quality of life over time; and
- Associated costs of each, measured in terms of health system resources used to deliver the interventions and perhaps also some measure of the wider resource implications.

An evaluation that has all of these ingredients can provide decision makers with relevant insights into efficiency and, in some respects, also equity. An analysis that misses one or more of these ingredients, for example, one that looks only at comparative outcomes and ignores costs, or stacks up the costs of different policy options without assessing the outcome implications, might still be useful, but it "cannot" provide evidence on efficiency.

Cost-effectiveness evaluations come in different forms, as we describe below, but they have a lot in common. They share a common approach to the conceptualization, definition, and measurement of costs. They tend to differ in how they define and assess outcomes, and this is primarily because they seek to answer slightly different policy or practice questions. In the subsections that follow, we therefore describe the different questions that a cost-effectiveness study might address, and then turn to the measurement of costs and outcomes. The key ingredient is to understand how trade-offs are made between costs and outcomes. Two further subsections examine the slightly more technical issues of utility and benefit measurement, both of which are becoming increasingly relevant, not just in how health economic evaluations are conducted, but also in how decision makers utilize the evidence that is generated.

Question and Perspective

If the question to be addressed by an economic evaluation is about improving health in a particular clinical context—for example, what is the most appropriate treatment for a child with particular mental health needs in particular family circumstances—then information will be needed on the comparative costs of the different treatments available, including the option of not treating at all, and the comparative outcomes (measured in terms of symptom alleviation, improved functioning and quality of life and so on). A CEA would then be an appropriate type of economic evaluation (see the subsection on effectiveness measurement).

The decision maker's question might actually be broader: they might need to choose whether to treat more children with behavioral or emotional problems rather than spending the funds elsewhere in the health system, say in pediatrics or cardiology. The decision maker would then need to know the costs of each of the different options—just as they did for the previous question—but now they need an outcome measure that allows them to compare the impact of treating behavioral or emotional problems with treatment in the pediatrics or cardiology fields. For this comparison they need a common metric that has validity across different health domains. The most common metric employed in health economics is a generic measure of "utility" or a measure of overall disability, and the type of analysis now conducted is sometimes called a *cost-utility analysis* (CUA). We discuss utility measurement later in a devoted subsection.

An even wider decision-making perspective would be to ask whether it is better to increase expenditure in the health system to allow more people to be treated or whether to spend more money on (say) improving school education or to invest in a country's transport infrastructure. In this case, the decision maker again needs information on the comparative costs and impacts of the different options, but they now need an even broader measure of "impact," one that is relevant across each of these public policy areas. The usual choice for such a broad impact measure is money, leading to a form of evaluation that health economists call *cost–benefit analysis*. We come back to these monetary benefit measures later.

Linked to the specification of the research response to the policy or practice question that is to be addressed is therefore the *perspective* to be taken. Is the evaluative information needed to help resource allocation within a particular agency (such as a child and adolescent mental health service), or within a particular system (such as the health care system or education system) or within a broader public policy or societal setting. The breadth of perspective would determine the breadth of both cost and outcome measurement.

Cost Measurement

Some costs are directly associated with a disorder or its treatment, such as the money spent on medications and other health services. Other costs are indirect, such as lost productivity because of ill-health or the family cost of unpaid care. How broadly the costs are measured would depend upon the purpose and perspective of the study. In the examples we gave earlier there were both direct and indirect costs. Romeo et al. (2006) reported that only 5 percent of the total cost associated with supporting children with persistent antisocial behavior was carried by the health service, with the remainder falling to schools (especially special education), social care agencies, community voluntary organizations, families (disrupted parental employment, household damage etc.), and the welfare benefits system. In one of the longitudinal studies we described, the much higher adulthood costs for people who as children had a conduct disorder fell mostly on the criminal justice system (Scott et al., 2001). In these illustrations the indirect costs were high.

When an evaluation is carried out, data is needed on the services that individuals use as well as on the impacts on families. Information on service use might come from organizational billing systems, which record amounts transferred between purchasers and providers for mental health and other services used by individual children or families, or alternatively might be collected specifically for the purposes of research through interviews with children, parents or service professionals. One instrument that has been widely used is the Client Service Receipt Inventory (Beecham & Knapp, 2001; Chisholm et al., 2000).

The next task is to attach unit cost estimates to these service use data. These are the average costs for units of provision, such as the cost per family per session of psychological therapy or the cost per child per day in an inpatient adolescent ward. In England, an annual compendium of health and social care unit costs readily provides these figures (Curtis, 2010). In most other countries, however, unit cost data are not routinely available and so it is usually necessary for the decision maker (or the research economist) to calculate unit costs anew.

When carrying out cost-effectiveness evaluations in the child and adolescent mental health field, the main cost categories that would need to be included in calculating a unit cost are as follows:

- Salaries of staff employed in prevention
- Treatment and care services
- Facility operating costs (e.g., cleaning, catering)
- Overhead costs (e.g., personnel, finance)
- Capital costs for buildings and durable equipment

Effectiveness Measurement

As we noted above, probably the most intuitively familiar type of economic evaluation is CEA which measures costs, as set out in the previous subsection, and measures outcomes along dimensions that would be immediately recognized by clinicians and other service professionals—such as changes in symptoms, behavior and functioning. A CEA can then help decision makers choose between interventions aimed at specific health needs, such as two different treatments for childhood depression. For each outcome measure in turn, a CEA computes and compares the difference in costs between two interventions and the difference in the outcome. If one intervention is both more effective and also less costly than its comparator, then it would clearly be seen as the more cost-effective of the two. But, if one intervention is both more effective and more costly than the other, then a trade-off has to be made (see the following subsection).

Usually there is more than one outcome that needs to be compared. The economist will then compute cost differences and a number of effectiveness differences, one for each relevant outcome dimension. This approach is sometimes called *cost-consequences analysis*. It has the advantage of breadth, but poses a challenge if one intervention is found to be better than the alternative intervention on one outcome measure but worse on another. It is then not immediately obvious which one of these two interventions is to be preferred, and a decision maker would need to weigh the strength of evidence, which inevitably introduces value judgments as to which outcome dimension(s) they believe to be of most importance. For this and other reasons, attempts have been made to find summary outcome measures that can range across all the dimensions (see the discussion on Utility).

Making Trade-offs

If an evaluation finds one intervention to be more effective but simultaneously more expensive than another intervention, which of them would be more cost-effective? A trade-off must be made between the better outcomes and the higher costs necessary to achieve them. The precise amount or threshold at which societies are willing to spend additional money for improved outcomes is a value judgment. It is not necessarily an arbitrary amount, but it is a value that comes from outside the evaluation context. The classical way of presenting the evidence from an economic evaluation so as to illustrate the nature of the trade-off is to calculate the *incremental cost-effectiveness ratio*. This ratio divides the extra cost associated with a new intervention by its additional effect. Health economists now employ the net benefit approach to explicate the nature of the trade-off. The point to emphasize is that there is no value-free scientific basis for trading off costs and outcomes: it is a question of someone (the decision maker somewhere in the system) deciding whether the better outcomes are *worth* the higher costs.

Utility Measurement

One way to overcome the potential problem of different outcome dimensions pointing in different directions is to employ a single, over arching measure. This is also the way to compare interventions in different diagnostic areas. Health economists have developed preference-weighted, health-related quality of life measures. The value of the quality of life improvement is gauged in units of utility, usually expressed by a combined index of the mortality and quality of life effects of an intervention. The best known such index is the Quality Adjusted Life Year (QALY). Values are elicited from the general public on the quality of life associated with different states of health, with 1 being time spent in perfect health and 0 representing death. In essence, the value of years of life lived is then adjusted to take account of the quality of life experienced during that time period. For instance, if living with severe depression is valued by the public as being 0.8 of time spent in full health then an additional 5 years of life lived with severe depression would be equivalent to 4 quality-adjusted life years.

A CUA then measures the outcome difference between two interventions in terms of QALY gain, and compares this with the difference in costs. CUAs have a number of attractions, including their use of a unidimensional, generic outcome measure that allows comparisons across diagnostic groups, based on an explicit methodology for weighting preferences and valuing health states. But the utility measure may be thought to be too reductionist and insufficiently sensitive to changes expected in some clinical areas. This has been argued to be the case in respect of some mental health treatments (Chisholm, Healy, & Knapp, 1997). Another outcome measure that endeavors to be valid across different health domains is the Disability Adjusted Life Year (DALY), which has been more widely employed than the QALY in low-income country evaluations. Cost-utility analyses produce estimates of cost per QALY gain from one therapy over another, which can then inform health care resource allocation decisions. We discuss this in the next section.

Monetary Benefits

Another approach to economic evaluation, cost–benefit analysis, values all costs and outcomes (benefits) in the same monetary units. If benefits exceed costs, the evaluation provides support for the intervention, and vice versa. With two or more alternatives, the intervention with the greatest net benefit (the monetary difference between outcomes and costs) would be deemed the more or most efficient.

Cost–benefit analyses are intrinsically attractive, as we noted earlier, because they can help decision makers to allocate resources across very different systems, for example, comparing investments in health care with those in housing, education or transport. There have been very few cost–benefit analyses of mental health care interventions because of the intrinsic difficulty of attaching monetary values to outcomes.

The Evidence Base

There are few completed economic evaluations in the child and adolescent mental health field, and even then some of the published studies are not very good in terms of quality, with methodological limitations such as small sample sizes and narrow cost measures. Romeo, Byford, and Knapp (2005) found only 14 published studies that could be described as economic evaluations. Five years later, Kilian, Losert, McDaid, Park, and Knapp (2010) found 21 cost-effectiveness studies in the child and adolescent mental health area (two on the topic of prevention and 19 on psychiatric or psychological interventions). Fourteen of these were based on new primary data collections and seven on simulation models, the latter focusing mainly on drug treatments and the former mainly on non-medical interventions. A further three modeling studies are described in Knapp, McDaid, and Parsonage (2011b), work that fed into the development of the new Mental Health Policy Strategy in England.

The small size of the evidence base about such a fundamental issue as the efficient way to use scarce resources is disappointing, and severely limits the information available to decision makers as they aim to make the best use of resources.

How can we judge the quality of these and other evaluations? Two immediate checks can be made, one in relation to costs and the other in relation to outcomes:

- *Have all the relevant costs been taken into account?* There can be many inputs to a mental health system broadly defined, including health, social care, education, housing, social security and other support. There are also other economic impacts, such as lost productivity, premature mortality and family burden. It might be necessary to measure all of these, depending on the policy or practice question that needs to be addressed and the perspective necessary for the evaluation.
- *Are all the dimensions of effectiveness taken into account?* Good mental health care is obviously not just about tackling clinical symptoms, but about improving young people's ability to function in ways that are valued by them (such as performing well at school and integrating with peers) and improving quality of life.

Most of the completed economic studies have been undertaken in North America, parts of Western Europe and Australia. But the results of economic evaluations often do not transfer well from one country or health/care system to another because of differences in structure, financing arrangements, incentives and relative price levels. There might also be differences in the appropriate choice of comparator—a new therapeutic approach might look attractive compared to current arrangements in one country but not in comparison to what is generally the norm elsewhere. It is infeasible and certainly unnecessary to carry out an evaluation every time a policy decision needs to be taken, but evidence-based decisions are generally thought to be better than evidence-free decisions. This could mean using the results from a study carried out in another country, or updating a previous study, or carrying out a modest adaptation to adjust for context.

Using Economic Evidence

As we have already noted, decision makers in health and related systems across the world are increasingly turning to economics for evidence to help inform, shape, and support their actions. We offer some brief examples here to illustrate how information on costs and cost-effectiveness evidence is being used.

Interest Group Lobbying and Marketing

Earlier in the chapter we described some of the cost impacts of child and adolescent mental health problems, and it has become common today, across the health field and across countries, to find studies that calculate the overall economic impact of a condition or disability. The aim of these so-called "cost-of-illness studies" is to add up the direct costs of treatment and support, together with the indirect costs of reduced productivity because of interrupted employment and the unpaid support provided by family members. Studies of this kind give lobbyists and advocacy groups the economic ammunition to argue the case for more attention and probably more resources to be allocated to improve prevention, treatment, and support.

A similar approach is often employed as a marketing strategy by pharmaceutical, medical devices, and other private sector companies. The aim again is to draw attention to what is considered to be a neglected set of needs, and in that way to encourage greater spending on meeting those unmet needs. In some countries there may be formal requirements, primarily for the manufacturers of new pharmaceuticals, to submit information on the cost-effectiveness of their medications to regulatory authorities (see the following subsection). Even where no such regulations exist, pharmaceutical companies may commission additional clinical and economic evidence to try to demonstrate that their product is both more effective and cost-effective than other available treatments. Consequently, economic evaluations sometimes get commissioned by companies for this purpose, some of them of good quality and some not. Of course, treatments that do not have proprietors, such as psychological therapies, may lose out in the battle to convince budget holders how and where to spend their money.

Policy Development and Monitoring

A major and growing use of economic evidence is in the formulation and monitoring of policy, and this has been a core theme running through our discussion in this chapter so far. For example, the Department of Health in England commissioned a series of studies from our research center in order to see whether there was an economic case for mental health promotion and mental illness prevention (Knapp et al., 2011b). Among the studies included in our report were economic models of parenting programs where a family had a child with conduct disorder, school-based social and emotional learning programs, anti-bullying interventions in schools, and early intervention services for psychosis. Another example is the *Mental Health Pact* produced by the European Commission and the EU Member States, again to help promote mental well-being and address the needs of people with mental health problems. In developing the case for the Pact, the Commission puts much emphasis on arguments highlighting the economic impacts of poor mental health (McDaid, 2008). At a broader international level, the World Health Organization (WHO) has invested in cost-effectiveness evidence within its Choosing

Interventions that are cost-effective programs. This endeavor has collated information for each of the 17 WHO sub-regions on the costs and impact on population health and cost effectiveness of different health interventions (Hutubessy, Chisholm, Edejer, & WHO-CHOICE, 2003; Chisholm, Sanderson, Ayuso-Mateos, & Saxena, 2004; Chisholm, van Ommeren, Ayuso-Mateos, & Saxena, 2005).

Guideline Development

A growing number of high-income countries have set up mechanisms to formally consider the cost-effectiveness of new technologies, in order to inform reimbursement and coverage decisions, and/or to draw up treatment guidelines. The National Institute for Health and Clinical Excellence (NICE) in England and Wales is perhaps the best known of these national bodies; it evaluates specific technologies and develops clinical guidelines which are then used to shape practices across the national health services. Once NICE decides to appraise an intervention or "technology" (a treatment, device or therapy), an expert committee examines the synthesis of information on both the clinical effectiveness and potential cost-effectiveness of the intervention. Usually it asks for an estimate of the cost per QALY gained compared with current treatment as part of its appraisal. Effective interventions that are seen to have an affordable cost per QALY gained are likely to be recommended. Although a cost-per-QALY threshold is often quoted for NICE decisions (currently around £30,000), in fact decisions and recommendations are not quite so straightforward (e.g., taking account whether the absence of treatment could have catastrophic consequences or if the intervention has a major contribution to make to reducing health inequalities). It is a small step from such appraisals to the development of clinical guidelines.

Commissioning

Economic evidence can also be used to help shape the commissioning of therapies above and beyond the issuing of clinical guidelines. For instance, it might be thought that offering specific bonus payments and other financial incentives would encourage adherence to such guidelines, as has been the practice in relation to primary care doctors in the UK for a few years (Department of Health, 2004). Payments might additionally be offered to encourage the targeting of treatments on particularly vulnerable population groups (such as ethnic minorities and poorer communities).

Since many mental health services are funded and delivered outside the health care system (e.g., in the social care, education, employment, and housing systems), another area where economics can help is in improving collaboration across system and sector boundaries. As part of a drive to help empower people with mental health problems, some health care systems have also evaluated use of various forms of consumer-directed payment schemes, where consumers themselves can decide how to spend public resources on services that best meet their needs (Glendinning et al., 2008; Shen et al., 2008).

Resource Barriers

Even when there is an evidence base—that is, even when there is a good appreciation of efficient ways to enhance child and family health and quality of life or improve the overall efficiency of a child and adolescent mental health system—there could be "barriers" in the way (Knapp et al., 2006). One of the most challenging problems is *resource insufficiency*—child and adolescent mental health services across most of the world are under-funded, and sometimes grossly so. This is clearly a major issue for countries where the proportion of national income devoted to health care is low, as in most of the poorer countries of the world, or where the proportion of the health budget allocated to child and adolescent mental health is minimal. If funds are not allocated it is clearly very difficult to build a service system.

Increasing the resources available for child and adolescent mental health care would help overcome these challenges, but even when resources are committed, available services might be poorly distributed, available at the wrong place or time relative to the distribution of needs. They may be available as only delivered by specialist clinics or particular schools, or concentrated in urban areas, or available only to certain population groups (usually those with higher incomes). This is what we have called the *resource distribution* barrier, and it is often related to how a health (or other system) is financed or structured.

A more general difficulty is when available services do not match what is needed or what is preferred, which we can call *resource inappropriateness*. For example, treatment or support arrangements may be too rigidly organized, leaving service systems unable to respond to differences in individual needs or preferences, or to differences in community circumstances. Inflexibility of this kind is common when there is little or no epidemiological information, or when families have few opportunities to participate in treatment decisions, or when there is deep-rooted reluctance to move away from hospital-based services.

A linked challenge is when services are potentially available to meet individual and family needs, but they are poorly coordinated. This resource dislocation can be compounded by professional rivalry or "silo budgeting." Improved coordination might be achieved by reducing budgetary conflicts between agencies, rewarding efficiency and equity improvements, and encouraging individual and family participation in decision making, although these solutions have their own (transaction) costs. A linked barrier could be timing—most intended improvements when put to practice take a long time to work their way to improved health outcomes, cost-effectiveness gains or fairer access. There could be transitional or longer-term difficulties recruiting suitable professionals, or opening new facilities. Decision makers must also be encouraged to think long, so far as this is possible.

Conclusion

The starting point for an interest in economics is recognition of the pervasive scarcity of resources relative to needs and demands. The need for careful choices about how those resources are to be deployed has led to examinations of a number of criteria, and in this chapter we have highlighted two that are particularly associated with economics: efficiency and equity. We devoted a large part of the chapter to cost-effectiveness analysis, describing how such an evaluative approach can be pursued. Balancing outcome improvements with higher costs is not at all easy. Many economic evaluations across the health spectrum today find that new interventions offer better outcome profiles than currently prevalent interventions, but they do so only at a higher cost. The decision maker then faces a difficult trade-off: Are the better outcomes from the new intervention worth the higher cost of introducing it?

We described how the evidence that is generated might be used to inform or guide practice and policy development. Among the uses we discussed were interest-group lobbying and marketing, policy development and monitoring, evidence appraisal and guideline development, and commissioning. But even when there is an evidence base, there could be barriers in the way. Economic analysis certainly does not have all the answers, but what it can offer is a coherent framework and a set of empirical techniques that can provide decision makers with evidence to inform their responses to that challenge.

References

Beecham, J., & Knapp, M. (2001). Costing psychiatric interventions. In G. Thornicroft (Ed.), *Measuring mental health needs* (2nd ed., pp. 200–224). London: Gaskel.

Chisholm, D., Healey, A., & Knapp, M. (1997). QALYs and mental health care. *Social Psychiatry and Psychiatric Epidemiology, 32*(2), 68–75. doi: 10.1007/BF00788923

Chisholm, D., Knapp, M., Knudsen, H. C., Amaddeo, F., Gaite, L., van Wijngaarden, B., & the EPSILON Study Group. (2000). Client socio-demographic and service receipt inventory—EU version: Development of an instrument for international research. EPSILON Study 5. *British Journal of Psychiatry, 177*(39), 28–33.

Chisholm, D., Sanderson, K., Ayuso-Mateos, J. L., & Saxena, S. (2004). Reducing the global burden of depression: Population-level analysis of intervention cost effectiveness in 14 world regions. *British Journal of Psychiatry, 184*(5), 393–403.

Chisholm, D., van Ommeren, M., Ayuso-Mateos, J. L., & Saxena, S. (2005). Cost-effectiveness of clinical interventions for reducing the global burden of bipolar disorder. *British Journal of Psychiatry, 187*(6), 559–567.

Curtis, L. (2010). *Unit costs of health and social care 2010*. Canterbury, UK: University of Kent, Personal Social Services Research Unit.

Department of Health. (2004). *Quality and outcomes framework: Guidance*. London: Department of Health.

Foster, E. M., & Connor, T. (2005). Public costs of better mental health services for children and adolescents. *Psychiatric Services, 56*(1), 50–55.

Glendinning, C., Challis, D., Fernández, J. L., Jacobs, S., Jones, K., Knapp, M., & Wilberforce, M. (2008). *Evaluation of the individual budgets pilot programme: Final report.* York, UK: Social Policy Research Unit, University of York.

Glied, S., & Cuellar, A. E. (2003). Trends and issues in child and adolescent mental Health. *Health Affairs, 22*(5), 39–50. doi:10.1377/hlthaff.22.5.39

Hutubessy, R., Chisholm, D., Edejer, T., & WHO-CHOICE. (2003). Generalized cost-effectiveness analysis for national level priority setting in the health sector. *Cost Effectiveness and Resource Allocation, 1*, 8. doi:10.1186/1478-7547-1-8

Kilian, R., Losert, C., McDaid, D., Park, A. L., & Knapp, M. (2010). Cost-effectiveness analysis in child and adolescent mental health problems. *International Journal of Mental Health Promotion, 12*(4), 45–57.

Knapp, M., Funk, M., Curran, C., Prince, M., Grigg, M., & McDaid, D. (2006). Economic barriers to better mental health practice and policy. *Health Policy and Planning, 21*(3), 157–170. doi: 10.1093/heapol/czl003

Knapp, M., King, D., Healey, A., & Thomas, C. (2011a). Economic outcomes in adulthood and their associations with antisocial conduct, attention deficit and anxiety problems in childhood. *Journal of Mental Health Policy and Economics, 14*(3), 122–132.

Knapp, M., McDaid, D., & Parsonage, M. (Eds). (2011b). *Mental health promotion and mental illness prevention: The economic case.* London: Department of Health.

McDaid, D. (2008). Mental health reform: Europe at the cross-roads. *Health Economics, Policy and Law, 3*, 219–228.

Romeo, R., Byford, S., & Knapp, M. (2005). Economic evaluations of child and adolescent mental health interventions: A systematic review. *Journal of Child Psychology and Psychiatry, 46*(9), 919–930. doi: 10.1111/j.1469-7610.2005.00407.x

Romeo, R., Knapp, M., & Scott, S. (2006). Economic cost of severe antisocial behaviour in children—and who pays it. *British Journal of Psychiatry, 188*(6), 547–553. doi:10.1192/bjp.bp.104.007625

Scott, S., Knapp, M., Henderson, J., & Maughan, B. (2001). Financial cost of social exclusion: Follow up study of antisocial children into adulthood. *British Medical Journal, 323*(7306), 191–194. doi:10.1136/bmj.323.7306.191

Shen, C., Smyer, M., Mahoney, K. J., Simon-Rusinowitz, L., Shinogle, J., Norstrand, J., & del Vecchio, P. (2008). Consumer-directed care for beneficiaries with mental illness: Lessons from New Jersey's Cash and Counseling program. *Psychiatric Services, 59*(11), 1299–1306. doi: 10.1176/appi.ps.59.11.1299

SECTION 2

Clinical Case Studies

2

Childhood and Adolescent Depression

Raman Deep Pattanayak
Manju Mehta

Introduction

Depression is a disabling and serious mental disorder which can occur at any age. Depression in children and adolescents has the potential to interfere with the cognitive, emotional, and social development occurring at a young age. The manifestation of depressive symptoms is influenced by the age, developmental stage, and cultural background. Childhood and adolescent depression remains an under-recognized entity leading to substantial morbidity and mortality. There is a need for policies and effective steps aimed at prevention and early detection of depression in the young population. This chapter will discuss the childhood and adolescent depression in clinical practice, in addition to cultural considerations and implications for policy.

Historical Perspective

Historically, the concept of childhood depression was considered to be implausible due to absence of a fully mature superego in children. This was questioned by the description of anaclitic depression among infants separated from their primary caregivers. Subsequent researchers proposed that depression in young age was primarily masked, evident only through behaviors such as conduct problems, somatic symptoms, school refusal, and poor scholastic performance. The concept of masked depression was gradually sidelined, as the overt, directly observable nature of childhood depressive symptoms became clearer.

Diagnostic Issues and Controversies

A lot of disagreements surround the diagnosis of childhood and adolescent depression. So far, adult criteria are used for diagnosis of childhood and adolescent depressive disorders. A few age-appropriate variations have been allowed in *Diagnostic and Statistical Manual of Mental Disorders, Fourth Edition* (DSM-IV; American Psychiatric Association, 1994). These include the presence of irritable rather than depressed mood and failure to have expected weight gain, rather than weight loss, in case of major depression in children and adolescents. In case of dysthymia, there may be a presence of irritable rather than depressed mood, and the minimum duration can be one year instead of two years.

It is still unclear if depression in young should be characterized as a discrete categorical entity or a continuum of symptoms. The subsyndromal symptoms are associated with marked impairment and may interfere with normative developmental trajectories in childhood. Children often have depressive symptoms that are of concern but may fall short of meeting the formal criteria, emphasizing the need for a more flexible approach to diagnosis. Further, there are several cultural variations in the symptomatology, for example, somatic symptoms are a common expression of depressed mood in children from Asian cultures. Concerns have been raised about the cultural insensitivity of criteria to detect the symptom manifestations in children and adolescents.

Epidemiology

General Trends

Rates of depression have increased gradually over the past century. There has been a steady increase in the reported incidence rates for depression in childhood and adolescence along with a progressive decrease in the age of onset for each successive generation (Birmaher et al., 1996). This phenomenon has been most evident in studies on mild to moderate depression and cannot be simply explained by a larger cohort of children and adolescent population.

Prevalence

The prevalence rates differ according to the population, setting, informants or diagnostic instruments. The community population studies have shown prevalence rates of major depressive disorders to be 0.3–1.1% for preschool children, 1–2% for school-age children and 3–8% for adolescents (Birmaher et al., 1996) (see Table 2.1). The cumulative probability of having a depressive episode by late adolescence is as high as 10–20%, approaching the adult prevalence.

Incidence studies, though scarce in number, have found the rate to be 2.7–3.3 per thousand per year for depression and 3.4 per thousand per year for dysthymia (Garrison et al., 1997; Malhotra, Kohli, Kapoor, & Pradhan, 2009). Subsyndromal symptoms are far more common and disabling, but are likely to remain under-detected. For example, Cooper and Goodyer (1993)

Table 2.1 Prevalence of Depressive Disorders

	Major Depressive Disorder (%)	*Dysthymia (%)*
Preschool	0.3–1.1	NA
School age children	1–2	0.6–4.6
Adolescents	3–8	1.6–8.0

Source: Tabulated by author.

reported that 20.7 percent of the 11–16-year-old female sample had significant symptomatology, which fell short of a diagnosis of major depressive disorder. Nonetheless, there is considerable distress associated with these symptoms and such population is in need of a mental health intervention, even if they do not meet the formal criteria.

Gender Differences

In children, the depressive disorders occur at the same rate in girls and boys whereas in adolescence, females are twice as likely to have a depressive disorder (Birmaher et al., 1996). The most critical time for gender differences to emerge is the period when adolescents are aged 15–18 years, when the rate of depression in females grows to twice the prevalence rate for males. The severity or recurrence of disorder appears to be similar for both genders.

Socioeconomic Status

Children from low socioeconomic status have a nearly a twofold increase in lifetime risk for major depression compared to those from the high socioeconomic background (Gilman, Kawachi, Fitzmaurice, & Buka, 2003). Social disadvantage may not comprise only of lower income but chronic stress, racial discrimination, blocked access to opportunities, and greater environmental adversities.

Ethnic Differences

Ethnic differences appear to play a role in childhood and adolescent depression. Mexican American youth had a higher prevalence of depression (6.6 percent), compared to youth of American and Asian-American origin, for example, 1.6 percent in adolescents of Chinese descent (Siegel, Aneshensel, Taub, Cantwell, & Driscoll, 1998). Depression was found to have a relatively lower prevalence (0.5 percent) in an Indian community-based study of children and adolescents (Srinath et al., 2005).

Etiology

Psychological Factors

Depressed children often have a negative attribution style, which means that the negative outcomes are attributed to inadequacy of self and internal factors, while the positive outcomes are attributed to external factors. Cognitive distortions are common in young children, who may attach a different interpretation to seemingly innocuous events. For example, a child may feel sad and lonely immediately after the birth of a sibling as parents devote more attention to the newborn. The perceived incompetence and lack of self-esteem have been found to be strong mediators in development of depression. Adolescents are quite conscious of their bodily appearance and looks, and are in the process of developing their self-image. Even a minor skin problem, such as acne, may make them vulnerable to low self-esteem. The onset of adolescence is marked by a variety of changes, including puberty, need for autonomy, self-identity, and peer group affiliations. Psychosocial events such as change of school or rejection in romantic relationships are common in adolescence, and coping with these events could be determined by the healthy development of self-image and self-esteem. The combination of negative self-concept, stressful life events, and maladaptive coping has been shown to be predictive of depression in youth (Wagner & Brent, 2009).

Familial and Social Factors

The family stressors in early life interfere with key developmental tasks such as development of a healthy sense of self and acquisition of emotional regulation and coping, thereby increasing the predisposition to depression. Physical or sexual abuse in childhood is a profound risk factor for onset and recurrence of depression. Familial discord, lack of cohesion, parent–child conflict, parental substance abuse, and criminality are associated with depression in the child (Kaufman et al., 1998). The depressed youths react and contribute to disruption in their close relationships. Particular interpersonal styles and social deficits of depressed youth elicit negative responses from others, which maintain or exacerbate depression (Joiner, 1999).

In traditional societies, the joint family system ensures a strong role of extended family members in the upbringing of children. Living with grandparents, uncles, and cousins in the same house leads to strong emotional ties and social support for life. In the past few decades, several socioeconomic changes like urbanization, migration, and consumerism have contributed to an increase in nuclear families, stress levels, and higher rates of divorce. Time is increasingly viewed as a precious commodity, and there is little time left for a family get-together alongside a busy work life. Children in families with working parents or a single parent may face loneliness and isolation. The emotional unavailability of parents in childhood is likely to have long-term psychological consequences in the form of low self-esteem and vulnerability to depression.

School Factors

In the recent times, school education has become a tremendously competitive field. The admission cut-offs for various streams of higher education are on a constant rise with each academic year. The marks which were considered good in the past are no longer good enough for securing admission. These unrealistically high targets are difficult to achieve for the vast majority, leading to stress and depression. Parental pressure to over-perform or enormous expectations of the child is a frequently seen stressor in clinical practice. The term examination is a fairly common life event predating the onset of depression in school-going adolescents (Garg, 2004), especially in the months of February and March when the semester ends in most Indian schools. Headache is a common presentation among adolescents who are high achievers in school, with rigid and perfectionistic traits (Kayal, 2006). At times, the child may struggle hard to be a topper in order to seek parental approval. Many a times, in clinical practice, a child who has secured a second or third position in a competitive event presents with depression and guilt. Constant comparison between siblings and parental affection conditional on child's achievement promotes unhealthy competition between the siblings and acts as a stressor.

Life Events and Stressors

Depressed children and adolescents report significantly more stressful life events compared to healthy youth. The commonly reported life events at a young age are illness or death of a family member, interpersonal conflicts or scoldings, academic stressors like failure in examination, and change of residence or school (Sagar, Pattanayak, & Mehta, 2012). Parental divorce is another stressor frequently seen in depressed adolescents presenting to child and adolescent clinics. In addition to the emotional component, the depression is often mediated by secondary factors and stresses, such as, decline in socioeconomic status and change of residence which are linked to depression (Aseltine, 1996). Children of divorced parents residing with the mother who is not economically independent, may find it hard to adjust to a life with financial hardships and inability to maintain a standard of living they were earlier used to. It may further translate to peer rejection, low self-esteem, and change of school or residence, all of which may pose additional stress.

Low popularity with peers is related to depressive symptoms in children and adolescents. Children who are bullied are at increased risk for onset of depression. Some studies show that the bullied and the bullies have higher prevalence of depression compared to normal controls (Ivarsson, Broberg, Arvidsson, & Gillberg, 2005). It is important to assess the socioeconomic stressors faced by an adolescent, e.g., parental unemployment, poverty, racial discrimination which may lead to chronic stress and depression. The gender atypical behavior in adolescence may lead to peer rejection, parental disapproval, inner conflicts, and depression. The same-sex identification and homosexual orientation may be a source of significant distress in adolescent years. The adolescents with different orientation may feel rejected and lonely, and are at a greater risk for substance use, depression, and suicide (Russell & Joyner, 2001).

The intensity of stressors may range from major life events (death of a parent) to chronic stressors (parental restrictions, conflicts with authority) to daily hassles (school and home work). The major life events appear to exert their effects on psychological well-being at least partially by creating daily stressors, and by weakening the personal and social resources for coping (Kirmayer, 2001). On the other hand, positive affiliation to peers and family integration are protective for depression.

Genetic Factors

High familial loading of depressive disorders is an especially strong predictor for development of a major depressive disorder in a child or adolescent (Wasserman, Cheng, & Jiang, 2005). Twin studies have shown that depression is moderately heritable, with 31–42% rates. The child of a depressed parent is at a two to four times higher risk than the general population to develop a depressive disorder. Further, adolescent depression has been found to be relatively more heritable than prepubertal depression (Birmaher & Brent, 2007). The possible role of genes such as serotonin transmitter gene is being explored.

Neurobiological Factors

Hypothalamo–pituitary–adrenal (HPA) axis abnormalities have been demonstrated along with an evidence of non-suppression in stimulation studies. Studies suggest that depressed adolescents tend to have elevated cortisol around sleep onset (Goodyer, Park, & Herbert, 2001). Alterations in serotonergic and noradrenergic pathways have been linked to early-onset depression (Wagner & Brent, 2009).

Structural neuroimaging studies have found a smaller volume of amygdala and a blunted response to fearful faces in depressed children compared to health controls (MacMillan et al., 2003). Polysomnography studies have failed to consistently show decreased rapid eye movement (REM) latency seen in adult depression (Birmaher et al., 1996). Depressed children and adolescents have been found to be more vulnerable to the effects of emotion-induction paradigm in Functional Magnetic Resonance Imaging (fMRI) studies and a reduced reward-related circuitry when participating in the reward paradigm (Kyte, Goodyer, & Sahakian, 2005; Forbes et al., 2006).

Developmental Differences in Clinical Presentation

The core features of major depression in children and adolescents are broadly similar to adult depression, however the recognition and diagnosis of the disorder may be more difficult in youth (Birmaher et al., 1996). This is because the way in which a symptom is expressed depends on the cognitive, emotional, and social development of children as shown in Table 2.2.

Table 2.2 Depressive Symptoms at Different Developmental Stages

Infancy
Distress, crying, screaming, withdrawal, and dejection
Separation anxiety, sleep disturbance, and weight loss

Childhood
Anhedonia; somatic presentation (*headache, stomach ache, pain in body*)
Low self-esteem (*"I am not a good child," "I am not as smart as my sister"*)
Feeling of worthlessness (*"I can't get good grades," "nobody loves me," "my teacher hates me"*)
Hallucinations

Adolescence
Depressed or irritable mood; anhedonia
Hopelessness, feelings of guilt, suicidality, delusions
Endogenous/melancholic symptoms (extreme psychomotor retardation, diurnal variation, etc.)
Atypical symptoms (increased appetite, hypersomnia)

Source: Author.

Children have a limited verbal capacity to express their thoughts and feelings. For example, instead of communicating how bad they feel, they may act out and be irritable, which may be interpreted as misbehavior or disobedience. Children with depressive disorders may not be able to report a sad mood, but may present with a depressed appearance. There may be feelings of low self-esteem and worthlessness, manifested in statements such as, "I am not a good child." Somatic presentation is quite common in depressed children and they commonly complain of general aches and pains, headaches, or stomach aches (see Box 2.1). The limited language skills or immature cognitive structure of young children makes them less likely to comprehend guilt or hopelessness. The melancholic or endogenous symptoms are extremely uncommon in children. Children with psychotic depression have hallucinations much more frequently compared to an adolescent or adult.

With progression of age, the symptoms common to childhood depression decrease in frequency. Symptoms such as subjectively depressed mood, hopelessness, guilt, atypical, and melancholic symptoms make their mark in adolescent depression. They may also present with irritable mood, boredom, conduct problems, relationship difficulties, and may attempt to take substances in

Box 2.1   Case Illustration: Childhood Depression

> A 10-year-old boy was presented to the clinic with complaints of "tiredness," "stomach aches," and "dull headache" over the past few months. His parents were particularly concerned about the decline in his academic performance and came for a consultation on the teacher's insistence. The boy had become quarrelsome in class, did not complete work assignments and appeared uninterested in studies. On probing further, parents remarked that he no longer played cricket with his brother and preferred to stay indoors. He would complain of heaviness of head, occasional "stomach ache" and inability to study. Many a times he would say, "I am not good in class," "I am dumb," "Classmates don't like me; everybody loves a smart person." He had missed several days at school and would sleep in till late. He kept his face lowered through the interview, answering in a low tone. When asked about problems at school, he said, "I don't know what has happened in the past year, but I have turned from a brand new BMW car to a Suzuki car."

order to feel better. Suicidal ideation is also common, and when present, there is a higher likelihood of attempted and completed suicide as compared to children.

Cultural Context

There are wide cross-cultural variations in the way depressive symptoms are expressed, and interpreted. The intensity of social response to depressive symptoms may also vary across cultures. The understanding of these cultural factors is important for clinical practice. The cultural variations in child-rearing practices and parent–child relationships can prime and shape the affective responses of a child. Cultural context may make some feelings more salient and others a bit more difficult to articulate. The ways in which cultural background influences the regulation of emotion has implications for expression of depressed affect in clinical settings (Kirmayer, 2001).

The conceptualization of depression differs across cultures, with implications for manifestation and description of depressive symptoms. The emotional symptoms in Asian cultures are often explained as a social or moral problem, rather than a mental health problem. Consequently, children and adolescents from Asian cultures are more likely to be taken to a religious, spiritual or community leader rather than a mental health professional. Further, there is a tendency to minimize the psychological component of depression in favor of more socially acceptable somatic symptoms.

Culture influences the behavior of the adolescent toward the mental health professional. They may make a minimal eye contact and not initiate the conversation with the treating professional, as a mark of respect towards the authority figure as commonly seen in eastern cultures. Children and adolescents in western countries may be more vocal about their feelings, and open to discuss sensitive issues with the therapist, while those from Asian countries like India and Japan may find it difficult to discuss their personal issues with a person outside the family. The mental health professionals need to be aware of these differences and adopt a more culturally sensitive approach to assessment.

Culture has implications for validity and utility of scales for assessment of depression in youth from different cultural backgrounds. Linguistic and cultural concerns are not addressed by mere translation. These culturally sensitive scales have a higher emphasis on culture-specific presentation and expression of depression.

Course and Psychosocial Sequelae

Over 90 percent of children and adolescents recover from an initial episode of major depression within 1–2 years of onset (Birmaher & Brent, 2007). The treatment appears to restrict the duration of a depressive episode. Family stressors such as parental substance use, marital discord, lower socioeconomic status are associated with poor treatment response (Birmaher, Arbelaez, & Brent, 2002; Kayal, 2006). Prolonged and chronic episodes tend to occur in them with a severe episode, comorbid disorder, parental depression, and psychosocial stressors. Although the majority recovers from the depressive episode, recurrence is very common. It has been estimated that 20–60% of the depressive episodes recur within a year and up to 70 percent within five years (Birmaher & Brent, 2007). With each successive episode, the potency of psychosocial factors necessary to trigger a new depressive episode decreases so that a relatively minor stressful situation can lead to the onset of depression.

Depression may impair the development of a child's emotional, cognitive, and social skills and affect the family relationships (Birmaher et al., 1996). Depressed children and adolescents are at an increased risk of obesity, risky sexual behaviors, problematic social relationships, and educational underachievement. Children and adolescents with depressive disorders are also at high risk of substance abuse and legal problems. Suicide attempts and completion are among the most significant and devastating sequelae of depression with approximately 60 percent reporting suicidal ideation and 30 percent actually attempting suicide (Birmaher & Brent, 2007). Some researchers have suggested that persistent depression in children may lead to persistently altered brain functions, that is, chemical and physiological "scars" (Sokolov and Kutcher, 2001).

Depressive disorders of children and adolescents often persist into adulthood. Higher rates of adult depression, anxiety, and bipolar disorders have been seen in the depressed children and adolescents as compared to controls. The change of diagnosis to bipolar disorder is much more frequent in children and adolescent depression (20–40%) as compared to the adult depression (5–18%) within five years of onset (Birmaher & Brent, 2007). Those with familial loading, earlier onset, psychotic episodes, and psychomotor retardation are at higher risk (Geller & Luby, 1997).

Children with dysthymic disorder often have had symptoms since preschool years. They have a protracted course for several years characteristically with both good and bad days, but never good weeks. When the depressive episode is superimposed on dysthymia, it is known as double depression and usually occurs within five years of the onset of dysthymia (Kovacs, Akiskal, Gatsonis, & Parrone, 1994).

Comorbid Conditions

Presence of depression in children and adolescents increases the chance of finding comorbidity by at least 20 times. Approximately, 40–90% of depressed children and adolescent have a comorbid psychiatric disorder (Birmaher & Brent, 2007). Among preschool children, the common comorbid conditions include attention deficit hyperactivity disorder (ADHD), oppositional defiant disorder (ODD) and anxiety disorders. In adolescent depression commonly found comorbid conditions include anxiety disorders, conduct disorders, substance abuse, and personality disorders. The disruptive disorders are more likely comorbid disorders in boys with depression, while eating disorders are common in girls with depression. From a clinical perspective, it is important to look closely for any comorbidity in all cases of childhood and adolescent depression and vice versa.

Differential Diagnosis

The main psychiatric diagnoses that must be distinguished include bipolar disorders, anxiety disorders, adjustment disorders, substance use disorders, ADHD, conduct disorders, and learning disorders. Because of overlap of symptoms as well as frequent comorbidity, the differentiation may be quite challenging for the clinician. It is also important to evaluate carefully for the presence of subtle or short duration hypomanic symptoms because these symptoms often are overlooked and these children and adolescents may be more likely to become manic when treated with antidepressant medication.

Another important differential diagnosis which must be considered in adolescents is the presence of medical disorders (e.g., hypothyroidism/hyperthyroidism, mononucleosis, anemia, diabetes, autoimmune diseases, premenstrual dysphoric disorder, and chronic fatigue syndrome) closely mimicking depressive disorders. The use of medications such as stimulants, corticosteroids, and beta blockers can also induce depression-like symptomatology. Complete history including temporal sequence of events should be taken in all cases.

Clinical Evaluation

Children and adolescents of different ages and developmental stages differ in their emotional and cognitive capacities. Therefore, the developmental stage of a child must be kept in mind during the interview. The clinical evaluation may comprise of a combination of direct observation, questioning, discussion, drawings, or play. Information from multiple sources should be sought, e.g., parents, child, teachers, and peers to ascertain the child's behavior and functioning in various settings. Parents are better informants about behavioral symptoms such as irritability and social withdrawal, while children and adolescents can report about their inner experiences and thoughts. An attempt should be made to engage the child in the evaluation. All the children and adolescents should be asked directly about their emotional state and feelings. Special attention should be paid to delineate any familial or environmental stressors during the interview. If a particular theme recurs in the interview or play with the child, it should be gently probed.

Children may not be able to verbalize their thoughts and feelings and therefore it is important to pay attention to the nonverbal behavior. Manifestation of themes via imaginary play is of immense utility especially in young children. Persistent death and suicide themes in play can be useful indicators of suicidal ideation. If present, a detailed suicidal risk assessment should be conducted and a session with parents is warranted regarding the explanation of risk and precautionary measures. Due respect should be given to confidentiality of adolescent patients, who may not like to discuss sensitive matters such as romantic relationships and substance use in the presence of parents. Attention should be paid to collect information for associated comorbid disorders like anxiety or conduct symptoms. Some useful points for evaluation of depressed children and adolescents are shown in Box 2.2.

Box 2.2 Clinical Interview: Some Useful Points

- Establish rapport and take a sensitive, nonjudgmental approach.
- Questions should be put according to age and developmental stage.
- Try to focus on the social and cultural context of the illness behavior.
- Closely observe nonverbal behavior, like facial expression and posture, which may provide clues to depression.
- Combination of verbal exchange with play is quite useful for young children.
- Drawings of faces with downturned lips or tears can be used in assessing young children.
- If there is no subjective depressed mood, consider offering alternate word choices to the child, for example, sad, down, disappointed, bored, lonely, etc.
- Assess for presence of any familial or environmental stressors, for example, parental discord, physical abuse or "best friend moving away."
- Interviewing the adolescent alone may help in exploring the confidential or sensitive issues.
- Explore for any substance use in older children and adolescents.
- Assess for suicidal ideation and if present, conduct a risk assessment.

ABC Chart

Careful analysis of antecedents, behavior, and consequences (ABC) provides insight into the purpose or function of a behavior. Antecedents include triggers in the form of event or activity that immediately precedes a problematic behavior, for example, irritability or self-harm. Consequences are the events that immediately follow a behavior. Antecedents and consequences together often go a long way toward explaining the child's behaviors. The ABC Chart allows the mental health professional to record descriptive information about the depressed child or adolescent in a systematic and organized way. It can help in forming a hypothesis statement and identifying the underlying reasons to maintain a problem behavior.

Mood Diary

Mood diary helps in recording the variations of mood in a chronological fashion and can be used as a simple tool of assessment. The intensity of the depressed mood is rated using numbers or graph in the diary, which is seen by the mental health professional in subsequent visits. Mood charting puts together important pieces of information such as mood state, stressful events, and diurnal variations. Simply recording the information on mood chart helps in identifying the emerging patterns that may otherwise be difficult to identify.

Projective Tests

Projective tests are often used in children to reveal hidden emotions and inner conflicts. The Children's Apperception Test (CAT) is appropriate for prepubertal children and is intended to explore their inner psychological and emotional conflicts. The child is presented a series of pictures and asked for an imaginary description of the situation and create a story about the people or animals in the picture. The pictures are meant to encourage the children to tell stories related to competition, illness, injuries, body image, family life, and school situations and in the process, children project their unconscious attitudes and motivations onto the picture. At the time of analysis, special attention should be paid to protagonist (main character) of the story, his or her primary needs, and relationship to environment. The pictures draw out a child's anxieties, fears, and psychological defenses, thereby assisting in the evaluation of depression. The cultural adaptations of CAT have been developed for various countries including Japan, India, and Indonesia (Bellak, 1992).

The Draw-a-Person (DAP) test requires the child or adolescent to draw a man, a woman or themselves, with no detailed instructions to guide the drawing. The findings can be based on a psychodynamic interpretation of the figure drawn, such as the size, shape, complexity, clothing, and background and can provide useful clues to inner conflicts and emotions (see Figure 2.1).

Childhood and Adolescent Depression   **33**

Figure 2.1   An Eight-year-old Girl's Drawing Depicting Herself in a DAP Test

Source: Drawn by a patient visiting Child and Adolescent Clinic, Department of Psychiatry, All India Institute of Medical Sciences.
Note: The drawing appears regressed for her age. The child is shown as unhappy, with downturned lips. The posture and pointed fingers suggests presence of aggressive tendencies. The small legs compared to rest of body points to a sense of incompetence in self.

Several versions and modifications of the projective test are available, depending on which a child may be asked to draw themselves, person of the opposite sex, house, tree, person, or a kinetic family drawing in which the family is drawn doing something together. The language barriers which may be faced in clinical interview are not encountered in drawings, and children may find it more appealing and non-threatening.

Diagnostic Instruments and Rating Scales

Several semi-structured instruments are available, mainly used in research settings. These include Preschool Age Psychiatric Assessment (PAPA); Kiddie Schedule of Affective Disorders and Schizophrenia for School-age Children—Present and Lifetime (K-SADS-PL); and Child and Adolescent Psychiatric Assessment (CAPA). The National Institute of Mental Health (NIMH) Diagnostic Interview Schedule for Children (DISC), and Diagnostic Interview for Children and Adolescents (DICAs) are highly structured interviews useful for epidemiological studies. The validity of instruments for a particular cultural setting must be established before its use in research.

Rating scales are used for screening or measuring severity after a diagnosis is made. The most widely used scales are the revised versions of Childhood Depression Rating Scale (CDRS) (Poznanski, 1979), and Childhood Depression Inventory (CDI) (Kovacs, 1992). These can easily be used in clinical situations to monitor the progress and treatment response.

Approach and Strategies

The choice of the initial treatment depends on several factors such as age, severity and number of episodes, chronicity, and contextual issues (e.g., family conflict, academic problems, and exposure to negative life events). Table 2.3 summarizes the various treatment interventions for childhood and adolescent depression.

Table 2.3 Summary of Interventions for Childhood and Adolescent Depression

Effective in Controlled Trials	Effective in Noncontrolled Trials
Mild to moderate • Cognitive Behavior Therapy (CBT) • Interpersonal Therapy (IPT) *Severe or complicated* • CBT or IPT • Selective serotonin Reuptake Inhibitors, preferably Fluoxetine	• Psychoeducation • Supportive therapy • Family therapy • Group psychotherapy (except group CBT) • Electroconvulsive therapy • Repetitive Transcranial Magnetic Stimulation (rTMS)

Source: Author.

Mild depression in children and adolescents should be managed with either of the two forms of psychotherapy, namely, cognitive behavior therapy (CBT) or interpersonal therapy (IPT), both of which have been found to be effective in a variety of cultural and ethnic groups. Supportive therapy and psychoeducation can be routinely provided to all cases. The older children and adolescents must be present in psychoeducational sessions along with their parents. It is important to remember that depression in children and adolescents often occurs in a psychosocial context and hence, the familial and environmental problems should be addressed. Sessions on problem solving, coping skills, and social skills can be conducted for adolescents to help them deal effectively with familial and social stressors.

In case of moderate to severe depression, a combination of antidepressant medication and psychotherapy is an appropriate choice. If the risk of suicide is present, admission as an inpatient should be considered strongly and high-risk management should be implemented. In view of the chronic and recurrent nature of depressive disorders, treatment should be continued for a further 6–12 months after remission. This continuation phase of treatment comprising either booster psychotherapy sessions or antidepressant medication, or both, helps in minimizing the risk of recurrence. In case of multiple prior episodes or high familial risk, maintenance treatment should be considered strongly and should be continued for a few years.

In light of the US' Food and Drug Administration (FDA) clearance of repetitive transcranial magnetic stimulation (rTMS) for adult major depression, there is an increasing interest in rTMS as a novel treatment for adolescent depression. In a recent review of studies involving the treatment, comprising a total of 19 subjects less than 18 years of age, no adverse events were found (D'Agati, Bloch, Levkovitz, & Reti, 2010). However, more research is needed.

Special Treatment Considerations

For psychotic depression, atypical antipsychotics should be added to antidepressant medication, and tapered off following remission of symptoms. Anxiety disorders are frequently comorbid with depressive disorders, and treatment with selective serotonin reuptake inhibitors (SSRIs) tends to address both sets of symptoms. It has also been seen that patients with comorbid anxiety disorders respond better to CBT. Treatment of depression with comorbid ADHD is very challenging. Of the two conditions, management priority is given to the one having relatively severe symptoms or more impairment. Once it improves, the clinical re-evaluation is done to govern further decision making.

Implications for Policy

Adequate mental health at a young age prepares the children for a larger and meaningful role in society. The preservation of their mental health is, therefore, a matter of national priority. Unfortunately, a vast proportion of depressed children and adolescents remain unrecognized and untreated especially in developing countries. Policies and programs are not geared to identify or prevent depression in youth. For instance, in a study by Aaron et al. (2004) of a southern part of India, suicide was responsible for 25 percent of deaths in boys and 50–75% of deaths in girls aged between 15 and 24 years, in contrast to the global average, with suicide accounting for 9.2 percent of youth mortality (Wasserman et al., 2005). Yet, there is no mental health policy in the country. Ideally, there should be a separate child mental health policy to provide a developmental framework to enhance mental health resources, guide services, advocacy, and access to care for youth depression.

As depression in youth is triggered by situational factors and biological vulnerability, significant opportunity exists for multiple levels of interventions aimed at primary and secondary prevention. There is increasing evidence to suggest that intervention programs directed at high-risk groups (*selective prevention*) as well as those directed towards subsyndromal symptoms (*indicated prevention*) can successfully prevent or delay the onset of depression. School-based interventions can identify the at-risk population and impart life skills training to promote mental health. Most programs have used cognitive behavioral techniques in addition to problem solving and stress reduction. The school-based programs can reach otherwise healthy children to develop resiliency and enhance coping. Teachers and school counselors can be sensitized to recognize the early signs of depression and provide appropriate help and support. Similar intervention efforts should also be directed at prevention of youth suicide, which include skill building, screening and crisis intervention centers, media campaigns, and public educational campaigns.

The categorical and single problem-focused interventions may be limited in their potential effects in view of frequent comorbidity. The interventions which target problems that co-occur with depression, such as substance abuse, and are comprehensive in their approach are likely to be more effective with adolescent depression. It is important to integrate efforts for child and adolescent mental health with the ongoing efforts for general health and welfare of children and adolescents. There is a need to train the primary care physicians and community health workers to identify depression and reach out to the larger community. There is a need to integrate and collaborate with primary health care, social welfare, and educational sectors for a multimodal approach to combat depression in youth. The preventive efforts are likely to be cost effective in the long run by reduction in morbidity and disease burden.

Future Directions

Efforts are being made to reach a consensus for developmental modifications in the diagnostic criteria. It is important to identify potential intermediate phenotypes, such as impaired neuropsychological functions, for future research. Such identification will facilitate the monitoring of high-risk persons, providing a scope for early intervention to match patients to a particular treatment and guide the sample selection for genetic studies. High-risk populations, for example, those with history of physical abuse or stressful events, need to be studied further. Research should focus on public health interventions for prevention of depression in youth.

Conclusion

Depressive disorders in childhood and adolescence are common, chronic and recurring disorders, often with comorbid psychiatric conditions as well as psychosocial, academic, and interpersonal dysfunction. Children and adolescents need a careful assessment in accordance with their developmental stage. There is a significant role for psychotherapy in childhood/adolescent depression. Pharmacotherapy, whenever indicated, should be initiated keeping the safety issues in mind. Interventions for prevention of depressive disorders directed at the community in general, and high-risk, vulnerable groups specifically, would prove to be immensely beneficial.

References

Aaron, R., Joseph, A., Abraham, S., Muliyil, J., George, K., Prasad, J., & Bose, A. (2004). Suicides in young people in rural southern India: *Lancet, 363*(9415), 1117–1118. doi:10.1016/S0140-6736(04)15896-0

American Psychiatric Association. (1994). *Diagnostic and statistical manual of mental disorders* (4th ed.). Washington, DC: American Psychiatric Association.

Aseltine, R. H. Jr. (1996). Pathways linking parental divorce with adolescent depression. *Journal of Health and Social Behavior, 37*(2), 133–148.

Bellak, L. (1992). *The T.A.T., the C.A.T, and the S.A.T. in clinical use* (5th ed.). Boston: Allyn & Bacon.

Birmaher, B., Arbelaez, C., & Brent, D. (2002). Course and outcome of child and adolescent major depressive disorder. *Child & Adolescent Psychiatric Clinics of North America, 11*(3), 619–637.

Birmaher, B., & Brent, D. A. (2007). Practice parameters for the assessment and treatment of children and adolescents with depressive disorders. *Journal of American Academy of Child Adolescent Psychiatry, 46*, 1503–1526.

Birmaher, B., Ryan, N. D., Williamson, D. E., Brent, D. A., Kaufman, J., Dahl, R. E., & Nelson, B. (1996). Childhood and adolescent depression: A review of the past 10 years. Part I. *Journal of the American Academy of Child & Adolescent Psychiatry, 35*(11), 1427–1439. doi:10.1097/00004583-199611000-00011

Cooper, P. J., & Goodyer, I. (1993). A community study of depression in adolescent girls. I: Estimates of symptom and syndrome prevalence. *British Journal of Psychiatry, 163*(3), 369–374. doi: 10.1192/bjp.163.3.369

D'Agati, D., Bloch, Y., Levkovitz, Y., & Reti, I. (2010). rTMS for adolescents: Safety and efficacy considerations. *Psychiatry Research, 177*(3), 280–285. doi:10.1016/j.psychres.2010.03.004

Forbes, E. E., Christopher May, J., Siegle, G. J., Ladouceur, C. D., Ryan, N. D., Carter, C. D., & Dahl, R. E. (2006). Reward-related decision-making in pediatric major depressive disorder: An fMRI study. *Journal of Child Psychology and Psychiatry, 47*(10), 1031–1040. doi: 10.1111/j.1469-7610.2006.01673.x

Garg, R. (2004). *Clinical study of psychosocial factors and comorbidity in major depressive disorder in adolescents* (Unpublished Master's thesis). All India Institute of Medical Sciences, New Delhi.

Garrison, C. Z., Waller, J. L., Cuffe, S. P., McKeown, R. E., Addy, C. L., & Jackson, K. L. (1997). Incidence of major depressive disorder and dysthymia in young adolescents. *Journal of the American Academy of Child & Adolescent Psychiatry, 36*(4), 458–465. doi:10.1097/00004583-199704000-00007

Geller, B., & Luby, J. (1997). Child and adolescent bipolar disorder: A review of the past 10 years. *Journal of the American Academy of Child & Adolescent Psychiatry, 36*(9), 1168–1176. doi:10.1097/00004583-199709000-00008

Gilman, S. E., Kawachi, I., Fitzmaurice, G. M., & Buka, S. L. (2003). Socio-economic status, family disruption and residential stability in childhood: Relation to onset, recurrence and remission of major depression. *Psychological Medicine, 33*(8), 1341–1355. doi: 10.1017/S0033291703008377

Goodyer, I. M., Park, R. J., & Herbert, J. (2001). Psychosocial and endocrine features of chronic first-episode major depression in 8–16 year olds. *Biological Psychiatry, 50*(5), 351–357. doi:10.1016/S0006-3223(01)01120-9

Ivarsson, T., Broberg, A. G., Arvidsson, T., & Gillberg, C. (2005). Bullying in adolescence: Psychiatric problems in victims and bullies as measured by the youth self report (YSR) and the depression self-rating scale (DSRS). *Nordic Journal of Psychiatry, 59*(5), 365–373. doi: 10.1080/08039480500227816

Joiner, T. E. (1999). A test of interpersonal theory of depression in youth psychiatric patients. *Journal of Abnormal Child Psychology, 27*(1), 77–85. doi: 10.1023/A:1022666424731

Kaufman, J., Birmaher, B., Brent, D., Dahl, R., Bridge, J., & Ryan, N. D. (1998). Psychopathology in the relatives of depressed-abused children. *Child Abuse & Neglect, 22*(3), 171–181. doi:10.1016/S0145-2134(97)00170-1

Kayal, M. (2006). *Familial predictors of treatment outcome in adolescents with depression* (Unpublished Master's thesis). All India Institute of Medical Sciences, New Delhi.

Kirmayer, L. J. (2001). Cultural variations in the clinical presentation of depression and anxiety: Implications for diagnosis and treatment. *Journal of Clinical Psychiatry, 62*(Suppl. 13), 22–28.

Kovacs, M. (1992). *The Children's Depression Inventory Manual.* New York: Multi-Health Systems Inc.

Kovacs, M., Akiskal, H., Gatsonis, C., & Parrone, P. (1994). Childhood-onset dysthymic disorder: Clinical features and prospective naturalistic outcome. *Archives of General Psychiatry, 51*(5), 365–374.

Kyte, Z. A., Goodyer, I. M., & Sahakian, B. J. (2005). Selected executive skills in adolescents with recent first episode major depression. *Journal of Child Psychology and Psychiatry, 46*(9), 995–1005. doi: 10.1111/j.1469-7610.2004.00400.x

MacMillan, S., Szeszko, P. R., Moore, G. J., Madden, R., Elisa, L., Jennifer, I., & Rosenberg, D. R. (2003). Increased amygdala: Hippocampal volume ratios associated with severity of anxiety in pediatric major depression. *Journal of Child and Adolescent Psychopharmacology,13*(1), 65–73. doi:10.1089/104454603321666207

Malhotra, S., Kohli, A., Kapoor, M., & Pradhan, B. (2009). Incidence of childhood psychiatric disorders in India. *Indian Journal of Psychiatry, 51*(2), 101–107.

Poznanski, E. O., Cook, S. C., & Carroll, B. J. (1979). A depression rating scale for children. *Paediatrics, 64*(4), 442–450.

Russell, S. T., & Joyner, K. (2001). Adolescent sexual orientation and suicide risk: Evidence from a national study. *American Journal of Public Health, 91*(8), 1276–1281.

Sagar, R., Pattanayak, R. D., & Mehta, M. (2012). Clinical profile of pediatric mood disorders at a tertiary care centre. *Indian Pediatrics, 49*(4), 21–24.

Siegel, J. M., Aneshensel, C. S., Taub, B., Cantwell, D. P., & Driscoll, A. K. (1998). Adolescent depressed mood in multiethnic sample. *Journal of Youth and Adolescence, 27*(4), 413–427. doi: 10.1023/A:1022873601030

Sokolov, S., & Kutcher, S. (2001). Adolescent depression: Neuroendocrine aspects. In I. M. Goodyer (Ed.), *The depressed child and adolescent* (pp. 233–266). Cambridge, UK: Cambridge University Press.

Srinath, S., Girimaji, S. C., Gururaj, G., Seshadri, S., Subbakrishna, D. K., Bhola, P., & Kumar, N. (2005). Epidemiological study of child and adolescent psychiatric disorders urban and rural areas of Bangalore, India. *Indian Journal of Medical Research, 122*, 67–79.

Wagner, K. D., & Brent, D. A. (2009). Depressive disorders and suicide. In B. J. Saddock, V. A. Sadock, & P. Ruiz (Eds), *Kaplan & Sadock's Comprehensive Textbook of Psychiatry* (pp. 3652–3662). Philadelphia, PA: Lippincott Williams & Wilkins.

Wasserman, D., Cheng, Q. I., & Jiang, G. (2005). Global suicide rates among young people aged 15–19. *World Psychiatry, 4*(2), 114–120.

3

Suicidality among Children and Adolescents: Complexities and Challenges

Latha Nrugham
Vandana Varma Prakash

This chapter provides a glimpse into the complex terrain of suicidality among children and adolescents in four parts. The first section is on the numbers related to suicidal phenomena among children and adolescents. The next section discusses the definitions of these phenomena and the inherent difficulties of arriving at globally acceptable definitions from both perspectives, research and clinical. The third section focuses on the risk factors of suicidal phenomenon among children and adolescents. The last section is about prevention and intervention at the clinical practice and policy levels.

In each section, important studies on the topic are reviewed. They are primarily quantitative in design and from the Western world. Case vignettes from India, a geographically non-Western yet to a certain extent culturally Westernized nation, are presented. These cases reveal that although cultural contexts differ from the Western nations, certain identifiable and manageable psychosocial constructs related to suicidality remain the same. However, as the contexts in which the risk factors manifest themselves differ, identification and management may also differ.

The Numbers

In a systematic review of 128 studies comprising 513,188 adolescents, suicidal ideation was reported by 29.9 percent of adolescents in community samples and attempted suicide by 9.7 percent (Evans, Hawton, & Rodham, 2005). In the age group of 10–24 years, 6 percent of all deaths were suicides in many countries (Patton et al., 2009). Almost one-third of all cases of suicide worldwide were found in China and India (Bertolote & Fleischmann, 2009). However, the bulk of available statistics and empirical research on suicidality among children and adolescents comes from developed nations, such as the US, Canada, New Zealand, Australia, Japan, and West and North Europe. Statistics compiled by the World Health Organization (WHO) shows that with increasing age, suicide rates are higher and that the sharpest increase is among youth (World Health Organization, 2002).

Box 3.1   Case Study 1

S was a 15-year-old boy studying in Class 9 of a public school and the only child of his parents from a well-to-do family. His father was an engineer and his mother a homemaker. He was brought to the Child Guidance Clinic of the hospital with complaints of disturbed sleep and disruptive and quarrelsome behavior in school. Although these symptoms had been present for a long time, they had exacerbated in the last six months. Precipitating factors were not elicited. His case history revealed frequent complaints from school like disruptive behavior in class, bullying behavior with classmates and younger children on the school bus, and playing truant by hiding in the washroom during classes he disliked.

As the only child, most of his demands had been promptly fulfilled from early childhood. His parents found him a difficult child to raise due to the disturbances in his circadian rhythm, adaptability, attention span, and quality of mood. Since infancy, he slept for just five to six hours. He would wake up several times at night. When he was six years old he was diagnosed as suffering from borderline attention deficit hyperactivity disorder (ADHD). However, he was never treated for it. His hyperactivity decreased with age but his attention span continued to be short, particularly distractibility. Since childhood he was easily irritable and did not respond well to visitors at home. His academic performance was average.

He was brought to the outpatient department when his school threatened to suspend him for poor behavior. The mental status examination revealed only poor adjustment. Cognitive functions were grossly normal and attention span (digit span test) was adequate. Family history of any psychiatric disorder was reportedly absent. He was advised to come the following day for a detailed psychological evaluation and psychiatric consultation for sleep disturbance. The very same evening, his father developed angina pain and was admitted to another hospital. Consequently, the patient could not be evaluated as planned. During his father's hospital admission he behaved responsibly. His mother experienced him as being supportive during this family crisis. However, his sleep was disturbed and he appeared to be restless. This was attributed to expected anxiety about his father's health. On the 12th day, S went to visit his father in the hospital. On the way back he seemed happy that his father would be discharged in a couple of days. He planned a surprise holiday for his father and appeared in good spirits, chatting with his mother and paternal grandfather.

Nonetheless, soon after lunch, he suddenly locked his mother in her room. He found a rope, tied it to a window, climbed on a sofa, called out to his mother saying that he was ending his life and hung himself. No significant event or symptom could be elicited from the parents that could have had led to suicide except sleep disturbance and restlessness.

Discussion: *Bearing in mind the history of poor adjustment, latent depression cannot be ruled out. Young boys are known to externalize their distress by displaying it as aggressive behavior or direct it inwards as depressive behavior. Persistent sleep disturbances here could be due to depression.*

(Box 3.1 contd.)

(Box 3.1 contd.)

> *Temperamentally, the patient appeared to have cyclothymic disposition with anxiety sleep disturbance, sensitivity to separation and increase in interpersonal aggressive behavior with age. Such cases reveal that it is difficult to disentangle temperamental dispositions from other psychopathology and effects of parenting styles.*

The Definitions

Many suicides among children and adolescents occur under circumstances in which timely discovery would be considered realistically possible and death can be seen as an attempt gone wrong (Shaffer & Waslick, 2002). Due to the complex and sensitive nature of the phenomenon, a globally accepted definition of suicide or attempted suicide does not exist despite concerted efforts (Silverman, Berman, Sanddal, O'Carroll, & Joiner, 2007). Shneidman (1985), considered as the father of suicidology, defined suicide as "a conscious act of self-induced annihilation, best understood as a multidimensional malaise in a needful individual who defines an issue for which suicide is the best perceived solution" (p. 203). The use of inadequate and contradictory definitions of suicidal behavior is a limitation of suicide research and communication (Silverman, Berman, Sanddal, O'Carroll, & Joiner, 2007). Among children and adolescents, the definition of attempted suicide is more complex than among adults (Shaffer & Waslick, 2002). Clear differences between adolescent attempters and completers are absent, apart from the gender differences in the choice of method. Adolescent and adult males choose irreversible methods such as guns while the females choose reversible ones such as poisoning. Adult completers have higher suicidal intent than adult attempters. It is pertinent to note that in a nationally representative sample, two-thirds of the Norwegian adolescents who responded positively to deliberately harming themselves also stated that one of the motives of the act was to die (Ystgaard, Reinholdt, Husby, & Mehlum, 2003).

Clinicians would rather err on the side of safety (Wagner, Wong, & Jobes, 2002). They assume that the clinically insignificant manifestations of suicidality may not be unimportant and could lead to a tragic outcome, although it is quite probable that the outcome may be far better. Among children and adolescents, the interlocking of suicidal ideation, attempts, and completion is even more complex than among adults. Despite the lowered lethality of suicide attempts among children and adolescents, their intent is high (Nrugham, Larsson, & Sund, 2007; Hjelmeland & Grøholt, 2005; Ystgaard et al., 2003; Shaffer & Waslick, 2002). Medical lethality indicates the method better than the intent (Shaffer & Waslick, 2002). Access to means such as tablets or guns for the method can lead to medical intervention as compared to methods such as a failed drowning or hanging. Unsupervised access to high places such as high-rise buildings may remove the need for medical intervention due to the sheer and instant lethality of the method.

The Columbia Classification Algorithm of Suicide Assessment (6–17 years of age), for pediatric suicidal risk analysis, defines a suicide attempt as follows:

> A potentially self-injurious behavior, associated with at least some intent to die, as a result of the act. Evidence that the individual intended to kill him/herself, at least to some degree, can be explicit or inferred from the behaviour or circumstance. A suicide attempt may or may not result in actual injury. (Posner et al., 2007, p.1037)

These acts were differentiated from preparatory acts toward imminent suicidal behavior, which may be either aborted or interrupted (Posner, Oquendo, Gould, Stanley, & Davies, 2007). The Diagnostic and Statistical Manual of Mental Disorders I (DSM-I) (American Psychiatric Association, 1952) excluded psychiatric disorders of children while DSM-II included only behavioral disorders of children. Operationalized criteria defined in the 1970s and 1980s for depressive syndromes in adults were applied to younger patients by clinical researchers (Shaffer & Waslick, 2002). It was consistently found that children and adolescents reported similar concurrent constellations of emotional, cognitive, and behavioral symptoms, including suicidal behaviors that were difficult to distinguish from adult depressive syndromes. Early research publications on suicidal phenomena among children and adolescents were clinical in nature, focusing on inpatients (Shaffer et al., 1996; Pfeffer, Klerman, Hurt, Kakuma, Peskin, & Siefker, 1993; Pfeffer, Newcorn, Kaplan, Mizruchi, & Plutchik, 1988). Outpatient adolescent samples were rarely studied (Kovacs, Goldston, & Gatsonis, 1993). Epidemiological studies (Lewinsohn, Roberts, Seeley, Rohde, Gotlib, & Hops, 1994; Lewinsohn, Rohde, & Seeley, 1996; Lewinsohn, Rohde, Seeley, & Baldwin, 2001) and psychological autopsy studies followed in the wake of these clinical studies (Kjelsberg, Neegard, & Dahl, 1994; Grøholt et al., 1997; Grøholt, Ekeberg, Wichstrøm, & Haldorsen, 1998; Grøholt, Ekeberg, Wichstrøm, & Haldorsen, 1999).

Pfeffer (1986) in her groundbreaking book *The Suicidal Child*, writes about clinical problems in identifying suicidal behavior among children. The secrecy within the family that surrounds a suicidal child which may be understood as guilt of own role or/and fear of social stigma. Such secrecy leads to a minimization of the situation. Additionally, the ordinary clinician neither has the training nor the expertise required to elicit and manage suicidal behaviors among this vulnerable group. Compounding these inadequacies, clinical lore supports beliefs that children lack the cognitive development required to understand the finality of death, despite evidence to the contrary (Pfeffer, Conte, Plutchik, & Jerrett, 1979; Orbach & Glaubman, 1978; Orbach & Glaubman, 1979). A small, but well-designed early clinical study described below, showed that suicide was understood as irreversible among suicidal preschoolers whose motives were self-punishment or escape, while those suicidal preschoolers who had reunion or rectification as their motives saw death as reversible (Rosenthal & Rosenthal, 1984). The lack of adequate communication skills, including appropriate vocabulary among suicidal children and adolescents support these hesitancies among the adults, whether researcher or clinician. When this situation is coupled with the cognitive confusion among the children and adolescents about the process of planning, such as unrealistic assessments of lethality and the probabilities of being rescued, "attempts" may easily be fatal.

Platt et al. (1992) refer to the definition of attempted suicide adopted by the WHO/EURO multicenter study on parasuicide:

> An act with non-fatal outcome, in which an individual deliberately initiates a non-habitual behaviour that, without intervention from others, will cause self-harm or deliberately ingests a substance in excess of the prescribed or generally recognized therapeutic dosage and which is aimed at realizing changes which the subject desired via the actual or expected physical consequences.

A two-dimensional and directly proportional approach toward the definition of a suicide attempt is now gaining acceptance, as seen in the definitions above. The relationship between these two dimensions, medical lethality and suicidal intent, is not as clear as this relationship changes with age, gender, context, and the individual.

Medical Lethality

One definition of medically serious suicide attempts is that they require hospitalization for treatment for more than 24 hours in a specialized unit or surgery under general anesthesia (Beautrais, 2003). Suicide attempts by adolescents are usually less medically lethal than by adults for which various explanations have been offered, including lack of comparable cognitive development (Hjelmeland & Grøholt, 2005). Due to the low lethality, the magnitude of suicide attempts among adolescents would not have been known without the efforts made by epidemiological researchers who are also clinicians. The bulk of research on suicidality among this age group is either on the general population sample or the inpatient sample, not the outpatient sample. The attainability or the ease of access and availability or readiness for use can be decisive in the choice of a particular method for suicide, for example jumping from tall buildings in New York, insecticides in Sri Lanka, firearms in the US and Norway, especially when the range of alternatives is limited (Maris, Berman, & Silverman, 2000; Thoresen & Mehlum, 2006).

Suicidal Intent

Suicidal intent was researched by Beck and colleagues (Beck, 1971; Beck, Brown, Steer, Dahlsgaard, & Grisham, 1999) and is now accepted as the seriousness or intensity of a person's wish to terminate his or her life. A small sample of 16 suicidal preschoolers aged between two and a half to five years referred to a university child psychiatry outpatient clinic were compared with as many behaviorally disordered children matched by age, sex, race, and parental marital and socioeconomic status (Rosenthal & Rosenthal, 1984). The suicidal group showed significantly more non-suicidal self-directed aggression, loss of interest, morbid ideas, depression, impulsivity and hyperactivity, and running-away behavior. The authors report that this group showed significantly less pain and crying after injury. Most of the children were unwanted, abused, or neglected by parents. These children not only talked about wanting to kill themselves, they had made plans such as jumping from high places, ingesting poisons, and hanging themselves. Among adults in a clinical sample, suicidal intent at the time of self-harm was associated with the risk of subsequent suicide, especially within the first year and among female patients (Harriss, Hawton, & Zahl, 2005). In another clinical study, suicidal intent among adolescents was found to be comparable with adults, despite lower medical lethality (Hjelmeland & Grøholt, 2005).

Ambivalence

The presence of deep ambivalence in suicidal behavior was documented by Shneidman and Farberow (1957) while studying suicide letters written by persons who had died by suicide. Yet, ambivalence has not gained acceptance value in research settings, where certainty of suicidal intent has a higher value and is considered as the cut-off mark for clinical threshold in diagnostic interviews (Nrugham, Larsson, & Sund, 2008a). Clinicians, however, are in no doubt about the worth of ambivalence in their daily work with suicidal patients. It gives clinical work a platform to stand on and provides a time–space window. Therefore, the detection of the presence of ambivalence, its maintenance and expansion, are among the core tasks of clinical risk assessment and management of suicidal patients. However, among children and adolescents, this is even more difficult than among adults.

Box 3.2   Case Study 2

> *P is a 16-year-old boy from an upper-middle-class family, preparing to take the competitive entrance examinations for engineering. His parents are professors in an engineering college living on the college campus. The environment of the campus is one of competition and immense value is placed on academic achievements. He has a younger brother who is studying in class 8. Both siblings are high achievers.*
>
> *He was brought by his parents to the Child Guidance Center after he attempted suicide by consuming household pesticide. There was no precipitating factor, apparently. His parents reported that he had shown aggressive and regressive behavior alternatively since the last 4–5 months. Once, after a small argument he beat up his younger brother of whom he had always been overprotective.*

(Box 3.2 contd.)

(Box 3.2 contd.)

On another occasion he tore off all the sketches that he had made and displayed on the walls of his room. Several times in the night he would insist on sleeping with his parents. The parents often found him crying in his sleep. The parents presumed that he was stressed about the forthcoming examinations as he had failed to clear the examinations the previous year. They increased their efforts to help him in his studies but it appeared to make matters worse. Mental status examination revealed sad mood, anhedonia, hopelessness, helplessness, worthlessness, suicidal ideation, and an earlier suicidal act.

Psychopharmacological treatment had been started as his father felt that psychotherapy is not helpful. Within four weeks P showed improvement. However, after six weeks of medication, he attempted suicide again. This time he consumed rat poison and immediately called his parents who rushed him to the hospital. His condition stabilized after a stomach wash. The event alerted his mother that her son was far from well. His suicidal intent was high despite the lethality being low for this act. His parents brought him back to hospital where it was decided that a psychological evaluation needs to be done.

Personality tests (Eysenck Personality Questionnaire [Revised] and High School Personality Questionnaire) and projective tests were administered. Findings indicated an unstable extrovert with high anxiety, poor ego and superego strength, poor adjustment, and high creativity. The Sentence Completion Test and Thematic Apperception Test both indicated conflicts related to career choice, parental and self-expectations for achievement, and a sense of helplessness about his circumstances. Since childhood he had dreams of becoming a painter or an artist, and having his own exhibitions. However, due to parental and peer pressure he had been led to believe that one's worth was associated only with an engineering degree. He firmly believed that he was a failure and a good-for-nothing if he did not become an engineer.

A counseling session was held with the parents to tone down their expectations and help P to think of alternative career choices. The mother was receptive. The father was adamantly negative and expressed his displeasure and contempt by terming him "weak" and "paint dabbler." When an alternative career in computer graphics was suggested for his son, he was vocal about less earnings and lack of respect. He feared becoming a laughing stock on the campus if his son was not an engineer.

Psychotherapeutic sessions using ventilation as the first technique were started. P was helped to express his desires and long suppressed wishes. From the fourth session onwards, Cognitive Behavior Therapy (CBT) was introduced. After five sessions of CBT, P learnt not to evaluate himself purely in terms of being or not being an engineer. He started feeling relatively better and more independent. However, psychotherapy was abruptly terminated as the father felt that the patient was becoming too independent in his thinking. The patient continues with antidepressants.

(Box 3.2 contd.)

(Box 3.2 contd.)

> **Discussion**: *The adolescent's personality was being formed but had not yet attained individuality and independence. An additional factor was that his personality was characterized by unstable extrovertism (high score on extroversion and neuroticism) with high anxiety and poor ego, super-ego control, and poor adjustment. As he found his circumstances overwhelming and had a poor repertoire of coping skills, he could not withstand these intrapsychic and interpsychic conflicts. The combination of high intent and low lethality was considered serious enough to use double treatment modality of psychopharmacology and psychotherapy. The repeated suicidal attempts were a cry for help as the conflict between inner desires and external pressures was not resolved. Since the conflict continues to remain unresolved, the chances of future suicidal attempts remains in either condition—failure to get selected for the engineering entrance examinations or a poor academic performance later.*

Risk Factors of Suicidality among the Young

While all suicides cannot be prevented, many can be. Guidelines for the clinical assessment of suicide risk among adolescents and adults exist on the foundations of research findings of statistically significant associates and predictors collectively known as risk factors. Empirical research has shown consistently that history of a suicidal act and a depressive episode are the most prominent predictors of completed suicide and suicidal behavior among youth (Apter & King, 2006). Yet, it is not possible to predict who will follow which path with unerring precision. Several theories attempt to explain suicidal phenomena without specifically including or excluding children and adolescents. The stress-diathesis model of suicidal behavior (Mann, Waternaux, Haas, & Malone, 1999) proposes that a vulnerability or predisposition (diathesis) is activated during interactions with the environment (stress) and leads to suicidality. Durkheim's analysis of suicide (1951) and the cognitive model elicited by Beck (1971) are other theoretical perspectives. There is enough evidence to assume that suicide and attempted suicide are expressions of a continuum of self-harming behaviors with suicidal intent determining the position of the behavior on the continuum (van Heeringen, Hawton, & Williams, 2000). This stand is supported by the strongly increased risk of suicide following attempted suicide and the co-variance of attempted suicide and suicide rates. Up to 24 percent of teenagers who completed suicide had made a prior attempt (Grøholt, Ekeberg, Wichstrøm, & Haldorsen, 1997).

Mood disorders are reported to contribute substantially to the risk of completed and attempted suicide in both genders among adolescents (Bridge, Goldstein, & Brent, 2006). The most significant risk factor of suicide among girls in a clinical sample was found to be major depression (Brent et al., 1994; Shaffer et al., 1996). In a community sample, when depression was controlled for, the gender difference in suicide attempts disappeared (Wichstrøm & Rossow, 2002). Cognitive depressive symptoms overshadowed other depressive symptoms as predictors and associates of attempted suicide among a female-dominated sample (Nrugham, Larsson, & Sund, 2008b). Apart from a previous attempt and psychiatric diagnoses (notably depression), increased age, female gender, family discord, non-intact families, a family history of suicidal behavior, high rates of parental psychopathology, life stressors (particularly interpersonal conflict or loss), childhood physical and sexual abuse, poor physical health, physical disability, functional impairment due to physical illness or injury, impulsive aggression, neuroticism, non-heterosexual orientation and same-sex attraction, exposure to suicide, and availability of lethal agents were the risk factors for attempted suicides among adolescents as concluded in three reviews (Evans, Hawton, & Rodham, 2004; Gould, Greenberg, Velting, & Shaffer, 2003; Bridge, Goldstein, & Brent, 2006).

Future attempts and psychiatric diagnoses have also been found to be the outcomes of a suicide attempt in adolescence (Lewinsohn, Rohde, & Seeley, 1996; Lewinsohn, Rohde, Seeley, & Baldwin, 2001; Fergusson, Horwood, Ridder, & Beautrais, 2005). When under-controlled or inhibited and well-adjusted three-year-olds were followed up to age 21 and compared, suicide attempt was a common factor among those not well-adjusted at age three (Caspi, Moffitt, Newman, & Silva, 1996). In a birth cohort followed from 1981 to 2005 self-reports of depression did not predict suicide and attempted suicide among males (Sourander et al., 2009). Instead, such suicidality among males was predicted by living in a non-intact family at the age of 8 years; psychological problems as reported by the primary teacher; or conduct, hyperkinetic, and emotional problems. The authors concluded that these findings indicate a trajectory persisting throughout the lives of the males.

Coping is now being examined as a part of research into how risk factors work among suicidal adolescents and adults. It is inherently logical that poorer coping skills, whether taken as a state or a trait, should be both associates and predictors of suicidality. At high levels of stress, adolescents with poor problem-solving skills experienced elevated suicidal ideation and were at greater risk of making a suicide attempt (Grover et al., 2009). Resilience protected adolescents against suicide attempts, even among those who were victims of violence and depression (Nrugham, Holen, & Sund, 2010). An adult report on suicidality and personality profiles among depressed adults using one of the most researched personality models, Cloninger's bio-psychosocial model examines the issue from another angle (Cloninger, Przybeck, Svarkic, & Wetzek, 1994). Low self-directedness (lack of conviction in being able to positively influence a difficult situation and solve a given problem), the main correlate of personality disorder, was found to be associated with suicide attempters and ideators in an outpatient sample of patients with major depression. However, the authors also found higher self-transcendence among them, which in combination with low self-directedness was explained as an indicator of illogical, immature, and suspicious behavior: Such individuals are particularly sensitive to external influences without the conviction of being able to control themselves or their environment. However, no such difference was found among depressed and suicidal adolescents when compared to "pure" depressives (Csorba et al., 2010). They found another temperament dimension—higher novelty-seeking—as the main personality correlate of addiction. If the difference was due to age and genuine, it could explain the high frequencies of repetitive self-harm behaviors among adolescents. However, Cloninger's model has also been criticized with respect to the underpinnings of its internal structure and new divergent findings which continue to add to them—novelty-seeking has been found to be associated with negative parental warmth among delinquents (Richter, Krecklow, & Eisemann, 2002). The current state of knowledge on personality and suicidality appears to be in an early phase and needs longitudinal studies.

What Can Be Done about Suicidality in the Young?

A suicide risk assessment is one of the most complex and intricate tasks within mental health and a part of emergency care. Clinical suicide risk assessments are a balancing act between the sensitivity and specificity of research results on the tightrope of available information and clinical experience woven together. This complexity and intricacy is amplified in the case of children and adolescents due to the differences and similarities between them and adults, such as developmental changes, impulsivity, and the role of depression. Suicidal adults respond differently to antidepressants than children and youth (Lam et al., 2009). Suicidal intent does not always differ between adults and adolescents (Hjelmeland & Grøholt, 2005). Suicidal phenomena among adolescents are not related to the socioeconomic characteristics of their families (Evans, Hawton, & Rodham, 2004) while such a relation is often, even if inconsistently, observed among adults (Strand & Knust, 2007; Burrows & Laflamme, 2010). In order for the intervention to have the desired impact, it is not enough to identify risk factors for suicidality—a deep understanding of how they work and influence the suicidal process is pivotal.

An effective therapy for suicidal behavior is yet to be found, despite committed and consistent efforts (Hawton et al., 2003). The avoidable tragedy of the loss, especially of young lives, is one that needs to be tackled urgently and prevention efforts need not be only psychological. Two strategies of suicide prevention have been found effective in a review: restriction of access to means, and training general practitioners to detect and treat depression rapidly (Mann et al., 2005). Both these strategies are comparatively easy to implement and monitor, as the mechanisms of how these efforts work are known. From this very brief sojourn through the most important research findings on this topic and the case studies, we see that both, the individual and the context, interweave in the development and resolution of suicidality. The cases from India reveal that although cultural contexts differ, certain identifiable and manageable psychosocial constructs related to suicidality remain the same. A distressed child is a distressed child, regardless of ethnicity and culture. With differing contexts, identification and management of risk factors may also differ. It is not practically possible for every distressed child to access or use the services of mental health professionals.

Three aspects provide clear indicators of the work remaining to be done: (*a*) The absence of a globally accepted definition of suicidality, (*b*) the absence of effective treatment for suicidal behavior, and (*c*) the presence of merely two effective preventive strategies. In order to address these critical issues of its citizens, its most important resource, each nation must have a national program for suicide prevention. Such programs imply the dedication of earmarked financial resources and reliable political support for the generation and dissemination of knowledge on suicidality.

The most promising therapies with adult and adolescent suicidal patients in the West today—Dialectical Behavior Therapy (DBT) with borderline patients (Linehan et al., 2006) and Mindfulness Based Cognitive Therapy (MBCT) with depressed patients (Williams, Duggan, Crane, & Fennell, 2006) draw upon Eastern philosophy. DBT has mindfulness as one of its core aspects while MBCT is based on mindfulness. Simply put, mindfulness is the holistic and full awareness of the present moment, equidistant from the past and the future, in a nonjudgmental and unconditional manner. Meditation is its key component—being able to stop, distance one's self from one's self, observe calmly, and suspend all judgments and the various trains of thoughts and emotions, including the very process of breathing. In other words, it suspends the need to cope immediately and it intersperses reflection between stimuli and response, whether internal or external. It is sourced by Western mental health professionals from Buddhism, which stems from the *Upanishads*. In Sanskrit, mindfulness is expressed by *saakshibhaav* or witnessing the mind. In the *Yoga Sutras* of *Patanjali*, concentration or meditation (*dhyanam*) is defined as the continuous flow of perception. To be stable in this state, one requires adequate training. This is a personal capacity, sensitive to and, therefore, amenable to change. Disturbed concentration is one of those depressive symptoms which consistently relates to suicidality in empirical research (Nrugham, Larsson, & Sund, 2008b). The search for answers to the questions raised by suicidality promotes the pooling of resources, across all known boundaries. The ability to meet and cope with adversities which come along as a natural part of life is an integral part of Eastern philosophy which inculcates an awareness of the eternal within the inner self in daily life, regardless of the external environment.

Among those considering reasons to die, their individual reasons to live may tip the balance in favor of life (Harris, McLean, Sheffield, & Jobes, 2010). As seen from the cases and the risk factors presented in this chapter, reasons to live may differ according to many factors, ranging from the individual's own temperament to the culture in which the person is. Norway was among the very first nations to work out a National Program for Suicide Prevention in 1994. A review of research into suicidality among Norwegian children and adolescents found that depression, previous suicidal behavior, alcohol use and non-intact parental unit were consistent significant risk factors for both, suicide and attempted suicide (Nrugham, Herrestad, & Mehlum, 2010). Human development, even if envisioned as modern material prosperity, cannot afford to leave behind as dead or dying the very humans it moves ahead for: children and adolescents. The step into progress must include the living, all of them.

Acknowledgment

Except for the cases and the section on management, this chapter is a shortened version of the first author's doctoral dissertation titled: "Associates and Predictors of Attempted Suicide among Adolescents—A 6-year Prospective Study," published by the Faculty of Medicine, Norwegian University of Science and Technology, the electronic version of which has the following ISBN number 978-82-471-2533-5, and the print version has the ISBN number 978-82-471-2532.

References

American Psychiatric Association. (1952). *Diagnostic and statistical manual of mental disorders* (1st ed.). Washington, DC: American Psychiatric Association.

Apter, A., & King, R. A. (2006). Management of depressed, suicidal child or adolescent. *Child and Adolescent Psychiatric Clinics of North America, 15*(4), 999–1013.

Beautrais, A. L. (2003). Suicides and serious suicide attempts in youth: A multiple-group comparison study. *American Journal of Psychiatry, 160*(6), 1093–1099.

Beck, A. T. (1971). Cognition, affect and psychopathology. *Archives of General Psychiatry, 24*(6), 495–500.

Beck, A. T., Brown, G. K., Steer, R. A., Dahlsgaard, K. K., & Grisham, J. R. (1999). Suicide ideation at its worst point: A predictor of eventual suicide in psychiatric outpatients. *Suicide and Life-Threatening Behavior, 29*(1), 1–9. doi: 10.1111/j.1943278X.1999.tb00758.x

Bertolote, J. M., & Fleischmann, A. (2009). A global perspective on the magnitude of suicide mortality. In D. Wasserman & C. Wasserman (Eds), *Oxford textbook of suicidology and suicide prevention: A global perspective* (pp. 99–104). New York: Oxford University Press.

Brent, D. A., Perper, J. A., Moritz, G., Baugher, M., Schweers, J., & Roth, C. (1994). Suicide in affectively ill adolescents: A case-control study. *Journal of Affective Disorders, 31*(3), 193–202. doi:10.1016/0165-0327(94)90029-9

Bridge, J. A., Goldstein, T. R., & Brent, D. A. (2006). Adolescent suicide and suicidal behavior. *Journal of Child Psychology and Psychiatry, 47*(3–4), 372–394. doi:10.1111/j.1469-7610.2006.01615.x

Burrows, S., & Laflamme, L. (2010). Socioeconomic disparities and attempted suicide: State of knowledge and implications for research and prevention. *International Journal of Injury Control and Safety Promotion, 17*(1), 23–40. doi:10.1080/17457300903309231

Caspi, A., Moffitt, T., Newman, D., & Silva, P. (1996). Behavioral observations at age 3 years predict adult psychiatric disorders: Longitudinal evidence from a birth cohort. *Archives of General Psychiatry, 53*(11), 1033–1039.

Cloninger, C. R., Przybeck, T., Svarkic, D. M., & Wetzel, T. (1994). *The temperament and character inventory: A guide to its development and use*. St. Louis, MO: Center for Psychobiology of Personality, Washington University.

Csorba, J., Dinya, E., Ferencz, E., Steiner, P., Bertalan, G., & Zsadon, A. (2010). Novelty seeking: Difference between suicidal and non-suicidal Hungarian adolescent outpatients suffering from depression. *Journal of Affective Disorders, 120*(1–3), 217–220. doi:10.1016/j.jad.2009.03.008

Durkheim, E. (1951). *Suicide: A study in sociology* (Trans. J. Spaulding and G. Simpson). New York: The Free Press.

Evans, E., Hawton, K., & Rodham, K. (2004). Factors associated with suicidal phenomena in adolescents: A systematic review of population-based studies. *Clinical Psychology Review, 24*(8), 957–979. doi:10.1016/j.cpr.2004.04.005

Evans, E., Hawton, K., Rodham, K., & Deeks, J. (2005). The prevalence of suicidal phenomena in adolescents: A systematic review of population-based studies. *Suicide & Life-Threatening Behavior, 35*(3), 239–250. doi:10.1521/suli.2005.35.3.239

Fergusson, D. M., Horwood, L. J., Ridder, E. M., & Beautrais, A. L. (2005). Suicidal behavior in adolescence and subsequent mental health outcomes in young adulthood. *Psychological Medicine, 35*(7), 983–993. doi:10.1017/S0033291704004167

Gould, M. S., Greenberg, T., Velting, D. M., & Shaffer, D. (2003). Youth suicide risk and preventive interventions: A review of the past 10 years. *Journal of the American Academy of Child and Adolescent Psychiatry, 42*(4), 386–405. doi:10.1097/01.CHI.0000046821.95464.CF

Grøholt, B., Ekeberg, Ø., Wichstrøm, L., & Haldorsen, T. (1997). Youth suicide in Norway, 1990–1992: A comparison between children and adolescents completing suicide and age- and gender-matched controls. *Suicide and Life-Threatening Behavior, 27*(3), 250–263. doi:10.1111/j.1943-278X.1997.tb00407.x

———. (1998). Suicide among children and younger and older adolescents in Norway: A comparative study. *Journal of the American Academy of Child and Adolescent Psychiatry, 37*(5), 473–481. doi:10.1097/00004583-199805000-00008

———. (1999). Sex differences in adolescent suicides in Norway, 1990–1992. *Suicide and Life-Threatening Behavior, 29*(4), 295–308. doi: 10.1111/j.1943-278X.1999.tb00525.x

Grover, K. E., Green, K. L., Pettit, J. W., Monteith, L. L., Garza, M. J., & Venta, A. (2009). Problem solving moderates the effects of life event stress and chronic stress on suicidal behaviors in adolescence. *Journal of Clinical Psychology, 65*(12), 1281–1290. doi:10.1002/jclp.20632

Harris, K., McLean, J., Sheffield, J., & Jobes, D. (2010). The internal suicide debate hypothesis: Exploring the life versus death struggle. *Suicide and Life-Threatening Behavior, 40*(2), 181–192. doi:10.1521/suli.2010.40.2.181

Harriss, L., Hawton, K., & Zahl, D. (2005). Value of measuring suicidal intent in the assessment of people attending hospital following self-poisoning or self-injury. *British Journal of Psychiatry, 186*(1), 60–66.

Hawton, K., Townsend, E., Arensman, E., Gunnell, D., Hazell, P., House, A., & van Heeringen, K. (2003). Psychosocial and pharmacological treatments for deliberate self harm (Cochrane Review). *The Cochrane Library, 3*. Oxford: Update Software.

Hjelmeland, H., & Grøholt, B. (2005). A comparative study of young and adult deliberate self-harm patients. *Crisis, 26*(2), 64–72.

Kjelsberg, E., Neegard, E., & Dahl, A. A. (1994). Suicide in adolescent psychiatric inpatients: Incidence and predictive factors. *Acta Psychiatrica Scandinavia, 89*(4), 235–241. doi:10.1111/j.1600-0447.1994.tb01507.x

Kovacs, M., Goldston, D., & Gatsonis, C. (1993). Suicidal behaviours and childhood-onset depressive disorders: A longitudinal investigation. *Journal of the American Academy of Child and Adolescent Psychiatry, 32*(1), 8–20. doi:10.1097/00004583-199301000-00003

Lam, R. W., Kennedy, S. H., Grigoriadis, S., McIntyre, R. S., Milev, R., Ramasubbu, R., & Ravindran, A. V. (2009). Canadian network for mood and anxiety treatments (CANMAT) clinical guidelines for the management of major depressive disorder in adults III, Pharmacotherapy. *Journal of Affective Disorders, 117*, S26–S43. doi:10.1016/j.jad.2009.06.041

Lewinsohn, P. M., Roberts, R. E., Seeley, J. R., Rohde, P., Gotlib, I. H., & Hops, H. (1994). Adolescent psychopathology II, Psychosocial risk factors for depression. *Journal of Abnormal Psychology, 103*(2), 302–315. doi: 10.1037/0021-843X.103.2.302

Lewinsohn, P. M., Rohde, P., & Seeley, J. R. (1996). Adolescent suicidal ideation and attempts: Prevalence, risk factors, and clinical implications. *Clinical Psychology: Science and Practice, 3*(1), 25–46. doi: 10.1111/j.1468-2850.1996.tb00056.x

Lewinsohn, P. M., Rohde, P., Seeley, J. R., & Baldwin, C. L. (2001). Gender differences in suicide attempts from adolescence to young adulthood. *Journal of the American Academy of Child and Adolescent Psychiatry, 40*(4), 427–434. doi:10.1097/00004583-200104000-00011

Linehan, M. M., Comtois, K. A., Murray, A. M., Brown, M. Z., Gallop, R. J., Heard, H. L., Korslund, K., & Lindenboim, N. (2006). Two-year randomized controlled trial and follow-up of dialectical behavior therapy vs. therapy by experts for suicidal behaviors and borderline personality disorder. *Archives of General Psychiatry, 63*(7), 757–66.

Mann, J. J, Waternaux, C., Haas, G., & Malone, K. (1999). Toward a clinical model of suicidal behavior in psychiatric patients. *American Journal of Psychiatry, 156*(2), 181–189.

Mann, J. J., Apter, A., Bertolote, J., Beautrais, A., Currier, D., Haas, A., & Hendin, H. (2005). Suicide prevention strategies: A systematic review. *Journal of the American Medical Association, 294*(16), 2064–2074. doi:10.1001/jama.294.16.2064

Maris, R. W., Berman, A. L., & Silverman, A. M. (2000). Suicide attempts and methods. In R. Maria, A. Berman, & A. Silverman (Eds), *Comprehensive textbook of suicidology* (pp. 284–310). New York: The Guilford Press.

Nrugham, L., Herrestad, H., & Mehlum, L. (2010). Suicidality among Norwegian youth: Review of research on risk factors and interventions. *Nordic Journal of Psychiatry 64*(5), 317–326. doi:10.3109/08039481003628364

Nrugham, L., Holen, A., & Sund, A. M. (2010). Associations between attempted suicide, violent life events, depressive symptoms, and resilience in adolescents and young adults. *Journal of Nervous and Mental Disease, 198*(2), 131–136. doi:10.1097/NMD.0b013e3181cc43a2

Nrugham, L., Larsson, B., & Sund, A. M. (2007). *A comparison of responses on the Suicide Intent Scale of Norwegian adolescents up to 15 years and between 15–20 years.* Paper presented at 25th World Congress of International Association for Suicide Prevention, Killarney, Ireland.

———. (2008a). Predictors of suicidal acts across adolescence: Influences of familial, peer, and individual factors. *Journal of Affective Disorders, 109*(1), 35–45. doi:10.1016/j.jad.2007.11.001

———. (2008b). Specific depressive symptoms and disorders as associates and predictors of suicidal acts across adolescence. *Journal of Affective Disorders, 111*(1), 83–93. doi:10.1016/j.jad.2008.02.010

Orbach, I., & Glaubman, H. (1978). Suicidal, aggressive, and normal children's perception of personal and impersonal death. *Journal of Clinical Psychology, 34*(4), 850–857. doi: 10.1002/1097-4679(197810)34:4<850::AID-JCLP2270340406>3.0.CO;2-S

———. (1979). The concept of death and suicidal behavior in young children: Three case studies. *Journal of American Academy of Child Psychiatry, 18*(4), 668–678. doi:10.1016/S0002-7138(09)62214-7

Patton, G. C., Coffey, C., Sawyer, S. M., Viner, R. M., Haller, D. M., Bose, K., & Mathers, C. D. (2009). Global patterns of mortality in young people: A systematic analysis of population health data. *Lancet, 374*(9693), 881–892. doi:10.1016/S0140-6736(09)60741-8

Pfeffer, C. R. (1986). *The suicidal child.* New York: The Guilford Press.

Pfeffer, C. R., Conte, H. R., Plutchik, R., & Jerrett, I. (1979). Suicidal behavior in latency-age children: An empirical study. *Journal of American Academy of Child Psychiatry, 18*(4), 679–92. doi:10.1016/S0002-7138(09)62215-9

Pfeffer, C. R., Klerman, G. L., Hurt, S. W., Kakuma, T., Peskin, J. R., & Siefker, C. A. (1993). Suicidal children grow up: Rates and psychosocial risk factors for suicide attempts during follow-up. *Journal of the American Academy of Child and Adolescent Psychiatry, 32*(1), 106–113. doi:10.1097/00004583-199301000-00016

Pfeffer, C. R., Newcorn, J., Kaplan, G., Mizruchi, M. S., & Plutchik, R. (1988). Suicidal behavior in adolescent psychiatric inpatients. *Journal of the American Academy of Child and Adolescent Psychiatry, 27*(3), 357–361. doi:10.1097/00004583-198805000-00015

Platt, S., Bille-Brahe, U., Kerkhof, A., Schmidtke, A., Bjerke, T., Crepet, P., & Sampaio Faria, J. (1992). Parasuicide in Europe: The WHO/EURO multicentre study on parasuicide I: Introduction and preliminary analysis for 1989. *Acta Psychiatrica Scandinavica, 85*(2), 97–104. doi:10.1111/j.1600-0447.1992.tb01451.x

Posner, K., Oquendo, M. A., Gould, M., Stanley, B., & Davies, M. (2007). Columbia Classification Algorithm of Suicide Assessment (C-CASA): Classification of suicidal events in the FDA's pediatric suicidal risk analysis of antidepressants. *American Journal of Psychiatry, 164*(7), 1035–1043. doi:10.1176/appi.ajp.164.7.1035

Richter, J., Krecklow, B., & Eisemann, M. (2002). Interrelations between temperament, character, and parental rearing among delinquent adolescents: A cross-validation. *Comprehensive Psychiatry, 43*(3), 210–214.

Rosenthal, P. A., & Rosenthal, S. (1984). Suicidal behavior by preschool children. *American Journal of Psychiatry, 141*(4), 520–525.

Shaffer, D., Gould, M. S., Fisher, P., Trautman, P., Moreau, D., Kleinman, M., & Flory, M. (1996). Psychiatric diagnosis in child and adolescent suicide. *Archives of General Psychiatry, 53*(4), 339–348.

Shaffer, D., & Waslick, B. D. (Eds). (2002). *The many faces of depression in children and adolescents.* Washington, DC: American Psychiatric Publishing.

Shneidman, E. S. (1985). *Definition of suicide.* Northvale, NJ: Jason Aronson.

Shneidman, E. S., & Farberow, N. L. (1957). Some comparisons between genuine and simulated suicide notes in terms of Mowrer's concepts of discomfort and relief. *Journal of General Psychology, 56*(2), 251–256.

Silverman, M. M., Berman, A. L., Sanddal, N. D., O'Carroll, P. W., & Joiner, T. E. (2007). Rebuilding the Tower of Babel: A revised nomenclature for the study of suicide and suicidal behaviours, Part 1: Background, rationale, and methodology. *Suicide and Life-Threatening Behavior, 37*(3), 248–263. doi:10.1521/suli.2007.37.3.248

Sourander, A., Klomek, A. B., Niemelä, S., Haavisto, A., Gyllenberg, D., Helenius, H., & Gould, M. S. (2009). Childhood predictors of completed and severe suicide attempts: Findings from the Finnish 1981 Birth Cohort Study. *Archives of General Psychiatry, 66*(4), 398–406.

Strand, B. H., & Kunst, A. (2007). Childhood socioeconomic position and cause-specific mortality in early adulthood. *American Journal of Epidemiology, 165*(1), 85–93. doi: 10.1093/aje/kwj352

Thoresen, S., & Mehlum, L. (2006). Suicide in peacekeepers: Risk factors for suicide versus accidental death. *Suicide and Life-Threatening Behaviour, 36*(4), 432–442. doi:10.1521/suli.2006.36.4.432

van Heeringen, K., Hawton, K., & Williams, J. M. G. (2000). Pathways to suicide: An integrative approach. In K. Hawton & K. van Heeringen (Eds), *The international handbook of suicide and attempted suicide* (pp. 223–236). Chichester, England: John Wiley & Sons.

Wagner, B. M., Wong, S. A., & Jobes, D. A. (2002). Mental health professionals' determinations of adolescent suicide attempts. *Suicide and Life-Threatening Behavior, 32*(3), 284–300. doi:10.1521/suli.32.3.284.22178

Wichstrøm, L., & Rossow, I. (2002). Explaining the gender difference in self-reported suicide attempts: A nationally representative study of Norwegian adolescents. *Suicide and Life-Threatening Behavior, 32*(2), 101–116. doi:10.1521/suli.32.2.101.24407

Williams, J. M., Duggan, D. S., Crane, C., & Fennell, M. J. (2006). Mindfulness-based cognitive therapy for prevention of recurrence of suicidal behavior. *Journal of Clinical Psychology, 62*(2), 201–210. doi:10.1002/jclp.20223

World Health Organization. (2002). Distribution of suicides rates (per 100,000) by gender and age, 2000. *World Health Organization, Programmes and Projects: Mental Health.* Retrived from http://www.who.int/mental_health/prevention/suicide/suicide_rates_chart/en/index.html

Ystgaard, M., Reinholdt, N. P., Husby, J., & Mehlum, L. (2003). Deliberate self harm in adolescents. *Tidsskrift for den Norsk Legeforening, 123*(16), 2241–2245.

SECTION 3

Special Contexts

4

Impact of HIV/AIDS on the Mental Health of Children and Adolescents in India

Shankar Das
Ashima Das
George Leibowitz

Children are our future. Through well conceived policy and planning, governments can promote the mental health of children, for the benefit of the child, the family, the community and society.
(WHO, 2005)

Introduction

The HIV pandemic has adversely impacted households worldwide and the most affected are children and adolescents. This has been demonstrated by researchers globally who have explored the widespread prevalence of the problem and the psychological, cultural, and socioeconomic impact of HIV/AIDS among young people. The children are particularly vulnerable to poverty; limited educational opportunities; stigma; sexual, physical, and emotional abuse; and inadequate health care, resulting in poor mental health.

Child and adolescent mental health is seen as comprising of sense of identity and self-worth, sound family and peer relationships, an ability to be productive and to learn, and a capacity to use developmental challenges and cultural resources to maximize development (Dawes et al., 1997). The growing burden of mental disorders among children and adolescents has emerged as a vital concern for researchers and policy makers around the world (World Health Organization [WHO], 2005). Children who experience a serious medical condition are particularly vulnerable, from the standpoint that there are developmental factors affecting their ability to cope with an illness early in life, when their identities are being formed. The need to uphold a developmental perspective, taking into account individual, family, and social factors, is central to understanding child and adolescent mental health. In addition, coping is intricately connected to the level of a family's adaptation, and a family's responsiveness and resiliencies associated with helping a child manage the psychological consequences of the illness (Sourkes, 1995; Webb, 2009).

The burgeoning HIV/AIDS epidemic is among several risk factors that contribute to mental health problems of children and adolescents. The researchers have begun to investigate and understand the impact of the disease in a developmental and social context. Recent statistics compiled by UNAIDS (2010) for the year 2008 revealed that globally there were 2.1 million children and 5 million young people (aged 15–24 years) living with HIV/AIDS. Further, it was estimated that 13 million children worldwide were orphaned and had lost their mother or both parents (Narain, 2004). This situation appears especially dire when we consider the fact that disproportionate numbers of marginalized and vulnerable groups are affected in developing nations. For many young people, the difficulties of managing a chronic health condition are compounded by poor economic conditions, discrimination, and mental health problems. The illness of the child or parent in the family system jeopardizes the fulfillment of basic needs, such as access to adequate health care, nutrition, sanitation, and education threatening even the right to survival. Children affected by HIV/AIDS are at risk for a negative self-identity, grief, anxiety, and depression, and the disease compromises the development of a positive family environment, which would otherwise nurture self-esteem and foster secure attachment in children (UNICEF, 2005).

A number of recent studies also suggest that HIV/AIDS has negatively impacted lives of millions of children globally (Demmer & Burghart, 2008; Mweru, 2008). Psychosocial and biological factors associated with the disease increase vulnerabilities in many life spheres, such as parental loss, poverty, lack of educational opportunities, stigma and isolation, and even early death (Foster, Makufa, Drew, Mashumba, & Kambeu, 1997) Many researchers have opined that in the absence of adequate coping skills and social support mechanisms, children were predisposed to clinically significant levels of depression, anxiety, withdrawal, and suicidal thoughts (Atwine, Cantor-Graae, & Bajunirwe, 2005; Cluver & Gardner, 2007; Landry, Luginaah, Maticka-Tyndale, & Elkins, 2007). These vulnerabilities and traumatic life events warrant the attention of mental health professionals and policy makers. Considering the growing spread of the pandemic of AIDS and its effect on mental health of children and adolescents, the authors of this chapter elucidate the various issues associated with the disease and suggest possible interventions with a particular focus on India.

The Indian Scenario

India has a population of more than a billion, of which approximately one-third (approximately 400 million) are children below 18 years (Government of India [GOI], 2010). The country ranks 127 on the Human Development Index (HDI) despite being the tenth largest economy of the world. The Subgroup Report on Child Protection in the 11th Plan (2007–12) underscored that if child rights indicators were to become a measure of the HDI, then the ranking would be much lower. The Asia Development Bank and UNAIDS (2004) hypothesized that HIV/AIDS transmission will impact the annual rate of poverty reduction in India by 23 percent between 2003 and 2015.

Even after six decades of Independence the mortality and morbidity rates of Indian children continue to be high, 53 per 1,000 live births (GOI, 2010). Despite the Constitutional provisions and child-related policies, the social, health, and educational needs of our children are largely unmet. Until now, a large number of children and adolescents do not attend school. Forty percent of the Indian population still lives below the poverty line; children in such poverty-stricken families are forced to work as cheap labor and thus refrain from attending school. The situation of children living in poverty and vulnerable circumstances such as streets, slums, remote rural areas, hilly terrains, and so forth is alarming. Further, with the burgeoning impact of HIV/AIDS epidemic on families, the child and adolescent population are confronted with an unprecedented threat to their health and well-being.

Table 4.1 illustrates the estimated number of adult and children living with HIV. Approximately 1.2 million children have lost their one or both parents to the disease. Recent statistics from UNAIDS (2010) revealed that rates of infection in India account for half of Asia's HIV prevalence. UNICEF (2004) reported that although the prevalence rates were highest in Southern Africa, the rates of increase were sharpest in Europe and central Asia, and absolute numbers were the largest in India and China. Further, they reported that the HIV crisis among children would persist for decades to come, and although an accurate estimation of prevalence rates in children is difficult to obtain (e.g., many are unaware of their diagnosis), it is clear the infection rates have been steadily increasing.

Table 4.1 HIV/AIDS Statistics: India

Estimated number of adults and children living with HIV/AIDS	5,700,000
Estimated number of adult and children deaths	680,000
Estimated number of AIDS orphans	1,232,131

Source: UNAIDS/WHO (2005).

The mode of infection among children has been largely through mother-to-child transmission (MTCT), other modes of transmission include sexual contact (sexual abuse), blood transfusion, and unsterilized syringes including injectable drug use (UNAIDS, 2004). Unfortunately, the prevention of mother-to-child transmission (PMTCT) services fail to reach most women in resource-poor countries. It was reported in 2008 that only 45% of HIV-infected pregnant women in low- and middle-income countries received drugs to protect their babies from infection (WHO/UNAIDS/UNICEF, 2009).

Revised estimates in 2006 combined data from multiple data sources, and the number of people living with HIV/AIDS (PLHA) was reported to be 2 to 3.1 million, 3.8 percent of whom were children (GOI, 2009). The National AIDS Control Organization (NACO) estimates suggest that 70,000 children below the age of 15 were infected with HIV and 21,000 children were infected every year through MTCT (Motihar, 2007).

As in the other parts of world, PLHA in India suffer from entrenched stigma and discrimination in several contexts: household, workplace, health settings, and communities (UNAIDS, 2001). Four characteristics of the HIV disease have been identified, which contribute to misunderstanding and prejudicial attitudes associated with the stigma. First, primary responsibility is imposed on an HIV/AIDS infected individual, given that the central mode of infection is associated with behaviors that are considered voluntary and avoidable. Second, the condition is still considered progressive and fatal by the public, despite scientific advances and the fact that the effectiveness of highly active antiretroviral therapy (HAART) has altered the perception of HIV in the medical community as a more manageable chronic condition that can be treated on an outpatient basis. Third, contagious diseases are often stigmatized by society in general. Lastly, conditions which are easily discernible by the face of it, for example, the advanced stages of AIDS are further stigmatized (Herek, 1999). The stigma and discrimination could result in psychological trauma and social exclusion in which children may be denied their basic rights (Kulkarni & Shukla, 2001).

Socioeconomic and Psychological Impact

The socioeconomic and psychological impact of AIDS on children was summarized by Bailey (1992), and is described in Table 4.2. This research focused on addressing the negative outcomes, social consequences, and mental health sequelae for children living in the world with the epidemic in the following contexts: (*a*) children living with HIV infection and AIDS, (*b*) children living with HIV-infected parents, (*c*) children orphaned by AIDS, and (*d*) children in a world faced with the HIV pandemic.

The impact of the disease could be both direct and indirect. The psychosocial circumstances of children affected by HIV/AIDS are such that they may be compelled to take on adult roles in order to accommodate an infected parent (Bauman, Foster, Silver, Berman, Gamble, & Muchaneta, 2006), and they must learn to interact with helping professionals, and manage chronic stress. In some cases, in addition to facing the emotional trauma of nursing an infected family member, they might be required to care for their younger siblings and/or other family members (USAID, 2003).

There is a paucity of research and information on the mental health challenges faced by each of these four groups of children and adolescents impacted by HIV infection (Scharko, 2006). Nicholas and Abrams (2002) reported that a considerable number of HIV-positive children in

Table 4.2   Impact of AIDS on Children

	The Child with HIV Infection and AIDS	The Child with HIV-infected Parent(s)	The Child Orphaned by AIDS	The Children in a World Faced with the HIV Pandemic
Health and nutrition, well-being and material support	Disease-stunted growth, disability, and death	Loss of family income, priority allocation of available resources to support infected parents/siblings, poverty	Dependent on institutions/extended families or left alone to fend for themselves	Competing priorities within the health sector, competing priorities between health/social sector and other sectors, and impact of pandemic on availability of service and support
Emotional, affecting development	Children facing their own illness and death	Fear, loss of childhood, and living through parents' disease and death	Fear, loss of childhood, and psychological problems	Fear, loss of childhood
Education	Discontinued access to education, possible effect of HIV trauma on skill/knowledge acquisition	Reduced ability of parents to provide sustained support/guidance	Stigma/discrimination in school dropouts	Strained educational resources and absenteeism/illness of educators
Sexuality	Hopelessness, fear, and feeling of rejection	Street kids: survival and sexual abuse/injection drug use	Misperceptions resulting from absence of parental supervision or guidance	Misperception of risk/protection and misconception of sex

Source: Adapted from Bailey (1992, p. 669).

the child welfare system in the US displayed severe behavioral problems and developed mental illness during adolescence. Some of these children were aggressive and engaged in inappropriate sexual behavior, and quite a few landed in the criminal justice system (Freeman, 2004). Although the broader context and ecology related to adolescent aggression may vary across nations, the problems associated with growing up with the disease are of universal concern. Collins, Hollman, Freeman, and Patel (2006), in their systematic review, confirmed the high prevalence of mental disorders in HIV/AIDS care settings and treatment programs in developing countries. They did not find any studies that examined psychiatric co-morbidities among HIV infected children; however, their review included few studies (Boivin et al., 1995; Drotar et al., 1999), which examined the cognitive and neuro-developmental effects of the disease. All of these studies indicated that HIV infected infants and children experienced deficits in motor and cognitive development in comparison to HIV-negative children. Additionally, Scharko (2006) suggested that children and adolescents infected with HIV suffer high rates of psychiatric disorders, with prevalence rates of 28.6 percent for ADHD, 24.3 percent for anxiety disorders, and 25 percent for depression. Interestingly, Dowdney (2000) reported that childhood bereavement issues, that is, grief, depression, and dysphoria following parental death may be especially problematic for boys, and she found that the risk for psychiatric disorders is elevated when a mental health disturbance is present prior to parental death. Outcomes among bereaved children showed significant variance across populations, depending on the moderating factors that influence risk, with the greatest risk for less stable and more vulnerable children. Co-morbid depression and posttraumatic stress disorder was noted by Dowdney to interfere with family communication and the grieving process, a particularly important finding when considering appropriate interventions that target the family system (discussed later in this chapter).

Socioemotional and behavioral concerns have also been found to occur in children and adolescents who live with HIV infected parents and must cope with the death of parent/parents or close family members. For example, some researchers have found high levels of psychological distress among children and adolescents when their parents were terminally ill with HIV/AIDS (Foster & Williamson, 2000; Wild, 2001). A study by UNICEF (2003) reported that children are so burdened by taking on new roles as caregivers that they preferred solitude and experienced elevated distress in comparison to the control group. These additional responsibilities act as stressors and result in poor mental health. The way a child copes with illness is intricately connected to the family's emotional response and is dependent on the supports that are available in the child's social environment and culture.

The third category involves AIDS orphans who are also at increased risk of poor mental health outcomes. Regardless of the cause of the death of the parent, these children are at increased risk for depression, social withdrawal and low self-esteem (Dowdney, 2000). Cluver, Gardner, and Operario (2007) established that AIDS orphans had higher levels of psychological and behavioral problems compared with both non-orphans and other orphans (predominantly emotional difficulties, such as depression, suicidal ideation, and posttraumatic stress, as well as behavioral issues such as delinquency, as reported on standardized measures). Idoniboye (2008) reported that there was a greater likelihood of children becoming orphans at an age when they require adult supervision and guidance about sexual practices.

The positive role of communication between parents and children in HIV prevention has also been studied (Romo, Lefkowitz, Sigman, & Au, 2001; Lefkowitz, Kahlbaugh, Au, & Sigman, 1998). Corroborating previous research, Global Initiative on Psychiatry (2008) reported that children orphaned by AIDS were more likely to develop depressive symptoms, suicidal thoughts, problem with peer relationship, posttraumatic stress, delinquency and conduct problems than those orphaned by other causes and non-orphaned children. The AIDS-orphaned children are stigmatized and discriminated leading to psychological distress and drug addiction. These children become far more vulnerable to various forms of abuse and all forms of exploitations such as prostitution, beggary, and juvenile delinquency (Pandve, Bhawalkar, & Bhuyar, 2008). One study in Burundi established that children orphaned by AIDS were more likely to be malnourished, which in turn adversely affected their physical and intellectual development (Subbarao, Mattimore, & Plangemann, 2001). Additionally, educational competency is a critical component of child's development. UNAIDS (2008) reports that in 56 nations where there was availability of household survey data, orphans who had lost both parents were 12 percent less likely to attend school in comparison to non-orphans. In India, there were marked differences between HIV and non-HIV households regarding educational indicators, and the dropout rates were higher in children living in HIV households (Pradhan, Sundar, & Singh, 2006). These findings could have important implications for interventions and policy-related decisions, which are addressed in the subsequent sections of this chapter.

Figure 4.1 illustrates various psychosocial and economic consequences among children and families affected by AIDS. The cost of treatment and medical care for the infected person significantly impacts household income and savings. An HIV-household is severely compromised when the parent(s) die and the children are sent to relatives or placed in institutional settings (UNAIDS, 2002). In India, Duraisamy (2003) reported that 49 percent of a family's income may be spent on medical treatment, and in low-income families the expenses may be as high as 82 percent. In a study conducted in Maharashtra (amongst the six high prevalence states in India), Verma et al. (2002) found that households affected by HIV/AIDS related death had sold off their means of production to overcome the economic burden of the disease on the family. Another documented negative impact of the disease involved impediments to educational achievement and the withdrawal of children from schools (Pitayanon, Kongsin, & Janjaroen, 1997; UNAIDS, 2002; Whiteside, 2001). Gilborn, Nyonyintono, Kabumbuli, and Jagwe-Wadda (2001) contended that children infected or associated with HIV have been stigmatized and discriminated in educational settings in many countries where they are teased by their classmates. Mallmann (2003) reported that the teasing sometimes even led to physical bullying. In case of adolescents, the classmates and members of the community gossiped about the HIV/AIDS status of members of their families. Thus, the children and adolescents preferred to stay at home rather than attend school.

Orphanhood is often accompanied by prejudice and poverty, which interferes with educational attainment, and may result in the use of inadequate survival strategies in children, which in turn increases vulnerability to HIV infection (UNAIDS, 2008). It has been established that children orphaned by AIDS are prone to multiple stressors which could complicate the process of bereavement. Many of these children had to experience the death of the parent and had to witness the gradual loss of bodily functions as well as the accompanying mental illness (O'Olley et al., 2003).

Figure 4.1   Problems among Children and Families Affected by HIV/AIDS

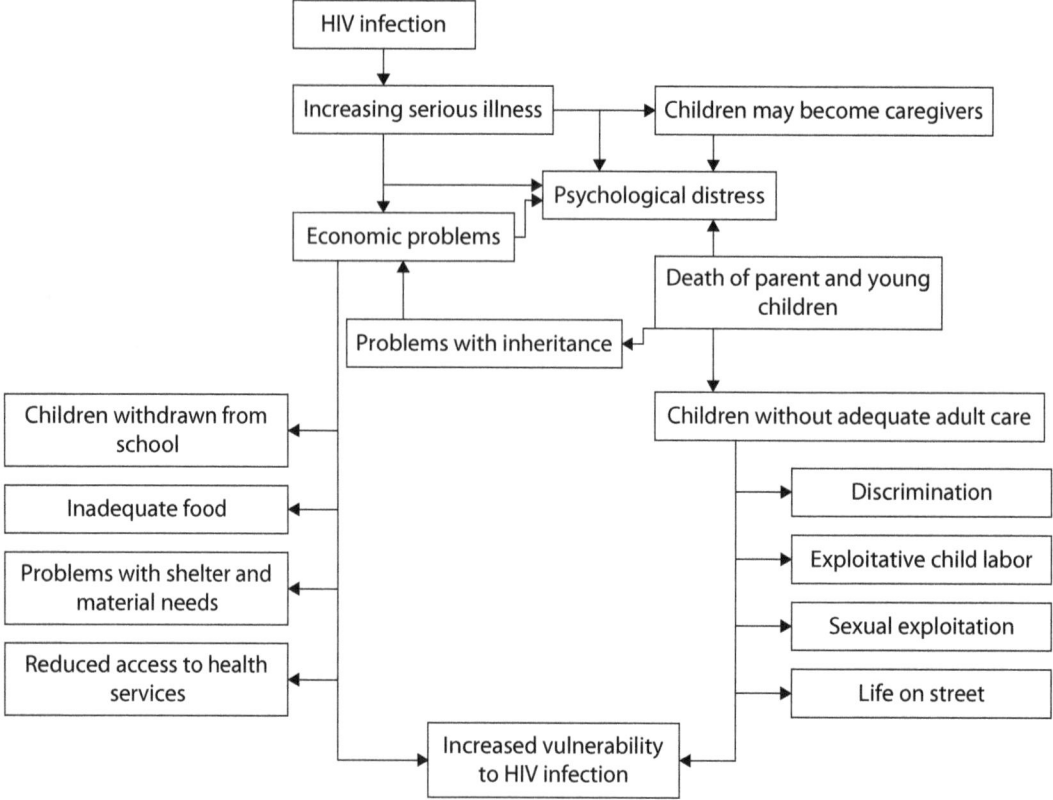

[Flowchart: HIV infection → Increasing serious illness → Children may become caregivers; Increasing serious illness → Economic problems and Psychological distress; Children may become caregivers → Psychological distress; Death of parent and young children → Psychological distress and Children without adequate adult care; Problems with inheritance → Economic problems; Economic problems → Children withdrawn from school, Inadequate food, Problems with shelter and material needs, Reduced access to health services; Children without adequate adult care → Discrimination, Exploitative child labor, Sexual exploitation, Life on street; all leading to Increased vulnerability to HIV infection.]

Source: Williamson (2005).

The AIDS epidemic may lead to numerous losses, such as loss of either or both parents and perinatally infected younger siblings. The caregivers of orphans also have been found to suffer from poor mental health (Manuel, 2002; Ferreira, Broderick, Keikelame, & Mosaval, 2001).

The following needs of children and adolescents affected by ongoing medical illness have been identified by the GOI (2009):

- Infected children and adolescents need specialized medical treatment and care, which could contribute in enhancing their quality of life.
- Children orphaned by AIDS often have psychological needs resulting from orphanhood or social exclusion/discrimination. The caregivers, which could be extended family members or foster families, must be provided with needed encouragement and support. Institutionalization must be considered as the last option and priority must be given to reintegration into society through placement in appropriate family care.

- Children and adolescents living with HIV-positive parent would benefit from appropriate medical intervention for the parent. This would delay orphanhood and would enable the parent to lead a productive life.

Psychosocial Interventions

The foregoing discussion highlights the vulnerability of children and adolescents infected and affected with HIV/AIDS to mental health problems. The literature suggests that therapeutic interventions for children and adolescents should be directed towards mitigating the effect of any adverse situations arising due to the disease and providing psychosocial supports for any negative mental health outcomes (Webb, 2009). Stigma and discrimination has been reported to be the major cause associated with weakening support systems, increasing vulnerability and dwindling economic status of the affected children (NACO, 2007). The interventions must therefore be multipronged and address individual, family, community, and policy levels. There is also a need to take a dynamic developmental perspective which takes into account changes over time at multidimensional levels as the reference point for developing intervention strategies and programs for child and adolescent mental health.

Individual and School-based Approaches

The use of psychotherapeutic and psychosocial interventions like psychotherapy, cognitive behavioral therapy (CBT), school interventions, outpatient counseling, and family therapy for the children and adolescents with mental health problems remain a better choice than using medications (WHO, 2003). Helping children and families cope with the stress of chronic HIV/AIDS-related illnesses involves enhancing cognitive self-appraisal and using restructuring to alter negative self-statements resulting from fear and loss (the focus of CBT), effective problem solving, and increasing social supports. CBT is used effectively in individual as well as group therapy settings and techniques are often adapted for PLHA self-help applications.

According to WHO (2001) school-based interventions could have an affirmative role in mental health promotion of young people. There is greater consensus that guidance and counseling should be a vital component of education of children with synchronized teacher training programs in this area. There is evidence that a positive school experience could strengthen the coping ability with transition and change, and that the school environment could act as a protective factor for positive mental health (Resnick et al., 1997; Anteghini, Fonseca, Ireland, & Blum, 2001).

The initiative, therefore, must be to create school inclusive cultures which recognize rights of vulnerable children and eliminate any sort of discrimination against any learner. The implementation of a coordinated response is imperative by preparing school counselors, social workers, administrators, medical professionals, and teachers to work together to assist children, parents, and the community to mitigate HIV/AIDS-related stigma, as well as to provide support to the child with ongoing medical issues (Griffith & Doyle, 2009).

In many places, children are increasingly affected by the epidemic. Apart from those themselves infected with HIV, they include children where one or both of the parents are either living with HIV or AIDS or have died of AIDS. These children have special counseling needs, such as the emotional trauma of seeing their parents ill or dying, discrimination by other children and adults, and emotional worries about their own continuing illness. Older children may need counseling related to sexual issues and on the avoidance of risk behavior. In such circumstances HIV/AIDS counseling has been proved valuable in different ways—it can help individuals make decisions about HIV testing, reduce HIV transmission (UNAIDS, 1997), and also solve intrapsychic problems. It could be started by reiterating values of good counseling practice and subsequently exploring various effective ways of communicating with children, for example, through play, storytelling, drawing, and role play. Counselors may need to address a number of issues before initiating the process, such as personal issues, belief systems, advocacy, talking about death with children, anonymity, and confidentiality.

Outpatient counseling, similar to treatment of other chronic conditions, like cancer, should be family-focused and collaborative (Davies & Webb, 2009) emphasizing traumatic bereavement counseling due to a loss of parent(s) to the disease, and helping a young person become aware of the issues surrounding HIV infection including safeguarding against infecting others and addressing substance abuse concerns (e.g., transmission through contaminated needles), and unprotected sex. Davies and Webb also identified several therapeutic perspectives for treatment, including an attachment perspective, and stress and trauma perspective. The former fostering secure attachments to help a child cope with stress associated with chronic diseases and learning to regulate, the latter, ensuring that the practitioner maintains a trauma-informed approach to address the symptoms of posttraumatic stress in both the child and the parent.

Family-based Approaches

Early research focused on the psychosocial impact of HIV/AIDS in the individual however, the focus has shifted to the family system (Webb, 2009). From an ecological point of view, families play a central role in the proximal social environment shaping childhood development, and researchers have identified positive family involvement as an important protective factor in preventing risky sexual behavior and HIV/AIDS among adolescents. Positive family relationships include communication regarding unsafe sexual behaviors and monitoring negative peer group influences (Perrino, Gonzalez-Soldevilla, Pantin, & Szapocznik, 2000).

Family systems approaches such as structural family therapy (Minuchin, 1974) that address enmeshed or disengaged boundaries; role reversals; cross generational coalitions; and spousal, child, and sibling subsystems, as well as coping strategies in the family (such as denial, guilt, and blaming) can be effective when working with families confronted with HIV and AIDS. Moreover, family-based approaches can be effective in targeting a young person's emotional challenges, grief issues, psychosocial, health related disorders due to substance abuse (the danger of contracting HIV/AIDS is higher among at-risk youth who abuse substances), and problem behavior (such as delinquency) resulting from stress, which is supported by the research (Liddle et al., 2001; Oman, Vesely, & Aspy, 2005). The notion that caregivers facilitate social learning and play an important role in preventing HIV among children is well supported in the literature (Perrino et al., 2000). Additionally, practitioners should explore the role of the extended family in supporting a young person orphaned by HIV-related death in resource limited nations (Ntozi, Ahimbisibwe, Odwee, Ayiga, & Okurut, 1999).

Community-based Approaches and the Third Sector

In the absence of a mental health policy for the children and adolescents infected and affected with HIV/AIDS, the third sector has emerged to be an active partner in safeguarding the rights of the children and adolescents and promoting their mental health. In so far as the broader field of sustainable development is concerned, nongovernmental organizations as providers of services are often engaged as an adjunct in the process. Despite the persistence to participate in the entire process, the national governments feel hesitant to share the decision making (Bagasao, 2004). Soderholm (1997) confirmed the vital role of NGOs as social advocates, and the growing and considerable numbers of national and international NGOs working in the field of HIV/AIDS. Considering the magnitude and complexity of the global pandemic, the NGO sector in India evolved over the last two and half decades. Their contribution in terms of innovativeness, development of practice-based knowledge, and activism has been the hallmark of nongovernmental sector in India. In light of the widespread complexity of the pandemic, there is a significant need for setting out the key principles, practice guidelines and evidence-based policy with special emphasis on mental health and comprehensive care of children and adolescents. In India, NGOs are committed to continuous improvement and may further benefit from national networks that aim to achieve the following initiatives that are imperative for successful responses to the HIV epidemic.

- Helping NGOs to develop quality and consistency of work.
- Assisting in developing accountability to partners and beneficiary communities.
- Fostering greater collaboration among the variety of active NGOs engaged in HIV prevention, control, and care program in communities.
- Empowering and capacity building of NGOs thus enabling them to commit to a shared vision of good practice in program implementation and advocacy.

Additionally, many community-based organizations (CBOs) are significantly engaged in HIV/AIDS prevention activities. CBOs may mainly include grassroots AIDS care and prevention organizations, primary health care agencies, drug rehabilitation centers, and community centers which are well known because of delivery of services to definite target population and their understanding of local communities and affiliation to the communities they serve (Chillag et al., 2002).

There could be several models of care and support for HIV affected children ranging from community-based support and rehabilitation to foster care to institutional arrangements run by faith-based organizations, and to temporary shelters run by NGOs (Kapadia-Kundu, 2006). A number of NGOs, CBOs, and international organizations are working actively in the field of HIV/AIDS, and have special programs for the infected and affected children in India. In the recent times the Peer Treatment Education (PTE) approach in the community has emerged as one of the effective practices and has become increasing popular strategy among network of PLHA as well as providers of care, support, and treatment. This is largely because the PTEs are closer to the people in the community and well aware of the local culture; with some amount of training they could effectively reach out to the PLHA and their families in their community (Das & Bharat, 2008).

Policy and Programs

It is vital to invest in the future of the children and adolescents, as they are the edifice for the future of the nation. For children and adolescents to achieve optimal psychological, social functioning and well-being, they must enjoy good mental health. Shatkin and Belfer (2004) reported that only 34 countries in the world (only 7% of the countries worldwide) have a child and adolescent mental health policy. In India, the prevalence rates of psychiatric disorders among children (1–16 years) who visit primary care facilities is 12.8% (WHO, 2005). Das and Leibowitz (2011) noted that several factors such as insensitivity, lack of resources, and trained personnel are jeopardizing the implementation of mental health policy in India.

The UN General Assembly (2006) adopted the Political Declaration on HIV/AIDS which restated and urged the governments to address

> as a priority the vulnerabilities faced by children affected by and living with HIV; providing support and rehabilitation to these children and their families, women and the elderly, particularly in their role as caregivers; promoting child-oriented HIV/AIDS policies and programs and increased protection for children orphaned and affected by HIV/AIDS; … and building, where needed, and supporting the social security systems that protect them. (p. 5)

Following this reiteration the Ministry of Women and Child Development and NACO released the Policy Framework for Children and AIDS in 2007. This policy emphasized the need to address rights of all children affected by HIV/AIDS and aimed to reach out to 80% of the children by 2010 (Ghanashyam, 2010). The policy is shared responsibility between NACO and NRHM,

Ministry of Social Justice and Empowerment, Ministry of Women and Child Development, and Ministry of Human Resource Development.

Freeman (2000) suggested that the mental health programs must be incorporated within other health priorities of the nation and must be considered as a pathway to general health care. A similar strategy was advocated for by WHO (2008) which recommended that a mental health component be incorporated within HIV/AIDS initiatives and programs, and this could bring about a remarkable improvement in the health of PLHA. To facilitate this process WHO developed a number of modules and training materials. The most significant is the guidance package (WHO, 2005) with a call for nations to develop a comprehensive mental health policy for children and adolescents and making their mental health care systems effective, affordable, and accessible. The primary steps involve an assessment of mental health disorders and their appropriate management. Primary health care providers and counselors must be trained to diagnose mental health problems and refer the patients to specialized services when need arises. As mentioned previously, effective multidisciplinary collaboration of mental health and HIV/AIDS professionals is crucial for prevention and effective treatment.

We elucidate an intervention plan (see Figure 4.2) for the children and adolescents. As the preceding discussion has established, the psychosocial and economic circumstances accompanied with the disease affects the mental health of the infected and affected individuals and their families.

Figure 4.2 Intervention for Infected and Affected Children and Adolescents

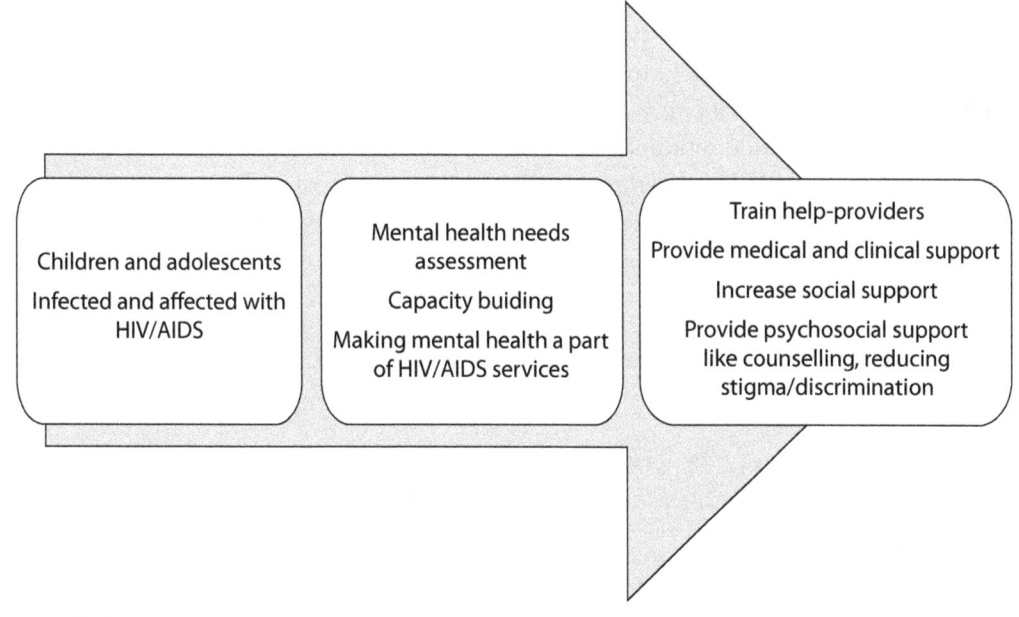

- Children and adolescents Infected and affected with HIV/AIDS
- Mental health needs assessment
- Capacity buiding
- Making mental health a part of HIV/AIDS services
- Train help-providers
- Provide medical and clinical support
- Increase social support
- Provide psychosocial support like counselling, reducing stigma/discrimination

Source: Authors.

For mental health promotion of the target population there are two kinds of service provision: at the macro level where the services and programs are more generic and at the individual level where it is specific and need based. It is important to assess the mental health of the infected and affected children and adolescents and provide support based on their status. Children and adolescents who are found to be suffering from any mental health problems require specialized and accessible treatment services. This necessitates that health care professionals be trained in mental health assessment and treatment in order to provide appropriate treatment and referral services to the needy. Effective services for children involve improving access to basic survival requirements like shelter, nutrition, education, and health. In the Indian context, it is especially important to mitigate stigma and discrimination prevailing in societies and health settings for improving mental health of the infected and affected children and adolescents.

Conclusion

The ramifications of HIV/AIDS on children and adolescents are manifold resulting in poor mental health. Thus, interventions must be planned and implemented at the level of the individual, family, and community as well as policy arenas; lessons must be drawn from the available evidence-based research data. The prevention of HIV, and ensuring access to treatment, must be among the foremost concerns of nations, which would significantly reduce the number of infected children and result in fewer AIDS orphans. However, in the present scenario there is paucity of evidence-based research data in the areas of mental health of children and adolescents affected and infected by HIV epidemics in India. There is exigent need for micro- and macro-level research to capture the actual multidimensional impact of HIV/AIDS on children and adolescents in families, schools, and communities vis-à-vis various emergent psychosocial and mental health needs. The larger issues of stigma and discrimination must be tackled within communities and nations to enhance quality of life of PLHA and their families. Moreover, mental health issues of children and adolescents are entangled with the overall psycho-socioeconomic conditions of the affected population and thus, apart from rendering specific services, programs and policies must be directed towards mitigating the impact of the disease at all levels.

References

Anteghini, M., Fonseca, H., Ireland, M., & Blum, R. (2001). Health risk behaviors and associated risk and protective factors among Brazilian adolescents in Santos, Brazil. *Journal of Adolescent Health, 28*(4), 295–302. doi:10.1016/S1054-139X(00)00197-X

Asia Development Bank & UNAIDS (2004). Asia-Pacific's Opportunity: Investing to avert an HIV/AIDS Crisis. ADB/UNAIDS Study Series.

Atwine, B., Cantor-Graae, E., & Bajunirwe, F. (2005). Psychological distress among AIDS orphans in rural Uganda. *Social Science and Medicine, 61*(3), 555–564.

Bagasao, T. M. P. (2004). NGOs in Asia: Key partners in the fight against AIDS. In J. P. Narain (Ed.), *AIDS in Asia: The challenge ahead* (pp. 19–41). New Delhi: SAGE.

Bailey, M. (1992). Children and AIDS: The shape of the pandemic, critical issues. In J. M. Mann, J. M. Daniel Tarantola, & T. W. Netter (Eds), *AIDS in the World: A global report, Part 4* (Indian ed., pp. 667–677). Mumbai: TISS and Harvard University Press.

Bauman, L., Foster, G., Silver, E., Berman, R., Gamble, I., & Muchaneta, L. (2006). Children caring for their ill parents with HIV/AIDS. *Vulnerable Children and Youth Studies, 1*(1), 56–70. doi:10.1080/17450120600659077

Boivin, M., Green, S., Davies, A., Giordani, B., Mokili J., & Cutting, W. (1995). A preliminary evaluation of the cognitive and motor effects of pediatric HIV infection in Zairian children. *Health Psychology, 14*(1), 13–21.

Chillag, K., Bartholow, K., Cordeiro, J., Swanson, S., Patterson, J., Stebbins, S., & Sy, F. (2002). Factors affecting the delivery of HIV/AIDS prevention programs by community-based organizations. *AIDS Education and Prevention, 14*, 27–37.

Cluver, L., & Gardner, F. (2007). Risk and protective factors for psychological well-being of children orphaned by AIDS in Cape Town: A qualitative study of children and caregivers' perspectives. *AIDS Care, 19*(3), 318–325.

Cluver, L., Gardner, F., & Operario, D. (2007). Psychological distress amongst AIDS-orphaned children in urban South Africa. *Journal of Child Psychology and Psychiatry, 48*(8), 755–763. doi:10.1111/j.1469-7610.2007.01757.x

Collins, P., Hollman, A., Freeman, M., & Patel, V. (2006). What is the relevance of mental health to HIV/AIDS care and treatment programs in developing countries? A systematic review. *AIDS, 20*, 1571–1582.

Das, S., & Bharat, S. (2008). *Evolving peer treatment education approaches in the networks of PLHA*. New Delhi: Population Foundation of India.

Das, S., & Leibowitz, G. (2011). Mental health needs of people living with HIV/AIDS in India: A literature review. *AIDS Care, 23*(4), 417–425.

Davies, D., & Webb, N. (2009). Outpatient counseling for children and youth with life threatening conditions, In N. B. Webb (Ed.), *Helping children and adolescents with chronic and serious medical conditions* (pp. 243–267). Hoboken, NJ: John Wiley & Sons.

Dawes, A., Robertson, B. A., Duncan, N., Ensink, K., Jackson, A., Reynolds, P., Pillay, A., & Ritchter, L. (1997). Child and adolescent mental health. In D. Foster, M. Freeman, & Y. Pillay (Eds), *Mental health policy issues for South Africa* (pp. 193–215). Cape Town: Multimedia Publications.

Demmer, C., & Burghart, G. (2008). Experiences of AIDS-related bereavement in the USA and South Africa: A comparative study. *International Social Work, 51*(3), 360–370. doi:10.1177/0020872807088082

Dowdney, L. (2000). Annotation: Childhood bereavement following parental death. *Journal of Child Psychology and Psychiatry, 41*(7), 819–830. doi:10.1111/1469-7610.00670

Drotar, D., Olness, K., Wiznitzer, M., Schatschneider, C., Marum, L., Guay, L., & Mayengo, R. (1999). Neurodevelopmental outcomes of Ugandan infants with HIV infection: An application of growth curve analysis. *Health Psychology, 18*(2), 114–121.

Duraisamy, P. (2003, April). *Economic impact of HIV/AIDS on patients and households in southIndia*. Paper presented at the 11th IAEN Face-to-Face Conference, Washington, DC.

Ferreira, M., Broderick, K., Keikelame, M., & Mosaval, Y. (2001). *Older women as carers to children and grandchildren affected by AIDS: Towards supporting the carers*. University of Cape Town: Institute of Ageing in Africa.

Foster, G., Makufa, C., Drew, R., Mashumba, S., & Kambeu, S. (1997). Perceptions of children and community members concerning the circumstances of orphans in rural Zimbabwe. *AIDS Care, 9*(4), 391–405.

Foster, G., & Williamson, J. (2000). A review of current literature of the impact of HIV/AIDS on children in sub-Saharan Africa. *AIDS, 14*(suppl. 3), S275–S284.

Freeman, M. (2000). Using all opportunities for improving mental health—examples from South Africa. *Bulletin of the World Health Organization, 78*(4), 508–510.

———. (2004). Mental health impacts of HIV/AIDS on children, *Journal of Child & Adolescent Mental Health, 16*(1), iii–iv.

Ghanashyam, B. (2010). India failing children orphaned by AIDS. *The Lancet, 375*(9712), 363–364. doi:10.1016/S0140-6736(10)60151-1

Gilborn, L., Nyonyintono, R., Kabumbuli, R., & Jagwe-Wadda, G. (2001). *Making a difference for children affected by AIDS: Baseline findings from operations research in Uganda*. Washington, DC: Population Council.

Global Initiative on Psychiatry. (2008). Mental health and HIV/AIDS: A challenging combination [Special issue]. *Mental Health Reforms, 1*. Retrieved from http://www.gip-global.org/p/28/133/ms9-0/mental-health-reforms

Government of India. (2009). *India 2009: A reference manual*. New Delhi: Ministry of Information and Broadcasting.

———. (2010). *Annual report to the people on health*. New Delhi: Ministry of Health and Family Welfare.

Griffith, S., & Doyle, R. (2009). School-based interventions for children and youth with medical conditions. In N. B. Webb (Ed.), *Helping children and adolescents with chronic and serious medical conditions* (pp. 105–119). Hoboken, NJ: John Wiley & Sons.

Herek, G. (1999). AIDS and stigma. *American Behavioral Scientist, 42*(7), 1106–1116. doi: 10.1177/0002764299042007004

Idoniboye, G. (2008). A call for mental health needs assessments in HIV positive children. *Perspectives in Public Health, 128*(5), 240–241. doi:10.1177/1466424008092800

Kapadia-Kundu, N. (2006). *Rapid assessment of children affected and vulnerable to HIV/AIDS in Maharashtra*. New Delhi: USAID. Retrieved from http://www.saathii.org/ovc/context_and_response/Maharastra_OVC_Report_March06.doc

Kulkarni, S., & Shukla, A. (2001, October). *Are we the reason for their social death? A HIV positive children's dilemma*. Poster presented at the Sixth International Congress on AIDS in Asia and the Pacific, Melbourne.

Landry, T., Luginaah, I., Maticka-Tyndale, E., & Elkins, D. (2007). Orphans in Nyanza, Kenya: Coping with the struggles of everyday life in the context of the HIV/AIDS pandemic. *Journal of HIV/AIDS Prevention in Children & Youth, 8*(1), 75–98. doi:10.1300/J499v08n01_05

Lefkowitz, E., Kahlbaugh, P., Au, T., & Sigman, M. (1998). A longitudinal study of AIDS conversations between mothers and adolescents. *AIDS Education and Prevention, 10*(4), 351–365.

Liddle, H., Dakof, G., Parker, K., Diamond, G., Barrett, K., & Tejeda, M. (2001). Multidimensional family therapy for adolescent drug abuse: Results of a randomized clinical trial. *American Journal of Drug and Alcohol Abuse, 27*(4), 651–688.

Mallmann, S. (2003). *Building resilience in children affected by HIV/AIDS*. Namibia: Catholic Aids Action.

Manuel, P. (2002). *Assessment of orphans and their caregivers' psychological well-being in a rural community in central Mozambique* (Unpublished master's thesis). London: Institute of Child Health.

Minuchin, S. (1974). *Families and family therapy*. Cambridge: Harvard University Press.

Ministry of Women and Child Development. *Sub Group Report: Child Protection in the Eleventh Five Year Plan (2007–2012)*. New Delhi: Government of India.

Motihar, R. (2007). Children and young people affected by HIV/AIDS in India: Challenges and emerging issues. *Exchange on HIV/AIDS, Sexuality and Gender, 2*, 10–11.

Mweru, M. (2008). Women, migration and HIV/AIDS in Kenya. *International Social Work, 51*(3), 337–347. doi:10.1177/0020872807088080

NACO. (2007). Policy framework for children and AIDS: India. *NACOonline.org*. Retrieved from http://www.nacoonline.org/upload/Publication/Treatment%20Care%20and%20support/PolicyFramework%20Aug_31.pdf

Narain, J. P. (2004). AIDS in Asia: The epidemic profile and the lessons learnt so far. In J. P. Narain (Ed.), *AIDS in Asia: The challenge ahead* (pp. 19–41). New Delhi: SAGE.

Nicholas, S., & Abrams, E. (2002). Boarder babies with AIDS in Harlem: Lessons in applied public health. *American Journal of Public Health, 92*(2), 163–165.

Ntozi, J., Ahimbisibwe, F., Odwee, J., Ayiga, N., & Okurut, F. (1999). Orphan care: The role of the extended family in northern Uganda. In I. O. Orubuloye, J. Caldwell, & J. P. Ntozi (Eds), *The continuing HIV/AIDS epidemic in Africa: Responses and coping strategies* (pp. 225–236). Canberra: Health Transition Centre.

O'Olley, B., Gxamza, F., Seedat, S., Theron, H., Taljaard. J., Reid, E., & Stein, D. (2003). Psychopathology and coping in recently diagnosed HIV/AIDS patients: The role of gender. *South African Medical Journal, 93*(12), 928–931.

Oman, R., Vesely, S., & Aspy, C. (2005). Youth assets, aggression, and delinquency within the context of family structure. *American Journal of Health Behavior, 29*(6), 557–568.

Pandve, H. T., Bhawalkar, J. S., & Bhuyar, P. A. (2008). AIDS orphans: An ignored issue in India. *Indian Journal of Sexually Transmitted Diseases and AIDS, 29*, 47–48.

Perrino, T., Gonzalez-Soldevilla, A., Pantin, H., & Szapocznik, J. (2000). The role of families in HIV prevention: A review. *Clinical Child and Family Psychology Review, 3*(2), 81–96. doi:10.1023/A:1009571518900

Pitayanon, S., Kongsin, S., & Janjaroen, W. (1997). The economic impact of HIV/AIDmortality on households in Thailand. In D. Bloom & P. Godwin (Eds), *The economics of HIV/AIDS: The case of South and South-East Asia* (pp. 53–101). New Delhi: Oxford University Press.

Pradhan, B., Sundar, R., & Singh, S. (2006). *Socio-economic impact of HIV and AIDS in India*. New Delhi: NACO (National AIDS Control Organisation), NCAER (National Council of Applied Economic Research) & UNDP (United Nations Development Programme).

Resnick, M., Bearman, P., Blum, R., Bauman, K., Harris, K., Jones, J., & Udry, J. (1997). Protecting adolescents from harm: Findings from the national longitudinal study on adolescent health. *Journal of the American Medical Association, 278*(10), 823–832. doi:10.1001/jama.1997.03550100049038

Romo, L., Lefkowitz, E., Sigman, M., & Au, T. (2001). Determinants of mother-adolescent communication about sex in Latino families. *Adolescent & Family Health, 2*, 72–82.

Scharko, A. (2006). DSM psychiatric disorders in the context of pediatric HIV/AIDS. *AIDS Care, 18*(5), 441–445. doi:10.1080/09540120500213487

Shatkin, J., & Belfer, M. (2004). The global absence of a child and adolescent mental health policy. *Child and Adolescent Mental Health, 9*(3), 104–108. doi:10.1111/j.1475-3588.2004.00090.x

Soderholm, P. (1997). *Global governance of AIDS: Partnerships with civil society*. Lund, Sweden: Lund University Press.

Sourkes, B. (1995). *Armfuls of time: The psychological experience of the child with a life-threatening illness*. Pittsburgh: University of Pittsburgh Press.

Subbarao, K., Mattimore, A., & Plangemann, K. (2001). Social protection of Africa's orphans and other vulnerable children: Issues and good practice program options. *African Region Human Development Working Paper Series*. African Region: The World Bank.

UNAIDS. (1997). Counselling and HIV/AIDS, UNAIDS Technical Update, November. *UNAIDS.org*. Retrieved from http://www.unaids.org/en/media/unaids/contentassets/dataimport/publications/irc-pub03/counstu_en.pdf

———. (2001). India: HIV and AIDS related discrimination, stigmatization and denial. In S. Bharat, P. Aggleton, & P. Tyrer (Eds), *UNAIDS best practice collection* (pp. 1–66). Geneva: UNAIDS.

———. (2002). *Report on the global HIV/AIDS epidemic*. Geneva: UNAIDS.

———. (2004). *Report on the global AIDS epidemic*. Geneva: UNAIDS.

UNAIDS. (2008). *Report on the global AIDS epidemic.* Geneva: UNAIDS.
———. (2010). *Annual report 2009.* Retrieved from http://www.unaids.org
UNAIDS/WHO. (2005). Global HIV/AIDS Online Database. Epidemiological Fact Sheets on HIV/AIDS and Sexually Transmitted Infections. Retrieved from http://www.who.int/GlobalAtlas/predefined Reports/EFS2004
UNICEF. (2003). *Africa's orphaned generations.* New York: UNICEF.
———. (2004). *The state of the world's children 2005: Childhood under threat.* New York: UNICEF.
———. (2005). *Children: The missing face of AIDS.* New York: UNICEF.
United Nations. (2006). General Assembly, Distr. General, June 15, 2006, Sixtieth Session, Agenda Item 45. Page 1–8. Retrieved from http://data.unaids.org/pub/Report/2006/20060615_hlm_politicaldeclaration_ares60262_en.pdf
USAID. (2003). *USAID project profiles: Children affected by HIV/AIDS* (3rd ed.). Washington, DC: USAID.
Verma, R., Salil, S., Mendonca, V., Singh, S., Prasad, R., & Upadhyaya, R. (2002). HIV/AIDS and children in Sangli district of Maharashtra (India). In G. Cornia (Ed.), *AIDS, public policy amd child well-being.* Florence, Italy: UNICEF-IRC.
Webb, N. B. (Ed.). (2009). *Helping children and adolescents with chronic and serious medical conditions: A strengths based approach.* Hoboken, NJ: John Wiley & Sons.
Whiteside, A. (2001, July). *The economics of HIV/AIDS.* Plenary paper presented at the International AIDS Economics Symposium, Barcelona.
Wild, L. (2001). The psychosocial adjustment of children orphaned by AIDS. *Southern African Journal of Child and Adolescent Mental Health, 13*(1), 3–22.
Williamson, J. (2005). *Finding a way forward: Principles and strategies to reduce the impacts of AIDS on children and families.* In G. Foster, C. Levine, & J. Williamson (Eds), *A generation at risk: The global impact of HIV/AIDS on orphans and vulnerable children* (pp. 254–277). Cambridge, MA: Cambridge University Press.
World Health Organization. (2003). *Caring for children and adolescents with mental disorders: Setting WHO directions.* Geneva: WHO.
———. (2005). *Mental health policy and service guidance package: Child and adolescent mental health policies and plans.* Geneva: WHO.
———. (2008). HIV/AIDS and mental health. Report by the Secretariat.
EB124/6 November 20, 2008. Retrieved from http://www.who.int/gb/ebwha/pdf_files/EB124/B124_6-en.pdf
WHO/UNAIDS/UNICEF. (2009). Towards universal access: Scaling up priority HIV/AIDS interventions in the health sector. Retrieved from http://www.who.int/hiv/pub/2009progressreport/en/index.html

5

Youngsters, Antisociality, and Violence: The Case of Norway

Ragnhild Bjørnebekk

Introduction

Historically and contemporaneously, nations vary in prevalence of violence and antisociality in their societies. What is common is that risk and protective factors exist and are distributed on three levels that ecologically interact with each other:

1. Macro-level factors are embedded in society and culture. Risk and protective factors are external to most inhabitants. Some risk factors, such as climate, are static. Most are dynamic political factors, embedded in the open and hidden structures of society. Poverty, inequality and autocracy, weak polity and structures are risk factors that put uncontrolled and high strain on society's inhabitants, cultural traits, legitimate violence, and hostility. Protective factors represent their opposite.
2. Meso-level factors are embedded in local communities, in its institutions; social groups; arrangement of neighborhoods, architecture, and street- and leisure-time cultures. Risks are related to disordered neighborhoods and institutions, presence of gangs, crime, violence, and drug dealing. Protective factors are related to gentrification, to well-functioning and integrated communities with healthy social control. At this level too, the risk and protective factors are external to most individuals and dynamic.
3. Micro-level factors are embedded in relations and interactions between children—their constitutions, strengths, vulnerabilities, and resilience—and their primary persons. Risks arise when children's basic needs and individual traits are not attended to in appropriate ways. Protective factors such as loving and thoughtful care, understanding of children's needs and development are exhibited by caretakers. Risk and protective factors at this level are both internal and external, but mostly dynamic. Even internal static factors are positively susceptible to influence, depending on surroundings and nutrition. Epi-genetic research suggests that optimal interactions between child and environment may prevent activation of even serious internal risks or vulnerabilities (Tremblay, 2009).

This means that rates of violence and antisociality will vary considerably between societies and cultures, local communities, as well as families according to how many and what kind of risk and protective factors exist and how they are handled in the interactions between the social units. Violence and antisociality are to a great degree dependent on a society's social policy.

Defining Violence and Antisociality

Derived from WHO's definition, in the Norwegian context violence is defined as "the intentional use of physical force or power, threatened or actual—against oneself, other person, or against a group or community—that either results in, or has a high likelihood of resulting in injury, death, psychological harm, maldevelopment, or deprivation" (Krug, Dahlberg, Mercy, Zwi, & Lozano, 2002, p. 5).

Antisocial behavior is used as a collective term of behavior patterns included in diagnostic criteria of conduct and behavior disorders. According to DSM-IV-TR (APA, 2000, pp. 68–69), the problematic pattern has to be repetitive, persistent and manifested by presence of at least three of the following criteria in the 12 months prior to it:

1. Aggression to people and animals, as bullying, threatening, or intimidating others; initiating physical fights, even using a weapon that can cause serious harm to others; being physical cruel to people and animals; stealing while confronting a victim; or forcing someone into sexual activity.
2. Destruction of property, as deliberately engaging in arson with the intention of causing serious damage, or have deliberately destroyed others' property.
3. Deceitfulness or theft, as breaking into someone else's house, building or car; lying often to obtain favors, goods or obligations from others; or stealing items of nontrivial value without confronting a victim.
4. Serious violation of rules, as staying out at night despite parental prohibitions (beginning before age 13); running away from home overnight (at least twice, or once without returning for a lengthy period) or often truant from school (starting before the age of 13).

Except self-directed violence in the WHO's definition, the other violence forms are included in the diagnostic description. WHO's definition stresses more clearly on collective violence. Not directly included in WHO's definition are (*a*) violence toward animals and (*b*) vandalism (destruction of property). It is a near relation between aggression toward humans and animals, both behaviorally and when it comes to causes (Linzey, 2009). Studies on vandalism show it as instrumental, often as revenge which targets persons or agencies, and sometimes involving serious injuries (e.g., arson) (Goldstein, 1996). These categories are to be included in a definition to grasp the phenomenon of violence.

Deceitfulness or theft and serious violating rules represent more typical antisocial behavior, which fall outside the phenomenon of violence. Except for vandalism, intentionality is only indirectly present in the diagnostic descriptions. This non-appearance allows for including acts that cause involuntary harm to people. Our definition consists of the definition by WHO and includes aggression to animals and vandalism described in the diagnostic criteria of antisocial behavior.

For teenagers who have developed antisocial behaviors that include violence, we use the term "youngsters out of control." The antisocial pattern involves violating the rights of others and of societal norms and rules. Included in our definition is also that the youngsters themselves and adults around them have not managed to stop their violating behavior.

Theories on development of antisociality, delinquency, and violence include two specific onset-types:

1. An early childhood-onset type is where the onset is at least prior to age 10. It consists of two pathways: One child-limited, where antisociality persists till the child is a teenager; and the other life-course persistent, where the child develops chronic antisociality. The life-course-persisters' antisocial pattern consists of a range of different delinquency, often characterized as cafeteria type.
2. An adolescent-onset type is one in which antisociality starts and peaks during the teenage years. Usually their delinquency is not cafeteria type, and their crime profile is not as serious as the early-onset type of persisters. Usually they desist from antisociality when reaching adulthood.

Identification of the two types is important. They need different kind of prevention and treatment to be able to desist. The early childhood-onset type is in need of extensive and multifaceted programs. The adolescent-onset type needs smaller specific interventions (Loeber & Farrington, 2001; Loeber, Farrington, & Washbusch, 1998; Moffitt, 2003; APA, 2000).

Young Delinquents: Relation between Violence/Antisociality and Mental Health

A presentation of empirical research (Maniadaki, Kakouros, & Karaba, 2010) on relationship between juvenile delinquency and mental health disorders in the US and Europe concludes that the exact number of mental disorders in juvenile offenders is unknown. Results from several studies have estimated that almost 80 percent has at least one disorder or specific problem, many have more than one. Mental disorders and specific problems in delinquents most often reported are:

1. Learning disabilities: Results from different correctional settings vary between 9 percent and 76 percent.

2. Attention deficit and disruptive behavior disorders (ADHD, ODD, and CD): The results vary between 40 percent and 90 percent. Longitudinal studies show substantial evidence for a relationship between ADHD and juvenile delinquency. Children with ADHD and aggressive behavior followed until adolescence were more likely to develop delinquency and substance use compared to their normal counterparts.
3. Substance abuse disorders: Studies show that all crime types are associated by substance use disorder. The rate for substance use disorder among young offenders is between 25 percent and 50 percent.
4. Mood and anxiety disorders (depression, anxiety, posttraumatic stress disorder, mania, and several more seldom disorders): Results from different studies vary from 17 percent to 78 percent, depending on what kind of, or how many different kinds of mood disorders were studied.

Co-morbidity is found between different problems and disorders. There is substantial support for a relation between violence and mental health. Whether violence leads to mental health problems or vice versa or there are co-occurrences between the two, is unclear.

Violence and Antisociality: Contributing and Mitigating Factors

There are static and dynamic external factors, some of which may be seen as contributing to and others as mitigating the violence and antisociality in the country.

The Climate

The country's climate is harsh. In northern parts, the winter is long and cold, snowy and dark through all 24 hours. This acts as a stressor on humans, but contributes to strength and patience too. Through centuries, Norwegians have been forced to plan thoroughly and rationally for the future in order to survive. This involves learning processes which strengthen self-control and prevent impulsivity, traits that buffer violence and antisociality. It is not clear if the cold is a stressor influencing violence directly, as heat does. Darkness, however, may generate a polar-night depression, indirectly influencing internal as well as external aggression. Finnmark, the darkest and most scattered part of Norway, is actually an area with more violence than any other. Together with the capital, it is where most youngsters are exposed to violence (Schou, Dyb, & Graff-Iversen, 2007), and where males show high rates of suicide (Norgeshelsa, 2011). Sami people experience more bullying and cultural conflicts than average Norwegians, and report bullying related to mental health problems as anxiety and depression (Hansen, 2011). How the climate and their stressors actually work with other factors is unclear. Both buffers and stressors are related to the climate.

What is clear, is that youngsters living under the toughest climate in Norway, experience more violence than others and that males conduct more internal violence. Treatment and prevention of the polar-night depression, with possible related internal and external aggression, belong to the health departments and take the form of light or medical therapy.

Social Indicators

According to the United Nation's Human Development Index, Norway is among the best nations to live in, despite its unfriendly climate. The index contains different quality of life factors as general life-satisfaction and satisfaction with everyday activities, work and personal health, life expectancy, income, equality, education, employment-rate, and level of democracy. It includes scores on crime and safety (UNDP–HDI Index, 2010). With the exception of crime, Norway gets high scores on almost every factor. Research shows that children too, enjoy a high standard of living and quality of life (Berntson & Köhler cited in Kivivuori, 2007). Almost 90 percent of young students report they enjoy school (Topland & Skaalvik, 2010). According to classical criminology, factors included in UN Index represent macro factors that cause violence and antisociality.

Macro factors influencing antisociality are also important when framing the Norwegian situation. Green (2008) describes Nordic democracies as multiparty political systems, based on consensus-building and compromises, in contrast to majoritarian democracies of England and the US. Majoritarian models usually imply cultures of polarity and populism. Consensus models imply cultures with fewer incentives to politicize and polarize complex subjects such as delinquency and punishment. Discourses on delinquency in political debates and in media are more responsible, balanced, and less passionate, with lesser focus on penal populism and more on restorative and rehabilitative perspectives. This contributes to lower imprisonment and fear of crime, and helps to build public trust. Norway has neither had a history of feudalism nor aristocracy. Egalitarian concern for the common good is deeply rooted. Norwegians accept high taxes to finance free health care, education, and high quality social security to all inhabitants. Poverty is almost nonexistent (Green, 2008; Stjernø, 2005). All these factors represent protection against development of violence and antisociality, and opportunities for optimal surroundings, few risk factors, and healthy development for all children including vulnerable ones.

Research confirming Norway as a consensus nation is characterized by low level of social repression and imprisonment, and high level of general trust toward authorities (Kivivuori, 2007). Comparisons between Norwegian and English ways of handling children committing serious violence show that while Norway relies on treatment, protection, and rehabilitation, England relies more on repression and penology (Green, 2008). United Nation's Committee on Rights of Child (2007) evaluated UNCRs juvenile justice core, which contains best interest of the child, custody as last resort, separation from criminal adults, and principles of respect and dignity for the child. The report recommended every state—except Norway—to give more consideration to the implementation of the core principles (Maniadaki et al., 2010). This suggests that the Norwegian system of juvenile policy has managed to bring into action factors that secure the Child Convention's core principles. By that Norway contributes to rehabilitation, protection, and development that buffers relapse of crime and antisociality.

In Norway, the police get the highest rating on trust (Runhovde, 2010). Widespread and high trust in the agency that regulates law and maintains order and safety makes it difficult to explain away the legalized disorder and lawbreaking. Trust builds bridges between conventional society and its norms. Together with the focus on treatment and rehabilitation versus repression, it contributes to powerful prevention of unlawful activity.

This indicates that collective violence embedded in society is a small part of violence in Norway. The Norwegian welfare society has succeeded in building a political and social culture where the main dynamic as well as the static societal factors generating crime and violence, are not present or are put out of circulation. Few Norwegian children of today are influenced by classical external macro risk factors that generate violence and antisociality.

Modern media and technology may, however, represent a macro factor generating a form of structural violence. Structures in social media, Internet, and mobiles have created new arenas that allow for intentional and harmful use of power against persons, groups, and communities. Violent content presented in media may also result in harm for vulnerable persons. Research documents effects of aggression from media violence on children and youth. Characteristics related to the child and her or his situation represents mediating factors which strengthen or buffer negative influences (Bjørnebekk, 1998, 2001; Hagen & Wold, 2009; Anderson et al., 2003; Möller & Krahé, 2009; Strasburger, Wilson, & Jordan, 2009). Norwegian children's high quality of life situation may function as a protective factor moderating negative impact on ordinary kids, but not necessarily on vulnerable ones. Whether violent media-content is a part of the violence definition may, however, be questioned. To satisfy the definition, intention has to be present. Our position is that the special kind of violent content in films, television programs, and video games that research has documented to be "dangerous," has so often been communicated to the media industry that it is impossible for them not to be aware of it. When the industry, for its own benefit, continues to produce and even escalate violent expression, even when they know some will suffer because of it, then it has to be seen as an intentional act and fulfill the definitional criteria of violence.

Social Policy

Norway is inhabited by about 5 million people distributed along a long, wild coast, in mountains and the countryside. There are a few big cities, only eight out of which have more than 50,000 inhabitants. Oslo, the capital and biggest city, has half a million people. More than 50 percent of the municipalities have less than 4,500 inhabitants, a challenging situation when it comes to giving everybody access to social services needed to protect mental as well as physical health. To meet this challenge, the ministries have built flexible links from national health and research institutions to specialized regional competence centers and local communities and agencies. In this way, most public services—including evidence-based programs on preventing and treatment of violent and antisocial development—are provided to individuals, families, and schools all throughout the nation (Ogden, Kärki, & Teigen, 2010). There are well-established structures and linkages at the macro level, which effectively offer necessary services to all Norwegian inhabitants.

A History of Nonviolent and Peaceful Culture

Research establishes Norway as a safe place, with low rates of violence and crime. Even historically Norway has been safe for children. In spite of harsh climate and being one of the poorer nations in Europe, problems related to health and death in childbirth have been a far more widespread threat than violence. Norway has been involved in few wars and violent conflicts. During the Nazi-occupation in World War II the nation experienced traumatic burnings and bombings of civilian homes (Alnæs, 1996; Skodvin, 1995). However, the war did much to forge a sense of solidarity, which is a prominent trait of Norwegian political culture and social policy of today. The occupation also turned out to be a protection for vulnerable youngster attracted to racist and neo-Nazi groups. In contrast, Sweden, which was not occupied, such groups have been a considerable problem to date (Green, 2008; Stjernø, 2005; Lööw, 1997).

Laws function as a primary means of violence prevention. Today almost all kinds of violence are forbidden. It is unlawful to chastise or punish a pupil at school. Parents are not allowed to punish their children (Næshagen, 2002). The laws protect children from any form of spanking, given for educational or other reasons.

The low rates of violence in Norway were broken between 1960 and 2008, a surprising trend because this was a period of growing welfare. A similar increase was observed in many industrial societies. In Norway, violent crime investigated by police increased by more than 13 times. Today, the rate of homicide is less than 1 case per 100,000 inhabitants a year, while occurrence of other violence is 5.5 cases per 100,000 inhabitants (KRIPOS, 2010; Thorsen, Lid, & Stene, 2009; Næshagen, 1995a, 1995b, 2005). Police-recorded violence during the last five years shows increase in domestic and dating violence of about 300 percent, and for rape, sexual abuse, and sexual crime against children of about 75 percent. Some of this reported increase is not real (e.g., Politiet, 2010). Due to political agendas and education of the police in tackling intimate violence, more hidden micro level violence has been discovered. The increase is so big that it is reasonable that only a part of it is real. It is of concern that the increase is in categories involving children as victims, witnesses, and offenders, which in turn may influence the cycles of violence.

The increase of violence in a society where most external risk factors are removed and welfare is growing is difficult to explain. In the US, the increase in the 1960s is associated with turbulence and friction in the society and consequently, a decrease in the legitimacy of institutions and society. The Vietnam War contributed to this loss of legitimacy. The next period's increase is explained as a cohort phenomenon. The baby-boom generation had reached the critical age of 14–25 years for conducting crime (Blumstein & Wallman, 2000). This macro explanation may also partly explain the Norwegian pattern. Five new traits that involve new risks may also explain some of the increase:

1. Children have experienced more family break-ups than earlier.
2. Children have been exposed to more risky media violence more often. New media technologies are introduced, offering new platforms to adult and youth offenders to sexually assault and harass, stalk, bully, and violate others.
3. Alcohol and drugs have become more widespread and drinking alcohol starts at an earlier age.
4. Emigration and flight have put children in vulnerable situations, in collision between social norms, expectations, and cultures. Some children have been exposed to serious violence and have lived with little protection before entering Norway.
5. During the 1980s and 1990s, multi-ethnic street gangs, One Percent Motor Cycle gangs, and racist gangs came into existence in Norway. Gang culture, inspired by gang and mafia movies, developed; violence and vendettas became a substantial part of it (Bjørgo, Carlsson, & Haaland, 2001; Bjørnebekk, 1999, 2001; Carlsson, 2005; Lien, 2004; Livingstone, Haddon, Görzig, & Ólafsson, 2011; Shannon, 2007; Nelander & Shannon, 2010; Rørhus, 1999; SIRUS statistikk, 2011).

These traits and developments occur at all levels. The cohort-phenomenon, society's loss of legitimacy, emigration and flight, and media technology belong to structures and situations at macro level which are difficult to influence. Violence perpetrated by new technology has been addressed by school programs on Internet safety and ethical communication. Direct "red" electronic links to police investigators have been installed for use if experiencing threats or sexual communication on Internet, along with devices to block violent content. Expert groups have developed film and videogame age-ratings as evaluation devices for parents. A comprehensive strategy focusing on gang ecology and individual problems such as aggression replacement training and family programs such as multi-systemic therapy are currently tried out on girl-gang problems in Oslo and on general gang-problems in other places. A broad group of experts cooperate with the police and follow gang-members tightly. Preliminary results seem promising. Others have implemented Exit-programs, and the police have focused on interventions and prevention of new recruitments. The strategies focus on both meso and micro levels. Police report the gang problem to be decreasing, although a couple of Pakistani and other minority gangs have transformed into organized criminal groups, and the One Percents have expanded and have established several clubs and prospect clubs around the country, despite being targets of police projects.

Prevention of youngsters' use of drugs and alcohol is being implemented at several levels. On a macro and meso level the authorities have, for a long time tried to minimize access nationally and locally by applying high taxes and sale monopoly. Schools have implemented a program, MOT (meaning "courage"), that among other issues also targets alcohol use. A recent evaluation shows that pupils in middle schools who participate in MOT postpone their alcohol onset and drink lesser alcohol than pupils in schools who not have implemented MOT (PROBA/MOT 2011).

Youngsters Out of Control

Exact figures on how many out of control youngsters there are in Norway are not available. Moffitt, Caspi, Rutter, and Silva (2001) suggest the group to be between 5 percent and 8 percent of the children. In Norway, the group is suggested to represent about 1–2% of the children (Sørlie, 2000).

A comparative self-report study on delinquent behavior perpetrated by 13- to 16-year-olds in Nordic capitals showed that adolescents in Oslo had significantly lower prevalence rates of all violent crimes. Fewer adolescents in Oslo had committed violence than in the other capitals, but they committed violence more often (Kivivuori, 2007). A school panel study in Oslo showed that about 6 percent of the boys and 1 percent of the girls belonged to a small group of chronic perpetrators (Bakken, 1999). The polarization between the ordinary children and the "wild" ones is large. During the last few years, empirical research shows, however, that the chronic group has diminished (Øia, 2007; Oslo Politiet/SALTO, 2011).

A study on prisoners shows that they had experienced a chain of severe risks during childhood: one-third reported being abused, one-third had been a childcare-client, and another one-third had had a close family member in prison. Only 40 percent had graduated from middle school, and 30–40 percent reported psychological illness (Friestad & Skog Hansen, 2004).

"Pathways to Violence—On Youngsters Out of Control"

Consisting of several interrelated sub-studies (Bjørnebekk, 1998, 1999, 2009a, 2009b) conducted between 1995 and 2007, this study is a qualitative, retrospective life-course study about youngsters out of control, and focuses on their current situation, as well as their years of upbringing. The sample consists of two groups: the target group with 34 youngsters (21 boys and 13 girls, one-third of them belonging to different minority groups, all of them with antisocial and violent problems) and a referential group consisting of 20 ordinary youngsters (12 boys and 8 girls, one-third from minority groups), randomly matched to the first 20 in the target group on age, sex, region, and type of school. The age varies from 13 to 19 years with the average being 17 years.

Interviews were conducted with the target group in clusters over time and across the country to secure their anonymity. A follow up study involving 11 of the 34 in the target group was also conducted during the same period.

I present some results from the qualitative structured life-history interviews (themes of Violence, Media, and Upbringing) which took up to five days for the target group and 5–6 hours for the referential group—along with content from official journals/documents, observations, and some unstructured interviews with only the target group.

The study uses the WHO's definition of violence when categorizing violence, and the DSM-V's description to categorize antisociality.

Results

The patterns of behavior seen in each group, which exhibit marked differences but a few similarities as well, are discussed here.

Similarities

Although the two groups vary markedly on several factors, there are a few similarities. Both groups reported almost the same socioeconomic background, except that none of the parents of the youngsters in the target group held high academic degrees. Some parents of youngsters in both groups belonged to the "third generation upper class family." Some of the upper class parents in the target group had "family-secrets," such as having been bankrupt and a mother being "a former hippie and now a pill abuser." In both groups there were parents whose main income was social security. When parents of the ordinary youngsters are on social security, it is on account of physical illnesses or difficult situations that do not necessarily influence upbringing negatively. When parents of the out of control youngsters are on social security, it is for other reasons such as the father being in prison, a parent's mental illness or substance abuse—conditions that may influence childcare in more serious ways. The risks are not so much related to poverty or inequities in the socioeconomic background of the youngsters, as to specific problems of their parents. This suggests that treating the risks and preventing negative pathways have to focus on the micro level.

Reactions to the question "What would you do if a friend was raped?" were similar. Both groups reporting that they would retaliate against the perpetrator in cruel ways. When it came to actually acting on this sentiment, only one boy in the target group reported retaliatory behavior in response to his girlfriend being abused by an older man when she was a child. He planned to kill him but was stopped. A girl in the same group reported that she gave a friend who had been raped, a pit-bull puppy as a weapon and for protection.

We also found similar results on a scale measuring conventional norms toward when and if it is acceptable to react aggressively. Members of both groups seemed to know what is acceptable or not, according to conventional social norms. However, when it came to acting, the differences between the two groups were big. In the target group all reported that they acted contrarily to what they knew was right, they legitimated their violence. In belonging to the deviant groups, the norms have been neutralized. This may be an example of the phenomenon described by Matza (2009) in his classical theory on delinquency and drift. During the process of becoming a delinquent, youngsters start with knowing the laws and what is considered right and wrong in mainstream culture. When they get affiliated to delinquent groups and start violating the norms, they gradually neutralize the norms and legitimate their lawbreaking.

The groups were also similar in their reflections on why they and their life had turned out as it had. Both groups perceived it as having to do with their family, friends, and school, as well as with how they themselves had met and resolved challenges—factors that have been recognized as risks for becoming antisocial (Loeber & Farrington, 2001). The differences between the groups lay in their explanation of each of the factors.

All members in the target group recognized that their life had turned out in a problematic way. Their explanations focused on traumatic events during their upbringing (father who had seriously sexually abused the children), destructive family interactions (ongoing conflicts with the mother), poor or absence of disciplining by parents (full freedom and no limitations of any kind), association with "bad" peers and gangs, school experiences (bullying and being bullied), and neurophysiological problems that had not been diagnosed and treated. Several attributed their problems to their own vulnerabilities ("I am born this way …") or to their temperament and problem with self-control ("I do not want to use violence, but I can't stop it" and "I am not able to stop my aggression … I become quite crazy …"). Several explained their problematic situation as their own choice: "… it was my decision, I started with drugs and I liked it" and "… things become what you decide them to be." No one mentioned poor local communities or poverty as explanations.

The majority of the referential group recognized that their life had turned out in good ways. The main reasons were protective, loving, and caring family and friends: "… it is because of my mother. She teaches me how to behave … has expectations about my school aspirations and sport, without putting any pressure on me …"; "I have always had someone who cares, who praises me and tells me what is wrong …"; "everything has been nice with my mother and with friends—at school and in my upbringing"; "… nice friends, no bad ones"; and "I know how to be successful at school." They also explained their good life as being a result of their own effort and achievements: "I have avoided trouble. I reflect a lot …" and "I have been focused on managing things in good ways …"

The last set of similar results was with respect to dreams for the future. The majority in both groups dreamed of being married, with two children, a nice house, and an ordinary job—although a few in the target group proclaimed that it would pay them more to be a successful crook! To have a future-time orientation toward a conventional life and routines may serve as a strong motivational factor for the target group to desist from antisociality and start working toward their dreams.

Behavior Patterns of the Ordinary Youngsters

Although the focus is on the target group, it is nevertheless important to emphasize results from the analysis of the referential group (ordinary youngsters) which varies significantly. The ordinary youngsters live mostly harmonious and stable lives in well-functioning intact families, experiencing thoughtful care and monitoring. Most of them have lived in the same place and are strongly attached to their caretakers. They reported positive events and moments from their childhood history. Almost everyone had adults to contact and talk to when in trouble, and a network of prosocial friends. Most of them reported healthy interests such as sports, fishing, music, and dancing in which their parents participated as coaches and supporters. Almost all had idols from sport, music, or film. Almost all had some models they looked up to and valued. The most popular models were parents or other family members.

Several reported that they had broken laws during childhood. Their offences were trifle such as petty larceny, and mostly isolated incidences. They correct their behavior when talked to. One had been involved in organizing gang-fights for a short period of time, and subsequently also in fraud. In contrast to the out of control youngsters, his remorse was complete and serious. When the ordinary ones are involved in risk behavior it is not of an antisocial nature. One girl experienced serious bullying at school that once triggered a physical attack on her teacher and afterwards a dramatic suicide attempt. Together with her mother, they started to learn about bullying to be able to understand, to debrief, and to be able to help other victims. In spite of her two collapses, her ability to empathize was intact.

Among the reference group, there were individuals with problematic backgrounds. Three of them seemed to jump on what Moffitt (2003) has described as an adolescent-limited pathway, where the antisociality begins during adolescence and ends on reaching adulthood. She suggests that the reason to this antisociality is antisocial peers, crises just before the time of youth, or the maturity gap between their biological maturity and the roles offered to them in the society. One of them was a member of a satanic death metal band. His clothes, style, and behavior were provocative. Although he was involved in drug use and ritual activity, he was not causing violence to others. Rather, his behavior made him the target of both physical and bullying attacks. He spoke about experiencing two factors which Moffitt (2003) suggested as a cause to adolescent-limited antisociality: a broken family and involvement with a marginalized peer group. Two other boys were seemingly early starters, but their pathway suddenly ended when their situation was turned around. One desisted from crime when his mother died from an overdose and he moved to his father's, who lived in another city with his new family. This proved to be his turning point. At the time of the interview he was a very active young boy, doing pro-social work for the benefit of his local community. His teachers took pride in his behavior.

Another lived as a child in a street gang, without any family in South American country. One day he was adopted by a Norwegian family and moved to Norway. His situation changed dramatically; a turning point for the young seven-year-old boy. External risks were removed and the child got thoughtful care and protection from psychological and physical harm and deprivation. His basic needs were satisfied—important inhibitors of antisocial development and negative outcomes. On reaching adolescence, he reported a new antisocial development by starting a gang and engaging in experiences he earlier had left. He decided to desist when corrected by the police. One of the girls reported that she had a parent with serious social psychological problems, creating harm in the family. When she was injured in a car crash caused by her drunk-driving father, it became the family's turning point. Her mother decided to divorce her husband to protect her children from harm. Others also reported risks created by one parent, but of the other parent taking action and caring for the young boy or girl's life. This seems to counterbalance risks, and protect the child from violent and risky pathways.

Behavior Patterns of the Out-of-control Youngsters

All the youngsters in the target group could be placed in the category of children with conduct problems—or as antisocial. Their antisocial pattern had lasted for more than a year (for most of them, even longer) had been both persistent and repetitive, and their behavior satisfied at least three of the criteria in the diagnostic system. Except for three boys, the others had been placed compulsorily or voluntarily in a treatment house because of escalating behavior problems. Their antisocial behavior was difficult to break by less radical treatment.

The antisocial and violent behavior, and dangerous situations they reported being engaged in shows a serious and extensive pattern. A summary of the behavior and perpetrator pattern is presented as follows:

- Hostage-taking, using firearms to threaten hostages in order to get their own wishes fulfilled.
- Attacks on people (officials, teachers, social workers, children from other ethnicity groups, and peers) often triggered by what is interpreted as a provocation by knives or other pointed objects, striking or electrical weapons, or by beating and kicking (almost all).
- Physical attacks on or threats to parents, caretakers, and siblings such as kicking a pregnant mother's stomach, using a gun, "throwing my mother into the wall," "kicking and beating stepfather" (almost all).
- Involvement in severe organized adult crime or teenager mafia-like groups where severe criminal acts as rape, smuggling and prostitution, selling drugs, organized burglary had happened.

- Vagabonding with peer group after being turned out from or leaving home.
- Involvement in criminal gangs or neo-Nazi groups, where violence, drug, reputation, respect, and revenge is a part of ganging (almost all).
- Involvement in gang-fights, kicking, and beating persons out of claimed territory, participating in racist/anti-racist attacks (almost all).
- Perpetrating robbery (person robbery of child and elderly on the street and in homes, and commercial robbery of gasoline station, shops, etc.), burglary, and theft. For some the activity is systematic: "morning burglary" in homes and "afternoon burglary" in university and schools (most of the boys and several of the girls).
- Vandalism (tagging, smashing windows, shooting inside house targeting objects).
- Meaningless and spontaneous attacks on foreigners passing by.
- Sexual abuse (about one out of eight had sexually abused others).

Several reported drug and alcohol use which may categorize them as having a substance abuse disorder. Most of them had an early onset for cigarette smoking, alcohol, and drugs. Most were using a cocktail of different drugs.

Such a pattern—or even anything similar to it—was not reported by any of the youngsters in the reference group. Their "biggest crime" was shoplifting or stealing "a very big chocolate." This is a clear indicator that the out of control children differ greatly from the ordinary youngsters. It is as if they live in two entirely different worlds.

Twenty-nine of the out of control youngsters were early starters, with cafeteria-like criminality on their criminal records. Five seemed to belong to the adolescent-limited group, but their criminality over a period of time has been so serious that they fall into the category of conduct and antisocial disorders. Some have been diagnosed with neurophysiological disturbances such as ADHD and Tourette's syndrome; some others were suspected of having it because of their hyperactivity and problems to concentrate and focus.

Family Experiences

About 80 percent reported that as victim or witness they had experienced serious often repeated violence from their caregivers or as perpetrator themselves. Almost ten had experienced homicide in their family or near-friend's. Childhood for most of them—not all—is characterized by many family break-ups and moving and living in foster care and in institutions. Some reported living in 15 different places until they were 15–16 years of age. Their families deviate greatly from ordinary families when it comes to disciplining and style of upbringing, health, social problems, and substance abuse. Some parents are reported as being extremely authoritarian, others as having a laissez-faire style. Most of them are inconsistent in their monitoring.

Many claimed that they did what they wanted to do (e.g., stay outdoors till late, with whoever they wished to be with—even with older persons who might be a danger to them), and if hindered, they threatened their parents to accept or just walked away. Several had run away from home several times. They were characterized by being very mobile for their age and heeding no restrictions—except those enforced by their gangs. Many had difficulty remembering nice events and situations during childhood. Remembered histories were often very traumatic ones. Several reported little protection from negative events and revealed that their parents or stepparents were the organizers of the negative experiences.

Sexual Abuse

About 30 percent reported that they had been sexually abused during childhood, usually by a stepfather or stepbrother, but sometimes also by members in their gang. Being raped by a stranger and sexually used by groups of friends was also reported. Some boys and girls prostitute themselves at a young age. Others had experienced that near relations had sexually abused/raped others than themselves, or that some near relation had been a victim. This means that almost 50% of them had been touched by sexual violence as a victim, a perpetrator, or a bystander. For the reference group, there is no report of any kind of sexual abuse.

Peer Influence

Everyone had antisocial friends, but most of them had pro-social ones earlier. Gradually, they lost contact with them, strengthened their relationship with troubled friends, and got more involved in antisocial activity. Almost everyone is a member of gangs or troubled groups who perpetrate violence and crime and use illegal substances. They use and often also sell a mixture of drugs, and have no rules that regulate their use. Several reported they had a room at their home or a house where they, together, smoked hashish and watched "drug movies" to strengthen the drug effect.

School Experiences

In addition to all these problems and risks, we also found that many had a negative school history, with truancy, oppositional behavior, reading and writing problems, being the scapegoat of the school, and conflicts with teachers and school authorities. A few said their teacher had stood up for them when they were accused, and helped them when in a conflict with teachers and school authorities. A few got treatment in school for their ADHD problems, mostly by means of some educational strategy. They were usually the problematic underachieving students, in constant conflict with teachers and school authorities. "I was the boss at the school, everyone was afraid of me and respected me. I organized fights and decided what was allowed to be done in the class and the schoolyard." Several had attacked their teachers physically. One because she thought the teacher was unfair to another pupil, another because she interpreted a "how are you today" as an ironic comment.

Influence of Media

The media history of these youngsters deviates in risky ways from that of the ordinary youngsters. From early childhood they had been exposed to an overload of violent content, and their caretakers had regulated their media exposure to a lesser degree. Many had encountered pornography early in life. Afterwards, they preferred movies with content that has been proved to influence the young public in negative ways: rewarding (or failure in punishing) the aggressor; violence without consequences, uncriticized or justified; and revenge as a motivating aspect of the story (Strasburger et al., 2009). At a point in time, they start to use media content and media technology with intent to build competence in violence, as well as to learn how to develop an effective gang. They look at specific fighting scenes again and again, often in Kick Boxer and Blood Sport movies and train themselves in the kicking and beating technique used by the hero. Afterwards, in the streets, when provoked by someone and "getting the blood fog in my head," they may model the technique viewed and developed in an automatic copycat manner. Some reported that they learnt how to build structures and norms in their gang and how to manage revenge and sanctions from mafia movies. A girl in a criminal organized group got her nickname from Matrix and copied the style, weapons, dress, and manners. In this way, media content are used intentionally to construct, to style, for violence and criminal behavior, and culture, as well as to build networks with groups that inspire them. This suggests that youngsters out of control experience risk for a greater part from the macro culture and are protected from its negative influence to a lesser degree than are ordinary youngsters.

The results from the study show youngsters out of control as an antisocial group with serious behavior disturbances. They have an over-representation of external risk factors, such as these:

Family and primary groups

- Many transitions (e.g., moving home, family break-ups and disruptions)
- Child abuse (physical and sexual violence)
- Poor monitoring
- Antisocial fathers
- Mental illness and substance abuse

Friends

- Member of a gang
- Antisocial peers

School

- Dropouts
- Oppositional behavior

Media

- Exposure to an overdose of "dangerous" depictions of violence
- Reception of violent content in a problematic manner

There is an over-representation of internal risks and vulnerabilities as well:

- Neuro-physical disturbances
- Intense and high aggressive feelings
- Low provocation tolerance

These results are in accordance with results from the life-course development on antisocial development and criminal carrier studies (Moffitt, 2003; Moffitt et al., 2001; Loeber & Farrington, 2001). Moffitt has suggested two main hypotheses for antisocial development in the early-starter group who are at risk of life-course persistent antisociality. One is that the causes are internal vulnerability consisting of neuropsychological disturbances in interaction with external risk factors. The other is an over-representation of external risks in children's life. Loeber and Farrington (2001) do not explain risks as causes, they are factors applied to child delinquency. The greater the risk factors and the fewer the protective ones, the higher are the chance to develop antisociality. Our study is not designed to explain causes, but the target group may fit into both of Moffitt's hypotheses and the contribution assumption of Loeber and Farrington. The youngsters themselves explain their problematic life in terms of corresponding external and internal factors as Moffitt and Loeber and Farrington do, but some strongly emphasize their own contribution to the situation, which is more in correspondence with the rational thinking tradition. In doing that they also place themselves as subjects of their antisocial development, a result also found in a Norwegian cultural study on how violent girls explain their violence (Natland, 2009).

Responses to Youngsters Out of Control: Social Policy and Treatment

A national research institute, established by central ministries and linked to Oslo University, offers the most effective evidence-based international programs to a nationwide network of regional centers, linked to local services. They educate specialists who carry out the programs, do research on implementation, and on follow up studies on the effectiveness of the programs. The institute is at the same time related to the international research community on evidence-based programs and the science of implementation. In this way they are able to bridge the gap between policy, research, and practice and to nurture both practice and research (Ogden et al., 2010). These institutional linkages and way of organizing the prevention of violence and antisocial development have proved to be effective and have enabled high-quality programs all over the country.

In our study we found serious, complicated, and deep problems faced by the target group. Most of them had been given different kinds of treatment—moved from foster care to foster care, from open and liberal institutionalized treatment to radical encroachment and strong treatment. Usually they had not been given any evidence-based treatment. Their care and treatment was based on experience, not on careful evaluation of effectiveness. Their antisociality had escalated so much that they had climbed up the treatment ladder. At the time of the interview they were in the most radical institutions.

At present they are likely to be involved in evidence-based programs and followed carefully by experts. Most of the programs and interventions used in Norway today to prevent and treat antisocial development are based on cognitive social learning theory—particularly, Patterson's coercion hypothesis of negative reinforcement that develops and maintains deviant behavior; Bandura's notions of modeling and self-efficacy; Piaget's developmental interactive learning methods; and on cognitive strategies for challenging angry, negative, and depressive self-talk and increasing parental self-esteem and confidence.

Several programs have shown to be effective in reducing problem behavior, to improve parental functioning and build positive relations between parent and child, and even to reduce the problem behavior related to ADHD in Norway (Hagen, Ogden, & Bjørnebekk, 2011; Bigland & Ogden, 2008; Ogden & Halliday-Boykins, 2004; Ogden et al., 2010; Ogden & Sørlie, 2009). Most of them are offered nationally.

Conclusion

I have argued that the Norwegian welfare society has succeed in building a political and social culture where the main dynamic as well as static societal factors that generate crime and violence on macro level are not present or are put out of circulation. The factors that remain are those related to structures in old and new media, and to moving patterns that create vulnerabilities in children. Few Norwegian children of today are influenced by classical external macro risk factors that generate violence and antisociality. The risks belong mainly at the meso and micro levels. The results from the "Pathway to Violence—on Youngsters Out of Control" study confirm this assumption, both by means of the analysis of the risk and protective factors and what the youngsters themselves report as explanations. Prevention and treatment have to focus on these levels to address the problems. In spite of a high quality of life in Norway, some children develop serious chronic violence and antisocial patterns. Their problems are complex and deep and have to be treated as such. Norway has built linkages between central authorities, national research institutes that educate experts needed to implement evidence-based programs, regional competence centers, and local communities and agencies. The linkages bind theory and practice together and make it possible to offer effective evidence-based programs to prevent and treat violence and conduct problems across the nation if the programs are implemented as prescribed.

References

Alnæs, K. (1996). *Norge*. Oslo: Gyldendal.
American Psychiatric Association. (2000). *Diagnostic and statistical manual of mental disorders* (4th ed., Text revision). Washington, DC: American Psychiatric Association.
Anderson, C. A., Berkowitz, L., Donnerstein, E., Rowell Huesmann, L., Johnson, J. D., Linz, D., & Wartella, E. (2003). The influence of media violence on youth. *PsychologicalScience in the Public Interest, 4*(3), 81–110.
Bakken, A. (1999). Ungdomstid. En *Ungdom og kriminalitet* (pp. 119–134). PHS, Forskning.
Bigland, A., & Ogden, T. (2008). The evolution of evidence-based practices. *European Journal of Behavior Analysis, 9*(1), 81–95.
Bjørgo, T., Carlsson, Y., & Haaland, T. (2001). *Generalisert hat polariserte fellesskap*. Oslo: *NIBR Pluss-serie* 4/2001.
Bjørnebekk, R. (1998). Violence against the eye. *News on children and violence on the screen, 2*(2–3), 7.
———. (1999). Gjenger, ran og vold: 90 tallets kriminalitets-treenighet? In *Ungdom og Kriminalitet* (pp. 135–174). Oslo: PHS Forskning.
———. (2001). "Volden for øyet" Unge, Vold, Medier og Oppvekst. En K. Øverland *Antisosial atferd og risikofaktorer i familien*, Delrap 3 av "Volden for øyet", pp. 5–19, PHS.
———. (2009a, June). Youngsters out of control: Involvement in violence and theft offending. Paper presented at the Stockholm Criminology Symposium, Stockholm, Sweden.
Bjørnebekk, R., & Bjørnebekk, G. (2009b). Alvorlige atferdsproblemer og antisosialitet. Bilder av ungdom i trøbbel— og som skaper trøbbel. In K. Haanes & R. Hjermann (Eds), *Barn* (pp. 238–261). Oslo: Universitetsforlaget.
Blumstein, A., & Wallman, J. (Eds) (2000). *The crime drop in America*. New York: Cambridge University Press.
Carlsson, Y. (2005). *Tett på gjengen: En evaluering av gjengintervensjonsprosjektet "Tett På" i Oslo*. Oslo: Norwegian Institute for Urban and Regional Research.
Friestad, C., & Skog Hansen, I. L. (2004). *Living conditions among inmates* (Fafo-report 429). Oslo: Fafo.
Goldstein, A. P. (1996). *The psychology of vandalism*. New York: Plenum Press.
Green, D. A. (2008). *When children kill children: Penal populism and political culture*. Oxford: Oxford University Press.
Hagen, I., & Wold, T. (2009). *Mediegenerasjonen: Barn og unge i det nye medielandskapet*. Oslo: Det Norske Samlaget.
Hagen, K. A., Ogden, T., & Bjørnebekk, G. (2011). Treatment outcomes and mediators of parent management training: A one-year follow-up of children with conduct problems. *Journal of Clinical Child & Adolescent Psychology, 40*(2), 165–178. doi:10.1080/15374416.2011.546050
Hansen, K. L. (2011). *Ethnic discrimination and bullying in relation to self-reported physical and mental health in Sami settlement areas in Norway: The SAMINOR study*. Tromsø: Institute of Community Medicine, University of Tromsø, ISM skriftserie (115).
Kivivuori, J. (2007). *Delinquent behaviour in Nordic capital cities* (Publication 127). Scandinavian Research Council for Criminology, National Research Institute of Legal Policy, Helsinki, Finland.

KRIPOS. (2010). *Drapsoversikt*, Oslo. Retrieved from https://www.politi.no/kripos/statistikk/drap
Krug, E. G., Dahlberg, L. L., Mercy, J. A., Zwi, A. B., & Lozano, R. (Eds). (2002). *World report on violence and health*. Geneva: World Health Organization.
Laub, J. H., & Sampson, R. J. (2003). *Shared beginnings, divergent lives: Delinquent boys to age 70*. Cambridge: Harvard University Press.
Lien, I. L. (2004). *Ugripelig ung* (Rapport 2004:14). Oslo: NIBR.
Linzey, A. (2009). *The link between animal abuse and human violence*. Brighton: Sussex Academic Press.
Livingstone, S., Haddon, L., Görzig, A., & Ólafsson, K. (2011). *Risks and safety on the Internet: The perspective of European children: Full findings*. London: LSE, EU Kids Online. Retrieved from http://eprints.lse.ac.uk/33731/
Loeber, R., & Farrington, D. P. (2001). The significance of child delinquency. In R. Loeber & D. P. Farrington (Eds), *Child delinquents: Development, intervention and service needs* (pp. 1–22). Thousand Oaks, CA: SAGE.
Loeber, R., Farrington, D. P., & Washbusch, D. A. (Eds). (1998). *Serious and violent juvenile offenders: Risk factors and successful interventions*. Thousand Oaks, CA: SAGE.
Lööw, H. (1997). *Utsatthet för etnisk och politisk relaterat våld m m, spridning avrasistisk och antirasistisk propaganda samt attityder till demokratin m m bland skolelever*. Stockholm: CEIFO förlag.
Maniadaki, K., Kakouros, E., & Karaba R. (2010). *Psychopathology in juvenile delinquents*. Hauppauge, NY: Nova Publishers.
Matza, D. (2009). *Delinquency and drift* (5th ed.). New Brunswick, NJ: Transaction Publishers.
Moffitt, T. E. (2003). Life-course-persistent and adolescent-limited antisocial behavior: A 10-year research review and a research agenda. In B. B. Lahey, T. E. Moffitt, & A. Caspi (Eds), *Causes of conduct disorders and juvenile delinquency* (pp. 49–75). New York: The Guilford Press.
Moffitt, T. E., Caspi, A., Rutter, M., & Silva, P. A. (2001). *Sex differences in antisocial behavior*. Cambridge, MA: Cambridge University Press.
Möller, I., & Krahé, B. (2009). Exposure to violent video games and aggression in German adolescents: A longitudinal analysis. *Aggressive Behavior, 35*(1), 75–89. doi: 10.1002/ab.20290
Næshagen, F. L. (1995a). *The drastic decline of Norwegian homicide rates between 1550 and 1800*. Paper presented at the American Society of Criminology Annual Meeting, Boston.
———. (1995b). *Kriminell ikke-dødelig vold fra 1500-tallet til idag*, Norsk Politihistorisk Årsskrift. Oslo: NPHS.
———. (2002). Private law enforcement in Norwegian history: The husband's right to chastise his wife. *Scandinavian Journal of History 27*, 19–30.
———. (2005). Den kriminelle voldens U-kurve fra 1500-tall til nåtid, *Historisk Tidsskrift, 3*, 411–427.
Natland, S. (2009). *Volden, horen og vennskapet*. Trondheim, Norway: Tapir Akademisk Forlag.
Nelander, K., & Shannon, D. (2010). *Mobbning kan kopplas till sexuell utsatthet på nätet*, Apropå, 2. BRÅ., Stockholm.
Norgeshelsa. (2011). *Kunnskap for folkets helse*. Retrieved from http://www.fhi.no
Ogden, T., Forgatch, M. S., Askeland, E., Patterson, G. R., & Bullock, B. M. (2005). Implementation of parent management training at the national Level: The case of Norway. *Journal of Social Work Practice, 19*(3), 317–329.
Ogden, T., & Halliday-Boykins, C. A. (2004). Multisystemic treatment of antisocial adolescents in Norway: Replication of clinical outcomes outside of the US. *Child and Adolescent Mental Health, 9*(2), 77–83.
Ogden, T., Kärki, F. U., & Teigen, K. S. (2010). Linking research, policy and practice in welfare services and education in Norway. *Evidence & Policy, 6*(2), 161–177.
Ogden, T., & Sørlie, M. A. (2009). Implementing and evaluating empirically based family and school programmes for children with conduct problems in Norway. *The International Journal of Emotional Education, 1*(1), 96–107.
Øia, T. (2007). *Levekår og sosiale forskjeller* (Rapport 6/07). Oslo: NOVA.
Politiet (2010, 2011), Kommenterte STRASAK-tall, 2010, Kommenterte STRASAK-tall, 2011, Politidirektoratet, Seksjon for analyse og forebygging, Oslo.

PROBA/MOT. (2011). *Evaluering av "MOT" i ungdomsskolen*. Sluttrapport.
Rørhus, K. (1999). *Ride to live—live to ride: En oversikt over sentral forskning om outlawbikerkulture* (PHS Research Report No. 4). Oslo, Norway: Police Academy.
Runhovde, S. R. (Ed.). (2010). *Tillit til politiet* (PHS Research Report No. 4). Oslo: Police Academy.
SALTO: *Barne- og ungdomskriminaliteten i Oslo,* Salto-rap. 2008, 2009, 2010, 2011, Oslo kommune, Politiet.
Schou, L., Dyb, G., & Graff-Iversen, S. (2007). *Voldsutsatt ungdom I Norge* (Rapport 8). Oslo: Folkehelseinstituttet.
Shannon, D. (2007). *Vuxnas sexualla kontakter med barn via internett: Omfattning, karaktär, åtgärder*. Stockholm: BRÅ.
SIRUS statistikk. (2011). Sirus.no/nor/Statistikk/ and sirus.no/filestore/import_vedlegg/sirusrap.5.09.pdf
Skodvin, M. (Ed.). (1995). *Norge i krig*. Oslo: Aschehoug.
Sørlie, A. (2000). *Alvorlige atferdsproblemer*. Oslo: Praksis forlag.
Stjernø, S. (2005). *Solidarity in Europe: The history of an idea*. New York: Cambridge University Press.
Strasburger, V. C., Wilson, B. J., & Jordan, A. B. (2009).*Children, adolescents, and the media*. Thousand Oaks, CA: SAGE.
Tendenser i kriminaliteten. (1999–2009). Utfordringer I Norge 2010-2012, Seksjon for analyse og forebygging, Politiet. Politidirektoratet, Mai 2010.
The Minister of Justice and Police and the Minister of Children, Equality and Social Inclusion. *Alternative to Prison for Youngsters under the age of 18, June 2011*. Press release.
Thorsen, L. R., Lid, S., & Stene, R. J. (2009). *Kriminalitet og rettsvesen*. Oslo: Statistics Norway.
Topland, B., & Skaalvik, E. M. (2010). *Meninger fra klasserommet: Analyse av elevundersokelsen, 2010*. Kristiansand, Norway: Oxford Research AS.
Tremblay, R. E. (2009). The development of chronic physical aggression: Genes and environments matter from the beginning. In R. E. Tremblay, Marcel A. Gvan Aken, & W. Koops (Eds), *Development and prevention of behaviour problems: From genes to social policy* (pp. 113–130). New York: Psychology Press.
UNDP–HDI Index. (2010). *undp.org*. Retrieved from http://hdr.undp.org/en/reports/global/hdr2010

6

Mental Health for the Media Generation: Balancing Coping and Riskiness

Usha S. Nayar
Ingunn Hagen
Priya Nayar
Dan Y. Jacobsen

The massive presence of media and the time spent on media technologies[1] by children are clear indicators that there is a shift in lifestyles and priorities for our new generation. Children spend over five-and-a-half hours daily using media in the US (Roberts & Foehr, 2004). This average, although alarmingly large, seems rather a matter of fact in 2011. Children across countries are spending more and more time in front of television sets, computer screens, and on cell phones making media a central part of their lives. Advertising, communications, as well as education have a brand new social networking image to make it accessible and reachable to children.[2]

Importance may vary depending on social class, culture, and the geographical regions where these young people come from. Nevertheless, because new media technologies are so integrated in young people's lives, they are also valuable resources to promote mental health; to develop a distinct identity; to give opportunities for social networking; and to provide scaffolds for constructing new forms of self-directed, interest-driven activities, peer-based communication, learning, and support.

Keeping this at the forefront, this chapter will examine healthy media use during childhood and adolescence and the parameters for media use so that it leads to good mental health and

---

[1] Such media technologies or information and communication technologies (ICTs) include computers, laptops, digital television, cellular phones or smart phones, game consoles like play station, Vii and X-box, mobile game consoles like Nintendo or PSBs, mp3 players, iPads, etc.

[2] When we talk about young people in this chapter, we refer to children and adolescents, that is, people under 18 years of age. We are, of course, aware that media use habits vary among those who are younger and older within this age group.

well-being. We will also examine the role of various mediators—such as peers, teachers, parents, community, and state to assist with cultivating sound media use habits and finding a balance in the everyday user pattern.

Although media technologies are a resource for children and adolescents' mental health, its intense use leads to questions concerning young people's capacity and interest to bring balance in physical and mental activity. A Kaiser Family Foundation Study looked at media use in very young children (0 to 6 years) and concluded that these children spend as much time with a screen as they do playing outside (Rideout, Vandewater, & Wartella, 2003). This study and many others draw links between media use and increase of health issues, such as obesity and other physical and mental health problems. It is not uncommon for health care professionals to use terms such as media-addiction implying media as the source of mental illness, dependency, obsessive-compulsive behaviors, concentration problems, and other attention disorders. Besides these physical and health risks there are safety concerns in media-heavy communities—issues such as cyber bullying, young children being exposed to extreme violence, sexually explicit material, as well as other extreme behaviors are being highlighted. The world at large, including the deviances of society, is much closer and easily accessible with media tools and other technologies.

This chapter examines children's well-being and their use of media following the guidelines of child participation and child protection within the framework of the United Nations Convention of Child Rights. Evidences of media immersion by children, their experiential power and control over children's lives, and the agencies that support this immersion are weighed against a child right's perspective. It is important to note that with changing media forms and new technology and tools there is a shift in how young people socialize, learn, and establish their relationships that ought to be addressed by psychologists, educators, parents, childcare workers, and policy makers.

Media Generation, Users, and Generators

> As anyone who knows a teen or a tween can attest, media are among the most powerful forces in young people's lives today. Eight- to eighteen-year-olds spend more time with media than in any other activity besides (maybe) sleeping—an average of more than 7½ hours a day, seven days a week. The TV shows they watch, video games they play, songs they listen to, books they read and websites they visit are an enormous part of their lives, offering a constant stream of messages about families, peers, relationships, gender roles, sex, violence, food, values, clothes, and an abundance of other topics too long to list ... Understanding the role of media in young people's lives is essential for those concerned about promoting the healthy development of children and adolescents, including parents, pediatricians, policymakers, children's advocates, educators, and public health groups. (Rideout, Foehr, & Roberts, 2010, p. 1)

There are many popular names given to identity generations. The Baby Boomer Generation led to Generation X, where researchers record birthdates from 1961 to the latest in 1981 (Armour,

2005). The demographic cohort following Generation X is called Generation Y, Generation Next, or Echo Boomers. These youngsters' birthdates are from late 1970s to somewhere in the late 1990s and are often known as the MTV Generation (Huntley, 2006), or as in this chapter, the "Media Generation" (Roberts, Foehr, & Rideout, 2005). This is a generation known for their expertise in playing video games, their instinctive use of mobile phones, computers, laptops, mp3 players, and virtual social platforms. Most importantly, however, they are the child and adolescent population that spend a large portion of their everyday life interacting with media technology for play, entertainment, school, social networking, and relaxation.

We understand the media generation as the youth that live in a hyper-media environment. In many countries, including India, access is an important concern due to inequity especially as media technologies (or information and communication technologies [ICTs]) are regarded as important resources for the future (Nayar & Bhide, 2008). Parents and other stakeholders are concerned with the potential negative aspects of media use on young people. These negative aspects can be simple, potentially harmful content, risk of excessive screen media use leading to less physical activity, or relatively newer phenomena such as cyber-bullying or "sexting." The Internet is also becoming the medium of choice for pedophiles to contact children anonymously and track addresses and other contact information (Livingstone & Haddon, 2009; Medietilsynet, 2010; Rideout et al., 2010).

Academic researchers are codifying not just access to media but also media content. Questions like whether there is censorship and who is responsible for media content are being asked. Who can make media, who may not? Media content such as a YouTube video, Facebook upload, Twitter, blogs, virtual forums, chat rooms, podcasts, online radio, and so forth are all part of this large Internet world and everyone can be a user and a generator of the content. We call the media creators, "media generators" and generators can be anyone with access and tools to make media messages. For children, these generators include friends, family, community, cultural influences, market, and state. There is a wide belief that the media generation is a product of nuclear families (two working parents), city life, and globalization. However, media generators such as cultural influences, family priorities, lifestyle, socioeconomic power, as well as peer and popular choices play an important role in the creation and sustenance of this new generation (Nayar, 2011).

Children's Participation and Protection

It is worth taking note of the recent trend in romanticizing children as pioneers with a "natural gift" for media use or alternatively as particularly vulnerable to new media (Hagen & Wold, 2009). Neither of these views is strictly accurate; children are both more cautious and conservative than adults perceive them to be. They possess a certain amount of resilience or at least are able to cope with many of the posited risks online or via new media (Livingstone & Haddon, 2009). It is important to acknowledge both—young people's immersion and experience with the

Internet and other new media technologies, as well as their need for empowerment and guidance (Dunkels, 2007).

There is a kind of frenzy about control, access, and use. On the home front parents install software to monitor Internet usage on computers, but access to media is so large and sometimes entirely subtle that it is not possible to completely or effectively monitor children and adolescent's media use. Moreover, parents are often reluctant to restrict children's media use, as especially computers and Internet are regarded as tools for learning; an educational aid backed by school and university systems and one of many methods of communication that has now grown into an overwhelming Internet and Intranet connectivity. However, an issue that ought to now concern the generators is that media do not only stimulate the young population but also create dependence. This poses an urgent question as to what kind of side effects this would lead our youth to, and what is the potential role of peers, parents, teachers, community, and state.

Contextualization

Children and young people's media use needs contextualization if this practice is to be understood properly (cf. Hagen 2004/1998; Livingstone, 2002). First of all, children's everyday life, which includes their home situation, their school, and their leisure activities, provides a context. Cultures and their norms are also contexts to consider when understanding the role of new media and ICTs in children's lives. Media use has to be related to young people's social context, such as family, community, and friends or peer groups.

Media landscape which includes traditional media is also the context for how new ICTs are appropriated. Children's use and reception will mediate the potential impact of media exposure. The consequences of media use can be extensive and may affect how children use their time, socialize, and even view the world. Thus, young people's media use can be a factor in how they experience themselves and their lives.

Recently, Leena (name changed), a 12-year-old from a suburb in New Delhi, who subscribes to YouTube, has been uploading videos of her re-enacting dance moves of popular music celebrities. She sings about romance, longing, break-ups, and other subjects that are often sung by pop music icons. Leena gets over ten thousand hits on her channel. She receives comments on her singing and dancing from viewers all over the world. Culturally, she comes from a protected and simple background where her singing and dancing may not seem in any way harmful. However, her fans have access to her directly by way of email and other communication and she writes freely about her personal life. It is hard to imagine this kind of free access to a 12-year-old without the help of a media platform. While the risks of this kind of access are high, the responsibility of such consequences is a grey area. Many can blame the child, her parents/guardians, the users who access, or YouTube. None of these "responsible" parties are the ultimate answer to media gatekeeping (see Figure 6.1).

Figure 6.1 Roles of Media Mediators for Children's Media Use

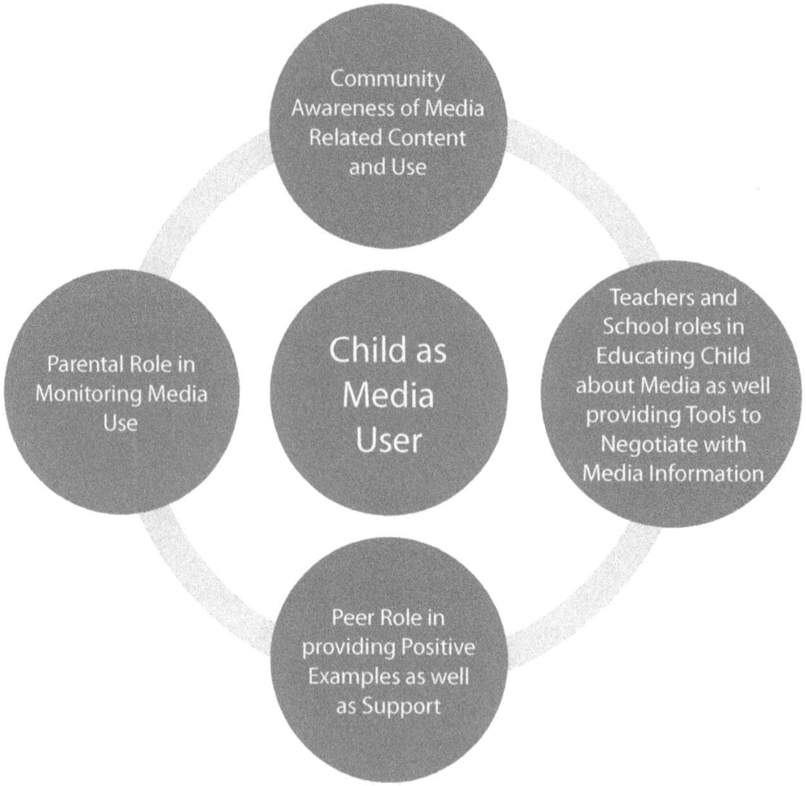

- Community Awareness of Media Related Content and Use
- Parental Role in Monitoring Media Use
- Child as Media User
- Teachers and School roles in Educating Child about Media as well providing Tools to Negotiate with Media Information
- Peer Role in providing Positive Examples as well as Support

Source: Authors.
Note: This figure specifies central actors in children's social context that can play a role to mediate children's media use. For example, while small children need guidance, young people may need informed discussion and negotiation partners.

Child Rights Perspective

Children have a basic right to grow in a healthy environment where they can realize their full potential. ICT has provided a new opportunity to explore and test their autonomy (Hagen, 2007). From a child rights perspective, children have a right to experience and experiment with new communication tools (UNICEF, 2005). In fact, children are agents for their learning through media use, and their participation in production will be an important milestone to highlight children's perspectives. Children can and ought to be empowered to use media creatively and to learn skills that can negotiate with the hypermedia environment. Keeping in mind the age and developmental stage of children, policies and practices have and must keep up with the uses, risks, and other causal effects of new technology and media.

Children's Changing Media Habits

Understanding children today involves understanding children's relationship to the media landscape. A number of studies in recent decades have confirmed that although young people are pioneers in adopting and using new media, their use of the newest technologies tend to enter into their existing lifestyles and use of media. Children are expanding their media mix, rather than replacing old media with new ones (Livingstone & Bovill, 2001; Rideout et al., 2010; Roberts et al., 2005). Children's media habits change in direct relationship to the ease with which new media integrate into their existing preferences for social interaction, for communication, and for play (Ito et al., 2009).

Generally, there are differences in media use during childhood that depend on age, gender, and accessibility. Television viewing is a key activity for children under 12 years in most countries. The significance of personal computers (PCs) and the Internet increases with age as the children grow outwards and peer-oriented (Hagen & Wold, 2009). In this process, the mobile phone also becomes more important for children and youth. SMS, chat, and e-mail are important communication tools in the peer culture of youngsters.

Changes in children's social environment are directly reflected in children's media use (Livingstone & Bovill, 2001). Personal media content often changes borders between public and private and allows for multitasking in a unique social way. A young person can be available socially for his or her friends while they are at home. While children and young people have intense negotiations on media use with their parents, having their own TV or PC in their rooms allows for more "free space" from parental control (cf. Hagen, 2007). Moreover, the increasing availability of portable media including laptops, iPads, video games, and mobile phones with Internet access makes it increasingly difficult for parents to monitor what websites their children visit, who they communicate with, and what they post about themselves online.

Private information and pictures can be available for almost anyone when they are posted online. It appears that increased multiplicity of media content and forms also result in more individualized lifestyles. Yet, patterns in children and adolescents' media use determined by age gender, ethnicity, national background, and region are evident. Children's use of the Internet continues to grow. Net users are increasingly younger, while parents are catching up with young people (Calvert, 2005). Gender differences are disappearing with the more communicative turn in Internet use. However, socioeconomic differences still exist in most countries.

Coping with the Internet

Children today are growing up in a "connected" world, for them the PC and the Internet are tools of communication. As noted by Livingstone, Haddon, Görzig, and Òlafsson (2011), "The rapidity with which children and young people are gaining access to online, convergent, mobile and networked media is unprecedented in the history of technological innovation" (p. 11).

The age at which children are starting to use the Internet and mobile phones is getting younger and younger. The younger the child, the more vulnerable he/she is and less able to navigate and negotiate impact of media messages on his/her emotions independently. However, to cope with the Internet is a precondition for being successful as a young person today socially, academically, and almost in all spheres of life. This can be a dilemma for parents as well as teachers.

A similar trajectory follows video games. Playing games—fictional games like action and shooting games, role play games, adventure games, and strategy games—are especially popular among young people (Hagen & Wold, 2009). When popular movies are launched for children, they are soon followed by games as is the case for *Harry Potter, Pirates of the Caribbean, Lego Star Wars, Lego Indiana Jones, Avatar,* and so forth. Players can be the main characters in the game (e.g., an avatar in one of the popular *SIMs* games) and can act towards other characters and objects. The games contain sound effects and music, just like in a movie. Thus, games can be very involving, such as the popular online game *World of War Craft*. In games such as these, players are also part of a team so they are socially committed to spend time on the game (Karlsen, 2011).

Surfing the web provides young people with access to different types of websites with enormous amounts of information including entertaining genres that are popular from other media, like music and film. YouTube has been one of the fastest increasing websites in recent years, where children and youth can see film and video clips. They can also search for information online related to school, homework, leisure, and hobby activities. Many children report that they use the Internet alone, more so than acknowledged by their parents (Medietilsynet, 2010). Chatting is also popular among young people, as they can stay in touch with their friends continuously while also doing other things. Using a web camera is often part of such chats.

Children tend to use all aspects and all genres of the PC and Internet, such as play games, search information for school homework, download music, write e-mail, surf websites, chat, and so forth. There are, however, differences in use according to age: playing games is the key activity for young children and news reading, e-mail, chatting, and communicating is a teenage year activity (Hagen & Wold, 2009). In addition, viewing film, TV, or video clips is popular. Both girls and boys use chat and other messenger clients, e-mail, and social networking sites extensively. Thus, the general picture is that these genres or platforms have become very important in the social relations of young people (Turkle, 2011).

In these forums, children and adolescents can to some extent play with their identity and often appear as idealized versions of themselves. They use these arenas both to maintain existing relationships and friendships and to get new contacts (Hernwall, 2003). The increased significance of Internet among young people tends to reinforce social differences among children in terms of competence, social networks, and intellectual resources (Seiter, 2005). Internet use in school often tends to reinforce existing social differences rather than bridging the gaps (Buckingham, 2007).

The Internet may also provide opportunities for participation and civic engagement. It provides youngsters with possibilities for being creative through numerous kinds of user-generated content

(Kalmus, Runnel, & Siibak, 2009; Davidson, 2011). Moreover, the Internet also provides young people with arenas for identity expression, social connections, and sharing experiences (Ito et al., 2009). In fact, the results from the latest EU Kids Online survey suggest that as many children and youth find it easier to "be themselves" online than offline (Livingstone et al., 2011). The challenges are to understand in new ways how children can develop sound coping mechanism related to their media use.

Internet Use—Some Related Risks

For most children, the Internet is a great resource and a source of entertainment, communication, and information. However, there are also risky aspects of Internet use by children and young people, and as it has been documented in the EU Kids Online project there seems to be a positive correlation between use and risk (Livingstone & Haddon, 2009). Such risks include, in rank order, giving out personal information (the most common risk), encountering online pornography, being exposed to hateful or violent material, online bullying, and receiving unwanted sexual comments. The last risk, meeting online contacts offline is the least common, but potentially the most dangerous.

The idea of privacy and personal information is still porous for a child. This may be attractive in the virtual world, especially for actors who target commercial messages as well as actors with dishonest intentions (Hagen & Wold, 2009; Nayar, 2011). Yet, children are more careful with giving out personal information when they have been taught about safe use (Medietilsynet, 2010). Older boys seek out explicit sexual content on the web. Girls are more likely to receive unwanted sexual comments (Brandtzæg, Staksrud, Hagen, & Wold, 2009). Boys tend to search for violent material, while girls tend to be emotionally upset when faced with similar material. Cyber-bullying is making headlines across the world; an estimated 10% of children have experienced virtual bullying according to a recent study (Medietilsynet, 2010).

Excessive use of screen-related activities leads to social isolation where young people find it difficult to relate to their peers in a traditional face-to-face communication model. Internet dependency is a growing risk for the media generation. In media coverage of dependency online games and virtual worlds, *World of War Craft* and *Second Life* are often mentioned. Young (1998), a psychologist, defines Internet dependency as an impulse-control disease without drugs. In order to distinguish Internet dependency from heavy use, this lack of control is central.

For young people the mobile phone is the lifeline of their social life—their way of keeping in touch with their peers (Hagen & Wold, 2009). As stated by Haddon (2004), "In many countries the mobile phone has also become a tool to support peer networking" (p. 45). Mobile phones are increasingly converging with other media, such as web browsing, pictures, games, playing music, and listening to the radio, in addition to calling and texting. For adults it is easy to underestimate the social significance of the mobile phone of today's adolescents, making constant availability possible. Young people bring the mobile phone along everywhere for constant status updating, coordination, and documentation with their peers (Stald, 2007). The mobile phone can also be used negatively for bullying others, for example, by sending SMS messages with unwanted content or embarrassing pictures.

Media Technologies and Mental Health

The integration of new media in young people's lives can effectively promote mental health for children. Children develop identity, explore new knowledge, develop new ways of problem solving, develop resilience, new techniques of manipulation, increase their focused attention, and develop openness to experiences (Hagen, 2010a). However, to achieve the optimal positive benefits of this integration, media generators and mental health professionals need to not only understand new media and its many uses but also find effective tools that help navigate this environment.

The intense use of media has led to questions about its consequences on the health of children. For example, there is a relationship between media intensive lifestyles and dependency, low academic achievement, low sensitivity to injury and pains of others, learning of antisocial skills and aggressiveness (cf. Strasburger, Wilson, & Jordan, 2009). There are attempts to examine the relationship between excessive media use and overweight and also ADHD (Vaughanbell, 2006). To find a balance between media use and other activities is important for young people's health and mental health (Hagen, 2009). The same goes for being able to use media in such a way that young people feel a sense of well-being and control over their own lives. Good health includes healthy interpersonal relations, social interactions, age-appropriate emotional maturity, identity, resilience, flexibility, and sense of control on their own lives. In terms of risks potentially affecting mental health some aspects of media use needs to be reduced amongst children: extensive use (especially if there are dependency issues); bullying (in Indian context the term commonly used is teasing); being bullied; being exposed to violence, substance abuse, or aggressiveness.

The Internet can be a valuable resource related to young people's mental health, especially in terms of help lines; hotlines; Question and Answer-options; and websites related to lifestyle, well-being, and typical youth challenges and problems (Hagen, 2009). Websites which focus on mental health can provide supportive environments for adolescents to discuss topics related to identity and well-being like their body, friendship and love, sexuality, family conflicts, temptations (to alcohol, nicotine, and drugs), experiences related to violence or threats, loneliness, and how to get further help. Such websites can be great resources for young people who can discuss their challenges with other youth, moderators, professionals, or voluntary workers. However, such websites can also be risky for young people if they are supporters and promoters of unhealthy lifestyles and values. For example, anorexia websites take a positive stance towards anorexia and present it as a lifestyle rather than an illness. These user-generated websites offer "thinspiration" where young girls get advice about how to lose weight and how to camouflage this from their parents (Wold, Aristodemou, Dunkels, & Laouris, 2009). Internet can provide valuable resources related to mental health where websites, blogs, discussion forums, and chat groups can be arenas for emotional support. However, websites like the pro-anorexia, suicide, and self-harm sites also demonstrate the potential dangers.

For children, relating to other people is an important part of their development. As much as 59 percent of 9- to 16-year-old European children have a social networking profile (Livingstone et al., 2011). Social networking sites focus on building and reflecting social networks or relations among people virtually. These networks are of people who share interests and/or activities; they create profiles, share pictures, blogs, calendar of events, and so forth. Among the media generation, the top social networking sites include Facebook, YouTube, MySpace, Twitter, Yahoo!, Orkut, and Bebo. References to these are made on television, in newspapers and magazines, and links to their website are available freely when using the Internet. Mobile phones now sync these social networking sites seamlessly onto the user's handheld device so that easy access is simply one touch, push, or click away.

For example, Facebook syncs a user's phonebook directory with its own so that contacts are backed up virtually, provided every person in the contact list also has a Facebook account. But, it is not that the media generation uses only one social networking site—they use several, and hours are spent in updating, refreshing, observing status messages, photos, mobile uploads, game applications, and so forth. MySpace, a popular destination before Facebook is now famous for new artists, musicians, and bands who, in addition to their own website, cross market themselves using Twitter feeds, YouTube subscriptions, Facebook, and Yahoo! Groups, and text message updates.

However, in the case of 12-year-old Leena we mentioned earlier, the promotion of her musical talent on YouTube may translate to real-life risky and dangerous behavior. Leena obtained a YouTube account, possibly by lying about her age. She sings and dances in her bedroom, living room, and neighborhood, answers emails from fans. With the help of her parents, she edits and uploads these video links not only on YouTube but also on Facebook, Twitter, local social networking sites, and other music talent websites. Among her fans and followers are adult men who she corresponds with regularly on a seemingly innocent basis (Nayar, 2011). This kind of interaction with strangers who are not peers would not have been possible without the YouTube platform and somewhat naïve parental support. But these are still anomalies in the virtual world. Social networking sites have expanded the world view for the media generation who now talk cross-culturally, geographically, and without the language barrier. Short forms for expressions and popular emoticons are understood across the board. The media generation understands and speaks a language that is constantly stimulated—often at the risk of over-stimulation. Video games that are one-dimensional like the *Mario Brothers* or *Packman* were a lost cause to boredom and replaced easily by the likes of *Halo, Final Fantasy,* and *Grand Theft Auto* which not only engage the user but also allow users to interact with other users who are playing the same game, as opponents.

Figure 6.2 A Framework to Guide the Media Generation

Extensive-use → increseased risk and potential harm

Riskiness factors:

Exposure to risks (like giving out personal information, encountering pornography, violence or hateful information, online bullying, unwanted sexual comments, meeting online strangers offline → harm

Guided use → More coping and balance

Protective factors include:

Regulation/supportive policy, support from mediators, digital media literacy encouraging children's participation in other creative and physical activities

Source: Authors (including the risk factors identified in reports by the *EuKidsOnline Network*, see http://www2.lse.ac.uk/media@lse/research/EUKidsOnline/Home.aspx)
Note: This figure shows some of the riskiness factors that children may be exposed to when they use media technologies, especially Internet. The figure also includes potentially protective factors that may increase young people's coping and being able balance use of media technologies with other aspects of their lives.

Reducing Risk and Increasing Balance

For the reduction of risk among young media users the role of protective factors is significant. These include:

Availability and Regulation

New media technologies have become cheaper and more mobile, and are thus more widely distributed in populations in Europe, North America, urban India, and many other countries around the world especially among children and young people. Thus, it is not surprising that children's use of Internet continues to grow and mobile phone users are becoming younger and younger. TV with its increasing number of channels also has a central place in the life of children. The increased availability and ease of access to media makes it more challenging for parents to regulate children's media consumption habits (Hagen, 2007). As already mentioned, the rise of a "bedroom culture" where children consume media in their own very media-equipped bedroom makes parental guidance of media use more difficult. Use of new media is closely related to young people's sense of autonomy, and with increasing age they are expecting greater freedom in their media use.

New media have permeated young lives and youth culture to the extent that they are "always on"; in constant contact with their friends via SMS, instant messaging, mobile phones, and Internet connection (Ito et al., 2008). This may impact their sense of identity and autonomy in yet unforeseen ways. These new media allow young people to extend their friendships and interests, and also facilitate new forms of self-directed and peer-assisted learning (Jacobsen, 2006). Researchers emphasize that when young people "hang out" online—they use media in social and recreational ways (for friendship-driven and interest-driven activities)—they also pick up essential social and technological skills necessary for their full participation in society. Ito et al. (2008, 2009) claim that new media forms have changed the ways young people socialize and learn—something that needs to be taken on board and addressed by educators, parents, and policy makers.

Children today need to use the Internet in order to be socially included for purposes of education and a future job, in fact for being able to function in today's technological world. Thus, too strict rules and regulations by state or caretakers will restrict young people's communication rights and potentials when it comes to career, friendships, and citizenship. Rather, meaningful guidelines and rules in the best interest of young media users may be worked out according to their use and navigation abilities and in dialogue with young people themselves.

Empowerment through Digital Media Literacy

If media is to be used in healthy and balanced ways and to function as resources to promote mental health then children need to develop digital media literacy. Digital media literacy means "the ability to access, understand and create communications in a variety of contexts" (O'Neill & Hagen, 2009). Adolescents need to learn about ICT risks and safe use, how to cope with online risk and to reflect about their own lifestyles. However, parents and teachers should also be involved in guidance, mediation, and continuous dialogue with children regarding the online aspects of their lives.

Such empowerment is also needed by parents and teachers, who cannot be less literate about ICT than their children if they are to guide children in this fast changing ICT and media environment. The case of Leena mentioned earlier is an example of a parental role which needs to be played with appropriate knowledge and awareness to protect children from the risks. Educational institutions as well as other actors in the community and media industry need to play a central role in promoting such digital media literacy and promoting child mental health and well-being. Children's media experiences, competencies, and expressed needs should be taken into consideration when developing digital media competencies and health related programs (cf. Hagen, 2009).

Privacy, Policy, and Responsibility

Policies at national level in various contexts are in place for action. Mostly, these policies are related to educational settings where schools can address mental health problems of children related to media use. At the school level there is emphasis on promotion of positive mental health and prevention of mental illness, and related activities and approaches are needed to improve socio-emotional competencies of children. Except for bullying and perhaps commercial pressure (children being exposed to continuous marketing efforts and advertising online and through media) the other problems linked with media use or abuse are not so apparent in school settings (Hagen, 2010b). Thus, the issue of policy and responsibility of child protection is much more complex than linking with only educational institutions.

The recognition of linkage between the use of media by children and related mental health issues in terms of attention deficit, compulsiveness, aggression, emotional sensitivity, sexual abuse, "grooming," bullying, and self-esteem are the ones that are to be talked about, communicated, and discussed in platforms of parent child meetings and school counselors. Thus, multi-setting literacy and mental health problems concerns, prevention, and promotion strategies are to be at school, home, and community levels.

Conclusion

The challenges are to simultaneously maximize children's opportunities for access and use, while also minimizing the potential risks. Policies to achieve this balance between providing media access opportunities whilst minimizing risks require an evidence-based approach. Such evidence in form of research is unevenly distributed across Europe and all over the world. Thus, there is a need for more research on how children and youth use new media as resources in their lives, what children perceive as online risks, and what strategies they develop to cope with such risks (Dunkels, 2007).

Children's Internet use continues to grow, also among the younger age groups (Livingstone et al., 2011). With this growth there will also be an increased exposure to risks, such as giving out personal information, encountering online pornography, violent or hateful content, being bullied, or experiencing sexual harassment at an earlier age. Cyber-bullying is an emerging threat to children in Europe and elsewhere, and needs to be combated (Brandtzæg et al., 2009). Cyberbullying is the risk that upsets children the most. Still, more bullying seems to occur offline than online. The question is how positive use can be facilitated and how one may empower children to deal with the problematic and risky media and online use.

To summarize, the key concerns for the media generation are integration of media with everyday life of children at home, school, and community. With different media being so integrated in children's everyday lives, providing them with constant messages, entertainment, and communication and taking up so much of their time, this new media environment has a great impact on children's lifestyles and selfhood. In some parts of the world, equal access is a primary concern. In India, for example, the disparity of the access to media between the low, middle, and high income is phenomenal. The other concern has been parental and educators' media literacy so that they can understand, communicate, guide and monitor use of media among children.

In liberal economies as well as in these global competitive environments, to create child appropriate media production and tools is desirable—the challenge is who is responsible for it: market, family, and/or state? From a child protection viewpoint the risks of over use of Internet and going to unprotected sites carries mental health risks for children. Thus parents and child caretakers need to be media literate in order to guide and have dialogues with children and teenagers. While increased use leads to increased digital competence and coping skills among children, the increasingly younger children online is a reason for concern, since they tend to lack the necessary skills (Livingstone et al., 2011).

Understanding children as participators is important. Involving children both in media productions and use is in the best interest of the children. Child protection is the responsibility of adults; state, parents, and teachers need to be proactive in respecting the resilience and innovativeness amongst children. The risks are managed if parents work with their children as partners in appreciating the ease with which children and young people enjoy using these media for a variety of purposes, and empowering children to protect themselves from those who could be harmful to them by "grooming," bullying, and other means.

References

Armour, S. (posted 11/06/2005, updated 11/08/2005). Generation Y: They've arrived at work with a new attitude. *USA Today*. Retrieved from http://www.usatoday.com/money/workplace/200511-06-gen-y_x.htm

Brandtzæg, P. B., Staksrud, E., Hagen, I., & Wold, T. (2009). Norwegian children's experiences of cyber bullying and harassment when using different technological platforms. *Journal of Children and Media, 3*(4), 349–365. doi: 10.1080/17482790903233366

Buckingham, D. (2007). *Beyond technology: Children's learning in the age of digital culture*. Cambridge, UK: Polity Press.

Calvert, S. L. (2005). Media and early development. In K. McCartney & D. Phillips (Eds), *Blackwell handbook of early childhood development* (pp. 508–530). Malden, MA: Blackwell Publishing,

Davidson, C. N. (2011). *Now you see it: How the brain science of attention will transform the way we live, work, and learn.* New York: Viking Penguin.

Dunkels, E. (2007). *Bridging the distance: Children's strategies on the Internet* (Doctoral thesis), Umeå University, Umeå, Sweden. Retrieved from http://urn.kb.se/resolve?urn=urn:nbn:se:umu:diva-1340

Haddon, L. (2004). *Information and communication technologies in everyday life: A concise introduction and research guide.* Oxford: Berg.

Hagen, I. (2004/1998). *Medias publikum. Frå mottakar til brukar?* (Media's audiences: From receivers to users?). Oslo: Ad Notam Gyldendal.

———. (2007). We can't just sit the whole day watching TV: Negotiations concerning media use among youngsters and their parents. *Young, 15*(4), 369–393. doi:10.1177/110330880701500403

———. (2009). The role of new media technologies and the internet in the promotion of mental health of children. In *Background document for the thematic conference: Promoting of mental health and well-being of children and young people—making it happen.* Stockholm: Swedish National Institute of Public Health.

———. (2010a). Children and young people in a changing media environment: Some challenges. In S. Kotilainen & S. B. Arnolds-Granlund (Eds), *Media literacy education: Nordic perspectives* (pp. 29–40). Göteborg, Sweden: Nordicom.

———. (2010b). Growing up in a commercial world: Reflections on media, marketing and young consumers. In U. Carlsson (Ed.), *Children and youth in the digital media culture: From a Nordic horizon* (pp. 113–127). Göteborg, Sweden: Nordicom.

Hagen, I., & Wold, T. (2009). *Mediegenerasjonen: Barn og unge i det nye medielandskapet* (The media generation: Children and youth in the new media landscape). Oslo: Det Norske Samlaget.

Hernwall, P. (2003). *Barn@com – att växa upp I det nya mediasamhället* (Children@com – A growing up in the new media society). Stockholm: HLS Förlag.

Huntley, R. (2006). *The world according to Y: Inside the new adult generation.* Sydney: Allen & Unwin.

Ito, M., Baumer, S., Bittanti, M., Boyd, D., Cody, R., Herr-Stephenson, B., & Tripp, L. (2009). *Hanging out, messing around, and geeking out: Kids living and learning with new media.* Cambridge, MA: MIT Press.

Ito, M., Horst, H. A., Bittanti, M., Boyd, D., Herr-Stephenson, B., Lange, P. G., Pascoe, C. J., & Tripp, L. (2008). *Living and learning with new media: Summary of findings from the Digital Youth Project.* Retrieved from http://digitalyouth.ischool.berkeley.edu/files/report/digitalyouth-WhitePaper.pdf, 6.13.2012

Jacobsen, D. Y. (2006, August). *Student response—What does it mean?* Paper presented at the International Human Science Conference, John F. Kennedy University, Pleasant Hill, California.

Kalmus, V., Runnel, P., & Siibak, A. (2009). Opportunities and benefits online. In S. Livingstone & L. Haddon (Eds), *Kids online: Opportunities and risks for children* (pp. 71–82). Bristol, UK: Policy Press.

Karlsen, F. (2011). Entrapment and near miss: A comparative analysis of psycho structural elements in gambling games and massively multiplayer online role playing games. *International Journal of Mental Health and Addiction, 9*(2), 193–207. doi:10.1007/s11469-010-9275-4

Livingstone, S. (2002). *Young people and new media: Childhood and the changing media environment.* London: SAGE.

Livingstone, S., & Bovill, M. (Eds). (2001). *Children and their changing media environment: A European comparative study.* London: Lawrence Erlbaum.

Livingstone, S., & Haddon, L. (2009). *EU Kids Online: Final report.* London: LSE, EU Kids Online. Retrieved from http://eprints.lse.ac.uk/24372/

Livingstone, S., Haddon, L., Görzig, A., & Òlafsson, K. (2011). *Risks and safety on the internet: The perspective of European children: Full findings.* London: LSE, EU Kids Online. Retrieved from http://eprints.lse.ac.uk/33731/

Medietilsynet (Norwegian Media Authorities). (2010). *Barn og digitale medier 2010: Fakta om barn og unges bruk og opplevelse av digitale medier* (Children and digital media 2010: Facts about children and young people's use and experience of digital media). Fredrikstad, Norway: Medietilsynet.

Nayar, P. (2011). *Innocent young girls and new media: Case studies in India.* Unpublished manuscript, The New School For Public Engagement, Media Studies, The New School University, New York.

Nayar, U. S., & Bhide, A. (2008). Contextualizing media competencies among young people in Indian culture: Interface with globalization. In D. Kristen & S. Livingstone (Eds), *The international handbook of children, media and culture* (pp. 328–335). Thousand Oaks, CA: SAGE.

O'Neill, B., & Hagen, I. (2009). Media literacy. In S. Livingstone & L. Haddon (Eds), *Kids online: Opportunities and risks for children* (pp. 229–241). Bristol, UK: Policy Press.

Rideout, V. J., Foehr, U. G., & Roberts, D. F. (2010). *Generation M2: Media in the lives of 8-18 year-olds* (Research Report No. 8010). Menlo Park, CA: Henry J. Kaiser Family Foundation.

Rideout, V. J., Vandewater, E. A., & Wartella, E. A. (2003). *Zero to six: Electronic media in the lives of infants, toddlers and preschoolers* (Research Report No. 3378). Menlo Park, CA: Henry J. Kaiser Family Foundation.

Roberts, D., & Foehr, U. (2004). *Kids and media in America.* Cambridge, MA: University Press.

Roberts, D. F., Foehr, U. G., & Rideout, V. J. (2005). *Generation M: Media in the lives of 8-18 year-olds* (Research Report No. 7251). Menlo Park, CA: Henry J. Kaiser Family Foundation.

Seiter, E. (2005). *The Internet playground: Children's access, entertainment and mis-education.* New York: Peter Lang.

Stald, G. (2007). Mobile identity: Youth, identity and mobile communication media. In D. Buckingham (Ed.), *Youth identity and digital media* (pp. 136–157). Cambridge, MA: MIT Press.

Strasburger, V. C., Wilson, B. J., & Jordan, A. B. (2009). *Children, adolescents and the media* (2nd ed.). Thousand Oaks, CA: SAGE.

Turkle, S. (2011). *Alone together: Why we expect more from technology and less from each other.* New York: Basic Books.

Vaughanbell. (2006, April). Electronic media causing ADHD? (Weblog post). Retrieved from http://mindhacks.com/2006/04/20/electronic-media-causing-adhd/

Wold, T., Aristodemou, E., Dunkels, E., & Laouris, Y. (2009). Inappropriate content. In S. Livingstone & L. Haddon (Eds), *Kids online: Opportunities and risks for children* (pp. 135–146). Bristol, UK: Policy Press.

UNICEF. (2005). *The media and children's rights manual.* Retrieved from http://www.equityforchildren.org/the-media-and-childrens-rights-manual-387/index.html

Young, K. S. (1998). *Caught in the net: How to recognize the signs of internet addiction—and a winning strategy for recovery.* New York: John Wiley & Sons.

SECTION 4

Schools and School Climate

7

Are Schools Injurious to Health?*
The Implicit Curriculum and Its Relation to Mental Health

Matthijs Cornelissen

Introduction

Educational theories and policies tend to include noble and inspiring ideals regarding "all-round development" of the students. The practice lives, however, rarely up to the intent. More often than not, the content of the curriculum and the manner in which it is transacted are such that a negative effect on the healthy development of the students is almost inevitable. Children all over the world tend to spend a considerable part of their day in schools, and there are many good reasons why this is almost universally considered a good thing. Children themselves, especially when they are very young, tend to take their time in school seriously, and accept their successes and failures at school as the yardstick for assessing how well they manage their lives in general. Schooling is, however, not an unmixed blessing. There are many aspects of school life that can hardly be considered conducive to the healthy development of either child or teacher. This chapter attends to some of these factors and suggests the direction in which a solution might be found.

---

*The provocative title of this article originated during a discussion with Larry Dossey, in which he shared some impressive scientific evidence suggesting that the psychological practices used in standard and mainstream schooling have a larger negative impact on physical health, than smoking and heredity combined. As we talked, we happened to pass by one of New Delhi's best private schools, and we wondered how it would look if schools would be compelled to fix a large statutory warning above the entry asserting, "SCHOOLING IS INJURIOUS TO HEALTH." Somehow that image never left me.

Pathogenic Elements of the Implicit School Curriculum

It is often said that what really matters in education is what remains once you've forgotten all they have tried to teach you. In its absoluteness, this is no doubt an exaggeration, but it is hard to overestimate the influence of what is known as the implicit curriculum: what children learn from the educational context, from the way the explicit curriculum is transacted. The effect from the educational environment is bound to be strong, if only because it hardly differs from year to year, or from subject to subject: It exerts more or less the same influence during each and every class, each and every day, and each and every year a child goes to school. Given how many hours children spend in school and how much importance they and their parents attach to this attendance, schools are rather likely to play a major role in "building the character" of the students. The question is, however, whether the type of character schools build is what the individual and the society really need. To get some grip on this question, we'll look in the first part of this chapter at what Watzlawick, Bavelas, and Jackson (1967) called *the pragmatics of communication*. In other words, we'll look at what happens to children when they attend school, not from an ideal or formal perspective, but from a pragmatic and psychological one.

The difficulties with what one could call the "standard school environment" are quite well known. They have been described with great insight over forty years ago by authors like Ivan Illich (1971) and John Holt (1964). It is also true that at least in Europe and North America, most nursery and primary schools do not follow this pattern any longer. But it is still holding out in the developing countries,[1] and its effects are likely to haunt humanity for many years to come. I'll try to summarize here some of the most serious problems in as concise a form as I can. Interestingly, many of them arise out of the typical classroom layout. It is such a classic, with such widespread acceptance, that virtually every educated human being will immediately recognize Figures 7.1 and 7.2 as a traditional classroom arrangement.

As Figure 7.2 shows, the arrangement allows (almost) all students to see the teacher, who, by walking a little to the left and right, can keep an eye on every child. If education had been nothing but instruction, and learning nothing but a passive absorption of predigested knowledge, all would have been well. This, however, is not the case.

---

[1] It is interesting to speculate why, up to very recently, schools in countries like India have changed much less than similar schools in Europe and America. One reason might be that in India, the English system of education was not home-grown but imposed from the outside, with the result that teachers didn't feel that they "owned" the system: they had the duty to execute it, but not the authority to change it. It is only in the last few years, since India is recovering her economic and political self-confidence that local educators have begun to feel that they have the power to make radical changes.

Are Schools Injurious to Health? **117**

Figure 7.1 Neatly Ordered Desks with Each Child Behind a Desk and the Teacher in Front of the Classroom

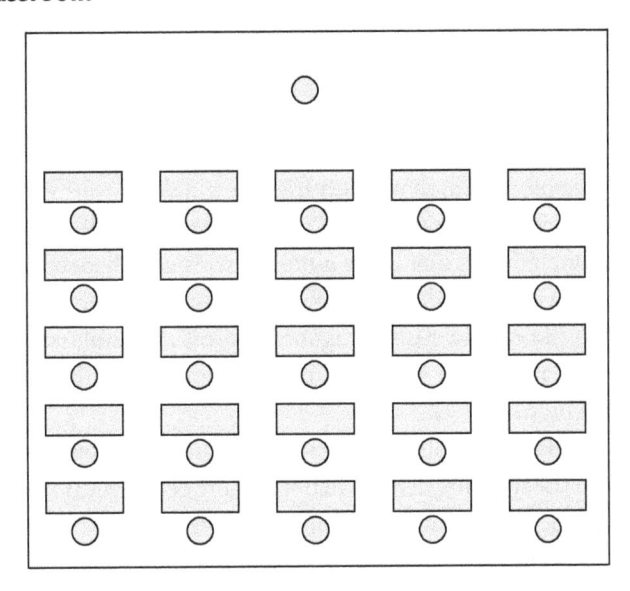

Source: Author.

Figure 7.2 All Children in the Teacher's Line of Vision

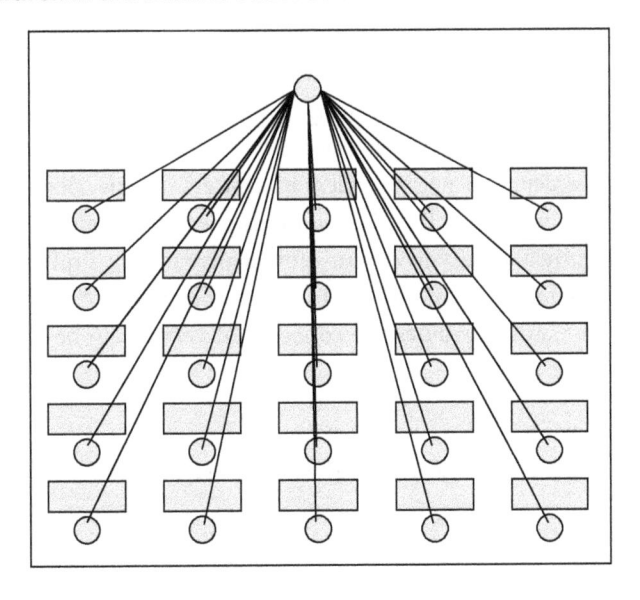

Source: Author.

Pervasive Lack of Trust and Harmony

Problems with the standard classroom layout arise mainly from the simple fact that it is not at all natural for children to spend their days sitting quietly behind little desks. The most visible victims of this arrangement are the increasing numbers of children with attention deficit disorder (ADD) who are nowadays routinely treated with drugs, while the vast majority of them would be quite fine with a bit more physical activity (and friendly hugs). The difficulties are, however, not limited to this increasing yet still relatively small group. They affect all children, and they seem to be primarily due to the antagonism that arises almost intrinsically between—on the one side, the children who are forced to do what they don't like, and on the other side, the teachers who are responsible for imposing the system. This antagonism forms the unpleasant backdrop for several educational practices that are bound to have a negative impact on the mental health of whole generations of human beings.

The next and perhaps strangest thing about the standard classroom layout is that it inhibits communication between the students. Even when in a more economical arrangement students are grouped in twos on every bench, communication between them is still looked at as a disturbance, and on many occasions, as cheating. In other words, to the extent that the students are obedient and conform to the system, they will learn to consider their peers (and to some extent even themselves) primarily as a potential source of conflict and disturbance. This is a highly peculiar, antisocial attitude towards self and others, and hardly something any well-meaning educationist would like to foster, but this is the attitude that flows naturally from the basic, physical setup. The need to communicate with others is a very deep-rooted and irrepressible part of human character. So suppressing this need for too many hours a day, leaves children in a permanent state of inner conflict and unease, a state in which they have to be always on their guard, distrusting their own and their peers' natural impulses. It is not hard to recognize traces of this unease in the adult population.

If a student does not accept this negative view of himself and his friends, he has very few options: the only simple way to stay loyal and close to his peers is to defy the teacher's authority, in one way or another. In other words, given the conflict that is built into the situation, the child can only remain socially connected by siding with the authority or by ganging up with the other kids against it. These are hardly attitudes the educational system can be happy to promote; and yet it does.

Competing for Secondary Gains: A Corruption of the Will

The traditional classroom setup has another negative effect that has far-reaching consequences. The child has little to look forward to in the standard arrangement except for whatever little warmth and appreciation he or she can elicit from the teacher. The teacher, who has a large group of children to motivate, will be inclined to present this appreciation as a scarce commodity the students have to compete for. For the sake of convenience and "objectivity," this appreciation then tends to get formalized as grades. As a result, children learn, systematically, during virtually every minute of their school-going life, to compete with their peers for the scarce and purely symbolic commodity of "top grades," or, if they know they cannot manage this, at least for grades that are considered "sufficient." In other words, they learn to do whatever the system demands in fierce competition with others, and in total disregard of more natural and more human sources of happiness and satisfaction.

Training Incompetence

A quality that is exceedingly difficult to cultivate in the traditional classroom arrangement is individual initiative. Power, control, and initiative are so completely centralized in the teacher, that even a well-meaning teacher can hardly create space for individual students to initiate their own work. Unfortunate as this is in its own right, it also has several untoward and entirely unnecessary consequences.

The most well-known difficulty is that the uniform arrangement of the benches in the classroom makes it difficult for teachers to offer different assignments to students with different interests, learning styles, and levels of capacity. Yet, if the teacher is incapable of providing worthwhile activities for different students at the same time, many of them will find it hard to find anything worthwhile to do. The less gifted children will learn to spend their time in an overwhelming and threatening environment, which they can neither understand nor control. The more gifted students will get bored, and as they can be rudely interrupted any time, they will find it safer to play silly games, than to do whatever they're really interested in doing. Being stumped or playing meaningless games to pass time can hardly be habits teachers would like children to develop, yet this is exactly what the system encourages.

Interestingly, even within the narrow range of behavior that is both constructive and compliant, the scope for developing useful mental capacities and mental skills is small. If a teacher leaves half the period for student responses, and if there are less than 30 students in the class—and in most countries these are completely unrealistic conditions—each student can still hardly expect to speak for more than one minute during a one-hour period. Yet, active engagement is crucial for effective learning, and for language learning, the need to speak is essential. If a language is taught only during one period a day, then a-minute-a-period means a-minute-a-day, and this is obviously not enough to acquire mastery. As a consequence, in a traditional classroom setup there is simply no realistic possibility for children to learn a language that is not already spoken—and spoken well—at home. The same difficulty mars effective learning of many other skills or mental capacities a school is supposed to teach. Especially when student–teacher ratios are high (in Indian government schools it is often 60:1) most of the actual learning has then to take place outside school hours with the help of parents and tutors, a development which seriously hinders the aim of socioeconomic equality which compulsory universal schooling is supposed to serve.

Training Opportunism: A Corruption of the Mind

In spite of what well-intentioned educationists and administrators may claim and hope for, and in spite of all the efforts individual teachers may make, the traditional education system, as a system, is still solidly syllabus-centered. Individuals and entire administrations may do their level best to introduce more activity-based learning and child-centered education, but in practice teachers are still duty-bound to "transact the curriculum," and they are judged on how well the students master its content. Once again, had schooling involved only a small part of a child's life, all would have been well, but going to school is for most children a full-time job. As a result, students hardly get much of a chance to develop, for example, the all-important life-skill of making free choices in areas that really matter to them. Nor do they develop the ability to evaluate and take full responsibility for what they have chosen. (The one exception is the choice between compliance and defiance, but, as we discussed earlier, that choice has no satisfactory answer.) As they are not self-motivated to do what they are supposed to do in the class, they have to be cajoled into collaboration by a carrot-and-stick system. We saw already that in a more formal setting these tend to come in the form of grades; low grades as a deterrent and high grades as encouragement. Where the teacher has a strong and dominating personality, he or she may manage to get a class to do what he or she wants even without using grades, but the principle remains the same: the children learn to do whatever is asked from them as long as it delivers the secondary rewards they have learnt to seek for.

The habit of working for secondary gains has a deeply corrupting influence in the area of motivation and will, but when this secondary gain is based on the evaluation of one's work, the corrupting influence extends to the area of perception and judgment. When evaluation is used as motivator, there arises in the child and in itself quite erroneous perception that there is an inherent conflict between what is desirable and what is true. This is, of course, not to claim that that conflict never arises naturally, but when evaluation is persistently used as the main source of motivation, it is kind of hammered into the child's mind that there is a conflict between what is true and what is pleasant and the child is almost bound to conclude that this conflict is inherent and pervasive. When evaluation is used as motivator, the corruption that takes place has its effect on both sides of the equation: on the side of the motivation that leads to the action and on the side of the evaluation that follows the action. In other words, there is then not only the subversion of a child's natural eagerness to learn, but there is also a direct attack on the child's willingness and, subsequently, the ability of impartial judgment of his own actions. To say it somewhat plainly, it is hard to be honest if there is too much self-interest at stake.

This pressure in the direction of opportunism is greatly reinforced by constant evaluation. The fact that children are continuously judged on criteria that are not of their own making conveys at least two implicit messages: (*a*) There is a clearly defined right and wrong way of thinking and doing things, which is implied by the fact that if this were not the case, the entire evaluation process would lose its meaning and validity; and (*b*) What is right and what is wrong cannot be determined by the student but is decided either by the teachers or by "the system," something rather vague and unaccountable that's even above their teachers. If education had been nothing but simple instruction of certain skills, this might have been relatively innocent. However, compulsory universal schooling has grown way beyond: a boy who is good at spelling and solving math problems is not perceived as only being good at spelling or math, but as a "good boy." Neither students, nor teachers, nor parents see evaluation as concerning only the student's performance in a limited domain; the complete personality of the student is judged. It is hard to accept that blind faith in "higher-ups" and "the system" is an acceptable outcome of a sane system of education.

There is another, more subtle problem with the imposition of a fixed syllabus. Teachers often ask questions to their students. These questions, however, are only rarely genuine questions in the sense that the teacher doesn't know the answer to his own question. Teachers are taught to ask, as much as possible, open-ended questions. Yet, even when they do so, these seemingly "open questions" are hardly ever about something that is genuinely open to a variety of different answers. Almost always, the teacher knows the "correct" answer beforehand and asks the question only to check whether the students can produce that specific answer. This can create for the students a number of difficult dilemmas, for which only a few can always find constructive answers. The nature of the dilemma depends on whether the question is about facts or opinions. The border between facts and opinions is of course fluid and to quite an extent a matter of attitude. Some people live in a world where almost everything is definite and well defined this way or that. Others live in a much more fluid world where "it all depends." For most children, the difference is clear—there are things that are straightforward, like math and geography, and other areas, like values, relationships, and feelings where it is far more difficult to be sure of what is "right" and what is "wrong."

When the question is "factual," in the sense that there actually is, or at least seems to be one clearly correct answer, the situation is still comparatively simple. John Holt has described with great perspicuity what happens in such situations. Those children who are considered bright by the teacher—and by themselves—make a genuine attempt at producing the right answer. They trust that even if they get it wrong, they will still be treated with respect on the basis of their standing reputation. John Holt observed that in fact, such students are often given a second chance. Those children, however, who are considered dumb by the teacher—and often by themselves—cannot trust at all that they will be treated so generously. They have, first of all, a greater chance of making a mistake, and they suspect, often correctly, that if they get it wrong, they will be derided in front of the whole class. Doing your best and then losing can be pretty frustrating, so they are tempted to avoid the risk. They tend to try this first by getting at the correct answer by stealth, and if this doesn't work, they may give, on purpose, a wrong answer. The incorrect answer does of course guarantee defeat, but the shame of the defeat is compensated for by the satisfaction of having been in charge of the entire chain of events leading to it. Though the teacher has the apparent victory, the student knows that behind the scene, it is the student who has pulled the strings. Making such negative choices is obviously disastrous for the intellectual growth of the child, but anecdotal evidence suggests that it is fairly common. Once this habit has established itself in a child, it is not hard to imagine how easily this habit can invade other areas of life and how disastrous the results can be.

When the answers do not have one factual answer, the situation gets more complex. The question that then arises is what the child should do when the answer that comes up in her own mind differs from the one the teacher expects. If the child is very clever, she can keep the two separate by giving the teacher what he expects and yet remembering and treasuring her own answer. This is however rare, and the few children who manage it tend to come from homes where they get full support from their parents to keep up their own individuality. For most children this is not the case, and so they are faced with an existential dilemma. If they stick to their own answer, they are in trouble because most teachers consider it their duty to teach, and they don't appreciate "recalcitrant," "stubborn," "uncooperative," or simply "unintelligent" students. For most students, compliance is thus far more likely to lead to attractive results, and so the vast majority of them gives in, and tries to answer what the teacher wants to hear. Now this is once more far more nefarious than it may look at first sight, for what happens is somewhat similar to what happens when evaluation is used as motivator: the child learns to suppress what is true, for the sake of what is convenient. To look at it from a slightly different angle, the child is trained to be other-directed (if not plain opportunistic) and in the process gradually loses the ability to distinguish for himself what is true and false.

To summarize the argument so far, the traditional classroom arrangement virtually prohibits learning how to build constructive relationships, how to respect differences between people, how to feel at ease with oneself and others, how to recognize one's own and others' strengths, how to pool these for a good common cause, how to make one's own value judgments, and work constructively together towards some meaningful end. One could well argue that this is a caricature, and that good teachers can manage to create an atmosphere of cooperation and common purpose even in a traditional classroom. This is no doubt true, but to the extent that this succeeds, it is an individual achievement, which is brought about in spite of the system. The factors mentioned above still play their antisocial and pathogenic role as undercurrents inherent in the system.

What Are the Alternatives?

Fortunately, there are effective and viable alternatives to the type of authoritarian schooling described above. For an outdated but still interesting exposition, one could consult, for example, *Freedom to Learn for the 80's* (Rogers, 1983), which contains an insightful discussion of the reasons some experiments succeeded while others failed. My own experience with the development of a radically different approach to education based on the work of Sri Aurobindo has convinced me that it is well possible to design and implement a system of education in which all participants—students, teachers, and management—learn and grow as human beings while staying true to themselves. For some excellent third person assessments of the same project, see Raina and Sibia (1999) and Sibia (2011), and for a detailed description Huppes (2002). Moreover, comparing our own work with that of others, it looks to me that the basic, underlying principle of such alternatives is so utterly simple, that it is almost embarrassing to mention it: the one thing needed to improve education is *respect from the teachers for the students*. The only additional condition is that this respect must be genuine, soul-based and applied systematically and rigorously to all aspects of the educational enterprise.

Over the years we have asked hundreds of psychologists, teachers, educationists, and parents about their strongest memories from their own school-going years. Interestingly, both their best and their most painful experiences had almost always to do with the presence or absence of respect from the side of their teachers. In other words, the single attitude, or one should perhaps say, the single quality that can make up for the defects of "standard," class-wise schooling seems to be a genuine, soul-based respect for the students. In an ideal world, the whole system of education should be built on such respect, but in practice it hardly is. Even if the system as a whole is not, individuals can sometimes still keep up the right spirit, but it is not made easy for them. For one single teacher, for example, it is exceedingly difficult to do good work within a school system that does not support it. From our experience it appears that the minimum grouping in which genuine educational reform can take place consists of one or more good teachers, a willing principal, and a supportive management, but much depends, of course, on how much freedom the local laws and culture allow.

For a solution on a larger scale we are confronted with a peculiar problem that has to do with the initial qualifiers: the respect must be "genuine and soul-based," but what is that? As an innocent, naive human individual, I "kind of know" what "genuine" and "soul-based" mean, but is there place for such ethereal concepts in science, and thus in public life? To answer this question we have to have a look at the very foundations of science and the role science has played, and still plays, in education.

Education and the Scientific Method

A highly respected professor in Educational Innovation once told me in total earnest that whatever can be researched is useless for educational practice, and that whatever really matters in education is beyond the scope of research. As he was clearly committed to the field of education, I asked him what made him stick to his job at the university. His response was that because of the research he did at the University, people believed what he said in public lectures and government committees, but that *what* he said there was not at all based on the kind of research he did. I thought this was rather shocking, and one could probably argue that his low opinion of research in education is exaggerated, but many in the field will recognize the basic problem. There can be little doubt that science has become the official knowledge system of our global civilization, and that within science it is psychology that is responsible for the study of human nature. Psychology is thus the fundamental science on which our educational methods should be based. If psychological research is considered irrelevant by key players in the field, the question arises why this is so and what we can do about it.

I have no scientific proof for any of the negative effects of schooling on mental health that I have discussed in this chapter. This is, however, not for want of trying: the problem is that scientific proof in fields like mental health and education is extremely difficult to achieve. Issues of epistemology and methodology are complex and in the social sciences the subject of much debate, but it may still be interesting to attempt a very short overview of the main difficulties and possibilities, as these may give us a hint on how education might be taken forward more effectively. The behaviorist approach which is still responsible for the bulk of psychological research, is by choice and definition limited to external behavior. In its early forms, it had thus very little to say about most of the invisible things that are important in education and that make human life worth living, things like consciousness, feelings, values, and even meaning itself. Strangely, this did not prevent it from being used in education. Many of our modern learning theories have their origin in animal experiments in which rats, mice, and pigeons are taught to produce arbitrary behavior by presenting them with the right regime of rewards and punishments.[2] In such experiments the "negative reinforcement" typically consists of electrical shocks given to the animal's feet or tail; the "positive reinforcement" consists of food-pellets, and "motivation to learn" is regulated by depriving the animal subjects of the positive stimulus beforehand so that it can be quantified as the difference between their "free feeding weight" and their actual weight. There are many reasons to object to such studies, but the most serious problem with them is that they were generalized mindlessly to learning in children. The result was a strong endorsement of educational practices which replace the natural learning of children, which consists of happy, playful attempts at making sense of their existence in the world, by learning of for the child arbitrary, meaningless facts under pressure of a reinforcement regime that consists of deprivation, punishment, and *secondary* rewards. In other words, children are taught systematically, throughout their formative years, to do meaningless things in order to obtain "incentives" in an overall climate of deprivation. This is not a minor, innocent error. Though hard to prove or quantify, it seems likely that this has

---

[2]There are far too many of such researches to mention them individually, but typical examples might be Leslie (1977) and more recently, Baum (2010). The latter starts with a stunningly flippant generalization from the actual experiment on pigeons to human decision taking.

contributed considerably to the pattern of increasing alienation and obsessive production and consumption that is the hallmark of our global civilization. Later schools of behaviorism learned to deal with more subtle, not directly material things and as such they are an improvement. The problem is that they manage this through surveys that are based on lay introspection, a source that is notoriously unreliable. Their large-scale surveys, however sophisticated they may be, can thus only contribute to an epidemiology of "representative" but superficial and unreliable lay self-perceptions. A more radical step forward was taken by social constructionism. Its qualitative methodologies allow the researcher to be choosy in the selection of his subjects and, as a direct consequence, its findings tend to be more refined and humanly meaningful than those of behaviorism, but they are still limited to what sensitive, ordinary people have always known about human nature. For education, the biggest advantage of the constructionist paradigm has been that it allowed Piaget's ideas to become mainstream. This is a positive change because Piaget asserts that learning in humans does not consist only of simple training and a passive imbibing of ready-made answers, but also of actively reconstructing one's own mental universe. A large-scale adoption of Piaget's theory of learning can be expected to rectify many of the problems mentioned in this chapter, as it forces teachers to respect the individuality of their different students. But constructionism as such does not go deep enough. The reason for this is that constructions need a foundation and constructionism does not provide for this necessity. Without a foundation, constructions collapse, and when constructionism is applied to itself, it leads to the conclusion that "anything goes" (Feyerabend, 1975, as quoted in Skinner, 1985). The hard sciences don't have this problem; their dual foundation of physical experiments and mathematics suffices for almost all practical purposes. Both have something inevitable about them and it is very rare that major controversies remain unresolved in the hard sciences in the way they do in the social sciences.[3] It appears to me that the main reason that mainstream psychology has not found a solid methodological and ontological foundation for itself is the fact that it has not found a methodologically sound way to study the natural core of its subject-area: consciousness. Though consciousness has become again, after a long gap, a respectable subject in academic discourse, the mainstream position is still that it is an "epiphenomenon." In other words, consciousness is considered a causally ineffective side effect that—unexplainably—emerges from the complexity of the physical activities in the brain. This is completely incommensurate with the role consciousness plays in our human existence. Psychologically, we *are* our consciousness: without it we would not exist, or at least we would not know that we exist. Without consciousness, nothing, absolutely nothing would matter. And science would not exist at all.

---

[3]One might think that Quantum Mechanics is an exception, but this is not so. There is no dispute about the *science* of QM; the dispute is exclusively about its interpretation, which is part of the philosophy of science, a subject which, in the words of Willis W. Harman, "is of as much interest to scientists as ornithology to birds" (Lorimer, 2001, p. 11).

The one major civilization that has given consciousness the central position it deserves, right from the beginning of recorded history, is the Indian civilization. Transpersonal psychology has recognized this and with help from the various Indian traditions it has expanded the scope of psychology considerably, but it somehow misses the depth and solidity of its original sources. One of the reasons for this defect is that it has too often utilized the *findings* of Indian yoga and Buddhist meditation, but not the underlying culture and the rigor of its psychological inquiry. In the next and last section, we'll have a quick look at what the Indian tradition can contribute in these areas.

The Contribution from Indian Psychology

As a collective enterprise, science has not yet made full use of everything humanity has to offer. The global civilization is as yet global only in its reach, but not in its origin. Science, as the main knowledge system on which our civilization is built, makes extensive use of the Euro-American cultural tradition, but it has, till now, almost completely ignored what other cultures have to offer in terms of *knowledge generation*. "Mindfulness" practices, *hathayoga*, and meditation, for example, are increasingly used for stress relief and therapy, but the underlying knowledge system is ignored. We have not bothered to find out how the Indian tradition arrived at the detailed knowledge that gave rise to these clearly effective techniques. This is remarkable because these techniques are based on something that our global civilization desperately needs and yet clearly lacks: a rigorous and effective methodology to study consciousness. The Indian civilization has specialized in this area for thousands of years and it has developed in this domain a detailed mastery which is in many ways comparable to our modern mastery in the domain of electricity and electromagnetism. Yoga is, in its culture of origin, not only a fitness program that delivers physical beauty and mental relaxation. Neither is it only a soteriological endeavor aimed at individual liberation. Yoga, and especially *jnanayoga*, is also a method to arrive at valid knowledge, knowledge about ourselves and knowledge about how we are related to the universe and to that which is beyond the universe. As the basic principles of yoga are rooted in experience and have been systematized with admirable mental rigor and coherence, yoga deserves to be looked at as a science—and because it is effective also as a technology—of consciousness. Though this is not the place to give an exposition of the various Indian knowledge systems, there are two aspects of their possible use in psychology and education I would like to highlight.

When American psychologists came to the conclusion that introspection did not produce reliable knowledge, they did not discover anything new: the Indian tradition had known this since time immemorial. The difference is that while American psychology simply gave up on it and shifted its attention to the study of outer behavior, the Indian tradition put a tremendous collective effort into figuring out the cause of the unreliability. Its conclusion was that the root cause for the low quality of ordinary psychological knowledge is that our consciousness is too much entangled in the workings of our mind. As a result we are obsessed with the defense of our existence as one small creature in a large and dangerous world, we have vested interests, and so we cannot judge freely. Mainstream science has accepted this idea in the study of physical nature as the need for objectivity, for "a view from nowhere," to use the charming phrase coined by Nagel (1986). Science has not pursued this same principle with sufficient persistence for subjective, inner enquiry, probably because the methods for doing so were never developed with sufficient rigor within the Euro–American tradition. For the physical sciences it is sufficient to draw back from one's first impressions and habitual thoughts, and adopt a more disciplined style of thinking. For psychology one has to draw back further, one has to stand back completely from one's own thinking, feeling, and sensing, and watch all these inner movements from an entirely pure and uninvolved consciousness. The ancient Indian *rishi*s (seers) found—and anyone with sufficient mental discipline can confirm this—that humans can actually do this. We can withdraw our consciousness from its preoccupation with self-assertion and self-defense, and we can withdraw it from its normal involvement in thoughts, feelings, and even sensations. They also found, perhaps surprisingly, that our consciousness does not diminish in the process—it actually increases in clarity and intensity. In other words, they found that it is possible, though not necessarily easy, to fix one's consciousness in a position from where it can observe the workings of one's mind with complete impartiality. If one does so, it becomes possible to achieve levels of precision and detail that go far beyond those that can be reached in more ordinary states of consciousness. It may be noted in this context that science does not only progresses through experiments. It also progresses by refining its instruments, and in psychology the main instrument is human nature. Indian approaches to psychology offer thus the possibility of using yoga as a method to perfect our own inner nature as a kind of psychological observatory, as an inner "instrument of knowledge" (*antahkarana*) (Cornelissen, 2006, 2007, 2011). It is this that could give constructionism a solid foundation in terms of method.

The second point is related to the first, and it is that once we acknowledge and begin to use the possibilities of yoga as knowledge system, we'll discover that our human nature is far more complex—and far more beautiful—than mainstream psychology has been able to fathom with its present set of methods. The ability to change, relocate, and explore one's own consciousness at will, opens the possibility of exploring one's inner nature in a manner that is entirely beyond the scope of naive introspection and spontaneous experience. It makes it possible to study with perfect mental rectitude and full academic rigor, domains of human experience that mainstream science has been forced to relegate to the domain of institutionalized religion and personal belief. The secrets of our inner drives and motives, the origin and operations of intuition and other forms of direct knowledge, the original source of our sense of identity—all these can actually be studied in a systematic, rigorous manner. Issues like the soul, which till now were shunned by science as utterly beyond its ambit, can finally be "naturalized." The impact that such a development could have, not only on our individual lives but also on the society as a whole can hardly be fathomed. As for education, it could finally become what it should have been all along—the development of our nature as a trustworthy and effective instrument for the soul to express itself in the world.[4] It would not only increase our understanding of what life in this exceedingly complex and mysterious universe is actually about, but it would also increase the overall level of harmony in our global society, for the deeper one studies one's own consciousness, the more it becomes clear that we are ultimately all one. For in the end, there is only one consciousness, in which we all, each in his or her own different and limited ways, participate.

Conclusion

I hope to have shown in a perhaps unscientific but nevertheless convincing manner that there are quite a number of entirely unnecessary, yet still amazingly common practices in mainstream education that deserve to be described as deleterious to mental health, both at the individual and the collective level. Though cause and effect are difficult to assess in the social domain, there seems to be a direct link between those practices and some of the most serious ills that beset our global civilization. Eugene Taylor (1999, pp. 289–296) argues in *Shadow Culture*, his insightful book on the relation between spirituality and science in American history, that we can expect to see a growing influence of Indian ideas on the developing global civilization and especially a major shift in its basic epistemological assumptions, away from materialism and in the direction of Indian spirituality. If Taylor is right, and science does indeed move in this direction, then it may finally be able to help us develop the genuine, soul-based respect that our children need.

References

Baum, W. M. (2010). Dynamics of choice: A tutorial. *Journal of the Experimental Analysis of Behavior, 94*(2), 161–174. doi:10.1901/jeab.2010.94-161

Cornelissen, R. M. M. (2006). *Research about yoga and research in yoga: Towards rigorous research in the subjective domain.* Retrieved from http://ipi.org.in/texts/matthijs/mc-researchinyoga.php

———. (2007). In defence of rigorous subjectivity. *Transpersonal Psychology Review, 11*(1), 8–18.

———. (2011). What is knowledge? Reflections based on the work of Sri Aurobindo. In R. M. M. Cornelissen, G. Misra, & S. Varma (Eds), *Foundations of Indian psychology: Concepts and theories* (Vol. 1, pp. 332–360). New Delhi: Longman.

Holt, J. (1964). *How children fail.* New York: Pitman Publishing Company.

---

[4]For a detailed practical workbook showing how this can be done, see Huppes (2002); for a critical appraisal, Sibia (2011).

Huppes, N. (2002). *Psychic education: A workbook*. New Delhi: SAES. Retrieved from http://ipi.org.in/texts/neeltje/psychedu-all-10a.pdf
Illich, I. (1971). *Deschooling society*. New York: Harper & Row.
Leslie, J. C. (1977). Effects of food deprivation and reinforcement magnitude on conditioned suppression. *Journal of the Experimental Analysis of Behavior, 28*(2), 107–115. doi: 10.1901/jeab.1977.28-107
Lorimer, D. (2001). *Thinking beyond the brain*. Edinburgh: Floris Books.
Nagel, T. (1986). *The view from nowhere*. New York: Oxford University Press.
Raina, M. K., & Sibia, A. (1999). *Schooling in Mirambika: A case study*. New Delhi: NCERT.
Rogers, C. (1983). *Freedom to learn for the 80's*. Columbus, OH: Merrill Publishing Company.
Sibia, A. (2011). Education for life: The Mirambika experience. In R. M. M. Cornelissen, G. Misra, & S. Varma (Eds), *Foundations of Indian psychology: Practical applications* (Vol. 2, pp. 156–179*)*. New Delhi: Longman.
Skinner, Q. (1985). Introduction: The return of grand theory. In Q. Skinner (Ed.), *The return of grand theory in the human sciences* (pp. 1–20). Cambridge: Cambridge University Press.
Taylor, E. (1999). *Shadow culture: Psychology and spirituality in America*. Boston: Counterpoint.
Watzlawick, P., Bavelas, J., & Jackson, D. (1967). *Pragmatics of human communication: A study of interactional patterns, pathologies, and paradoxes*. New York: W. W. Norton & Company.

8

Mental Health of Urban School-going Children in India

Neharika Vohra
Esha Patnaik

These are times of extreme highs and lows. With the Indian economy growing at 8.6% according to the advance estimate of Central Statistics Office (CSO) and abundant opportunities opening up, this seems to be the perfect time for young people to grow up and claim their space in the world. Such times expect the youth to be risk taking, motivated, and forward-looking. To make the country a world leader, we need youth who are secure, happy, and confident. India has the largest youth population in the world (Goswami, Baruah, & Shukla, 2010). The draft report of the working group on youth affairs and adolescents' development for the 11th five-year plan (2007–2012) estimates the country's adolescent population at 225 million (Government of India, 2007). This group is in the enviable position of being potentially in demand across the globe for their skills and training. The world is looking at India as the supplier of trained manpower for its needs (Bhandari & Malik, 2008).

In the face of such an exciting scenario, while some of our young people are rising to the challenge and making the best use of available opportunities, many others are succumbing to the stresses and pressures of everyday living and are giving up too soon. Psychological maturity is a composite of bio-cognitive-social factors. When children are raised in an environment that promotes active exploration and learning, when the social setup around them is warm, understanding, and supportive, and when their physical and emotional needs are addressed, they become well-adjusted, constructively contributing members of society. While this is how we would like our children to be, the concern expressed by mental health professionals, parents, teachers, and young people themselves points to a different reality. The concerns indicate a generation that is becoming increasingly psychologically vulnerable. Mental health is being defined more by its absence than as a proactive process of development. Interactions with psychiatrists, clinical psychologists, and psychotherapists point towards factors ranging from parent–child relationship patterns to school systems and media as influencing healthy mental development during the formative years. Other correlational factors such as physical development and peer group interaction also have a role to play in the mental health of school-going children.

Malhotra, Kohli, Kapoor, and Pradhan (2009) cite WHO reports (2000, 2001) according to which 20% of children and adolescents suffer from a disabling mental illness worldwide, and suicide is the third leading cause of death among adolescents. The issue of childhood psychiatric morbidity is more serious in middle- and low-income countries which have a much larger proportion of child and adolescent population, much lower levels of health indices, and poorer infrastructure and resources to deal with these problems. Based on a 2001 World Health Organization report, Shastri (2008) put around 66 million children in the country as suffering from mental and behavioral disorders.

It has been found that the most commonly reported childhood psychiatric disorder in India is anxiety disorder (5%) followed by mood disorder (3%), hyperactivity (1–2%), and autism and schizophrenia (1%) (Srinath et al., 2005). At the National Institute of Mental Health and Neurosciences (NIMHANS) 9–10% of the children brought in are diagnosed with depression. A survey carried out by Maharashtra's Parent Teachers Association United Forum across Mumbai schools found that 26 out of 100 children aged between 8 and 10 years showed signs of depression (Kumar, 2001; Kapur, 2005). As natural and human calamities increase in frequency, children are also developing posttraumatic psychological problems.

Familial Relationship Patterns

Many of the parents and grandparents of school-going children today come from lower to middle class socioeconomic backgrounds. Their academic achievements were what helped them to rise above their conditions, earn a comfortable living, and obtain a secure future for their children. These parents now believe that their children would also succeed only if they excelled in academics, did not take undue risks, and acquired professional qualifications. Hence, the consequent emphasis on getting good marks in school and the accompanying expectations and pressures by parents on their children.

Let us take a quick look at the changes in the socioeconomic environment since the time India achieved independence. Those who studied science and engineering were imminently employable in the post-independence period of industrial growth. People progressed, based on their academic qualifications. Many jobs and opportunities were created by the opening of new industries and associated support services, establishment of a state administrative machinery, and new educational and health infrastructure. Even those who did not have professional degrees but were educated were gainfully employed in state-run organizations. Many had lost their land and possessions during Partition and in the attempts of the State to democratize by ridding itself of the landed gentry. The only practical solution that was available to them to do well was to obtain a formal education and become part of the growing salaried class of India. In a country where self-governance was being rediscovered along modern lines, better jobs were perceived as those that got people better salaries and higher position and status. As they achieved professional and financial security, they dreamed of their children finding better jobs and improving their lives.

Another factor that contributed to these parents' exclusive focus on the achievement of their children was their migration from the traditional joint family setup in their native places to the urban nuclear family environment in their search for better jobs and opportunities. These migrants worked hard, had a high achievement orientation, and became successful. This was a generation that formed a conscientious workforce. It had learned that the best way to exist was to work hard and focus on the education of their children such that it not only makes them self-reliant but also leads to their being wealthy and prosperous. However, where they lost out was in the emotional support that a traditional joint family system provides. A nuclear family environment brought in a sense of isolation and disconnect with relationships.

Over the next three decades certain economic and political policies began to adversely affect the education system, job opportunities, and developmental plans. Until 1990, there were just 208 colleges for engineering, medicine, and general education (Kapur & Mehta, 2004). The number of jobs in the public sector was limited and the private sector was either very small or nonexistent. Competition was intense for seats in professional colleges, job opportunities in good organizations became limited and lengthy bureaucratic procedures became the norm. This aggravated the perversities in the system and corruption became rampant. A daunting combination of power, interminable administrative procedures, and impractical laws made even basic facilities inaccessible to the ordinary citizen. Under such conditions, the salaried class, with no influential connections or resources to pursue administrative processes, realized that the only way for their children to grow and prosper was if they worked very hard, chose non-risky options, and competed aggressively for scarce resources in the form of limited college seats and job opportunities.

Post-liberalization in 1991, the markets opened up, the private sector was strengthened, development of information technology created thousands of jobs, and young professionals were able to earn many times more than their parents. This young generation of workers and parents came from families that had stressed on education and had programmed them to think that success in education and staying ahead of the competition was the only way to be, that taking risks was not wise. They encouraged their children to continue to work like they had, make similar decisions, and put immense pressure on their children to achieve and succeed.

Now we have dual income nuclear families which are financially secure, but continue to feel the threat of insecurity enough to push their children to constantly succeed in whatever they do. Sometimes the child's academic performance is taken as a measure of the parents' skills in child rearing.

Indian School Systems

The Indian education, research, and training systems have been unable to match step with global changes and advancements. The education system is characterized by limitations in capacity and scarcity of resources and teachers. A high student–teacher ratio in many urban schools puts undue pressure on the teacher and deprives students of personal attention and mentoring. School curricula often emphasize academic performance and competition, sometimes at the cost of learning and personal growth. In higher education there is fierce competition for limited seats. A college under Delhi University made news recently for having a 100% cutoff for admission into the commerce stream. The tough entry criterion and heavy competition encourage a skewed view of achievement and put immense pressure on students from an early age.

Box 8.1   Desperate Steps

> India has one of the highest suicide rates in the world. At least 40% of these cases seem to be adolescents. Basu (2010) reported an alarming figure of 26 juvenile suicides in four weeks in Mumbai during the month of January 2010 itself. Pressure to do well in school is the main cause, according to a *Times of India* report (*The Times of India*, 2010).
>
> In 2008, 516 children (up to 14 years) committed suicide across West Bengal. In 2007, 419 children killed themselves; in 2006, the number was 334 (De, 2010). West Bengal accounts for the highest percentage of suicides overall and among children aged up to 14 years in the country.
>
> Failure in examinations and family problems were among the leading reasons for suicide, in children less than 14 years, according to the most recent report of the National Crime Records Bureau (2009).
>
> Family problems; academic, family, or peer pressure; poor academic performance; failed romantic relationships; victimization through ragging, domestic, or sexual abuse; and substance dependency have been some of the identified causes for youth (15–29 years) suicides. Many of these causes are more prevalent in urban areas due their lifestyle connotations.

Trends in Education

Three generations of emphasis on competition created some very disturbing trends. For one, tuition classes started gaining prominence. Students who struggled to learn in a large classroom were offered private tuition, sometimes by the same teacher who taught them in school as well. What might have been started as a helpful measure to aid children who required additional mentoring, soon became a means merely for clearing exams. The focus shifted from learning to written notes offered by the tutor that were designed to aid in putting in a superior performance in year-end exams.

Let us take the example of preparation for admission to the Indian Institutes of Technology (IITs). Earlier, children worked hard for their grade 12 exams. Based on their performance they went to an engineering college in the discipline of their choice. With the increase in student population, limited seats, and high admission criteria, entrance tests were designed to choose eligible candidates. Preparation for entrance tests, along with the regular school curriculum, gradually became the focus of students in high school. To meet the needs of this group of students who wanted to prepare for entrance exams, entrepreneurs started offering coaching material by postal correspondence. *Brilliant* and *Aggarwal* (tutorial centers) were household names in the late 1970s and all through the 1980s.

As time progressed and competition became stiffer the concept of part-time coaching institutes emerged. After school, students attended coaching classes to prepare for engineering entrance exams. It was a matter of time before cities like Kota emerged as hubs for full-time coaching. Students registered in grade 11 did not attend classes and focused exclusively on their preparation for entrance exams. Schools and coaching institutes were more than willing to encourage students in this endeavor. The incentives for ensuring success in competitive exams were so high that unhealthy practices in teaching and getting around the requirement of having a certain level of attendance in school became commonplace. Coaching institutes even started conducting entrance exams in class 10 for selecting who they would coach. They wanted to accept only the best students so as to improve the chances of their students topping the entrance exams, and thus enhance the institute's reputation. Parents were willing to pay high sums of money for such guarantees. Famous for its high priority to technical education, Hyderabad is also known for its excessive emphasis on preparation for the IITs, with coaching beginning as early as from grade five (informal communication from parents and school principals in Hyderabad)!

The issue does not stop with just coaching classes. In recent times, private institutes have mushroomed, which offer to children everything from personality development, leadership skills training, and finishing school facilities to design education and enhancement of natural cognitive abilities. Parents with children as young as preschoolers are willingly lining up for such offerings in the hope of giving their child that extra edge in a highly competitive world.

Many schools follow a rote learning-based curriculum that does not encourage creativity and engagement with the subject. Trained and competent teachers are few in number, as compared to the requirement. Consequently, students miss educators who would inspire them to learn. With a large class size, teachers sometimes find it difficult to remember the names of all students, let alone provide individual attention and academic support. Competition is high, with the top students being projected as role models for their less academically inclined peers. This increases pressure and competition and reduces healthy peer group interaction. When children are unable to match up expected academic standards, the result could be low self-esteem, diffidence, social withdrawal, psychiatric disorders such as anxiety and mood disorders, and at times the extreme step of suicide.

School counselors are not always trained in early detection of psychiatric morbidity and may, for example, label a child with attention deficit hyperactivity disorder (ADHD) as "naughty" or a child who lags behind classmates as a "slow learner." Addressing diversity in the classroom in terms of differential learning abilities, cultural backgrounds, and introduction of innovative pedagogy are some of the issues schools grapple with, while developing a constructive learning environment for children.

A Lost Childhood

Often children are caught in a never-ending cycle of long hours of studying, rushing from one tuition class to the next, helicopter parents who keep a constant check on their child's every activity, denial of social interactions, withdrawal from meaningful relationships, and no time for engagement in leisure activities. Any activity that does not contribute towards tangible performance-oriented goals is considered a waste of time. Spontaneity, ability to explore and question, exploration of social relationships, development of hobbies, and cooperative and shared learning are lost in the process. When such children grow up, they have understandably, a one-dimensional perspective and a limited worldview. When they become parents they have a limited sphere of knowledge, are very focused on their work, have low risk taking abilities, poor relationship skills, and very little emotional connect with even family members.

Many parents who were not able to fulfill their aspirations see a second chance in their children, on whom they impose their choices and failed dreams. They are prescriptive of what and how their children should study and get upset if the child deviates from their well-planned scheme. Statistics from various sources indicate that 70 percent of urban parents force their children to take up professions or academic programs of their (parents') choice, as compared to only 15 percent in semi-urban and rural areas (Nallari, 2010). Children do not have the freedom to choose their own areas of interest. When children who are made to study subjects different from their interest and aptitude perform poorly, the education system's normative assessment criteria makes them feel incapable and lesser than their more academically successful peers.

Children growing up in such environments often also develop linear worldviews. As they grow up they are expected by the school and peers to develop cooperative, reciprocal, and emotionally sound relationships with people around them, while also performing well academically. Many children who have not experienced this in their home life have difficulty in adjusting. Articulation of feelings is an alien concept for them, not having witnessed it even at home. They internalize all these feelings, not knowing how to address them. These are the children in school who are most likely to feel lonely and depressed when they cannot seem to match up to the expectations of their adult role models, their parents, and teachers. Some children who might experience a disconnect are those who did not make it to the elite club in terms of having a private school education, affluent parents, and superior cognitive abilities. To rationalize their situation they are often dismissive of others' achievement and justify their own choices by showing deviant or antisocial behavior.

The rural–urban migration pattern has also contributed toward children experiencing psychological vulnerability. Couples move from a predominantly agrarian community to an urban setting in the hope of better employment and lifestyle. First generation city dwellers, the children of such couples often struggle in establishing their independent identity and status. They see no reason to hold onto their rural background, but continue to feel alienated in an urban context.

Economic independence, education and awareness, and career aspirations of both sexes have now made it possible for couples in unhappy relationships to terminate them and live apart. However, societal norms are slower to change than individuals. Divorce is still considered an extreme measure that goes against cultural sensitivities which advocate the permanence of relationships, irrespective of the costs involved. The children of such couples find themselves coping with not only separation and rejection, but also being labeled as deviant or non-normal by their peers.

Thus, a classroom in an urban middle to upper class school is a medley of children of parents who believe that the only way for their children to have a happy life is by performing well academically and staying one step ahead of others; of parents who wish to fulfill their quashed dreams through their children; of parents who are so caught up in their work that they do not have a life beyond it; of parents who are so engaged in their own lives that they have no time for their children; of parents who are first generation city dwellers; of parents who are divorced; of fairly rich but medium educated parents from business backgrounds. These children, coming from typically nuclear families with one or no sibling, bring with them a substantial baggage of expectations, loneliness, competition, and a need to access scarce resources. The dice is loaded against these children to experience a healthy, carefree, and natural life.

Developmental Tasks as a Correlate of Mental Health

Nutritional deficiency is a major concern across age groups. Young children are particularly susceptible to the detrimental effects of persistent malnutrition and under nourishment. Reflective of the extremes that exist in socioeconomic status among the Indian population, children's eating disorders range from obesity to malnourishment (Sengupta, 2006). In the lower socioeconomic segments, economic considerations deprive children of a proper diet. Malnourishment is a significant cause in physical weakness and underdevelopment in cognitive abilities. Among the upper socioeconomic classes, eating habits are more of a lifestyle concern. Influenced by media perceptions of physical attractiveness, young people adopt unhealthy dietary habits, leading to problems ranging from general weakness to disorders such as anorexia nervosa, bulimia, and obesity.

Statistics indicate that children are reaching puberty faster than in earlier times (Chawla, 2010). Several factors such as changes in lifestyle and nutrition have been considered relevant in this context. Irregular sleep and continuous exposure to artificial light beyond natural daylight hours have also been contributing factors (Parihar, Srivastava, & Shah, 2010). While physically the child may mature, cognitive development may occur at a slower pace. Society expects a young person who looks older to behave in a corresponding manner, putting stress on a young and sensitive mind.

While children are increasingly exposed to adult content in various media, a Parliamentary Committee on Petitions in 2009 (*The Times of India*, 2009) recommended withdrawal of sex education in schools, arguing that "our country's social and cultural ethos are such that sex education has absolutely no place in it." The committee suggested as an alternative the inclusion of appropriate chapters in the biology syllabus after class 10. Denied reliable information on the subject by schools and parents concerned about preserving culture, children grow up in ignorance about basic facts of life. Some children seek out information about sex and sexuality from questionable sources such as online resources, pornographic literature, or peers who may be equally misinformed. This, in turn, impacts their notions about gender, sexuality, and sexual behavior.

Media Effects on Mental Health

There has been a media explosion in the last one decade. Advertising, satellite television, cinema, the computer, and the Internet are becoming all pervasive in Indian urban societies. Their impact on impressionable minds has been more a matter of concern than approval. Television and the Internet have made the world a smaller place. Children can sit in the comfort of their homes and access information from around the world, which broadens their knowledge base. Simultaneously, they also pick up information which they may be, as yet, unable to filter for its authenticity or ethicality. Unsupervised access to social networking sites is bringing young children in contact with people from across the world, whose background and intentions are difficult to verify. Cyber-bullying, online stalking and pedophilia, downloading of pornographic material, and adoption of fictitious persona online are some of the concerns being expressed by parents, teachers, and mental health professionals working with children.

During the 1980s and 1990s television serials such as *Kachchi Dhoop* and *School Days* offered a voice to the experiences of children coming from middle-class homes. *Boy Meets World* was a novelty because of its western context while still finding resonance with the Indian child's dilemmas of growing up. With changes in lifestyle, reality television has now gained prominence. Instant success through numerous "talent hunts" makes even children as young as 4–5 years aspire to be a celebrity. Their young mind is drawn to the instant success that such programs appear to offer, and is unable to grasp the transience of such fame. When they fail to live that dream, the result is emotional distress and loss of hope.

Lack of open space for play, parents being too busy to take their children out, and not having friends of the same age group in the neighborhood makes many urban children spend most of their free time at the computer. Excessive Internet usage has been linked to reduced social involvement and lower psychological well-being (Subrahmanyam, Kraut, Greenfield, & Gross, 2001).

According to Chaudhry (2007) there has been a "democratization of fame." Social networking sites make it easy for children to project an image very unlike their real self. Everyone can be famous online. This leads to a distorted sense of self and reality and makes it difficult for the child to adjust to the real world. Net addiction, social withdrawal, and development of psychopathic symptoms are some of the possible fallouts of such unregulated use of online resources.

Proactive Measures—the Need of the Hour

> Psychologists and mental health experts are unanimous in their view regarding the influence of the environment on the mental health of children. Dr Prashant Bhimani, one such psychiatrist, spoke of the mental health issues faced by children today in an interview. The core issues revolved around value conflicts in the family, stress from unhappy parent–child relationships, and academic pressure. Parental pressure and expectations, the school environment, exposure to unfiltered material in different media were some of the influencers that precipitated mental health problems. According to Dr Bhimani, sensitizing parents goes a long way toward raising well adjusted children. Schools need a well-designed counseling program to help students cope with difficult life situations. Awareness about psychological health, access to professional help, and sensitivity also contribute towards ensuring the mental health of children.

Suggestions for Development and Maintenance of Mental Health

The situation for urban children in India suffering from mental health problems becomes even more complex because of low access to good quality mental health services. A morbidity of 58.2 per 1,000 was reported in a meta-analysis of 13 epidemiological studies covering 33,572 persons (Mohandas, 2009). Another meta-analysis of 15 epidemiological studies reported a total morbidity of 73 per 1,000. The bulk of those affected fall in the 15–45 years age group. Existing facilities to serve this affected group are limited. There are only about 0.2 psychologists per 1 lakh population and just 2 psychiatrists per 10 lakh population (Gururaj and Isaac, 2004; Math, Chandrashekar, & Bhugra, 2007; Mohandas, 2009).

Indian mental health infrastructure suffers on both counts—quantity and quality of trained psychologists and psychiatrists (Kapur, 2005). Less than 15% of Indian urban schools have appointed a full time psychologist or counselor (based on data collected by the first author from an informal survey with 300 school principals of urban private schools in India). Many principals are not aware of the importance of such a facility and others cannot find the appropriate personnel. Thus, usually, unless the child is suffering from a very severe visible mental illness she/he is not likely to receive help from school or home. Kapur (2005) mentions that there are only 100 clinics for mental health in India and almost all of them are concentrated in Mumbai, Bengaluru, and Delhi.

Development of a well adapted personality begins at home. The nature of parent–child relationship is significant in how children view themselves and the world around them. Asking for help for mental health issues in Indian society is considered taboo. A child suffering from fever may be taken to a doctor, but a child having low self-esteem is likely to be told to just get better rather than "act up." Cases of psychiatric morbidity go undetected and/or untreated because the person or family members are apprehensive of the stigma that gets attached to them the moment they come out in the open (Kennedy, 2010). Many parents would rather seek astrological or spiritual, rather than medical, advice for mental health related problems. Not only is there shame attached to asking for help, there is also shame around the fact that their child is suffering from a mental illness. It is often concealed and played down. In such scenarios, a child who could improve with the right support and medication is left to fend for him/herself.

It is suggested that school principals and teachers must be trained to recognize symptoms of mental illness. Arrangements must be made to help the child in a humane and dignified manner. Creative approaches will provide the much needed help to children in a timely fashion (Kapur, 2005). Parents must also be educated to recognize and deal with psychological problems. They also need to explore how their parenting styles may be precipitating factors for such problems. Schools can take a leadership role in arranging seminars for parents and grandparents on parent–child relationships. Psychology and psychiatry departments in educational institutes may offer Internet-based courses for teachers and parents.

Schools also need to focus on developing more learner-centered curricula that allow children to explore and innovate and which do not stress merely on academic performance and promotion. More trained teachers in schools will address the issue of mentoring and individual attention. The CBSE recently issued a directive asking schools to offer 12 hours of counseling during the academic year to every student. The aim is to be proactive in encouraging mental health and help children develop relevant life skills. This needs to be actively implemented in schools across the country.

It is also time for the country to urgently put efforts into increasing the number of mental health professionals in India. Child guidance clinics had been started in the country with an aim to provide children with professional guidance in addressing mental health issues and life skills development. However, they have been inadequate in addressing the magnitude of the situation (Shastri, 2008). More psychopharmacological aid is to be made available to children who require long-term care and treatment. There are hardly any accredited training programs conducted at the national level to train mental health professionals. The need of the hour is to engage more trained mental health professionals, psychologists, teachers, and social workers in developing sustainable models of mental health checkup and life skills training programs and taking it to larger segments of the youth population. As has been argued in the chapter, the possibility of many children suffering from undiagnosed mental health problems is very high in India and to address this need the country must put in action a plan to meet the potential need.

Acknowledgments

The authors would like to acknowledge the help provided by Ms Anuja Thakkar, Assistant Professor, GLS School of Management, Ahmedabad, and Ms Jenifer Khusroo Patel, Academic Associate, IIM Ahmedabad.

References

Basu, K. (2010, February 7). Childhood's end? *The Hindu*. Retrieved from http://www.hindu.com/mag/2010/02/07/stories/2010020750010100.htm

Bhandari, L., & Malik, P. (2008). *India's borderless workforce* (A Manpower India white paper). Retrieved from http://www.manpowergroup.com/common/download/download.cfm?companyid=MAN&fileid=249646&filekey=d65bfc06-7ecc-43dd-a8f6-7f19225061ec&filename=Manpower%20India_%20Borderless%20workforce_white%20paper.pdf

Chaudhry, L. (2007, January 29). Mirror, mirror on the web. *The Nation*. Retrieved from http://www.thenation.com/article/mirror-mirror-web

Chawla, H. (2010, June 22). Puberty much earlier. *India Today*. Retrieved from http://indiatoday.intoday.in/site/Story/102562/Lifestyle/puberty-much-earlier.html

De, H. (2010, January 3). Look, Ma, I am dead! *The Telegraph*. Retrieved on December 24, 2010 from http://www.telegraphindia.com/1100103/jsp/7days/story_11936513.jsp

Goswami, J., Baruah, P., & Shukla, R. (2010). *Dynamics of youth population: Impact of education expenditure* (Working paper 102). New Delhi: National Council of Applied Economic Research. Retrieved from http://www.eaber.org/intranet/documents/41/2415/NCAER_Goswami_2010.pdf

Government of India. (2007). *Draft final report of the working group on youth affairs and adolescents' development for formulation of 11th five year plan (2007–2012), Volume 1*. New Delhi: Ministry of Youth Affairs and Sports.

Gururaj, G., & Isaac, M. (2004). Psychiatric epidemiology in India: Moving beyond numbers. In S. P. Agarwal & D. S. Goel (Eds), *Mental health: An Indian perspective 1946–2003* (pp. 37–61). New Delhi: Ministry of Health and Family Welfare.

Kapur, D., & Mehta, P. B. (2004). Indian higher education reform: From half-baked socialism to half-baked capitalism (CID working paper no. 108). Cambridge, MA: Center for International Development at Harvard University. Retrieved from http://www.cid.harvard.edu/cidwp/pdf/108.pdf

Kapur, M. (2005). An integrated approach to the delivery of child mental health services. *Journal of Indian Association for Child and Mental Health*, *1*(1), Article 4. Retrieved from http://cogprints.org/4208/1/Jiacam05_1_4.pdf

Kennedy, M. (2010, August 11). In India, stigma of mental illness hinders treatment. *National Public Radio*. Retrieved from http://www.npr.org/templates/story/story.php?storyId=129091680

Kumar, N. (2001). Developments in mental health scenario: Need to stop exclusion-dare to care. *ICMR Bulletin, 31*(4). New Delhi: Indian Council of Medical Research. Retrieved on August 31, 2010 at http://icmr.nic.in/buapr01.pdf

Malhotra, S., Kohli, A., Kapoor, M., & Pradhan, B. (2009). Incidence of childhood psychiatric disorders in India. *Indian Journal of Psychiatry, 51*(2), 101–107. doi:10.4103/0019-5545.49449

Math, S., Chandrashekar, C., & Bhugra, D. (2007). Psychiatric epidemiology in India. *Indian Journal of Medical Research, 126*(3), 183–92.

Mohandas, E. (2009). Roadmap to Indian psychiatry. *Indian Journal of Psychiatry, 51*(3), 173–179. doi:10.4103/0019-5545.55083

Nallari, A. K. (2010, May 10). Suicides in India: A web extract report. *Newindia*. Retrieved from http://blogs.siliconindia.com/ashwinnallari/Suicides_in_India-bid-f8Fn4xey23218156.html

National Crime Records Bureau. (2009). *Crime in India*. Ministry of Home Affairs, India. Retrieved from http://ncrb.nic.in/CD-ADSI2009/ADSI2009-full-report.pdf

Parihar, R., Srivastava, M., & Shah, N. (2010, May 8). Tweeny boppers. *India Today*. Retrieved from http://indiatoday.intoday.in/site/Story/96368/Tweeny+Boppers.html?complete=1

Sengupta, S. (2006, December 31). India prosperity creates paradox; many children are fat, even more are famished. *The New York Times*. Retrieved from http://www.udel.edu/anthro/neitzel/India%20Prosperity%20Creates%20Paradox.pdf

Shastri, P. (2008). Future perspective of planning child guidance services in India. *Indian Journal of Psychiatry, 50*(4), 241–243. doi:10.4103/0019-5545.44744

Special Correspondent. (2011, February 7). Economy to grow at 8.6%: CSO. *The Hindu*. Retrieved from http://www.thehindu.com/business/Economy/article1164046.ece

Srinath, S., Girimaji, S., Gururaj, G., Sheshadri, S., Subbakrishna, D., Bhola, P., & Kumar, N. (2005). Epidemiological study of child and adolescent psychiatric disorders in urban and rural areas of Bangalore, India. *Indian Journal of Medical Research, 122*(1), 67–79.

Subrahmanyam, K., Kraut, R., Greenfield, P., & Gross, E. (2001). New forms of electronic media. In D. G. Singer and J. L. Singer (Eds), *Handbook of Children and the Media* (pp. 73–99). New Delhi: SAGE.

The Times of India. Parliamentary panel says no to sex education in schools. (2009, April 16). *The Times of India*. Retrieved from http://timesofindia.indiatimes.com/india/Parliamentary-panel-says-no-to-sex-education-in-schools/articleshow/4409307.cms

———. Kids driven to breaking point. (2010, July 12). *The Times of India*. Retrieved from http://timesofindia.indiatimes.com/City/Kolkata-/Kids-driven-to-breaking- point/articleshow/6156937.cms

World Health Organization. (2000). *The world health report 2000–Health systems: Improving performance*. Geneva: WHO.

———. (2001). *The world health report 2001–Mental health: New understanding, new hope*. Geneva: WHO.

9

Resilience and Resourcefulness of Disadvantaged Children: Lotus in the Mud

Ajit K. Dalal

Children who come from a socioeconomically impoverished background do not always perform poorly in schools. There are studies which have evidenced that many children from poverty background show a propensity to develop innate strengths and protective skills that help them deal with unpredictable and adverse life conditions (Richardson, 2002; Misra & Tripathi, 1980). By developing resiliency skills these disadvantaged children tend to focus more on their strengths than on weaknesses and focus more on problem solving than on defensive strategies. They become more resourceful in dealing with adverse childhood circumstances by developing social competence, autonomy, and sense of personal control (Capuzzi & Gross, 2000). These children from poverty background, at times, perform better than the other children in schools. The phrase "lotus in the mud" is metaphorically used for such high achieving children who typically come from poor and disadvantaged background. Such children are few but an in-depth study about them can reveal psychological dispositions and environment factors that turn adversity into advantage. The chapter is primarily aimed at identifying individual dispositions and developing a generic training model to enhance achievement of children from poverty background.

Poverty and Academic Performance

A host of child, family, school, and community-related factors place poor children at increased risk for academic failure. Such factors are congenital defects, social skills deficits, only child syndrome, impoverished family, parental psychopathology, insensitive and inconsistent parenting, peer rejection, lack of social support, and low teacher expectations (Fortin & Bigras, 1997; Grizenko & Fisher, 1992; Myers & Taylor, 1998). These factors are interrelated in complex ways within cultural ethos and adversely contribute to children's school performance (Brooks-Gunn, Klebanov, Liaw, & Duncan, 1995; Garmezy, Masten, & Tellegen, 1984). There is some progress in understanding developmental trends and processes through which the vicious cycle of poverty-performance continues but a clearer and comprehensive picture has yet to emerge.

Studies have shown that a close relationship between interest and personal skills develop as early as at 20 months of age (Chapman, Tunmer, & Prochnow, 2000; Crain-Thoreson & Dale, 1992). In the early school years, low-socioeconomic status (SES) children show self-confidence and positive school attitudes comparable to higher-SES children (Alexander & Entwisle, 1988; Stipek & Ryan, 1997), but they are more likely to lose interest in classroom learning within the first few years of school (Stipek & Tannatt, 1984; Wigfield, Eccles, Schiefele, Rosser, & Davis-Kean, 2006). Children's interest decreases with increasing recognition that their skills to cope with schooling are deficient and consequently, their motivation declines. Dweck's seminal work (Smiley & Dweck, 1994) shows that attitudes about failure and responses to subsequent fallout play significant role in sustaining motivation. Though Smiley and Dweck did not take poor children in their sample, their finding that those who attribute school failure to low ability also show low expectation and low interest in studies is relevant in this context. Other factors likely to exacerbate this problem for low-SES children include teachers' negative stereotypes about children and decreased expectations—parents' attitudes, values, and expectations, and especially as children get older peer influence accentuates (Ogbu, 1978; Steinberg, Dornbusch, & Brown, 1992).

In an important and much quoted study, Stipek and Ryan (1997) used a diverse battery of motivational measures that included children's feelings about school (i.e., perceived competence and attitudes toward school), emotions in school and task settings (child worry ratings, anxiety ratings, and enjoyment ratings), expectations for success, preferences for challenge, and dependency on the investigator in task settings. It was found that most of the children had positive motivational orientations at the time they enter school, regardless of their ethnic and economic status. Also, disadvantaged preschoolers and kindergartners maintained high motivation levels throughout the school years.

The relation between motivation and achievement manifests very early and grows stronger with time (Reynolds, 1989), and is expected to be stronger for low-SES children than their higher-SES peers (Stipek & Ryan, 1997). Since both core knowledge and motivation are critical for achievement, basic skills must be taught in a way that fosters motivation. This integrative approach might appear ambitious, but it is natural and feasible: Children learn better when interested, and are more interested when they know more.

The factor which exacerbates educational disadvantage is the teachers' expectations from economically poor and lower caste children. Rosenthal and Jacobson (1968) in their famous experimental study examined the effect of teacher's expectation on student performance. They arbitrarily selected a group of students and told the teacher that these children have extra potential for academic growth. At the end of the academic session, it was discovered that this group of children performed much better than other children in the class. Conducting research on these lines, Lal and Nahar (1978) and Singh (1980) found that teachers do not hold a positive opinion about Scheduled Caste students and do not expect them to do well in the examination. Sharma and Tripathi (1988) further observed that teachers maintain low expectations from low caste students by attributing their failure to dispositional factors, like lack of ability, effort, and so on and success to situational factors like, chance and the easiness of the task. These attributions about their school performance are internalized by the low caste students, who tend to blame themselves for their failure (Sharma and Tripathi, 1988), and thus fall into a trap of making self-defeating attributions.

Repeated Failure Leading to Learned Helplessness

When exposed to uncontrollable failure outcomes, not all poor and disadvantaged children would show the symptoms of helplessness. Many disadvantaged children persist against heavy odds to become successful learners. Some Western studies, investigating the consequences of the state of helplessness reported a facilitation effect, where, in the face of uncontrollable failure, disadvantaged children performed better on dissimilar tasks (Hanusa & Schulz, 1977; Roth & Bootzin, 1974). Yando, Seltz, and Zigler (1979) found that such children did poorly on traditional academic tasks, but their performance was better than that of middle-SES children on tasks requiring critical thinking. Wortman and Brehm (1975) asserted that lack of control does not always result in learned helplessness, but quite often causes reactance manifested in terms of anger and a sense of injustice. This happens when people blame others for their failure or when they feel that the reward which they deserved was unjustly denied to them. According to the reactance theory, in such conditions, motivation to achieve the outcome—which is denied—increases and greater effort is made to regain personal control over the outcome. Such reactions were found more frequently among elder (age 14–15 years) than younger (age 8–9 years) tribal children (Dalal, Sharma, & Bisht, 1983). Dweck and Goetz (1978) further showed that children who were mastery-oriented attributed their failure to lack of control and more vigorously pursued alternative solutions after encountering failure. They engaged in self-instructive and self-monitoring activities to achieve success. It was observed that despite clear negative feedback, the mastery-oriented children did not consider themselves failures. It may thus be argued that socioeconomic and ecological disadvantages do not always have adverse effects but many times motivate children to do better. In fact, in one study, Misra and Tripathi (1980) found that although on an average the high deprivation group did poorly, some highly deprived children showed superior performance than the less deprived children.

To conclude, low-SES children often suffer a negative cycle of failure and disinterest, whereby failure increases disengagement and disaffection fosters additional failure. Research shows that in comparison to pessimistic children, optimistic children are more likely to engage in a hope–success cycle (Yates, 2004).

Resilient Children

Fortunately, not all children who come from a poor and disadvantaged background fall in a trap of negative outcomes. There are a large number of success stories of famous people who came from abject poverty and yet accomplished remarkable feats. One of the ways to address this question is to recount success stories which are universally found in all societies, in all time frames. Psychologists have used these anecdotal evidences to highlight positive attributes which contribute to high achievement in adverse conditions. There are life stories of great people, like Abraham Lincoln, Thomas Alva Edison, and Ishwar Chandra Vidyasagar to name a few.

In 1980s, a new trend noticeable in educational psychology research was to systematically examine psychological factors which facilitate school achievement. A number of collaborative, international, interdisciplinary, and longitudinal studies were conducted to explore this phenomenon. These high achieving children were nicknamed "lotus in the mud" by Misra and Tripathi (1980). Like the lotus plant which grows in the mud, many poor children display inner strength and hardiness to withstand debilitating outcomes. They were found to be "invulnerable," "stress-resistant," "hardy," or to use a more popular term, "resilient." Resilient children are those who rather than succumbing, successfully overcome adverse life circumstances (Masten & Coatsworth, 1998).

Resilient children are characterized by innate personal competencies associated with successful development in the face of adverse circumstances. These are the children who bounce back from the problem with greater vigor and strength and cope effectively with difficult circumstances. Children who develop resiliency have a distinct advantage that they are capable of making adaptations necessary for positive outcomes. The concept of resiliency originally emerged from psychopathology and was based on the observation of children who not only overcame high-risk life situations, but in turn developed into productive people (Richardson, 2002). What these studies suggest is that highly resilient individuals will typically take effective problem-solving or self-correcting approach to overcome major difficulties. They inculcate such skills as resourcefulness, critical thinking, and insight. Academic resilience is defined as "high levels of achievement motivation and performance despite the presence of stressful events and conditions that place individuals at risk of doing poorly in school and ultimately dropping out of school" (Alva, 1991, p.19).

Academic resilience research increasingly emphasizes recognizing the strengths of children which promote achievement (Luthar & Zigler, 1991; Masten & Coatsworth, 1995). Resilience, coping competence, and related terms are at times defined and operationalized differently, but consistently refer to those protective factors that save the person from negative consequences of difficult and frustrating life conditions. Many such attributes are: good cognitive functioning, positive temperament, high sociability, close peer friendships, internal locus of control, sense of self-efficacy, high expectations for self, positive construal of negative life events, engagement in activities, close relationship with an adult, effective parenting, access to consistent and warm care giving, presence of positive adult role models, and positive association with school (Doll & Lyon, 1998).

Apart from dispositional and background factors there are many school and home related factors which protect a child from the debilitating consequences of poverty. Resiliency research has evinced that teacher's support and friendliness, classroom environment, administrative policies, and peer support can protect at-risk children (Wang & Gordon, 1994). Parenting can protect children from negative educational outcomes. Increased parent involvement in school reduces the negative effects of poverty on educational achievement and socio-emotional adjustment (Marcon, 1999; Reynolds, 1991; Shumow, Vandell, & Posner, 1999). Positive relationships with family, teachers, and other adults are strong protective factors (Masten, 1994) in providing guidance, mentoring, role models, feedback, and resources (Ladd & Burgess, 2001). How these factors collectively contribute to development of resilient personality is a conceptual and methodological challenge (Luthar, Cicchetti, & Becker, 2000). For instance, a protective factor protective for one child may be a risk factor for another and neutral for a third (Stouthamer-Loeber et al., 2002). Resiliency may reduce problems directly, lower risk factors, or interact with risk factors to diminish their influence. Furthermore, children may be successful in some areas but not others, suggesting that thinking of resilience in unidimensional terms may not be very useful (Luthar, 1993).

Resilience and Resourcefulness

Many times the terms resilience and resourcefulness are used interchangeably to denote individual disposition to effectively deal with adversities. Both are subjective concepts which are difficult to define. Both broadly refer to learned readiness to respond positively to a challenging situation. However, these two concepts have marked differences also and cannot be used interchangeably.

Resilience refers to the individual's ability to embrace the challenge of life and invulnerability to life stresses (Weiss, 2008). In contemporary research the term invulnerability has largely been replaced by resilience (Werner & Smith, 1992). Resiliency and invulnerability, though, are not equivalent. Resilience refers to the ability to spring back from adversity, it does not mean that one cannot be wounded—as the term "invulnerability" implies. Furthermore, resilience is largely taken as developmental–dispositional characteristics of an individual. Children acquire these coping skills in the developmental process to deal with their harsh environment.

Resilience research has primarily concentrated on the individual and has often ignored the role of community and social institutions (e.g., schools) in promoting or hindering resiliency (Goldstein & Brooks, 2005). As a result the question how resiliency develops and declines at some stage remains unaddressed. The concept of resourcefulness enlarges the scope of studying response to adversity in a broader sense. It focuses more on the process by which children from impoverished backgrounds acquire positive coping skills to thrive despite their adversities.

Educational Resourcefulness Model

The concept of educational resourcefulness is defined as an acquired repertoire of strategies and skills (mostly cognitive) by which existing opportunities to learn can be maximally utilized. The proposed educational resourcefulness model thus predicts that if failure is taken as a challenge, whereby future outcomes are perceived as controllable by self-efforts, it would result in performance improvement rather than impairment. Moreover, for a child high on educational resourcefulness, scholastic failures will have less deleterious effects and at times will impel the child to put forward his or her best.

The proposed educational resourcefulness model primarily focuses on creating a school environment for educationally disadvantaged children which prepares them to benefit maximally from the available opportunities. Merely creating better physical conditions, providing books and scholarships will not compensate for intellectual and motivational deficiencies. The effort to raise the standard and introduce tougher courses, without adequately preparing disadvantaged children further aggravates their plight. Thus, even in schools with good teaching facilities and supportive environment, without adequate psychological preparation to benefit from the available facilities and opportunities, most of the disadvantaged children continue to perform poorly. Earlier work in this area has supported many of these contentions which led to the formulation of the educational resourcefulness model (Dalal, 1991).

The educational resourcefulness model provides a theoretical basis for developing intervention programs. It posits that the cognitive orientation essential to induce educational resourcefulness should comprise self-esteem, sense of personal control, and planfulness. These three attributes create a psychological state essential to face failure and adversities in life. Studies show that self-esteem has high correlation with school performance, that is, the lower the performance, the lower the self-esteem (see Gerard, 1983). The attribution theory suggests that blaming one's disposition for poor performance lowers self-esteem (Dalal, 1988; Weiner, 1986), which in turn, again leads to poor performance on subsequent tests. It has been further shown that failure outcomes have greater negative impact on the motivation and performance of low self-esteem students than their high self-esteem counterparts (Brockner, 1979; Campbell & Fairey, 1985). One of the explanations given for more adverse impact on low self-esteem students is that these students tend to generalize the implications of their failure to the totality of their self-concept (Behar-Mitrani, 1985). Many recent studies have cast doubt about the positive consequences of inflated self-esteem. Research has indicated that inflating students' self-esteem has no positive effect on grades, and one study even showed that inflating self-esteem by itself can actually decrease grades (Baumeister, Campbell, Krueger, & Vohs, 2005).

The second attribute, sense of personal control, is a belief that one's own efforts will yield the desired outcome. The Coleman Report (1966) on the Head Start Program for black children concluded that the factor which has stronger relationship with achievement than all the school factors taken together is the belief among disadvantaged children that they have some control over their destiny and that they can influence their environment. In fact, as the Coleman Report revealed, sense of personal control accounted for maximum variance in school performance after background variables. Studying how students explain their own academic success and failure, Weiner (1986) has shown that their explanations tend to focus on three broad causal categories—ability, effort, and luck. Weiner demonstrated that, in general, those who attribute success to ability and effort tend to fare better in school than those who implicate luck or other external factors. Also more attribution to effort implies high sense of personal control.

Another dispositional characteristic essential for sustaining learning is *planfulness.* This refers to the ability to plan a behavioral sequence to achieve the desired outcome. This entails a sense of purpose and a future orientation—healthy expectations, goal-directedness, and success orientation. Planfulness requires people to act constantly on their environment and to make appropriate alterations in their coping strategy. A person high on planfulness is more sensitive to one's environmental demands and has better adaptability than someone low on planfulness.

Das (1984) considered planfulness to be the most essential cognitive skill to succeed in any sphere of life. The essential ingredient of planfulness is delayed gratification. The proposed educational resourcefulness model posits that all the three characteristics: self-esteem, sense of personal control, and planfulness are not independent but mutually influence each other. It is further conjectured that self-esteem and sense of personal control will determine the perception of self-efficacy (Bandura, 1982), a belief that one has behavioral skills necessary to produce a desired outcome. This efficacy–expectation determines how much effort people will expend and how long they will persist in the face of obstacles. Pajares (2009) observed that academic achievement is positively associated with self-efficacy, which in turn is critical to the life choices students go on to make.

A natural consequence of sense of self-efficacy is self-regulation of thinking and behavioral sequences. If children can become self-regulated, they can mediate the negative environmental influences they may encounter. Unless they believe they can produce desired results, children will have little incentive to persevere in the face of difficulty. Efficacy beliefs influence whether people think pessimistically or optimistically and in ways that are self-enhancing or self-hindering. Such children not only have internal locus of control but also greater control over their action tendencies. Descriptors of self-regulatory task-engagement behaviors included children's tendencies: (*a*) to spontaneously use outside resources to augment their performance, (*b*) to exhibit a sense of carefulness and reflective behavior, and (*c*) to be planful and independent in their task activities. There is research evidence to suggest that children's self-regulation skills, namely deliberate attempts to self regulate the quality and sequence of their behaviors in task settings, may enhance school achievement beyond the more general behavior-initiating effects of intrinsic motivation (Schunk & Zimmerman, 1994; Zimmerman, 1998). Lange, Farran, and Boyles (1999) solicited teacher ratings of general motivational tendencies as well as ratings of self-regulatory task-engagement behaviors for two cohorts of economically disadvantaged children. They found that at-risk children showed poorer abilities to regulate their task-attention than did low-risk children. In addition, younger at-risk children's achievement scores were predicted by their levels of attention-regulation abilities.

Sense of self-efficacy and self-regulation inoculate children from the adverse affective consequences of repeated failure. If these children get a supportive school environment their school performance would show an upswing. At some stage, this improvement in the school performance would itself augment educational resourcefulness and a self-sustaining good-performance cycle would take over. A conceptual model of learned resourcefulness is presented in Figure 9.1. Unless the school environment is perceived as supportive and stable, sense of personal control and planfulness will not have the intended consequences. More than the physical facilities, the supportive environment is defined in terms of the quality of student–teacher interaction. Since most of the reward contingencies are controlled by teachers, they play an important role in accentuating the positive consequences of educational resourcefulness. As a corollary, creating physical infrastructure without inculcating educational resourcefulness among the disadvantaged children will not, by itself, improve school performance.

Figure 9.1 Educational Resourcefulness Model

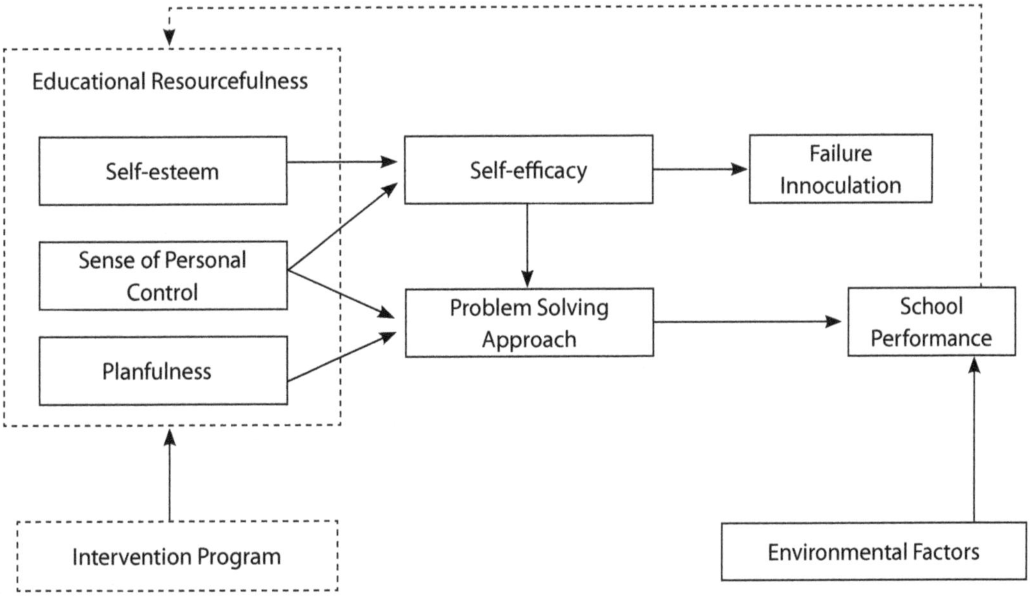

Source: Dalal (1991). Reprinted with permission.
Note: In this model, the school environment is viewed as a modulator of the influence of problem-solving orientation on scholastic performance.

Early Intervention Program

The challenge for educational researchers and practitioners is to identify practical and effective intervention programs to reduce poor students' chances of academic failure and their dropping out of the school at an early stage.

Any intervention programs to inculcate educational resourcefulness need to focus on both academic and social contexts. Experimental literature has demonstrated that emphasizing learning rather than performance, process rather than outcome, and effort rather than intelligence improves children's motivation and persistence (Kamins & Dweck, 1999; Mueller & Dweck, 1998). The emphasis in an early intervention program should be on changing the self-defeating causal attributions that children make for their failure. The study (Bempechat, 1999) supports the contention that low achievers are at risk for believing that their poor performance results from lack of ability. This belief is potentially debilitating, for if students do not think they have at least some ability, it makes little sense to them to invest effort in their learning. The challenge for teachers is to help their students maintain a healthy balance between believing that they have the ability necessary to learn, and knowing that effort will help them maximize their ability. This kind of reattribution training has been found effective in earlier studies. Dweck (1999) found that in failure situations resilient individuals tend to attribute failure to a lack of effort and are prepared to take effective remedial action while more helpless individuals attribute failure to a lack of ability and tend to give up. She developed a training program in which she taught helpless children to attribute failure to lack of effort. To a control group, only success experience was provided with no attribution training. The results indicated that the "success only" group did not improve upon their baseline performance, whereas the "reattribution" group showed significant improvement in their performance. Jain and Singh (1984) found confirmatory data for their hypothesis that the children (12–14 years) who received success with internal global attribution showed greater improvement in expectancy of future success, performance, and mood as compared to their counterparts who received external-specific attribution instructions for success.

The proposed attributional intervention makes use of teaching aids and classroom games specially designed for that purpose. Some simple indigenous teaching games can be developed in which good performance is contingent on effort expenditure than on anything else, and the criteria of success in such teaching games is kept somewhat vague so that success feedback is convincing during intervention. Effort, ability, and chance attributions are manipulated, such that in success condition either effort or ability (or both) attribution is present, whereas failure is associated with lack of effort or chance attribution. According to Martin and Marsh (2003), students develop a sense of control when they see that they are able to make choices and decisions in class that affect the way work is done. One way to do this is to provide students with choices over class objectives, assessment tasks, criteria for assessment, and due dates for work assigned.

Another variation of the intervention program aims at inculcating planfulness through delayed gratification training. This will also employ teaching games as part of the classroom activities. The children may be required to set proximal or distal goals in terms of the number of trials they would like to have, either for a smaller or a bigger reward. The complexity of the task is to be manipulated in such a manner that the children are required to take some strategic decisions at different stages of the teaching game to attain bigger rewards. The game should be purposely biased to give success experience more frequently than failure experience, when children forgo immediate reward. The exact nature of these teaching aids may be worked out from field experience.

The target group for such intervention should be preschool and first grade, school-going children, that is those children who have just joined school. These children will be in the age range of four to seven years, and should belong to lower castes and scheduled tribes. There are several advantages of selecting disadvantaged children who are in the first year of their schooling:

- This is a critical period of rapid growth and any intervention program to bring cognitive changes has greater likelihood of success at this stage than at any time later.
- The first year of schooling is a period of big transition in the life of a child. At this stage the child is more curious and open, and thus more amenable to change programs.
- A child's method of learning concepts, habit patterns, and interests are well established at a fairly early age (De Cecco, 1968). Thus, any change brought about at this stage will have a lasting effect on the child.

A good intervention program improves performance on achievement testing, lessens grade retention, and decreases utilization of remedial education. However, such intervention programs need to run for longer periods as the poor children continue to lag behind the not-poor children in their academic skills, and the positive effects of most interventions diminish over time (Lee, Brooks-Gunn, Schnur, & Liaw, 1990).

Making Bridges from Research to Practice and Policy

Given the massive problem of poverty in India, it is a big challenge to have an educational model which produces high achievers in the society. It is through sustained efforts at the school level where teachers are actively involved that such early intervention programs can be effectively introduced. There are many practical difficulties in introducing such programs at mass level. Often it is the question of monetary and human resources on a grand scale.

Taking the resourcefulness approach demands a shift in educational policies which focus on deficiencies and remedial intervention to develop strength. This alternative approach is fundamentally different in the sense that it focuses on building capacity rather than fixing problems. It would entail convincing a larger section of policy-planners and educationists who are more grounded in the conventional model of enhancing academic performance of poor and disadvantaged children.

Before introducing such programs, schoolteachers would need comprehensive training to understand the concept of educational resourcefulness and designing interventions appropriate for a particular school and group of children. Another major challenge is to involve parents and communities in these children-focused interventions at the school level. Factors influencing participation require explicit research, since families with multiple stressors are the least likely to participate. An understanding of portability, trainability, and the factors influencing implementation choices are essential. Little is known about the supports necessary to move programs successfully from research to applied settings. Given the multiple factors related to academic success, there is an urgent need to reform educational programs targeting the poor. It is not practical to intervene in all aspects of a child's life, and overly broad attempts may be either overwhelming or too diffuse. Research and theory need to guide the choice of key leverage points and strategies for continued support. Good research inputs could be useful to tailor programs to the specific needs of the targeted group of children. This needs a change both at the policy and attitude level.

References

Alexander, K., & Entwisle, D. (1988). Achievement in the first two years of school: Patterns and processes. *Monograph Social Research on Child Development, 53*(2), 1–157.

Alva, S. (1991). Academic invulnerability: Children's achievement attributions and self-reinforcement—Effects of self-concept and competitive reward structure. *Journal of Educational Psychology, 70,* 345–355.

Bandura, A. (1982). Social cognitive theory: An agentic perspective. *Annual Review of Psychology, 52,* 1–26.

Baumeister, R., Campbell, J., Krueger, J., & Vohs, K. (2005). Exploding the self-esteem myth. *Scientific American, 284,* 96–101.

Behar-Mitrani, M. (1985). Effects of repeated failure on self-esteem: An empirical study. *Journal of Asian Studies, 45,* 186–192.

Bempechat, J. (1999). Learning from poor and minority students who succeed in school: Children's views of success and failure have big impact on their learning. *Harvard Education Letter, 15*(3), 1–3.

Brockner, J. (1979). The effects of self-esteem, success-failure, and self-consciousness on task performance. *Journal of Personality and Social Psychology, 37*(10), 1732–1741.

Brooks-Gunn, J., Klebanov, P., Liaw, F., & Duncan, G. J. (1995). Toward an understanding of the effects of poverty upon children. In H. E. Fitzgerald & B. M. Lester (Eds), *Children of poverty: Research, health, and policy issues* (pp. 3–41). New York: Garland.

Campbell, J., & Fairey, P. (1985). Effects of self-esteem, hypothetical explanations, and verbalization of expectancies on future performance. *Journal of Personality and Social Psychology, 48*(5), 1097–1111. doi:10.1037/0022-3514.48.5.1097

Capuzzi, D., & Gross, D. (2000). *Youth at risk: A prevention resource for counselors, teachers, and parents* (3rd ed.). Alexandria, VA: American Counseling Association.

Chapman, J., Tunmer, W., & Prochnow, J. (2000). Early reading related skills and performance, reading self-concept, and the development of academic self-concept: A longitudinal study. *Journal of Educational Psychology, 92*(4), 703–708. doi:10.1037/0022-0663.92.4.703

Coleman, J. S. (1966). *Equality of educational opportunity.* Washington, DC: U.S. Office of Health Education and Welfare.

Crain-Thoreson, C., & Dale, P. (1992). Do early talkers become early readers? Linguistic precocity, preschool language, and emergent literacy. *Developmental Psychology, 28*(3), 421–429.

Dalal, A. K. (1988). *Attribution theory and research.* New Delhi: Wiley Eastern.

———. (1991). School performance of disadvantaged children: The educational resourcefulness model. *Indian Journal of Social Work, 42,* 313–323.

Dalal, A. K., Sharma R., & Bisht, S. (1983). Causal attributions of ex-criminal tribal and urban children in India. *Journal of Social Psychology, 119*(2), 163–171. doi:10.1080/00224545.1983.9922817

Das, J. P. (1984). Aspects of planning. In J. Kirby (Ed.), *Cognitive strategies and educational performance* (pp. 13–31). New York: Academic Press.

De Cecco, J. P. (1968). *Psychology of learning and instruction: Educational psychology.* New York: Prentice-Hall.

Doll, B., & Lyon, M. (1998). Risk and resilience: Implications for the delivery of educational and mental health services in schools. *School Psychology Review, 27*(3), 348–363.

Dweck, C. S. (1999). *Self theories: Their role in motivation, personality, and development.* Philadelphia: Psychology Press.

Dweck, C., & Goetz, T. (1978). Attributions and learned helplessness. In J. H. Harvey, W. J. Ickes, & R. F. Kidd (Eds), *New Directions in Attributions Research* (Vol. 2, pp. 158–181). Hillsdale, NJ: Erlbaum.

Fortin, L., & Bigras, M. (1997). Risk factors exposing young children to behaviour problems. *Emotional and Behavioural Difficulties, 2*(1), 3–14. doi:10.1080/1363275970020102

Garmezy, N., Masten, A., & Tellegen, A. (1984). The study of stress and competence in children: A building block for developmental psychopathology. *Child Development, 55,* 97–111.

Gerard, H. B. (1983). School desegregation: The social science role. *American Psychologist, 38*(8), 869–877. doi:10.1037/0003-066X.38.8.869

Goldstein, S., & Brooks, R. (Eds) (2005). *Handbook of resilience in children.* New York: Kluwer/Plenum.

Grizenko, N., & Fisher, C. (1992). Review of studies of risk and protective factors for psychopathology in children. *Canadian Journal of Psychiatry, 37*(10), 711–721.

Hanusa, B., & Schulz, R. (1977). Attributional mediators of learned helplessness. *Journal of Personality and Social Psychology, 35*(8), 602–661. doi:10.1037/0022-3514.35.8.602

Jain, U., & Singh, B. (1984). *Alleviation of learned helplessness* (Unpublished manuscript). University of Rajasthan, Jaipur, India.

Kamins, M. L., & Dweck, C. S. (1999). Person versus process praise and criticism: Implications for contingent self-worth and coping. *Developmental Psychology, 35*(3), 835–847.

Ladd, G. W., & Burgess, K. B. (2001). Do relational risks and protective factors moderate the linkages between childhood aggression and early psychological and school adjustment? *Child Development, 72*(5), 1579–1601.

Lal, S. K., & Nahar, U. (1978). *Higher education: Scheduled Caste and Scheduled Tribes.* Jodhpur: Jainsons Publications.

Lange, G., Farran, D., & Boyles, C. (1999, August). *Mastery behaviors and scholastic competence of at-risk children transitioning into school.* Paper presented at the Auburn University (NSF-sponsored) conference: Creating a Climate for Children's Learning: Families, Peers, and Teachers as Affordances and Constraints across the Transition to School, Birmingham.

Lee, V. E., Brooks-Gunn, J., Schnur, E., & Liaw, F. (1990). Are Head Start effects sustained? A longitudinal follow-up comparison of disadvantaged children attending Head Start, no preschool, and other preschool programs. *Child Development, 61*(2), 495–507. doi: 10.1111/j.1467-8624.1990.tb02795.x

Luthar, S. (1993). Annotation: Methodological and conceptual issues in research on childhood resilience. *Journal of Child Psychology and Psychiatry, 34*(4), 441–453. doi:10.1111/j.1469-7610.1993.tb01030.x

Luthar, S., Cicchetti, D., & Becker, B. (2000). The construct of resilience: A critical evaluation and guidelines for future work. *Child Development, 71*(3), 543–562. doi:10.1111/1467-8624.00164

Luthar, S., & Zigler, E. (1991). Vulnerability and competence: A review of research on resilience in childhood. *American Journal of Orthopsychiatry, 61*(1), 6–22. doi:10.1037/h0079218

Marcon, R. A. (1999). Positive relationships between parent school involvement and public school inner-city preschoolers' development and academic performance. *School Psychology Review, 28*(3), 395–412.

Martin, A., & Marsh, H. (2003). Fear of failure: Friend or foe? *Australian Psychologist, 38*(1), 31–38. doi:10.1080/00050060310001706997

Masten, A. S. (1994). Resilience in individual development: Successful adaptation despite risk and adversity. In M. C. Wang and E. W. Gordon (Eds), *Educational resilience in inner-city America: Challenges and prospects* (pp. 3–25). Hillsdale, NJ: Erlbaum.

Masten, A., & Coatsworth, J. (1995). Competence, resilience, and psychopathology. In D. Cicchetti & D. J. Cohen (Eds), *Developmental psychopathology: Risk, disorder, and adaptation. Wiley Series on Personality Processes* (pp. 715–752). New York: Wiley.

———. (1998). The development of competence in favorable and unfavorable environments: Lessons for research on successful children. *American Psychologist, 53*(2), 205–220. doi:10.1037/0003-066X.53.2.205

Misra, G., & Tripathi, L. (1980). *Psychological consequences of prolonged deprivation.* Agra, India: National Psychological Corporation.

Mueller, C.M., & Dweck, C. S. (1998). Praise for intelligence can undermine children's motivation and performance. *Journal of Personality and Social Psychology, 75*(1), 33–52.

Myers, H. F., & Taylor, S. (1998). Family contributions to risk and resilience in African American children. *Journal of Comparative Family Studies, 29*, 215–30.

Ogbu, J. (1978). *Minority education and caste.* San Diego, CA: Academic.

Pajares, F. (2009). Toward a positive psychology of academic motivation: The role of self-efficacy beliefs. In R. Gilman, E. Huebner, & M. Furlong (Eds), *Handbook of positive psychology in schools* (pp. 149–159). New York: Routledge.

Reynolds, A. (1989). A structural model of first-grade outcomes for an urban, low socioeconomic status, minority population. *Journal of Educational Psychology, 81*(4), 594–603.

———. (1991). Early schooling of children at risk. *American Educational Research Journal, 28*(2), 392–422. doi:10.3102/00028312028002392

Richardson, G. (2002). The metatheory of resilience and resiliency. *Journal of Clinical Psychology, 58*(3), 307–321. doi:10.1002/jclp.10020

Rosenthal, R., & Jacobson, L. (1968). *Pygmalion in the classroom.* New York: Holt, Rinehart and Winston.

Roth, S., & Bootzin, R. (1974). Effects of experimentally induced expectancies of external control: An investigation of learned helplessness. *Journal of Personality and Social Psychology, 29*(2), 680–691. doi:10.1037/h0036022

Schunk, D., & Zimmerman, B. (Eds). (1994). *Self-regulation of learning and performance: Issues and educational applications.* Hillsdale, NJ: Erlbaum.

Sharma, R., & Tripathi, R. (1988). Teachers' expectations and attributions: The self-fulfilling prophecy cycle. In A. K. Dalal (Ed.), *Attribution theory and research.* New Delhi: Wiley Eastern.

Shumow, L., Vandell, D., & Posner, J. (1999). Risk and resilience in the urban neighborhood: Predictors of academic performance among low-income elementary school children. *Merrill-Palmer Q., 45*, 309–331.

Singh, A. K. (1980). Social disadvantage and academic achievement. *Social Change, 10*, 15–19.

Smiley, P. A., & Dweck, C. S. (1994). Individual differences in achievement goals among young children. *Child Development, 65*(6), 1723–1743. doi:10.1111/j.1467-8624.1994.tb00845.x

Steinberg, L., Dornbusch, S., & Brown, B. (1992). Ethnic differences in adolescent achievement. *American Psychologist, 47*(6), 723–729. doi:10.1037/0003-066X.47.6.723

Stipek, J. D., & Ryan, R. H. (1997). Economically disadvantaged preschoolers: Ready to learn but further to go. *Developmental Psychology, 33*(4), 711–723. doi:10.1037/0022-0663.76.1.75

Stipek, J. D., & Tannatt, L. (1984). Children's judgements of their own and their peers' academic competence. *Journal of Educational Psychology, 76*(1), 75–84.

Stouthamer-Loeber, M., Loeber, R., Wei, E., Farrington, D., & Wikström, Per-Olof H. (2002). Risk and promotive effects in the explanation of serious delinquency in boys. *Journal of Consulting and Clinical Psychology, 70*(1), 111–123.

Wang, M. C., & Gordon, E. W. (1994). *Educational resilience in inner-city America: Challenges and prospects.* Hillsdale, NJ: Erlbaum.

Weiner, B. (1986). An attribution theory of achievement motivation and emotion. *Psychological Review, 92*(4), 584–573.

Weiss, L. G. (2008). Toward the mastery of resiliency. *Canadian Journal of School Psychology, 23*(1), 127–137. doi:10.1177/0829573508316600

Werner, E., & Smith, R. (1992). *Overcoming the odds: High-risk children from birth to adulthood.* New York: Cornell University Press.

Wigfield, A., Eccles, J., Schiefele, U., Rosser, R., & Davis-Kean, P. (2006). Development of achievement motivation. In W. Damon, R. Lerner, & N. Eisenberg (Eds), *Handbook of child psychology* (Vol. 3, 6th ed., pp. 933–1002). New York: Wiley.

Wortman, C. B., & Brehm, J. (1975). Response to uncontrollable outcomes: An integration of reactance theory and the learned helplessness model. In I. Berkowitz (Ed.), *Advances in experimental social psychology* (Vol. 8). New York: Academic Press.

Yando, R., Seltz, V., & Zigler, E. (1979). *Intellectual and personality characteristics of children: Social class and ethnic group differences.* Hillsdale, NJ: Erlbaum.

Yates, T. M. F. (2004). Resilience at an early age and its impact on children. *Youth and Society, 35*, 41–53.

Zimmerman, B. J. (1998). Developing self-fulfilling cycles of academic regulation: An analysis of exemplary instructional models. In D. H. Schunk & B. J. Zimmerman (Eds), *Self-regulated learning: From teaching to self-reflective practice* (pp. 1–19). New York: Guilford Press.

SECTION 5

Child Welfare

10

Family Group Conferencing: Engaging the Family Culture for Improved Children's Mental Health Outcomes

Jeanette Schmid

Introduction

Clinical interventions and child welfare responses have, in the Anglophone world, typically not made room for the integration of culture or the acknowledgment of diversity. Failing to do so has potentially compromised children's mental health. In this chapter, the shortcomings of the formal child protection system are briefly outlined.[1] Family Group Conferencing (FGC) is offered as a vehicle through which difference can be integrated into decision-making processes affecting children. The history, philosophy, and practice of FGC are described and examples are drawn from the children's mental health arena. I conclude the chapter by identifying how FGC potentially improves the mental health outcomes for children and its value in the context of development.

The Anglophone Child Protection System and Outcomes for Children's Mental Health

While the child protection system is not implemented uniformly across English-speaking countries and differences can be identified, clear commonalities exist in the histories and core principles, allowing a particular model of child welfare intervention to emerge (Freymond & Cameron, 2006). Anglophone child welfare systems were established in the late 1800s and early 1900s to rescue poor children from their misfortune (Margolin, 1997). Initially staffed by middle-class

---

[1] A more comprehensive critique of all child welfare approaches is offered in the chapter entitled *Child Welfare and Children's Mental Health Needs in the Context of Development: An Integrated (South African) Approach.*

female volunteers, these institutions now employ specialist social workers. The goal of the system is to prevent children from being abused and intervening where children have come to harm. More recently, the issue of neglect has become a central concern.

Despite its international currency, child protection as an orientation to child welfare has been found to be ineffective in many areas and have been critiqued by such authors as Blackstock, Trocme, and Bennett (2004); Cohen (2004); DeMontigny (1995); Ferguson (2004); Freymond and Cameron (2006); Horjesi, Craig, and Pablo (1992); Otway (1996); Mandell, Blackstock, Clouston Carlson, and Fine (2006); Margolin (1997); Merkel-Holguin (2004); Morris (2005); Parada (2004); Parton (1998); Reich (2005); Richardson (2003); Scourfield (2001a, 2001b, 2003, 2006); Swift (1995); Waldegrave (2006); and Waldfogel (1998a, 1998b). I rely on these writers for the following evaluation of the child protection system. The main focus of Anglo-American child welfare systems is the protection of vulnerable children. This imperative has promoted an intrusive approach that mandates social workers to closely monitor parents identified as inadequate. Because matters are decided in family court, workers tend to focus on deficits and potential risks—even when encouraged to consider strengths—so as to be able to present substantial proof of negligence or abuse. One effect of such an interrogative framework has been that the voice of the family (both nuclear and extended) has been marginalized in decision-making processes. Scientific language is used to create apparently objective and unassailable data from observations of children and parents' lived realities.

The shortcomings of the child protection system have impacted directly on issues of diversity and culture, and by extension on children's mental health. Constructions of both children and families conform to dominant norms. For example, because the nuclear family is normative, data protection and confidentiality clauses prevent information being shared with other family members without the parents' permission, thus undermining families guided by collective values. Prevailing gender constructions determine that women bear the primary scrutiny of the child welfare system. In this framework, child protection workers view children and parents as separate units. This position is reinforced by the children's best interest standard, which unintentionally but effectively pits the rights of children against those of their parents and concerned relatives. Child-rearing practices are expected to mirror middle-class traditions and norms, effectively marginalizing those who are poor and devaluing their parenting styles. Middle-class parenting failures are reframed or are frequently overlooked as these families have alternative resources. The value base informing child protection further results in cultural differences becoming either invisible or being interpreted as deviant. For example, children are expected to have one significant adult figure, typically their mother. Family cultures that value multiple attachments are often perceived as being irresponsible toward the child. Child protection responses tend to be standardized, allowing for little adjustment to particular family constellations or minority child-rearing practices. Diversity in terms of disability or sexual orientation is rarely taken into account.

Anglophone workers thus become overwhelmed when expected to deal with families where gender roles do not conform to what they see as normal, conflict is not resolved according to patterns familiar to them, particular information is shared with children that they do not approve of, or children are expected to take on household or familial tasks which they identify as adult responsibilities. Workers are confounded when families believe that their children do and should have relationships with a range of significant others. The child protection system struggles to engage with indigenous groupings who insist that a cultural identity is more critical than maternal attachment. Conflicts between parents and social workers, who typically represent different class backgrounds and racial profiles, are therefore *de rigueur*, but become represented as parental lack of cooperation and resistance rather than as cultural misunderstandings.

The child protection system is focused on parental dysfunction, remedial efforts being largely directed at failing caregivers. Preventive initiatives tend to prioritize parenting skills training. Structural factors affecting parenting capacity and the need for universal supports of families are generally disregarded, creating further bias when assessing the parenting capacities of poor and minority groups. Further, issues of diversity amongst personnel and the impact this has on worker–client relations are inadequately explored, leaving minority social workers vulnerable (Morrell, 2007).

While individual workers may be culturally sensitive, the child protection system as a whole is diversity-unfriendly. This is demonstrated by the profile of child welfare service users. In Anglo-American systems, those living under the gaze of child welfare are overwhelmingly minority groups, people of color and the poor (Hines, Lemon, Wyatt, & Merdinger, 2004; Gough, Trocmé, Brown, Knoke, & Blackstock, 2005). This bias is referred to as "disproportionality" in the US.

It is on this basis that the Maori of New Zealand challenged the dominant system in the 1980s. Maoris were acutely aware that because their children were overrepresented in the child protection and the young offender systems and were most often placed in settings managed by whites, they were losing their familial and cultural connections and becoming alienated and anchorless (Love, 2000).

The child protection system is in its racial and cultural bias, in many instances continuing its historical legacy as an agent of colonization and control (Bennet and Blackstock, 2006; Crichlow, 2002; Love, 2006, Tilbury, 1998). The well-known film *Rabbit-proof Fence* records how Australian aboriginal children were removed and placed in white families and institutions in an effort to erase their heritage and instill middle-class European values. Native Canadian children were forced to attend residential schools, typically remote from their communities of origin, where they were not permitted to speak their home languages, their culture and history was ignored or vilified and abuse was rife. Indigenous Canadians suggest that the contemporary child welfare system continues the tradition of the residential schools, First Nations children being overrepresented in the Canadian child welfare system and frequently placed in homes alien to their culture.

In summary, a significant failing of the Anglo-American child protection system is its inability to respond constructively to families who are poor or belong to minority groups. This particular approach to child welfare is oppressive to these groups both in the intense surveillance and the negative valuation of parenting in these communities. By frequently removing children from their family networks and disregarding their historical roots, children's sense of belonging, and security, their broader mental health is deeply affected.

It is critical to find a healing and liberatory approach to address child welfare concerns. Family group conferencing has emerged as such a potential alternative.

The Family Group Conferencing (FGC) Approach

FGC is a planning mechanism that engages the child and the immediate and the broader family network in a process of decision making with the service providers involved. First articulated through the Young Persons and their Families Act of 1989 in New Zealand, FGC has since been implemented at child welfare sites in the UK, the US, Canada, and Australia as well as places such as the Nordic countries, Holland, Hungary, and Israel. While the New Zealand legislation addressed both child protection and young offender decision-making procedures, I will focus only on the child welfare application.

In describing FGC I draw from the following authors: Bogue (2010); Burford and Hudson (2000); Holland, Scourfield, O'Neill, and Pithouse (2005); Merkel-Holguin and Wilmot (2005); Pennell and Andersen (2005); Nixon, Merkel-Holguin, Sivak, and Gunderson (2001); and Schmid and Pollack (2009) as well as my personal experience as a conferencing coordinator.

Principles of Family Group Conferencing

FGC assumes that the family network's knowledge of its own capacities and how it functions is critical in developing plans for children who have been abused or are at risk of being harmed, supplementing professional knowledge of the child and family. Another central belief is that the people who are or wish to be connected to the child should have a voice in the decision-making process. A third core assumption is that a child, to have a sense of rootedness or belonging, must maintain connections with her/his family and culture of origin. Fourth, it is believed that for an adequate safety plan to be arrived at, as many family members as possible need to participate. Widening the circle ensures that diverse perspectives are presented and all possible familial resources are made available. Family supports must be supplemented by formal resources to undergird the family's capacity to care for the child, and not to leave the family alone to carry the responsibility. A final assumption is that all conference participants must have voice. Thus, the child concerned must be able to express his/her opinions if he/she so wishes and his/her perspectives must be taken into account. This applies also to any other family member who may feel vulnerable.

These foundational principles are given shape through the unique process of conferencing. While there is a generic conferencing pathway, FGC has been adapted to suit local conditions in the many countries and settings it has been applied. The American Humane Association has produced an FGC manual,[2] presenting an "international" understanding of the essential elements of conferencing. Any site adapting conferencing to its needs and priorities should ensure the basic principles are adhered to, rather than slavishly following the procedure.

I describe the model followed in Toronto, Canada. This model has certain validity having been successfully implemented with an extremely diverse population.[3]

Phases of Conferencing

Conference practitioners agree on two broad phases of conferencing (the preparation and the conference itself) and that good outcomes are dependent on good preparation.

Preparation is the bulk of the conferencing process. A coordinator, who has no mandated role regarding the family, and who ideally is perceived as independent of child protection agendas, is responsible for adequately preparing all conference participants (service providers and family members) for the conference. Typically, the coordinator meets the prospective participant face-to-face for around an hour, usually in their home. The concerns and strengths expressed by the child welfare agency and other service providers, as well as any legal constraints to the decision making (e.g., a permanent plan for a child under one year has to be arrived at within a year) are covered. The coordinator checks who else is in the family circle so that these individuals can also be invited. If the participant has concerns (including safety issues) regarding the coming meeting, these are specifically discussed. The coordinator addresses logistical issues regarding the conference with the family members including arranging childcare and transport. The preparation process is not rushed, allowing every prospective participant to get ready. Allowing adequate time further ensures that the family as a group has had the informal conversation needed to be able to come together for a communal discussion.

The conference is held on a date jointly negotiated between all prospective participants. For maximum attendance, the meeting is often held on a weekend. Conferences mostly are completed in one day, but in particular circumstances and cultures, the deliberations may extend over two days. The meeting is held in a venue that all participants experience as neutral and accessible.

---

[2]Available as a free download from www.fgdm.org
[3]The manual can also be downloaded free from www.georgehullcentre.on.ca

Participants usually arrive with a mixture of apprehension and expectation. Maternal and paternal sides of the family may never have met one another, or may not have seen each other for extended periods of time. Often, such a family reunion is indeed a historic event.

The day itself moves through three distinct parts, namely the opening and information giving session, the family private time, and a review of the plan. The coordinator facilitates the first and the last parts of the day.

Information-giving Phase

The stage for the day's proceedings is set in the opening. The conference begins with a secular or religious ceremony chosen by the family group, communicating that this day belongs primarily to the family network. The coordinator welcomes everyone and provides an opportunity for introductions. In the Toronto model, both service providers and family members are asked to share their hope for the day as this promotes common agenda setting. There is no doubt that bringing together relatives and friends who have long and sometimes acrimonious histories with one another can create tension. It is thus useful to enable the participants to articulate conferencing guidelines, which reference the type of behavior that participants can expect from one another.

Once these preliminary processes are completed, the service providers have the floor. Each professional shares what he/she identified as strengths in the family group and why he/she is concerned about the child or children to be planned for. This is a restatement of the information the coordinator has already passed on to the family members during the preparation phase. Relatives and friends can ask the service providers questions of clarification. Sometimes, the family group also asks for an expert to speak to a particular challenge, for example, the impact of substance abuse on a child's sense of security, supporting children through the death of a parent, understanding the impact of bipolar disorder on parenting capacity, and so on.

The information-giving phase is normally concluded within an hour, unless translation has been needed. The family members need to be adequately informed but should not be overwhelmed with unnecessary detail. At this point, the service providers retire to another room and leave the family group to meet privately. The meal chosen by the family group and in some instances prepared by them is usually then served.

Family Private Time

The family private time allows the family group the space to discuss the service providers' reports and to develop a plan they deem appropriate for the child concerned. The family circle may choose someone to lead the process, but no external mediator or facilitator is in the room. Neither is this time ever interrupted by the coordinator or a service provider. This signals that the service providers believe in the family network's ability to manage their own affairs and also communicates a respect for private issues.

The family group takes as long as it needs to develop a safety plan for the vulnerable child. Some families are very clear about the goal and how to get there, where others may first need to build trust and alliances with one another. The decision-making process also varies from family to family, affecting the amount of family private time needed. Family members may seek out the service providers in order to have specific questions answered. These queries typically revolve around available agency resources.

Review of the Plan

Once the family circle has arrived at a plan, the service providers are invited back into the meeting room. The plan is reviewed together. Should the service providers believe the plan is good enough to ensure the child's future safety, the plan is formally accepted. In the Anglo-American child protection context, this step is necessary as child protection workers are mandated to ensure the children's safety. They are also required to present the agreed upon plan to the court if there has been statutory intervention.

Family groups may propose a short-term plan, making it necessary to develop a further phase of the plan at another point. Family groups may also decide to have a second conference to review how the plan is working.

The family network, including relatives and friends, has thus been given the opportunity to have a central voice in determining the future of the child that has been harmed or is deemed at risk. Their particular challenges, priorities, resources, needs, and life approaches have been respected and incorporated into the plan. In the conferencing process, issues of diversity are directly addressed. How this is done is covered in the next section.

Conferencing and Diversity

The family's unique culture stands in the forefront of the conferencing process. During the preparation, the coordinator expects to familiarize himself/herself with the prevailing values and norms of the particular family. This may be complex as families are not necessarily culturally homogenous and individuals may have different identifications with the formal culture. However, if the family culture is to have expression at the conference, the coordinator needs to understand what this might mean for the circle. It is useful for the coordinator to be informed of any migration stories the family carries and the impact of these on the family's way of doing things and its relationship to authority figures. The coordinator is aware of the power dynamics that may occur between the coordinator and various family members due to each individual's social location.

The coordinator may take on the role of "cultural translator" in helping the family group to understand the procedures and language of the child protection system or supporting workers in deconstructing the behavior of family members. For example, what a worker may see as over-intrusive behavior by a grandmother can be reinterpreted as a cultural expression of concern. Alternatively, a family group may feel victimized, but can be helped to see that this is routine and not directed at this family in particular.

A further role taken on by the coordinator is to encourage the family members to identify how the conference process can be shaped to match the family culture. A significant way in which this is done is through the opening (and if wished, the closing), where the family members can include expressions of their spirituality or belief systems. The family group will also choose what kind of food is to be served and in some instances will insist that they themselves prepare the food. The family's preferred language(s) is honored by providing appropriate interpretation and translation if required. How children should participate is negotiated with the family circle, though the principle that the child should have a voice in the process and his/her preferences taken into account remains. The private time allows the family group itself to form and direct the decision-making process in concurrence with the family's style of decision making.

The principle of inclusion is another conferencing aspect that speaks to diversity. A family member is only excluded by personal choice or if he or she is expected to be violent at the conference or threaten the safety of participants in the process leading up to or following the conference. Indeed, the preference is to include as many persons connected to the child as possible. There is no upper limit, the family circle itself deciding who ought to be included or not. One does not need to have blood ties to be part of the family group, and thus best friends, godparents, neighbors, and work colleagues may be asked to attend. No one is left out because of mental health or substance abuse issues, two typical reasons for exclusion in regular child welfare processes. Physical health or disability also does not preclude attendance. Arrangements are made to ensure full participation. Persons who are incarcerated may in certain situations be able to be physically present at the conference, and where this cannot be arranged, may participate by phone or by letter. The coordinator supports the individual and the family group to create the conditions necessary for participation. Such strategies may include more breaks, interpretation, physical support, visual aids, or greater preparation of the individual.

As alluded to earlier, the venue should also be accessible to all participants, both physically and emotionally. Families may choose to have the meeting at a cultural or religious venue. The pub has apparently been a favored venue for Scottish conferences!

Conferencing further facilitates diversity in ensuring that voices that are typically marginalized are heard and that the family members speak to their lived reality, rather than this being constructed by social workers. Children and vulnerable adults such as a mother who has been abused are carefully and thoroughly prepared for their role in the conference. Participation is always voluntary.

Inclusion is thus a cornerstone of the conferencing process. Having outlined the process of conferencing, I now provide examples of conferencing in addressing children's mental health issues.

How Does Family Group Conferencing Address Children's Mental Health Issues?

In this section, I present examples of how children's mental health issues were addressed in some of the family group conferences held in Toronto. All names have been changed in the case examples are quoted.

Broadly, two central issues are addressed through conferencing for children who are dealing with mental health challenges, namely safety and rootedness. The outcomes of conferencing demonstrate—both in the short and long term—that the at-risk child as well as his/her siblings, were more likely to be safe following an FGC intervention. Adults in the home also are less likely to be subject to violence in the future. Partly the family safety is increased because the threats to children and women are discussed directly and explicitly. Family members, with the support of service providers, must present a plan that will ensure safety. This may mean that the person who perpetrated the harm has to live outside of the home, and contact between him and the children or partner is supervised by relatives. The fact that more people are aware of the abuse that occurred and are better informed about the future risks and consequences and thus more people are actively monitoring the situation, also leads to a decrease in the potential for violence. One family network accordingly decided that the father could not return to the home, but that he would be able to have visits to his children, supervised by the children's grandmother.

Many children who have mental health issues may also feel insecure. The concrete display of family interest through the attendance of a wide circle of family members demonstrates to the child the concern that there is in the family circle for him/her. Children also get to know people in the family network with whom they may not have previously had contact. For example, a 10-year-old who had spent much of his life in care got to know uncles and aunts for the first time.[4] A young girl, also 10, stood in the middle of the family circle, her arms akimbo, and informed the coordinator that all these people loved her, and this was not even all of them!

The FGC process, in addition, promotes a cultural sense of belonging. The (anecdotal) experience in the Ontario program with native Canadian children is that children are reminded of their spiritual and cultural heritage through the conferencing process. Extended families have the opportunity to take care of their children, rather than these being placed with stranger families. This

---

[4]Family Voices Video, available from the American Humane Association.

is not to suggest that caregivers with a different cultural background cannot offer these children the necessary love and care. However, if children are able to find this in their communities of origin, there is less likely to be a sense of displacement. The cultural identity can be strengthened and the culture can become a source of power.

Conferencing in addition helps families address other mental health needs that children have. In one family, 14-year-old Alan who had some developmental delays found himself caught between the attentions of his grandmother and step-grandmother. His grandfather, also caught between these two women, tended to make the situation worse: he would give Alan mixed messages and the boy would be drawn into also trying to please both women. Unfortunately each grandmother had different ideas about what Alan needed. Alan would become quite stressed, and felt strongly that he was failing both. Through the conference process, the grannies were able to shift the focus away from their own conflict to Alan's needs. He reported later being able to enjoy both grandmothers and the support each offered him. I suspect that the grandfather also was much relieved!

In another instance, 16-year-old Desiree wanted to plan for her early adulthood. She had spent many years in care, but wanted to return to family. She suffered from rapid bipolar disorder and understood that for any family placement to last that the family member would need to appreciate the literal ups and downs of her mental health condition. A conference was held. I was disappointed as no concrete proposal emerged from the meeting. Desiree however was delighted, having reconnected with a range of family members, including her mother and two siblings. The next summer, she was able to visit an aunt, who it turns out is a psychiatric nurse. The holiday became a trial run for a permanent move a year later.

A conference was held for a teenager with autism because his elderly parents could no longer manage him. Tim would threaten his parents and they became quite afraid at his outbursts. Abandoning him in a home was however no option for them. Through the conference, Tim was able to understand somewhat how fearful he made his parents. He also understood that he was getting old enough to move out. The plan was for Tim to move into an independent but supported living arrangement where he could maintain contact with his parents and his siblings. The parents were relieved that Tim would be in an appropriate setting, but that they could still remain actively (but safely!) involved in his life. He was excited that he could begin a new chapter, one that was appropriate to his age and stage in life.

In another example, 11-year-old Jonathan, who was struggling to attend school on a regular basis, was the focus of the conference. Jonathan would become extremely anxious and being in the classroom was terrifying for him. His single mother, Julie, was becoming quite distressed. She felt increasingly isolated and unable to deal with the situation. Through the conference, it was agreed that Julie's sister would become more involved to provide the mother with direct support. An older cousin of Jonathan's said that he would pick him up in the morning and accompany him to school. Arrangements were made at the school to provide added supports to Jonathan during the school day. In this way, Jonathan was slowly able to reintegrate back into school life.

The relationship between him and his mother shifted from one of struggle and resistance to one where each could enjoy the other.

Conferencing can thus be successfully applied even where there are no official child protection concerns, but where the primary issue has to do with mental health challenges. In the UK, conferencing is also regularly used in the school environment to support children with behavioral or learning difficulties and to effectively increase both their attendance and academic performance.

All the examples referenced, however, are located in developed countries. Can FGC realistically be applied in less resourced contexts?

FGC for Developing Countries

The question to consider is whether the FGC approach can have any value in situations where both formal and informal resources are scarce. Conferencing is not without criticism, and these questions should also be answered for the development context. A concern that arises as soon as FGC is suggested in a development environment is cost. In practice contexts where placement outside the family is regularly resorted to, it is clear that family placement provides a much more financially viable alternative. (FGC, though, is not intended as a neoliberal option which simply places all responsibility for the child's care and safety with the family.) This is more difficult to demonstrate where services have been almost entirely absent.

Certainly, FGC is expensive at the front end. A coordinator with the necessary people and organizational skills must be employed. This person invests a minimum of 40 hours in preparing the participants for the conference, 8 hours for the conference day and another 5 in post conference activities including distributing the plan. (The time invested shifts upwards if the coordinator has to travel long distances to meet family members and where extended families are large.) In addition, funding is required for transporting family members to the conference, for food and refreshments during the meeting, as well as for childcare. (Children, namely the children being planned for as well as children of adult participants can attend the conference if they wish. Mostly, children come in and out of the meeting as determined by their and the adults' wishes.) Financing may also be needed for the conference venue. Post conference, poor, disadvantaged families particularly are likely to require formal state assistance. However, these short-term expenses must be considered against long term costs. FGCs tend to keep children with their families and in their community of origin. Usually there is no further abuse of the child previously harmed or of siblings. As noted earlier, family violence as a whole tends to be terminated. These outcomes ensure that critical concerns are formally addressed in the short term, thus avoiding long-term, costly remedial investments in children and families.

In trying to address the cost question, it is sometimes expressed that the FGC preparation process is too long and unnecessary, particularly the face-to-face contact. Experienced coordinators are however very aware that inadequate preparation results in participants being insufficiently informed regarding the concerns, their own role, and the role of other participants, this is turn leading to plans that have not been thoroughly thought through. These plans are vulnerable to failure, undermining the conference process altogether. Abridged "partnership" models have been proposed in North America and the UK. Merkel-Holguin and Wilmot (2005) caution that these processes, which are typically expert-led and -driven, do not in fact allow family members to determine the future welfare of their children.

The Role of Families and Child Welfare Authorities in Creating Safety

As a conference coordinator, I frequently have come upon critics who maintain that the family is unsafe for children and women and that permitting the family network to determine plans is irresponsible at least and dangerous at worst. This may indeed be so where violence has become the norm in the family as a collective and where this is further sanctioned through dominant values. However, the work of Pennell (2004, 2005) and Pennell and Burford (1997) in particular, demonstrates that conferencing can be successfully used in situations of domestic violence, though it requires that the coordinator be familiar with the dynamics of such violence and is able to support the family group in preparing for safety. Careful preparation also lifts out and strengthens the dissenting voices in the family circle and allows one to challenge what is often a myth about the "cultural" support of violence.

Others worry that certain families have become dysfunctional over generations and do not have the resources needed to create safety. Conferencing experience demonstrates that when the family circle is widened typically there are family members who can make positive contributions. The conferencing process also allows previously unwitnessed strengths to emerge.

It is regrettable to note that family group participation often ends at the point that the conference concludes, workers frequently falling back into directing the process, rather than allowing the family group to remain in the driver's seat. This is because the culture of professionalism is much stronger than the culture of family partnership and empowerment in Anglo-American child welfare agencies. The worker must remain sensitive to the fact that planning decisions may again be needed and the family as a whole (or representatives they themselves have appointed) need to be kept informed and involved. A worker with a large caseload (which tends to be the situation in developing countries) may find it too cumbersome to stay in touch with the family members, overlooking the fact that engaged family members are indeed relieving the worker of much responsibility toward the vulnerable child. It thus becomes critical when introducing FGC that there are changes within the organizational culture to support the individual worker in engaging family networks in decision-making processes.

Conferencing is indeed vulnerable where it is introduced in a subsidiary manner to the child protection approach, as pointed out by Maori authors such as Love (2000, 2006), Tauri, (2005), and Walker (1997). Walker argues that if a family group is invited to develop a plan, it must be accepted at face value and not be further interrogated by child welfare professionals as it undermines the family network's expertise. The discourse of safety which has been adopted into conferencing as well as the reliance on professional judgments of the family strengths and concerns further undermines the family group's decision-making power. While the expertise of the service provider may indeed be valued by the family group, the deferment to the child welfare authorities will always mean that a child protection discourse dilutes the empowerment discourse of FGC. It is extremely difficult to shift the dominant construction of families, children, and abuse. Ideally, conferencing should be introduced as a planning tool within a broad developmental welfare approach (discussed in another chapter in this Handbook) to children and families.

Conclusion

Bearing in mind the above critiques, I would argue that FGC is relevant and practical also in less resourced countries. First, the notion of the family circle coming together to make decisions is often culturally close where extended families still operate as the family unit, or where the memory of a collective family unit is not far away. Even where the family network has become eroded, for example, through AIDS, the cultural basis of joint decision making is still valued. Second, the impetus for community-based rather than institutional responses suggests that where children are at risk either because of abuse or because of their own mental health difficulties, FGC is more likely to provide a non-institutional outcome. (It must be said that certain family networks have considered their own resources and have opted for adoption as the preferred alternative. This is not seen as a failure in FGC terms as the family network themselves have come to this conclusion, rather than having a decision imposed on them.) Where decisions must be made for child headed households, FGC can play a significant role. Third, allowing families to make their own decisions, rather than service providers determining these for them, is important in social work, no matter what the context.

References

Bennett, M., & Blackstock, C. (2006). First Nations Child and Family Services and indigenous knowledge as a framework for research, policy, and practice. In N. Freymond & G. Cameron (Eds), *Towards positive systems of child and family welfare: International comparisons of child protection, family service and community caring systems* (pp. 269–288). Toronto: University of Toronto Press.

Blackstock, C., Trocme, N., & Bennett, M. (2004). Child maltreatment investigations among aboriginal and non-aboriginal families in Canada. *Violence Against Women, 10*(8), 901–916. doi:10.1177/1077801204266312

Bogue, D. (2010). Reversing the trend: Families resolving and responding to their own problems of living through family group conferencing. *International Journal of Narrative Therapy and Community Work, 1*, 23–31.

Burford, G., & Hudson, J. (Eds). (2000). *Family group conferencing: New directions in community-centered child and family practice.* New York: Aldine de Gruyter.

Cohen, B. J. (2004). Reforming the child welfare system: Competing paradigms of change. *Children and Youth Services Review, 27*(6), 653–666. doi:10.1016/j.childyouth.2004.11.016

Crichlow, W. (2002). Western colonisation as a disease: Native adoption and cultural genocide. *Critical Social Work, 3*(1). Retrieved from http://www.criticalsocialwork.com

DeMontigny, G. (1995). *Social working: An ethnography for front line practice.* Toronto: University of Toronto Press.

Ferguson, H. (2004). *Protecting children in time: Child abuse, child protection and the consequences of modernity.* Hampshire: Palgrave Macmillan.

Freymond, N., & Cameron, G. (2006). *Towards positive systems of child and family welfare: International comparisons of child protection, family service and community caring systems.* Toronto: University of Toronto Press.

Gough, P., Trocmé, N., Brown, I., Knoke, D., & Blackstock, C. (2005). Pathways to the overrepresentation of Aboriginal children in care (Information sheet). Toronto: Centre of Excellence for Child Welfare.

Hines, A. M., Lemon, K., Wyatt, P., & Merdinger, J. (2004). Factors related to the disproportionate involvement of children of color in the child welfare system: A review of emerging trends. *Children and Youth Services Review, 26*(6), 507–527. doi:10.1016/j.childyouth.2004.01.007

Holland, S., Scourfield, J., O'Neill, S., & Pithouse, A. (2005). Democratising the family and the state? The case of family group conferences in child welfare. *Journal of Social Policy, 34*(1), 59–77. doi:10.1017/S0047279404008268

Horjesi, C., Craig, B., & Pablo, J. (1992). Reactions by Native-American parents to child protection agencies: Cultural and community factors. *Child Welfare Journal, 71*(4), 329–342.

Love, C. (2000). Family group conferencing: Cultural origins, sharing and appropriation—a Maori reflection. In G. Burford & J. Hudson (Eds), *Family group conferencing: New directions in community-centered child and family practice* (pp. 15–30). New York: Aldine de Gruyter.

———. (2006). Maori perspectives on collaboration and colonization in contemporary Aotearearoa/New Zealand and family welfare policies and practices. In N. Freymond & G. Cameron (Eds), *Towards positive systems of child and family welfare: International comparisons of child protection, family service and community caring Systems* (pp. 237–268). Toronto: University of Toronto Press.

Mandell, D., Blackstock, C., Clouston Carlson, J., & Fine, M. (2006). From child welfare to child, family and community welfare: The agenda of Canada's Aboriginal peoples. In N. Freymond & G. Cameron (Eds), *Towards positive systems of child and family welfare: International comparisons of child protection, family service and community caring systems* (pp. 211–236). Toronto: University of Toronto Press.

Margolin, L. (1997). *Under the cover of kindness: The invention of social work.* Charlotteville: University Press of Virginia.

Merkel-Holguin, L. (2004). Sharing power with the people: Family group conferencing as a democratic experiment. *Journal of Sociology and Social Welfare, 31*(1), 155–173.

Merkel-Holguin, L., & Wilmot, L. (2005) Analyzing family involvement approaches. In J. Pennell & G. Anderson (Eds), *Widening the circle: The practice and evaluation of FGC with children, youths and their families.* Washington, DC: NASW Press.

Morrell, P. (2007). Power and status contradictions. In D. Mandell (Ed.), *Revisiting the use of self: Questioning professional identities* (pp. 71–86). Toronto: Canadian Scholars Press.

Morris, K. (2005). From "children in need" to "children at risk"—the changing policy context for prevention and participation. *Practice: Social Work in Action, 17*(2), 67–77. doi: 10.1080/09503150500148057

Nixon, P., Merkel-Holguin, L., Sivak, P., & Gunderson, K. (2001). How can family group conferences become family driven? Some dilemmas and possibilities. *Protecting Children, 18*(1, 2), 108–109.

Otway, O. (1996). Social work with children and families: From child welfare to child protection. In N. Parton (Ed.), *Social theory, social change and social work* (pp. 152–171). New York: Routledge.

Parada, H. (2004). Social work practices within the restructured child welfare system in Ontario. *Canadian Social Work Review, 21*(1), 67–86.

Parton, N. (1998). Risk, advanced liberalism and child welfare: The need to recover uncertainty and ambiguity. *British Journal of Social Work, 28*(1), 5–27.

Pennel, J. (2004). Should we invite her and his side of the family to the FGC? *Together: The Family Group Conference Network Newsletter,* 8–9.

———. (2005). Safety for mothers and their children. In J. Pennel & G. Anderson (Eds), *Widening the circle: The practice and evaluation of FGC with children, youths and their families* (pp. 163–181). Washington, DC: NASW Press.

Pennell, J., & Anderson, G. (Eds). (2005). *Widening the circle: The practice and evaluation of FGC with children, youths and their families.* Washington, DC: NASW Press.

Pennel, J., & Burford, G. (1997). Family group decision making: After the conference: Progress in resolving violence and promoting well being. *Protecting Children, 18*(1, 2), 108–109.

Reich, J. A. (2005). *Fixing families: Parents, power, and the child welfare system.* New York: Routledge.

Richardson, M. (2003). A personal reflective account: The impact of the collation and sharing of information during the course of a child protection investigation. *Child and Family Social Work, 8*(2), 123–132. doi:10.1046/j.1365-2206.2003.00274.x

Schmid, J. E., & Pollack, S. (2009). Developing shared knowledge: Family group conferencing as a means of negotiating power in the child welfare system. *Practice: Social Work in Action, 21*(3), 175–188.

Scourfield, J. B. (2001a). Constructing women in child protection work. *Child and Family Social Work, 6*(1), 77–87. doi:10.1046/j.1365-2206.2001.00189.x

———. (2001b). Constructing men in child protection work. *Men and Masculinities, 4*(1), 70-89. doi:10.1177/1097184X01004001004

———. (2003). *Gender and child protection.* United Kingdom: Palgrave Macmillan.

———. (2006). Gendered organizational culture in child protection social work. *Social Work, 51*(1), 80–82.

Swift, K. (1995). *Manufacturing bad mothers: A critical perspective on child welfare.* Toronto: University of Toronto Press.

Tauri, J. M. (2005). Family group conferencing: The myth of indigenous empowerment in New Zealand. In W. D. McCaslin (Ed.), *Justice as healing: Indigenous ways. Writings on community peacemaking and restorative justice from the Native Law Centre* (pp. 313–323). St. Paul, MN: Living Justice Press.

Tilbury, C. (1998). Child protection policy and practice in relation to Aboriginal and Torres Strait Islander children in Queensland in the 1990's. *Australian Social Work, 51*(2), 25–31. doi:10.1080/03124079808411215

Waldegrave, C. (2006). Contrasting national jurisdictional and welfare responses to violence to children. *Social Policy Journal of New Zealand, 27,* 57–76.

Waldfogel, J. (1998a). Rethinking the paradigm for child protection. *Protecting Children from Abuse and Neglect, 8*(1), 104–119.

———. (1998b). *The future of child protection: How to break the cycle of abuse and neglect.* Cambridge: Harvard University Press.

Walker, H. (1997). Whanua hui, family decision making and the family group conference: An indigenous, Maori view. *Protecting Children, 12*(3), 8–10.

11

Behavioral Parent Training with Abusive Parents*

Patricia L. Kohl

Child welfare systems are guided by the principles of safety, permanency, and child well-being (Pecora, Whittaker, Maluccio, Barth, & Plotnick, 2000; Webb & Harden, 2003). Services within this system of care are provided along a continuum; investigation of maltreatment reports, supportive and treatment services for maltreating and at-risk families, and temporary or permanent placement in substitute care are services along this continuum (Webb & Harden, 2003, p. 50). The ultimate aim of supportive and treatment services is the prevention of recurrent maltreatment; the promotion of child well-being is a secondary aim. Yet, little is known about how to effectively achieve these outcomes. This chapter discusses research and theory which establish the need for effective behavioral parent training (BPT) to be delivered within child welfare systems. The assertion is made that BPT, originally developed to target child behavior problems, has the potential to also prevent maltreatment recidivism.

Maltreatment and Child Behavior Problems

Disruptive behavior problems are common among children in the child welfare system. Some children have contact with this system due to child behavior problems (Barth, Wildfire, & Green, 2006), while the majority of children enter this system due to abuse and/or neglect. Regardless of grounds for entry, disruptive behavior problems are highly prevalent. A national study of children and families investigated for maltreatment in the US found that 45 percent of children age 4 through 15 years and 26 percent of children age two and three years met criteria for borderline or clinical levels of externalizing behavior problems (US DHHS, ACF, 2005). This represents a sizable number of children. According to statistics maintained by the federal government, about 3.3 million children were investigated or assessed following a report of child maltreatment in 2009 (US DHHS, ACF, 2010).

---

*Support for this chapter was provided by the National Institute for Child Health and Human Development (1R01HD061454-01A1).

Abuse and neglect place children at risk for the development of a plethora of adverse outcomes including disruptive behaviors, conduct disorder, global impairment, poor social competence, depression, substance abuse, and academic achievement (Flisher et al., 1997; Smith, Ireland, & Thornberry, 2005). The focus here will be limited to behavioral problems and disorders. It is well established that children who have been physically abused are more likely to demonstrate disruptive behavior problems than other children. Findings from the Lahey et al. (1996) Methods for the Epidemiology of Child and Adolescent Disorders study (n = 665 youth 9–17 years of age) provide support for this assertion. The adjusted odds ratios reveal that, compared to non-physically abused children, physically abused children were four times more likely to be diagnosed with any disruptive behavior disorder (CI: 2.0 to 9.0) and conduct disorder (CI: 1.8 to 10.3) (Flisher et al., 1997). In two cohorts of kindergarten-aged children, Weiss and colleagues (1992) found that harsh (physical) discipline was associated with school aggression, even when controlling for SES, child temperament, and marital violence. Among 99 youth aged 12 to 19, physical abuse experienced in adolescence made a unique contribution to the development of conduct disorder over and above other risks for adolescent psychopathology (Kaplan et al., 1998). The association between physical abuse and the development of behavior problems is robust, regardless of the child's age at the time of the abuse.

The development of disruptive behavior problems is commonly associated with physical abuse; neglected children, however, may also develop behavior problems. Neglected school age children can be more aggressive than their non-neglected peers (Erickson & Egeland, 2002, Scannapieco & Connell-Carrick, 2005). Furthermore, child neglect is associated with increased risk of adult criminality and violent offending (Widom, 1989). Hence, BPT should be considered as a potential treatment and prevention strategy with neglecting parents as well as with physically abusive parents.

In addition to maltreatment increasing the risk for child behavior problems, these behaviors place children who have had prior contacts with the child welfare system at risk for subsequent contact due to new allegations of maltreatment. Analysis of the National Survey of Child and Adolescent Well-being revealed that children with borderline or clinical behavior problems were significantly more likely to have a new maltreatment report over an 18-month period compared to children with behaviors in the normal range (Kohl & Barth, 2007). This research highlights the importance of training parents to address problem behaviors using nonviolent, positive parenting to improve both child disruptive behavior and safety outcomes.

Theoretical Perspectives on Parenting and Child Behaviors

In this section, the ecological-transactional model and coercion theory will be discussed to provide a framework for understanding parenting and child behaviors within a broader environmental context. These theoretical perspectives also inform the argument in favor of BPT as an intervention to address maladaptive parenting and child behavior problems, and to treat child maltreatment.

Ecological-transactional Model

The ecological-transactional model posits that the combined influence of factors within multiple nested levels (e.g., macrosystem, exosystem, and microsystem) with varying levels of proximity to the child influence the development of psychopathology (Lynch & Cicchetti, 1998). Risks at any level of the model interfere with the promotion of healthy child development (Cicchetti & Toth, 2005). Furthermore, it is a dynamic, interactional model with parent, child, and environmental characteristics coalescing to shape the developmental trajectory of the child (Scannapieco & Connell-Carrick, 2005).

Parenting has a salient influence on children and certain parenting behaviors have been shown to place children at risk of developing disruptive behavior problems. These negative parenting behaviors include parental negativity, harshness, use of coercion, and overuse of physical punishment (Bender et al., 2007; Coie & Dodge, 1998; Dodge, Bates, & Pettit, 1990; Dornbusch, Ritter, Leiderman, Roberts, & Fraleigh, 1987; Patterson, 2002), inconsistent parenting, especially in discipline (Dumas & Wahler, 1985; Wahler, Williams, & Cerezo, 1990), and parent's negative attributes and unrealistic views of their children (Bugental & Johnston, 2000; Sanders & McFarland, 2000).

Within the ecological-transactional framework, however, the influence of parenting has to be considered within a broader context. Many parents entering the child welfare system are distressed by cumulative hardships and blighted living environments. Poor families are overrepresented in the child welfare system (Coulton, Korbin, Su, & Chow, 1995; Drake, Jonson-Reid, Way, & Chung, 2003). Evidence suggests that this over-representation is based on need rather than bias; poor families are more likely to have family and neighborhood levels of risk for maltreatment (Jonson-Reid, Drake, & Kohl, 2009). At the neighborhood level, community violence which is pervasive in impoverished neighborhoods is associated with increased rates of maltreatment (Lynch & Cicchetti, 1998). Many family level conditions are also associated with poverty, as well with involvement in a child welfare system—such as substance abuse, homelessness, and parental incarceration (McGuinness & Schnieder, 2007). Intimate partner violence and mental illness are prevalent among families in the child welfare system and both are associated with increased risk of maltreatment (Chaffin, Kelleher, & Hollenberg, 1996; Kohl, Barth, Hazen, & Landsverk, 2005; Shepard & Raschick, 1999; Walsh, MacMillan, & Jamieson, 2002). Furthermore, these neighborhood and family level risks are typically comorbid.

Cumulative risk factors impact parents and their capacity to parent (Lynch & Cicchetti, 1998). Trentacosta et al. (2008) found that nurturing parenting mediated the relationship between cumulative risk and child externalizing problems. Cumulative risk was negatively correlated with nurturing parenting and this influence on parenting was the mechanism through which cumulative risk influenced child outcomes. Clearly, there is a complex interplay among multilevel factors which influence parenting, risk of maltreatment, and the development of disruptive behavior problems. As described below, BPT seeks to enhance emotional aspects of parent–child relationships; this includes nurturing. The findings of Trentacosta et al. (2008) strengthen the assertion that BPT is an auspicious intervention to reduce child behavior problems with families contending with cumulative risk factors, such as those within the child welfare system.

Coercion Theory

Coercion theory, as a way to understand child aggressive behavior within the broader environmental context, fits well within the ecological-transactional framework. This theory postulates that environment and social conditions result in between-individual differences in aggressive behavior (Snyder, 1995). Sequences of negative parent–child interaction and behavioral reinforcement by the parent contribute to the development and maintenance of conduct problems (Coie & Dodge, 1998; Patterson, 1995; Reid, Patterson, & Synder, 2002). The coercive process involves action–reaction patterns comprised of three steps: (*a*) parent directs child to stop an undesirable behavior (e.g., temper tantrum) or to engage in a behavior (i.e., pick up the toys), (*b*) child escalates behavior, and (*c*) parent surrenders (Cummings, Davies, & Campbell, 2000). The child's coercive behaviors are functional in that the child avoids punishment, gains attention, or otherwise gets his or her desires met (e.g., the candy bar at the grocery store) (Snyder & Stoolmiller, 2002). Furthermore, the reinforcement of the behavior inherent in this process operates to shape and maintain coercive behavior (Snyder, 1995). Fortunately, coercive patterns are malleable (Snyder & Stoolmiller, 2002) and BPT seeks to disrupt these patterns.

Need for Intervention to Prevent Exacerbation of Child Behavior Problems

Intervention is necessary to disrupt negative sequences of parent–child interaction. Children with disruptive behavior problems are at further risk to develop conduct disorder, and engage in delinquent behavior (Dodge et al., 1990; Loeber et al., 2005; Mersky & Reynolds, 2007), and have juvenile court involvement (Jonson-Reid, 2002, 2004; Jonson-Reid & Barth, 2000). For some children, adverse outcomes extend into adulthood. Childhood victimization is associated with violent offending in both adolescence and young adulthood (Loeber et al., 2005; Rivera & Widom, 1990; Thornberry, Ireland, & Smith, 2001), and maltreated children are twice as likely to be diagnosed with antisocial personality disorder in adulthood (Lutz & Widom, 1994) compared to non-maltreated children. Age at childhood victimization contributes to the development of problem behaviors (Thornberry et al., 2001) and children with earlier onset of delinquent and violent behavior are more likely to continue offending into adulthood than youth whose pattern of delinquency begins later (Coie & Dodge, 1998). The trajectory from childhood behavior problems to adult criminality and violent behaviors should be disrupted as early as possible, when behavior patterns are most malleable (Tremblay, 2006).

Unfortunately, child behavior problems often go untreated and very few children receive evidence-based interventions (Burns et al., 2004). There is, however, a growing recognition that children's mental health services need to be integrated into the settings where children receive other services—such as school and child welfare settings (Burns et al., 1995). Integrating appropriate and evidence-based mental health services into these other settings is perhaps the most promising strategy to assure that children receive the services needed to treat disruptive behavioral problems that often have lifelong consequence.

Evidence-based Parent Training and the Child Welfare System

Parent training is usual care within the child welfare system. A national survey revealed that parent training is included as a component of child welfare case plans in at least half of all cases served by county agencies (Hurlburt, Barth, Leslie, Landsverk, & McCrae, 2007). Evidence-based parenting programs are, however, rarely provided. Hurlburt et al. (2007) found that the five most commonly used parent training programs in child welfare were Active Parenting, Nurturing Parenting, Systematic Training for Effective Parenting (STEP), Parents as Teachers, and Tough Love. There was little evidence that the parent mediated interventions with the highest levels of empirical support were used. Incredible Years (1.4 percent) and Parent–Child Interaction Therapy (PCIT) (0.2 percent) were rarely used; Positive Parenting Program (Triple P) was not mentioned by any of the respondents. A review of several parent training programs and their applicability to child welfare also revealed that services typically provided lack empirical support, as well as applicability to a child welfare population (Barth et al., 2005).

Behavioral Parent Training Interventions

The reduction of early behavior problems is critical to improving long term outcomes for children in the child welfare system. Behavioral parent training—interventions where parents' behaviors are targeted for change—are the most empirically supported means to intervene to reduce child behavior problems (Weisz & Gray, 2008). Three parent training programs are consistently held up in the empirical literature as the gold standard in BPT: Triple P (Sanders, Markie-Dadds, &

Turner, 2003), PCIT (Eyberg et al., 2001), and Incredible Years (Reid & Webster-Stratton, 2001). Each has demonstrated empirical superiority over usual care or benign attention control conditions. Furthermore, the California Evidence-Based Clearinghouse for Child Welfare, which is a resource to identify evidence-based practices relevant to child welfare, gives each its highest ratings for scientific support of their effectiveness (see www.cebc4cw.org for additional information).

While each model has unique and distinguishing characteristics, similarities across models are clearly evident. First, each is grounded in social learning theory (Hurlburt et al., 2007). Second, therapeutic content is consistent across interventions (Garland, Hawley, Brookman-Frazee, & Hurlburt, 2008; Hurlburt et al., 2007). Parenting is a two pronged construct. One domain of parenting is control (related to discipline and monitoring), the other is emotional relationship (Cummings et al., 2000). BPT targets both. Parents are taught ways to change their interactions with their children and respond to disruptive behaviors in more positive ways. Each intervention trains parents in similar concepts, such as praise and reward to increase desired behavior, and non-violent discipline techniques such as ignoring or timeout to reduce undesired, challenging behaviors (Hurlburt et al., 2007). Additionally, the parent–child relationship is a focus of the intervention (Weisz & Gray, 2008). Third, service delivery strategies are analogous (Garland et al., 2008). Parents are given the opportunity to practice and refine the use of new techniques and homework assignments are a common element (Hurlburt et al., 2007; Kazdin, 2005). Each intervention also employs detailed materials to ensure fidelity to the model, and has built in evaluation techniques (Hurlburt et al., 2007).

Triple P

Triple P is a continuum of parent support and training that was developed over thirty years ago in Australia by Matt Sanders and his colleagues (Sanders et al., 2003). It provides parent management training techniques at different levels of intensity ranging from universal prevention (level 1) to indicated treatment (level 5). Level 4 Triple P is behavioral parent training which can be delivered in a group format or individually via home visits. Many studies of level 4 Triple P using a variety of research designs (e.g., experimental, quasi-experimental, and case studies) have been reported in the literature (Nowak & Heinrichs, 2008). Triple P has demonstrated efficacy; parenting practices have improved and disruptive behavior problems have declined and gains have been maintained (Bodenmann, Cina, Ledermann, & Sanders, 2008; Leung, Sanders, Leung, Mak, & Lau, 2003; Zubrick et al., 2005). Moreover, Triple P is beneficial with multiple parent populations, including parents of children with early onset conduct disorder, parents at risk of child maltreatment, depressed mothers, and parents experiencing marital conflict (Sanders, Markie-Dadds, Tully, & Bor, 2000; Sanders & McFarland, 2000; Sanders et al., 2003). The effectiveness of Triple P at improving parenting and reducing behavior problems has not yet been tested with a child welfare population. However, results from a small pilot study of level 5 Triple P suggest a good fit between the intervention and the system of care (Petra & Kohl, 2010). Level 5 Triple P is comprised of the level 4 BPT intervention, plus add-on modules that address parental anger, challenge negative parental attributes, and help parents identify the effect of harsh disciple on their children.

Parent–child Interaction Therapy

PCIT, developed by Sheila Eyberg, uses a two-staged approach to intervene with parents and children together (Eyberg et al., 2001). During both stages parents are observed and coached by a therapist as they play with their child. Stage 1, child directed intervention, is focused on building the emotional relationship between the parent and child. Stage 2, parent directed intervention, teaches parents to discipline children consistently and positively. PCIT has a wealth of evidence supporting its efficacy; it has a demonstrated capacity to enhance parent–child interactions and reduce child behavior problems (Eisenstadt, Eyberg, McNeil, Newcomb, & Funderburk, 1993; Eyberg, Boggs, & Algina, 1995; Schuhmann, Foote, Eyberg, Boggs, & Algina, 1998). Positive treatment effects have been maintained for multiple years following intervention (Eyberg et al., 2001; Hood & Eyberg, 2003). Emerging evidence also suggests that PCIT can reduce child behavior problems with maltreating parent–child dyads (Timmer, Urquiza, Zebell, & McGrath, 2005).

Incredible Years

The Incredible Years was developed by Carolyn Webster-Stratton and is a video-based training series with programs for parents, teachers, and children. It is delivered in a group format. Incredible Years has demonstrated success at increasing nurturing parenting, decreasing harsh parenting, and reducing child conduct problems (Webster-Stratton, 1998; Webster-Stratton & Hammond, 1997; Webster-Stratton, Reid & Hammond, 2004). Long term treatment effects have also been established (Drugli, Larsson, Fossum, & Morch, 2009).

Recent efforts are being undertaken to empirically test the effectiveness of Incredible Years with families in the child welfare system. A pilot study in which Incredible Years was delivered to parents in this system found that mothers who attended the training reported decreased levels of parental stress and reduced child behavior problems (Webster-Stratton & Reid, 2010). Knowledge of who benefits from an intervention is important information to glean and Incredible Years has been found to be equally useful for advantaged and disadvantaged families (Gardner, Hutchings, Bywater, & Whitaker, 2010). This reinforces that this is a relevant intervention for the child welfare population.

BPT and Maltreatment Prevention

Taken together, the research suggests that BPT can, or at least has the potential to, improve parenting and reduce behavior problems within the child welfare system. Whether or not BPT can prevent maltreatment recidivism is less clear. The BPT interventions reviewed above were developed to provide parents with the tools they need to deal with their children's behavior problems and were not developed with the intended objective of preventing child maltreatment or maltreatment recidivism (Barth, 2009). There is some indication, however, that maltreatment prevention may be an outcome of BPT.

A randomized control trial was conducted to determine if PCIT could prevent maltreatment recidivism (Chaffin et al., 2004). One hundred and ten parent–child dyads participated in the study; they were recruited upon entry into a child welfare system following confirmed physical abuse. Over the course of an approximate two year follow-up period, 19 percent of dyads in the treatment group compared to 49 percent of dyads in the comparison group, who received group-based standard care, had re-reports for physical abuse. This is promising evidence that PCIT can prevent maltreatment recidivism.

Promising evidence of Triple P's capacity to prevent maltreatment is also available. A randomized control trial of the Triple P system (i.e., included all five levels of Triple P) in 18 South Carolina counties demonstrated positive, large effects on three population-level indicators: substantiated child maltreatment, foster care placements, and maltreatment injuries (Prinz, Sanders, Shapiro, Whitaker, & Lutzker, 2009). Rates for each outcome were significantly lower in the treatment counties compared to the control counties. Post-intervention, rates of substantiated maltreatment cases per 1,000 children were 11.74 in the Triple P counties compared to 15.06 in the control counties. Rates of foster care placement per 1,000 children were 3.75 in the Triple P counties compared to 4.46 in the control counties. Rates of child maltreatment injuries per 1,000 children were 1.41 in the Triple P counties compared to 1.69 in the control counties.

Conclusion

The following facts provide strong arguments for the implementation of BPT interventions within child welfare settings: (*a*) child welfare systems serve large numbers of maltreated children with or at risk of developing disruptive behavior problems; (*b*) these disruptive behavior problems can carry lifelong consequences and put society at risk of violent crime; and (*c*) efficacious BPT interventions are available for preventing and treating these problems. While families who have contact with child welfare agencies are often contending with a multitude of problems and challenges that may not be reflective of families with whom the evidence-based parent training interventions were first tested, the overall aims of parent training are likely similar—enhanced parenting and improved child behavior (Hurlburt et al., 2007). Early evidence suggests that despite potential differences in the populations BPT may be able achieve similar treatment effects on these outcomes for abusive and non-abusive parents.

Despite the potential for successful outcomes, additional efforts are necessary before large scale implementation of BPT occurs within this system of care. Further evidence of effectiveness of BPT with this population and in this service setting are necessary to validate this small, but emerging, body of literature on BPT in child welfare. Research establishing the efficacy of interventions is conducted in highly controlled settings; treatments effects may be smaller or nonexistent when the intervention is provided within a "real world" child welfare system. As recommended by Barth (2009), effectiveness studies are necessary.

Given the complex interplay of family and environmental risks that abusive parents and abused children present with to child welfare systems, a better understanding is needed about for who and under what conditions BPT interventions are effective. BPT has actually been shown to reduce maternal depression (Hutchings, Appleton, Smith, Lane, & Nash, 2002; Kaminski, Valle, Filene, & Boyle, 2008; Lundal, & Harris, 2006; McCart, Priester, Davies, & Azen, 2006; Zubrick et al., 2005). Furthermore, changes in depression predict future changes in parenting (Patterson, DeGarmo, & Forgatch, 2004). This ability to alleviate depression and the influence that this mitigation has in achieving desired outcomes seems particularly relevant because of the high prevalence of maternal depression among the child welfare population. One in five (21 percent) of women who enter this system meet the diagnostic criteria for major depressive episode (Kohl, Kagotho, & Dixon, 2011). However, does BPT work equally for parents with and without substance abuse histories, or intimate partner violence, or community violence? What about comorbid conditions that are common in these families?

Knowledge about the capacity of BPT to prevent child maltreatment and maltreatment recidivism is even more scant. Child safety and prevention of abuse and neglect are the ultimate aims of child welfare services; hence, building the evidence base in support of their ability to target these outcomes, in addition to parenting and child behavior outcomes, should be a priority.

References

Barth, R. P. (2009). Preventing child abuse and neglect with parent training: Evidence and opportunities. *Future of Children, 19*(2), 95–118.

Barth, R. P., Landsverk, J., Chamberlain, P., Reid, J. B., Rolls, J. A., Hurlurt, M., & Kohl, P. S. (2005). Parent-training programs in child welfare services: Planning for a more evidenced-based approach to serving biological parents. *Research on Social Work Practice, 15*(5), 353–371. doi:10.1177/1049731505276321

Barth, R. P., Wildfire, J., & Green, R. (2006). Placement into foster care and the interplay of urbanicity, child behavior problems, and poverty. *American Journal of Orthopsychiatry, 76*(3), 358–366. doi:10.1037/0002-9432.76.3.358

Bender, H. L., Allen, J. P., McElhaney, K. B., Antonishak, J., Moore, C. M., Kelly, H., & Davis, S. O. (2007). Use of harsh physical discipline and developmental outcomes in adolescence. *Development and Psychopathology, 19*(1), 227–242.

Bodenmann, G., Cina, A., Ledermann, T., & Sanders, M. R. (2008). The efficacy of the Triple P—Positive Parenting Program in improving parenting and child behavior: A comparison with two other treatment conditions. *Behaviour Research & Therapy, 46*(4), 411–427. doi:10.1016/j.brat.2008.01.001

Bugental, D., & Johnston, C. B. (2000). Parental and child cognitions in the context of the family. *Annual Review of Psychology, 51*, 315–344. doi:10.1146/annurev.psych.51.1.315

Burns, B. J., Costello, E. J., Angold, A., Tweed, D., Stangle, D., Farmer, E., & Erkanli, A. (1995). Children's mental health services across sectors. *Health Affairs, 14*(3), 147–159.

Burns, B. J., Phillips, S. D., Wagner, H. R., Barth, R. P., Kolko, D. J., Campbell, Y., & Landsverk, J. (2004). Mental health need and access to mental health services by youth involved with child welfare: A national survey. *Journal of the American Academy of Child and Adolescent Psychiatry, 43*(8), 960–970. doi:10.1097/01.chi.0000127590.95585.65

Chaffin, M., Kelleher, K., & Hollenberg, J. (1996). Onset of physical abuse and neglect: Psychiatric, substance abuse, and social risk factors from prospective community data. *Child Abuse & Neglect, 20*(3), 191–203. doi:10.1016/S0145-2134(95)00144-1

Chaffin, M., Silovsky, J., Funderburk, B., Valle, L., Brestan, E., Balachova, T., & Bonner, B. (2004). Parent-child interaction therapy with physically abusive parents: Efficacy for reducing future abuse reports. *Journal of Consulting and Clinical Psychology, 72*(3), 500–510. doi:10.1037/0022-006X.72.3.500

Cicchetti, D., & Toth, S. L. (2005). Child maltreatment. *Annual Review of Clinical Psychology, 1*, 409–438. doi:10.1146/annurev.clinpsy.1.102803.144029

Coie, J. D., & Dodge, K. A. (1998). Aggression and antisocial behavior. In W. Damon & N. Eisenberg (Eds), *Handbook of child psychology* (5th ed., Vol. 3: Social, Emotional, and Personality Development, pp. 779–862). New York: John Wiley & Sons, Inc.

Coulton, C., Korbin, J., Su, M., & Chow, J. (1995). Community level factors and child maltreatment rates. *Child Development, 66*(5), 1262–1276. doi:10.1111/j.1467-8624.1995.tb00934.x

Cummings, E. M., Davies, P. T., & Campbell, S. B. (2000). *Developmental psychopathology and family process: Theory, research and clinical implications.* New York: Guilford Press.

Dodge, K. A., Bates, J. E., & Pettit, G. S. (1990). Mechanisms in the cycle of violence. *Science, 250*(4988), 1678–1683. doi:10.1126/science.2270481

Dornbusch, S. M., Ritter, P. L., Leiderman, P. H., Roberts, D. F., & Fraleigh, M. J. (1987). The relation of parenting style to adolescent school performance. *Child Development, 58*(5), 1244–1257.

Drake, B., Jonson-Reid, M., Way, I., & Chung, S. (2003). Substantiation and recidivism. *Child Maltreatment, 8*(4), 248–260. doi:10.1177/1077559503258930

Drugli, M. B., Larsson, B., Fossum, S., and Morch, W. (2009). Five- to six-year outcome and its prediction for children with ODD/CD treated with parent training. *Journal of Child Psychology and Psychiatry 51*(5), 559–566. doi:10.1111/j.1469-7610.2009.02178.x

Dumas, J., & Wahler, F. G. (1985). Indiscriminate mothering as a contextual factor in aggressive-oppositional child behavior: "Damned if you do and damned if you don't." *Journal of Child Psychology, 13*(1), 1–17. doi:10.1007/BF00918368

Eisenstadt, T. H., Eyberg, S., McNeil, C. B., Newcomb, K., & Funderburk, B. (1993). Parent-child interaction therapy with behavior problem children: Relative effectiveness of two stages and overall treatment outcome. *Journal of Clinical Child Psychology, 22*(1), 42–51. doi:10.1207/s15374424jccp2201_4

Erickson, M. F., & Egeland, B. (2002). Child neglect. In J. Myers, L. Berliner, J. Briere, C. Hendrix, C. Jenny, & T. Reid (Eds), *The APSAC handbook on child maltreatment* (2nd ed., pp. 3–20). Thousand Oaks, CA: SAGE.

Eyberg, S. M., Boggs, S. R., Algina, J. (1995). Parent-child interaction therapy—A psychosocial model for the treatment of young children with conduct problem behavior and their families. *Psychopharmacology Bulletin, 31,* 83–91.

Eyberg, S. M., Funderburk, B. W., Hembree-Kigin, T. L., McNeil, C. B., Querido, J. G., & Hood, K. K. (2001). Parent-child interaction therapy with behavior problem children: One and two year maintenance of treatment effects in the family. *Child & Family Behavior Therapy, 23*(4), 1–20.

Flisher, A. J., Kramer, R. A., Hoven, C. W., Greenwald, S., Alegria, M., Bird, H., & Moore, R. E. (1997). Psychosocial characteristics of physically abused children and adolescents. *Journal of the American Academy of Child & Adolescent Psychiatry, 36*(1), 123–131. doi:10.1097/00004583-199701000-00026

Gardner, F., Hutchings, J., Bywater, T., & Whitaker, C. (2010). Who benefits and how it works? Moderators and mediators of outcome in an effectiveness trial of a parenting intervention. *Journal of Clinical Child & Adolescent Psychology, 39*(4), 568–580. doi:10.1080/15374416.2010.486315

Garland, A. F., Hawley, K. M., Brookman-Frazee, L., & Hurlburt, M. S. (2008). Identifying common elements of evidence-based psychosocial treatments for children's disruptive behavior problems. *Journal of the American Academy of Child and Adolescent Psychiatry, 47*(5), 505–514. doi:10.1097/CHI.0b013e31816765c2

Hood, K. K., & Eyberg, S. M. (2003). Outcomes of parent-child interaction therapy: Mothers' reports of maintenance three to six years after treatment. *Journal of Clinical Child and Adolescent Psychology, 32*(3), 419–429. doi:10.1207/S15374424JCCP3203_10

Hurlburt, M. S., Barth, R. P., Leslie, L. K., Landsverk, J. A., & McCrae, J. (2007). Building on strengths: Current status and opportunities for improvement of parent training for families in child welfare. In R. Haskins & F. Wulczyn (Eds), *Using research to improve policy and practice* (pp. 81–106). Washington, DC: Brookings Institution Press.

Hutchings, J., Appleton, P., Smith, M., Lane, E., & Nash, S. (2002). Evaluation of two treatments for children with severe behavior problems: Child behavior and maternal mental health outcomes. *Behavioural and Cognitive Psychotherapy, 30*(3), 279–295. doi:10.1017/S1352465802003041

Jonson-Reid, M. (2002). Exploring the relationship between child welfare intervention and juvenile corrections involvement. *American Journal of Orthopsychiatry, 72*(4), 559–576. doi:10.1037/0002-9432.72.4.559

———. (2004). Child welfare services and delinquency: The need to know more. *Child Welfare, 83*(2), 157–172.

Jonson-Reid, M., & Barth, R. (2000). From maltreatment report to juvenile incarceration: The role of child welfare services. *Child Abuse & Neglect, 24,* 505–520.

Jonson-Reid, M., Drake, B., & Kohl, P. (2009). Is the overrepresentation of the poor in child welfare caseloads due to bias or need? *Children and Youth Services Review, 31*(3), 422–427. doi:10.1016/j.childyouth.2008.09.009

Kaminski, J., Valle, L., Filene, J., & Boyle, C. (2008). A meta-analytic review of components associated with parent training program effectiveness. *Journal of Abnormal Child Psychology, 36*(4), 567–589. doi:10.1007/s10802-007-9201-9

Kaplan, S. J., Pelcovitz, D., Salzinger, S., Weiner, M., Mandel, F. S., Lesser, M. L., & Labruna, V. E. (1998). Adolescent physical abuse: Risk for adolescent psychiatric disorders. *American Journal of Psychiatry 155*(7), 954–959.

Kazdin, A. E. (2005). *Parent management training: Treatment for oppositional, aggressive, and antisocial behavior in child and adolescents.* New York: Oxford University Press.

Kohl, P. L., & Barth, R. P. (2007). Child maltreatment recurrence among children remaining in-home: Predictors of re-reports. In R. Haskins & F. Wulczyn (Eds), *Using research to improve policy and practice* (pp. 207–225). Washington, DC: Brookings Institution Press.

Kohl, P., Barth, R., Hazen, A., & Landsverk, J. (2005). Child welfare as a gateway to domestic violence services. *Children and Youth Services Review, 27*(11), 1203-1221. doi:10.1016/j.childyouth.2005.04.005

Kohl, P., Kagotho, N., & Dixon, D. (2011). Parenting behaviors among depressed mothers in the child welfare system. *Social Work Research.*

Lahey, B., Flagg, E., Bird, H., Schwab-Stone, M., Canino, G., Dulcan, M., & Regier, D. (1996). The NIMH methods for the epidemiology of child and adolescent mental disorders (MECA) study: Background and methodology. *Journal of the American Academy of Child & Adolescent Psychiatry, 35*(7), 855–864. doi:10.1097/00004583-199607000-00011

Leung, C., Sanders, M., Leung, S., Mak, R., & Lau, J. (2003). An outcome evaluation of the implementation of the triple P—positive parenting program in Hong Kong. *Family Process, 42*(4), 531–544.

Loeber, R., Pardini, D., Homish, D. L., Wei, E. H., Farrington, D. P., Creemers, J., & Rosenfeld, R. (2005). The prediction of violence and homicide in young men. *Journal of Consulting and Clinical Psychology, 73*(6), 1074–1088. doi:10.1037/0022-006X.73.6.1074

Lundal, B., & Harris, N. (2006). Delivering parent training to families at risk to abuse: Lessons from three meta-analyses. *The APSAC Advisor, 18*(3), 7–11.

Lutz, B. K., & Widom, C. S. (1994). Antisocial personality disorder in abused and neglected children grown up. *American Journal of Psychiatry, 151*(5), 670–674.

Lynch, M., & Cicchetti, D. (1998). An ecological-transactional analysis of children and contexts: The longitudinal interplay among maltreatment, community violence, and children's symptomatology. *Development and Psychopathology, 10*(2), 253–257.

McCart, M. R., Priester, P. E., Davies, W. H., & Azen, R. (2006). Differential effectiveness of behavioral parent-training and cognitive-behavioral therapy for antisocial youth: A meta-analysis. *Journal of Abnormal Child Psychology, 34*(4), 527–543. doi:10.1007/s10802-006-9031-1

McGuinness, T., & Schnieder, K. (2007). Poverty, child maltreatment, and foster care. *Journal of the American Psychiatric Nurses Association, 13*(5), 296–303. doi:10.1177/1078390307308421

Mersky, J. P., & Reynolds, A. J. (2007). Child maltreatment and violent delinquency: Disentangling main effects and subgroup effects. *Child Maltreatment, 12*(3), 246–258. doi:10.1177/1077559507301842

Nowak, C., & Heinrichs, N. (2008). A comprehensive meta-analysis of triple P—positive parenting program using hierarchical linear modeling: Effectiveness and moderating variables. *Clinical Child and Family Psychology Review, 11*(3), 114–144. doi: 10.1007/s10567-008-0033-0

Patterson, G. R. (1995). Coercion as a basis for early age of onset for arrest. In J. McCord (Ed.), *Coercion and punishment in long-term perspective* (pp. 81–105). New York: Cambridge University Press.

———. (2002). The early development of coercive family process. In J. B. Reid (Ed.). *Antisocial behavior in children and adolescents: A developmental analysis and model for intervention* (pp. 25–44). Washington DC: American Psychological Association.

Patterson, G. R., DeGarmo, D., & Forgatch, M. S. (2004). Systematic changes in families following prevention trials. *Journal of Abnormal Child Psychology, 32*(6), 621–633. doi:10.1023/B:JACP.0000047211.11826.54

Pecora, P. J., Whittaker, J. K., Maluccio, A. N., Barth, R., & Plotnick, R. (2000). *The child welfare challenge* (2nd ed.). New York: Aldine de Gruyter.

Petra, M., & Kohl, P. L. (2010). Pathways triple P and the child welfare system: A promising fit. *Children and Youth Services Review, 32*(4), 611–618. doi:10.1016/j.childyouth.2009.12.008

Prinz, R. J., Sanders, M. R., Shapiro, C. J., Whitaker, D. J., & Lutzker, J. R. (2009). Population-based prevention of child maltreatment: The U.S. triple P system population trial. *Prevention Science, 10*(1), 1–12. doi:10.1007/s11121-009-0123-3

Reid, J. B., Patterson, G. R., & Synder, J. (2002). *Antisocial behavior in children and adolescents: A developmental analysis and model for intervention*. Washington, DC: American Psychological Association.

Reid, M. J., & Webster-Stratton, C. (2001). The Incredible Years parent, teacher, and child intervention: Targeting multiple areas of risk for a young child with pervasive conduct problems using a flexible, manualized, treatment program. *Journal of Cognitive and Behavior Practice, 8*(4), 377–386. doi:10.1016/S1077-7229(01)80011-0

Rivera, B., & Widom, C. (1990). Childhood victimization and violent offending. *Violence and Victims, 5*(1), 19–35.

Sanders, M., Markie-Dadds, C., Tully, L., & Bor, B. (2000). The triple P—positive parenting program: A comparison of enhanced, standard and self-directed behavioral family intervention for parents of children with early onset conduct problems. *Journal of Consulting and Clinical Psychology, 68*(4), 624–640.

Sanders, M. R., Markie-Dadds, C., & Turner, K. M. T. (2003). Theoretical, scientific and clinical foundations of the triple P—positive parenting program: A population approach to the promotion of parenting competence. *Parenting Research and Practice Monograph No. 1.* Retrieved from http://www.triplep.net/files/pdf/Parenting_Research_and_Practice_Monograph_No.1.pdf

Sanders, M. R., & McFarland, M. L. (2000). The treatment of depressed mothers with disruptive children: A controlled evaluation of cognitive behavioral family intervention. *Behaviour Therapy, 31*(1), 89–112. doi:10.1016/S0005-7894(00)80006-4

Scannapieco, M., & Connell-Carrick, K. (2005). *Understanding child maltreatment: An ecological and developmental perspective.* New York: Oxford University Press.

Schuhmann, E. M., Foote, R. C., Eyberg, S. M., Boggs, S. R., & Algina, J. (1998). Efficacy of parent-child interaction therapy: Interim report of a randomized trial with short-term maintenance. *Journal of Clinical Child Psychology, 27*(1), 34–45. doi:10.1207/s15374424jccp2701_4

Shepard, M., & Raschick, M. (1999). How child welfare workers assess and intervene around issues of domestic violence. *Child Maltreatment, 4,* 148–156.

Smith, C. A., Ireland, T. O., & Thornberry, T. P. (2005). Adolescent maltreatment and its impact on young adult antisocial behavior. *Child Abuse & Neglect, 29*(10), 1099–1119. doi:10.1016/j.chiabu.2005.02.011

Snyder, J. (1995). Coercion: A two-level theory of antisocial behavior. In W. T. O'Donohue & L. Krasner (Eds), *Theories of behavior therapy: Exploring behavior change* (pp. 313–348). Washington DC: American Psychological Association.

Snyder, J., & Stoolmiller, M. (2002). Reinforcement and coercion mechanisms in the development of antisocial behavior. In J. B. Reid, G. R. Patterson, & J. J. Snyder (Eds), *Antisocial behavior in children and adolescents: A developmental analysis and model for intervention* (pp. 65–100). Washington DC: American Psychological Association.

Thornberry, T. P., Ireland, T. O., & Smith, C. A. (2001). The importance of timing: The varying impact of childhood and adolescent maltreatment on multiple problem outcomes. *Development & Psychopathology, 13*(4), 957–979.

Timmer, S. G., Urquiza, A. J., Zebell, N. M., & McGrath, J. M. (2005). Parent-child interaction therapy: Application to maltreating parent-child dyads. *Child Abuse & Neglect, 29*(7), 825–842. doi:10.1016/j.chiabu.2005.01.003

Tremblay, R. E. (2006). Prevention of youth violence: Why not start at the beginning? *Journal of Abnormal Child Psychology, 34*(4), 481–487.

Trentacosta, C. J., Hyde, L. W., Shaw, D. S., Dishion, T. J., Gardner, F., & Wilson, M. (2008). The relations among cumulative risk, parenting and behavior problems during early childhood. *Journal of Child Psychology and Psychiatry, 49,* 1211–1219. doi:10.1111/j.1469-7610.2008.01941.x

U. S. Department of Health and Human Services, Administration for Children and Families. (2005). *National survey of child and adolescent well-being: Children involved with the child welfare services (Baseline Report).* Washington, DC: U.S. Department of Health and Human Services, Administration for Children and Families

———. (2010). *Child Maltreatment 2009.* Washington, DC: U.S. Government Printing Office.

Wahler, R. G., Williams, A. J., & Cerezo, A. (1990). The compliance and predictability hypothesis: Sequential and correlational analyses of coercive mother-child interactions. *Behavioral Assessment, 12,* 391–407.

Walsh, C., MacMillan, H., & Jamieson, E. (2002). The relationship between parental psychiatric disorder and child physical and sexual abuse: Findings from the Ontario Health Supplement. *Child Abuse & Neglect, 26*(2), 11–22.

Webb, M. B., & Harden, B. J. (2003). Beyond child protection: Promoting mental health for children and families in the child welfare system. *Journal of Emotional and Behavioral Disorders, 11*(1), 49–58. doi:10.1177/106342660301100107

Webster-Stratton, C. (1998). Preventing conduct problems in Head Start children: Strengthening parenting competencies. *Journal of Consulting and Clinical Psychology, 66*(5), 715–730.

Webster-Stratton, C., & Hammond, M. (1997). Treating children with early-onset conduct problems: A comparison of child and parent training interventions. *Journal of Consulting and Clinical Psychology, 65*, 93–109.

Webster-Stratton, C., & Reid, M. J. (2010). Adapting the Incredible Years, an evidence-based parenting program, for families involved in the child welfare system. *Journal of Children's Services, 5*(1), 25–42. doi:10.5042/jcs.2010.0115

Webster-Stratton, C., Reid, J. M., & Hammond, M. (2004). Treating children with early-onset conduct problems: Intervention outcomes for parent, child, and teacher training. *Journal of Clinical Child and Adolescent Psychology, 33*(1), 105–124. doi: 10.1207/S15374424JCCP3301_11

Weiss, B., Dodge, K. A., Pettit, G. S., & Bates, J. E. (1992). Some consequences of early harsh discipline: Child aggression, and a maladaptive social information processing style, *Child Development, 63*(6) 1321–1335. doi:10.1111/j.1467-8624.1992.tb01697.x

Weisz, J., & Gray, J. (2008). Evidence-based psychotherapy for children and adolescents: Data from the present and a model for the future. *Child and Adolescent Mental Health, 13*(2), 54–65. doi:10.1111/j.1475-3588.2007.00475.x

Widom, C. S. (1989). Child abuse, neglect, and adult behavior: Research design and findings on criminality, violence, and child abuse. *American Journal of Orthopsychiatry, 59*(3), 355–367. doi:10.1111/j.1939-0025.1989.tb01671.x

Zubrick, S. R., Ward, K. A., Silburn, S. R., Lawrence, D., Williams, A. A., Blair, E., & Sanders, M. (2005). Prevention of child behavior problems through universal implementation of a group behavioral family intervention. *Prevention Science, 6*(4), 287–304. doi:10.1007/s11121-005-0013-2

12

From Institutionalization to Family Settings: Rethinking Practices for Children and Youth with Mental Disabilities in Brazil

Irene Rizzini
Neli de Almeida

Institutionalization of Children and Youth with Disabilities

This chapter is based on a research project[1] which focused on children and adolescents with mental disabilities who are provided care by the State of Rio de Janeiro shelter system. The practice of placing children[2] in closed institutions has been strongly condemned in Brazil in the past few decades, particularly after the Statute on the Child and the Adolescent was approved in 1990 (Rizzini, 2007). According to Article 19 of the Statute which states that all children have the right to grow up in a family and community setting, as well as recent policy guidelines, every effort is to be made to avoid separating children from their homes. Due to these new guidelines, most of the large institutions for children have been closed down in Brazil and have been replaced by the "sistema de abrigos" or shelter system, composed of establishments designed to accommodate approximately 30 children for a short period of time. However, many children end up staying for years, often due to family lack of financial resources. This is particularly true for children with disabilities. This chapter examines the following four questions about these young people. Who are they and where do they live? What are the consequences of long-term stay in institutions? What are the possibilities for reuniting them with their families? How are these children with mental

---

[1] Carried out in 2006–2007 by CIESPI—The International Center for Research and Policy on Childhood, in association with the Pontifical Catholic University of Rio de Janeiro (PUC-Rio), selected by Notice MCT-CNPq/MS-SCTIE-DECIT/CT-Saúde 07/2005 (CNPq—The National Research Council and the Ministry of Health) (Rizzini, 2008).

[2] The use of the word "children" in this chapter refers to the age group 0–18 years and therefore encompasses adolescents as well.

disabilities referred to various services? Based on these questions, we examine the possibilities for keeping children out of institutions in more nurturing settings in the context of their right to be kept as far as possible in family and community settings. This survey was the first of its kind and therefore a critical first step for shaping a rights-based public policy.

Characterizing the Concept of Disability

The concept of mental disability is characterized by complexities. These complexities are the result of: (*a*) the specialized discourse about disability in the fields of medicine, education, law, and social assistance (Lobo, 2008); (*b*) the particular differences between the medical and social models and the organic and non-organic models (Medeiros & Diniz, 2004); and (*c*) the historical development of the idea of mental disability including the notion of insanity and institutionalization as a "starting point" (Foucault, 2006).

For the purposes of this study, we use as reference the concept of disability defined by the World Health Organization in 1981, and approved by the United Nations in 1982, when the World Program of Action Concerning Disabled Persons was released. In this document, disability is defined as "any loss or abnormality of psychological, physiological, or anatomical structure or function, generating the inability to perform an activity in the manner or within the range considered normal for a human being."[3]

This definition was adopted by Brazilian law with the help of the National Coordinating Center for the Integration of People with Disability (*Coordenadoria Nacional para Integração das Pessoas com Deficiência—CORDE*) in Decree no. 3.298/99. It was ratified in the Brazilian National Policy for People with Disability (*Política Nacional da Pessoa Portadora de Deficiência*) in 2002. These policies classify the following types of disability: walking, hearing, visual, mental, and multiple (a combination of two or more types of disability).

Measuring Disability

We used data from the national census 2000 to determine the extent of disability in the Brazilian population.[4] Census 2000 adopted the new definition of disability (Medeiros & Diniz, 2004; Néri, 2003; Néri & Soares, 2004), according to which 14.5 percent of the Brazilian population[5]

---

[3]World Health Organization. United Nations 1981, 1982 (ONU, 1982).

[4]The Census is conducted by the Brazilian Institute of Geography and Statistics, Instituto Brasileiro de Geografia e Estatistica (IBGE).

[5]This percentage amounts to 24,600,000 Brazilians. The Census is the only extensive survey done in Brazil on people with disabilities in Brazil.

had some type of disability. In the state of Rio de Janeiro with a population of 14.4 million, 2.1 million were identified as having some type of disability. This number represents 14.8 percent of the Rio population, a percentage very close to the national percentage. Almost 190,000 children were identified as having some form of disability, 8.9 percent) of whom were identified as having a permanent mental disability (IBGE, 2000).

The new measure of disability had the effect of including more people in the category "disabled"—especially older people. The increase generated an important discussion about seeing disability less as an attribute of an individual or a group and more as a phenomenon related to the life cycle. Some believe that this re-measuring may result in a new awareness of the importance of public policies for services at each phase of the life cycle (Medeiros & Diniz, 2004; Néri, 2003).

Children with Disabilities in Shelters in the State of Rio de Janeiro

As a first result of the mapping carried out of the shelter system in the state of Rio de Janeiro, we identified two types of institutions, which we chose to call *special purpose shelters* (intended exclusively for children with disabilities) and *mixed shelters* (intended for children considered at-risk, but which also include those with disability).[6] When we started the research there were no existing lists of the shelters that comprise the shelter system. As there were no public records of these children, we used phone books, professional contacts, and other sources to develop a list of the shelters. We identified 106 separate shelters in the state of Rio de Janeiro (see Table 12.1). In those we estimated that they were able to accommodate 2,088 children with disabilities. Eighteen of the shelters we contacted did not report the number of vacancies they had. It must be added that the total number of vacancies mentioned is an approximate number, obtained over the phone rather than through visits. It was comparatively easy to find the specialized shelters for children because there were only 13, all of which we visited for our work. There were 112 target children in these shelters. The mixed shelters provided a greater challenge because once we had constructed a list we had to ascertain by phone call whether or not they had children with disabilities. We identified 93 mixed shelters that housed children with disabilities. We then chose the municipalities with the greatest number of children with disabilities and visited nine institutions in those municipalities with the highest number of target children. This second sample added up to 61 children.

---

[6]Even though shelters are designated to assist children and youth exclusively, we verified the existence of a significant number of adults in the surveyed institutions. It is possible that many of those individuals became adults while in those shelters. This is an important issue, which requires further research.

Table 12.1 Number of Shelters that Reported Caring for Children With or Without Disability, and Vacancies by Region in the State of Rio de Janeiro, 2006/2007

Region	No. of Institutions	Total Vacancies Reported*	Vacancies by Region (%)
Central-South Fluminense	4	127	6.1
Costa Verde	3	83	4.0
Baixadas Litorâneas	8	110	5.3
Médio Paraíba	10	227	10.9
Metropolitan	52	926	44.3
Northeast Fluminense	2	70	3.4
North Fluminense	8	255	12.2
Serrana	20	290	13.9
Total	106	2008	100.0

Source: From institutionalization to a family setting: Changing the practice of institutionalizing children and youth with disabilities in the State of Rio de Janeiro. Rio de Janeiro: CIESPI—CNPq/MS, 2008.
Note: *Nineteen institutions did not report the number of vacancies available.

Table 12.1 shows a large concentration of accommodation for children with disabilities in the metropolitan region (44 percent). This is due to the fact that this is the most densely populated region in the state. The Northeast Fluminense region has the lowest population density and the least number of shelters in the state. In both, special purpose shelters and mixed shelters, there was predominance of males and of children in the age group of 10–18 years (60 percent in the special purpose shelters and 56 percent in the mixed shelters). There were also more children of color than white children.[7] The majority of residents entered the shelter system in the same municipality where they were born, and a large number of children and youth remained in the shelter they first entered. A high percentage of residents were excluded from the formal school network. The exclusion is partly due to the severity of some residents' condition and partly due to a lack of effort to enroll them in regular schools. Children in the mixed shelters are more likely to attend a regular school with 77 percent of the sample cases attending such schools.[8]

---

[7] The questionnaire used to describe the shelter population had five types of variables: (*a*) demographic data, (*b*) socioeconomic data, (*c*) institutional data, (*d*) clinical data, and (*e*) data describing the degree of autonomy for residents.

[8] A similar pattern is reported in studies on children and youth without disability, in shelters or in the streets (IPEA/CONANDA, 2004; Rizzini et al., 2003).

Contrasts and Similarities

What most distinguishes the residents of the two types of shelter is the degree of disability rather than any demographic variable such as age or color. The specialized shelters admit children with severe neurological and psychiatric conditions. In the mixed shelters there are many children who have not been given a precise diagnosis. Another noticeable difference is that in the specialized shelters the residents come from families with fewer family members and with a lower reported incidence of disability and mental disorder. It is the families themselves that usually initiate the entry of the children into the shelter system, particularly those approaching adolescence. Families managed to keep their children at home for several years after the children's condition became noticeable, but at some point the parents were no longer able or willing to cope with the children. One of the main reasons recorded for the admission of children into a shelter was the family's lack of material resources. Other important reasons were lack of treatment alternatives, other sources of care for children, and the lack of support for the families. Although we do not focus in this article on the burdens parents face coping with disabled children, this is a major issue and deserves more study (Santos, 2003).

In mixed shelters there was a greater variation in the family backgrounds of residents. In contrast to the specialized institutions, residents in mixed shelters came from larger families, with a greater number of siblings in shelters and more reported cases of disability and mental disorder. For these children, placement was most often requested by the Guardianship Councils and the major reason was violation of the children's rights, in particular mistreatment and neglect.

Diagnosis, Degree of Disability, and Capacity

The questionnaire we used to examine the situation of each child in the shelters also included a set of question about the degree of functioning of each of the residents. We noted that in the specialized shelters more than half of the children exhibited the lowest levels of functioning. They did not communicate, did not move around or eat on their own and did not have bladder control. These children relied on the help of others for basic daily functions.

Only 10 children out of a total of 112 scored at the highest level on the autonomy scale which included the ability to clearly communicate verbally and intelligently, to walk normally, to feed themselves, to bathe themselves, to have bladder and bowel control, to dress themselves, to use the shelters' furniture and utensils properly, to participate in household chores spontaneously, and use personal and shelter objects appropriately. We discovered that 56, or about half of the children cared for in the specialized shelters, had not been given a diagnosis at the time they entered the shelter (see Table 12.2).

Table 12.2 Children with Disabilities in Specialized Shelters According to Most Frequently Registered Diagnosis 2007 (n = 10)

Main Diagnoses	Number	Percent
Childhood brain paralysis (severe childhood encephalopathy)	47	43.1
Non-specified mental retardation	19	17.4
Epilepsy	17	15.6
Non-specified psychological development disorder	13	11.9
Behavior disorder	13	11.9
Hydrocephaly	11	10.1
Paraplegia and tetraplegia	10	9.2
Moderate mental retardation	10	9.2
Severe mental retardation	10	9.2
Deep mental retardation	9	8.3
Specific motor developmental disorder	9	8.3
Microcephaly	8	7.3
Blindness and subnormal vision	7	6.4
Minor mental retardation	6	5.5

Source: From institutionalization to a family setting: Changing the practice of institutionalizing children and youth with disabilities in the State of Rio de Janeiro. Rio de Janeiro: CIESPI—CNPq/MS, 2008.

Among those who had some diagnosis recorded in their case records, 27 (24 percent) showed "severe childhood encephalopathy," classified for this study in accordance with ICD10[9] as "childhood brain paralysis" (either as a single diagnosis or associated with other diagnoses). The second most frequent diagnosis was non-specified mental retardation which was found in 11 cases (10 percent). Taking into account the entire period of institutionalization, at least 97.3 percent of those in shelters had at least one diagnosis. Only three residents had no diagnosis at all. Among those with diagnoses, there were 47 cases (43 percent) of infant cerebral palsy, 19 cases of non-specified mental retardation (17 percent) and 17 cases of epilepsy (16 percent).

The situation was quite different in the mixed shelters where the children were able to function independently as defined by the survey. In the mixed shelters, more than half of the sheltered

---

[9]The International Statistical Classification of Diseases and Related Health Problems—ICD 10, published by the World Health Organization (WHO), provides codes to classify diseases and a wide variety of signs, symptoms, abnormal findings, complaints, social circumstances, and external causes of injury or disease.

children (35 out of 61 children) had no diagnosis recorded in their case records. This suggests that excluding the two cases where no diagnosis was appropriate, only 24 children had at least one diagnosis registered in their case records for the entire period they were institutionalized. Amongst the children diagnosed, there were five cases of non-specified mental retardation, four cases of non-specified psychological development disorder, four cases of epilepsy and three cases of hearing loss due to transmission disorder and/or neurosensory hearing loss.

In the next section we discuss some of the issues that should be considered for drafting new public policies for this group of children.

Some Implications for Public Policy

The Long Stay of Children in Shelters

Some factors emerged from the survey as contributing to a long stay for children in shelters. They include: lack of financial resources, lack of access to benefits that could provide financial support and enable families to keep their children at home, and the gradual detachment of families from the institutionalized children as time spent at the shelter increased. We know that these factors are not exclusive to the children that we researched. However, these factors combined with the children's conditions of disability tended to prolong the children's stay in shelters.

The Statute on the Child and the Adolescent asserts that placing children and youth in shelters should be a temporary and exceptional measure. But our data show that for most of the children with disabilities in the shelter system in the state of Rio de Janeiro, their residency is far from temporary. In our sample, 42 percent of the children who were in specialized shelters had spent more than half of their lives in the shelter system. In the mixed shelters, more than half of the children (59 percent) had the same tenure.

Non-Utilization of Benefits by Families of Sheltered Children

Although lack of material resources is a major reason why children enter shelters, the financial resource offered by the Continuous Cash Benefit Program (*Benefício de Prestação Continuada—BPC*[10]) had been used by only eleven families (10 percent) in the specialized shelters and in four

---

[10]BRAZIL. Law N. 8.742, dated December 7, 1993. The BPC (Continuous Cash Benefit Program or *Benefício de Prestação Continuada*) is guaranteed by the Brazilian Federal Government. It consists of a monthly payment of one minimum salary (about US$283.) to the elderly and people with disability who are permanently incapacitated, to help them lead an independent life and to work, if they do not have the means to provide for their own maintenance or do not have it provided by their families.

families (7 percent) in mixed shelters. An examination of why this benefit is not being sought by more families who have children with disabilities is necessary.

Another question that needs to be examined but was not within the scope of this study is whether that benefit has, in fact, enabled some children with disability to stay at home with their families. We would expect that if more families availed of the benefit, more children could remain at home. This resource could also be used by families whose children had to be placed in shelters to defray family expenses incurred in visiting their children in the shelters.

As Time Goes by, Children's Connections to Their Families Loosen

Besides examining the question of why children with disabilities enter shelters, there is a concern about whether children's connections to the outside world—particularly with their families—are maintained or lost as their time in placement increases. Our study indicated that most of the children in the sample were being looked after by relatives at the time they entered the shelter system. Seventy-six percent of the children in specialized shelters and 74 percent in mixed shelters were with family immediately prior to their admission. However, for many this link became frail or was lost during the course of their institutional life. In specialized shelters the proportion of children who maintained family ties declined significantly from the time of entrance into the system up to the last six months before this study which was the end point for the analysis.

We checked the case records of the children for information about people who were part of their lives when they entered their first shelter and the one that they were presently in, as well as for records of such contacts in the six months prior to the examination of their case records. The data revealed that 15 percent of the children in specialized shelters had no outside contacts they could depend upon at the time they entered the shelter system.[11] If we make the same calculation for the time the young people entered their current shelter that number increased to 30 percent. Taking the later time period of the six months before the examination of their case records that proportion further increased. By that time, one-third of the children in our sample lost all of the family contacts they had when they entered the shelter system. The data also showed that the longer the children stayed in the shelter system the more likely they were to remain in care.

In the mixed shelters, 10 of 61 children (16 percent) had no family contacts at the time that they entered the system. This number increased to 21 percent if calculated at the time of entry into the present shelter, but dropped down back to 16 percent at the point of six months from the current survey. It is not known why the number declined during this last time period, but would be important to understand the reason for it, in a future study.

---

[11]This percentage refers to 17 cases from a total of 112 children and youth in specific shelters. In four cases (3.6 percent), we were unable to obtain information on which those children and youth counted.

Visits: Family Connections that Last

While some of the shelter population lost contact with their families, a significant proportion of it maintained contact. Fifty-six percent of the children who lived in specialized shelters, and 69 percent who lived in mixed shelters, received visits from family members at their institutions in the 12 months prior to the examination of their case records. Including visits from friends/godparents and others in addition to family members, the percentages increased to 75 percent in the specialized shelters and 78 percent in the mixed shelters.

The flip side of the coin is that about one-fourth of that population was not visited by anyone in a one-year period. Moreover, even for those children who had visits, those visits were very sporadic. In the case of specialized shelters, the children on average received one visit per semester. However, the fact that most children do have visits from family and friends can serve as a basis for strengthening familial ties. In the majority of cases, data showed that it is the mothers who are the main presence in the lives of the young people. We also noticed that the loss of family connections is related to the length of period in the shelter system. These factors suggest that it is critical to start working with the mothers and other family members at the time of the child's entry into a shelter and to identify the types of support and strategies that would maintain connections and facilitate an early exit from the shelter. We cannot emphasize enough the importance of valuing families, many of whom despite great challenges, managed to maintain physical contact and emotional ties to their children. Maintaining these connections is a necessary condition for returning the children to their families and communities.[12]

Final Considerations: Steps for Building a Public Policy Agenda

Based on the data we have described, we suggest three major steps that can assist the development of public policies to promote family ties and the return of children with disabilities back to their homes.

A Clear Definition of Disability and Its Diagnoses

There is a clear need to revisit the concept of disability and the various definitions of different kinds of disability. There are competing definitions from specialists in different fields and different

---

[12] A key existing policy in the Ministry of Mental Health is the program *Going Back Home (De Volta para Casa)* which is being implemented since 2006. It consists of offering financial and psychosocial support to help institutionalized adults in psychiatric hospitals return to their families.

working definitions from people running institutions. These conceptual confusions result in ineffective treatments and harm to the young people.

Significantly Reduce the Reliance on Institutional Care

The reliance on institutionalization needs to be reduced particularly since many of our target groups of children spend a very long time in the shelter system. This institutionalization constitutes a violation of rights, most notably the right to live with families and the home community as set out in Article 19 of the Statute on the Child and the Adolescent.

Change of Paradigm: Need for Alternatives to Institutional Care

There has to be an emphasis on developing and implementing public policies that are guided by the legal mandate that all children are the "subjects of rights" (Almeida & Delgado, 2000). It is essential that practices are developed that give families the degree of support they need to care for children with mental disabilities. The institutionalization of children can only be reduced if alternatives are developed.

The key findings of the survey that are relevant to policy change include the following. Children with disabilities who are sent to specialized and mixed shelters remain there for a long period of time. Many of the children in our sample had been in shelters for more than half of their lives. Few children who enter the shelter system are reunited with their families. Some of the obstacles to reunification are the families' lack of material resources, the existence of reports of domestic violence, and the children's physical and psychological condition. We also found that while relationships with the family attenuate as the children spend more time in care, many children still maintain some connection to their families and so a bridge exists for rebuilding strong family ties.

These findings suggest a number of steps for policy change. The fact that children remain in institutional care for long periods of time points to the need for preventing the first placement as far as possible. Where institutionalization is unavoidable, planning should begin immediately to maintain the fullest possible contact between children and parents, and for the possibility of returning home. In cases where contact with family members erodes or disappears, ways to prevent the child becoming permanently institutionalized and "forgotten" are to be found.[13]

Another vital policy principle is to ensure that no child enters an institution solely because his or her parents lack material resources. A family needs to have or should be provided with resources sufficient to cover the special needs of the child including treatment, medication, and

---

[13] What constitutes a good out-of-the-home alternative to institutions will vary depending on the age and condition of the individual child. Adoption that comes with various supports is one option as are therapeutic homes.

various appropriate therapies. However, merely the existence of such benefits is not a sufficient condition to keep children out of shelters. For parents to have quick and easy access to the benefits is just as necessary. Improving practical access to resources is vital and maybe as simple as providing transportation in particular for children who have difficulty walking. Such a resource might make all the difference between a child getting and not getting help.

The heaviest responsibility for the care of children with mental disabilities falls on the family and particularly on the mother. They are the key to the children staying out of institutional care. For this reason, we need to be imaginative in developing and/or expanding the availability of other supports a family might need. These supports include psychological support, instruction about the disability and its treatment, and well-run daycare and education programs. These programs should be decentralized so that they are easy to access. Home visiting programs can provide some of the help parents need.

Any expenditure of public resources has a political aspect and the political issue which needs highlighting is the practice in Brazil of the arbitrary elimination of a useful program when a new municipal, state or federal administration comes into office. Although any new administration will want to examine its predecessors' programs and priorities, the elimination of a program simply because it was developed by a previous administration is destructive of good policies and practices.[14]

As we search for new ways to keep mentally disabled children in their families or in family-like settings, we should remember Brazil's long history of providing institutional care; care which consistently violated young people's rights. The search for alternatives will still encounter resistance from more traditional interests. So the search for developing and implementing alternatives that respect the mandate of Article 19 of the Statute on the Child and the Adolescent will demand not only creativity but also persistence and courage.

References

Almeida, N., & Delgado, P. (2000). *De volta à cidadania. Políticas públicas para crianças e adolescentes* [The return to citizenship. Public policies for children and adolescents]. Rio de Janeiro: IFB/FUNLAR.
Foucault, M. (2006). *Os anormais* [Abnormal-Lectures at the College de France]. São Paulo: Martins Fontes.
IBGE. (2000). *Censo Demográfico de 2000* [The 2000 Demographic Census]. Rio de Janeiro: IBGE.
IPEA/CONANDA. (2004). *O direito à convivência familiar e comunitária: Os abrigos para crianças e adolescentes no Brasil* [The right to live with family and community: Shelters for children and adolescents in Brazil]. Brasília: IPEA/CONANDA.
Lobo, L. F. (2000). A criança anormal no Brasil: Uma história genealógica [The abnormal child in Brazil: A genealogical history]. In I. Rizzini, Irma (Ed.), *Crianças desvalidas, indígenas e negras no Brasil: Cenas da Colônia, do Império e*

---

[14]For further discussion on this subject, please see Rizzini, Rizzini, Naiff, & Baptista, 2007.

da República (Destitute, indigenous and black children in Brazil: Scenes from Colonial, Imperial and Republican Eras). Rio de Janeiro: CESPI/EDUSU.

Lobo, L. F. (2008). *Os infames da história: Pobres, escravos e deficientes no Brasil* [Those whom history despised: The poor, slaves and the disabled]. Rio de Janeiro: Lamparina.

Medeiros, M., & Diniz, D. (2004). *A nova maneira de se entender a deficiência e o envelhecimento* [A new way of understanding disability and aging]. Brasília: IPEA.

Medeiros, M., Diniz, D., & Squinca, F. (2006). *Transferências de renda para a população com deficiência no Brasil: Uma análise do benefício de prestação continuada* [Income transfers for the disabled population in Brazil: An analysis of family benefits]. Brasília: IPEA.

Néri, M. C. (Ed.). (2003). *Retratos da deficiência no Brasil* [An account of disability in Brazil]. Rio de Janeiro: FGV/IBRE, CPS.

Néri, M., & Soares, W. (2004). Idade, incapacidade e o número de pessoas com deficiência [Age, incapacity and the number of people with disabilities]. *Campinas: Revista Brasileira de Estudos Populacionais, 21*(2), 303–321.

Rizzini, I. (2007). *O século perdido. Raízes históricas das políticas sociais para a infância no Brasil* [The lost century. Historical roots of the public policies for children in Brasil]. São Paulo: Editora Cortez.

———. (Ed.). (2008). *Do confinamento ao acolhimento. Institucionalização de crianças e adolescentes com deficiência: desafios e caminhos* [From institutionalization to a family setting: Changing the practice of institutionalizing children and youth with disabilities in the State of Rio de Janeiro] Rio de Janeiro: CIESPI—CNPq/MS.

Rizzini, I., Rizzini, I., Baptista, R., & Naiff, L. (2007). *Acolhendo crianças e adolescentes: Experiências de promoção do direito à convivência familiar e comunitária no Brasil* [Supporting children and adolescents: Experiences of promoting the right to live with family and community]. São Paulo: Editora Cortez. Segunda edição.

Santos, R. L. (2003). *Transtorno mental e o cuidado na família* [Mental disorder and care in the family]. São Paulo: Editora Cortez.

ONU. (1982). *Programa de ação mundialpara as pessoas deficientes* (The United Nations. Plan of global action for people with disabilities) United Nations Resolution n. 37/52, December 3, 1982).

13

Child Welfare and Children's Mental Health Needs in the Context of Development: An Integrated (South African) Approach

Jeanette Schmid

Introduction

The construction of *child welfare* varies amongst child welfare models. There is frequently a binary between child protection, in which children (and their families) are portrayed narrowly in terms of their safety needs and a broad definition of child welfare, where protection needs are overlooked. Focusing exclusively on child protection has created difficulties in responding to the needs of vulnerable children in South Africa, and would by implication also present challenges in other contexts where mass poverty, AIDS, and significant violence affect families. An alternative child welfare model that integrates protection issues with broader concerns regarding child wellbeing and that does not in turn marginalize children's mental health needs is required.

To offer such an alternative, it is necessary to understand the strengths and weaknesses of prevailing child welfare models. After introducing these, I describe the needs of South African children and their families and maintain that the dominant child protection model is unable to respond effectively to these needs. With the developmental social welfare approach as its base, I offer an integrated developmental child welfare model. In this chapter I focus on the South African situation, but argue that such an alternative response is required for all contexts of development.

Child Welfare Models

Policy makers, children's rights activists, and practitioners often assume a universal understanding of "child welfare issues." However, parochial assumptions about such notions as children, families, abuse, and responsibility shape local constructions and interventions regarding vulnerable children. The literature on comparative child welfare systems is limited, and I rely primarily on Freymond and Cameron (2006), who propose three types of child welfare responses in the Western world, viz., child protection, family services, and community care approaches. This typology of necessity draws out the commonalities while minimizing differences, ultimately offering rough stereotypes of the systems.

The child protection model characteristic of Anglophone countries responds to children who have been harmed or are at significant risk of being hurt. Parents are seen as primarily responsible for their children's care. Corrective parenting procedures are directed at the inadequate parent. The authority of social workers derives from the courts and workers formally investigating child abuse allegations. The system typically is distinct from health, education, and even welfare institutions resulting in single-point access being the norm.

Multiple criticisms are leveled against the child protection approach. It is seen as individualistic, overlooking collective relations and in its focus on the vulnerable child, and potentially creating a polarization between the needs of the child and of its parents (and by definition, broader family) (Burman, 2003). In a neoliberal climate, increasing attention has been paid to administrative and statutory procedures, face-to-face support of clients being compromised (Parada, 2004; Parton, 1998). The deficit-based approach is an intrusive and punitive one, closely surveilling especially mothers (Freymond, 2003; Scourfield, 2003). Preventive practice is almost entirely ignored, and where included, tends to be secondary rather than primary. As middle-class parenting methods are valued, minority group and/or poor families tend to be overrepresented (Hines, Lemon, Wyatt, & Merdinger, 2004). The structural issues impacting parenting capacity are largely invisible. Out-of-home placements are frequently used (Bunting & Reid, 2005).

Internationally, the extensive critique of child protection approaches has recently led to attempts at minimizing the discriminatory bias of the system and increasing family partnership activities (Katz & Pinkerton, 2003; Lohrbach & Sawyer, 2004). Legislative amendments, by offering time frames regarding permanent placements, aim to ensure that children are not left in limbo. Greater interagency and interdisciplinary collaboration has been promoted (Katz & Pinkerton, 2003). Differential response—a two-track system of either assessment or investigation, depending on the specific family's needs—has become increasingly popular (Merkel-Holguin & Wilmot, 2005). Alternative dispute resolution (ADR) mechanisms are being advanced (Schmid & Sieben, 2008). The positive systems (Cameron, Freymond, Cornfield, & Palmer, 2001) and "patch" (Adams, 2000) approaches aim at offering more holistic responses. However, Lonne, Parton, Thomson, & Harries (2009) are adamant that even with improvements this system fails children and families and must be fundamentally transformed.

Family services is Freymond and Cameron's (2006) next model, typifying the work with children and families in many European countries. Solidarity, a core cultural value, underpins this child welfare approach, the state sharing responsibility for child-rearing with parents. All families are assumed to potentially encounter difficulties, and hence various universal supports (such as day care, parenting support, and youth centers) are offered, tacitly acknowledging that structural factors may also contribute to child abuse. Child protection activities are integrated into broader welfare activities. The emphasis is on collaboration and joint problem-solving. Where child protection matters come to court, as in France, the judge adopts a conciliatory position (Waldegrave, 2006). Adoption is rare, and foster care is used only in exceptional cases of children and parents maintaining contact.

The family services model avoids certain pitfalls of the child protection model in that intervention is less stigmatizing or punitive. Further, the intersectoral response to troubled families allows for multiple access points. The emphasis on universal, primary prevention offers families support before they come into crisis. However, the needs of the child may become overshadowed by being "too" sensitive to parental needs (Agathonos-Georgopoulou, 1998). The approach is limited in addressing the needs of migrant (poor) populations (Andersson, 2006), suggesting that also here middle-class Western values determine how childhood and child-rearing are constructed. An individualist position is adopted (Bühler-Niederberger, 2007), focusing on nuclear families and individual family members. Although not described specifically, it seems that dominant gender relations are reflected in the family services approach.

The third model is that of community care, which operates in places such as New Zealand, Australia, the US, and Canada. This approach emerges out of efforts by indigenous communities to find child welfare responses that intersect more closely with their values and traditions and which explicitly acknowledge the impact of structural factors and oppression on parenting capacity. Intervention must address both structural and familial issues. The inclusion of the spiritual/cultural perspectives is viewed as essential. Family Group Conferencing legislated in New Zealand in 1989 and since implemented internationally, epitomizes the core assumptions of this approach:

- Children are inherently identified as part of and connected both to their immediate and extended family circle and culture.
- An inclusive, collective, and communal view is favored, inviting every family group member to have a voice in the collaborative decision-making process; particular attention is paid to how the voices of children and women can be heard.
- While "expert" input is valued, it is the family group's knowledge of their situation that is privileged.

As community care approaches have emerged where the child protection model is dominant, the focus has been on planning for the child who has been abused or is at risk of harm. This creates a tension between the dominant constructions which favor child protection and the community care construction, which inclines toward a holistic understanding of children's needs. The critical view of systemic influences on parenting capacity is thus often diluted. Love (2006) argues that indigenous approaches to vulnerable children and families need to be entirely decoupled from the dominant child protection model, as local practices and norms are essentially overridden and the intention of responding specifically to the situation of minority communities becomes compromised.

It is apparent that although each of the Western models is criticized for failing to adequately address the needs of minority groups and the poor, the child protection model seems most to entrench difference, individualistic paradigms, punitive responses, and curative interventions. Patel (2005) has stated that welfare orientations that favor individualistic, tertiary, and expert-driven responses cannot effectively address the needs of poor children and their families.

Before examining the child welfare approach in South Africa, it is necessary to understand the conditions with which South African children and their families are confronted.

Lived Reality of South African Children and Their Families

The majority of children in South Africa live in extremely difficult circumstances. Black South Africans were seriously disadvantaged during apartheid, with few having access to adequate health, education, and welfare services. Families and communities were negatively affected by the rural–urban migration. While service provision and the social security net has improved markedly post-apartheid (Triegaardt, 2005), many South African children and their families continue to lack access to basic necessities. Unofficial unemployment rates average around 40%. The AIDS epidemic, which by 2007 resulted in 20% of children losing one or both parents, has further compromised income levels (Pendlebury, Lake, & Smith, 2009). Tuberculosis and malaria, often in association with AIDS, continue to rob the health of South Africans. The pervasive violence, both domestic and public, has impacted children, leaving few safe spaces existing for them. Other societal ills also affect the lives of children, with many children, for example, not having relationships with their fathers (Richter, Manegold, Pather, & Mason, 2004) and informal supports increasingly becoming more fragile. The poverty–AIDS–crime complex potentially leaves deep emotional scars on children, compromising children's mental health, despite their resilience. An effective child welfare response must be able to support children and their families in this complicated environment, building on their inherent strengths and providing the necessary resources to minimize the gaps.

Dominant Child Welfare Model in South Africa

The Anglophone child protection model became the basis for intervention in South Africa initially through colonization (Allsopp, 2005; Patel, 2005). During the apartheid era, the tendency of traditional Western social work to utilize deficit-based approaches reinforced racial stereotyping and prejudice. Social work services were predominantly individualized, casework-based, treatment-oriented, and residual, prevention and early intervention services generally not being prioritized (Dutschke, 2006). These remedially oriented services tended to be located in urban areas, and were directed mostly at whites.

The child protection model continues to hold sway, being partly strengthened through globalization and international rights instruments. Even though the child protection system is in crisis due to severe underfunding as well as human resource shortages, academics (e.g., September, 2005) as well as practitioners such as Loffell (2008) argue that a system specifically built around child protection is needed, because child abuse is so prevalent and a diffused welfare agenda might result in only the most extreme misconduct being addressed. It is also argued that the new Children's Act (No. 38 of 2005) is in line with children's needs, introducing mandatory prevention, acknowledging children's connections to significant others in their family network, and expanding the definition of abuse to include neglect as well as the exploitation of children both in the labor and sexual arena alongside physical, sexual, and emotional abuse.

However, as noted earlier, the child protection paradigm is proving inadequate in resourced countries. Even a resourced and adapted child protection system is simply unable to respond to the needs of South African children and their families (Schmid, 2008), because it

- continues to direct (gendered) interventions at the individual actor, whether this is the "inadequate" parent/caregiver or the vulnerable child. Individual interventions are costly and ignore systemic issues that impact parenting capacity (Patel, 2005);
- defines vulnerability relatively narrowly collective poverty and its impact on children is not typically considered part of the child protection mandate;
- is skewed toward statutory rather than preventive interventions. Court processes are expensive, redirecting resources away from primary prevention (Loffell, 2008), and promoting antagonism between the family and the child protection worker. Secondary and tertiary prevention is less effective than primary prevention. Court-ordered participation typically results in reluctant participants.

If the child protection model cannot offer appropriate intervention is there potentially a more relevant framework?

An (Integrated) Developmental Child Welfare Model

I propose an alternative model for the South African reality, the hallmark of which is integration. This approach potentially has value in other contexts of development. I draw on developmental social welfare (DSW), as well as facets of the family service and community care models.

With the advent of the "new South Africa" in 1994, the welfare community required an alternative policy framework that built on the limited strengths of the previous system while avoiding replicating the fragmented, disjointed, and residual nature of apartheid welfare; acknowledged the dignity and needs of all South Africans; and responded effectively to the crises created by poverty, crime, and AIDS. The DSW policy, which is informed by social development theory, was adopted as the White Paper (Department of Welfare, 1997). Although the South African welfare community has struggled to fully implement a developmental approach (Patel, 2008), and though aspects of the policy have been criticized, the policy offers an integrated social work practice model which could be implemented not only in under-resourced countries but also in developed nations.

By reviewing the White Paper and articles by Bak (2004), Dutschke (2006), and Patel (2005) one can conclude that DSW is based on the premise of integration on a number of different levels. The primary focus is on *economic and social integration*. Challenging the conventional separation of these two spheres, DSW recognizes that economic and social development is interdependent. A strong social security system is core as a redistributive mechanism. Human capacity is enhanced through skill-building and training and the creation of meaningful and accessible employment opportunities. A second facet of integration is an *emphasis on rights* and the subsidiary principle of inclusion of the service users' voices in decision-making processes that affect them. Another level is the integration of *efforts by all stakeholders*, requiring collaboration between government, the voluntary welfare sector, and business, harmonious interaction between local, provincial, and national governments and intersectoral work by interdisciplinary teams work across health, education, housing, and so forth. Similarly, the *modes of intervention* ought to be integrated, even though DSW lays the emphasis on community development: prevention, early intervention, and treatment programs should be mutually reinforcing and utilized with the intent of building capacity and empowering individuals, groups, and communities. Community work builds on existing local, indigenous helping strategies, and integrating cultural perspectives into the social work response.

The DSW approach to service delivery is thus a multilevel response that acknowledges both structural and individual factors affect a person, family, or community's ability to cope. DSW offers a possible platform for the revisualization of child welfare practice. I have utilized the DSW principles to develop a multifaceted framework for integrated child welfare practice. Local realities must be considered in the application of this model.

The integrated developmental child welfare (IDCW) framework

- identifies that family difficulties frequently stem from social injustices;
- assumes that the state and families share responsibility for providing for the needs of children;
- is participatory, valuing the voice, expertise, spirituality and culture of families and communities;
- is communal, acknowledging that children are raised by and identify with a network of relatives and friends;

- is collective, recognizing the interdependence of children and the circles around them;
- is rights-based, drawing the connection between individual and group rights;
- is preventive, focusing on broad capacity building;
- is collaborative, bringing together diverse sectors and levels of government in unified service delivery; and
- is supportive, simultaneously addressing socioeconomic needs.

Emphasis on Prevention

A key issue in developing an integrated model for child welfare is related to the continuum of prevention, early intervention, and statutory work, areas seen as discrete in child protection discourse. In contrast, in the IDCW framework, points of intersection between prevention, early intervention, and statutory are recognized (Follentine, 2004), with the continuum weighted toward primary prevention. The service user is constructed as *community member* rather than "client" or "beneficiary," and the worker as *facilitator* rather than "helper."

The goal in IDCW is to develop social capital (Magongo, 2005) by building on naturally occurring helping systems to strengthen families and communities to face adversity and challenge structural inequalities. This goes beyond the currently popular "awareness-raising" programs in South Africa. Further, disadvantaged communities frequently require an infusion of external resources in order to meet parochial needs (Jackson et al., 2003), though Pinkerton (1994) warns that the competition for resources can divide communities.

The child protection emphasis on parental functioning disregards the resources of the family group. IDCW promotes a shift in focus from the parent or caregiver to the family network and the broader community. Family support services, though strengths oriented and home based, must be used cautiously as these tend to stigmatize by targeting families who are child welfare or potential clients and which, with their focus on resilience overlook structural contributors to family functioning (Katz & Pinkerton, 2003). These various constraints can be addressed through ensuring multilevel intervention, including macro-level advocacy and activism (Quiery, McElhinney, Rafferty, Sheehy, & Trew, 2003), and offering services on a universal basis (Andersson, 2003).

Underscoring prevention does not suggest that micro-practice is inappropriate or that only generic services should be considered. As the integrated approach carries a social justice focus (Patel, 1987; Pinkerton & Campbell, 2002), developmental goals can be achieved by integrating micro-approaches with social action on both a micro- and macro-scale (Elliot, 1993), resulting in multilevel interventions that address the total context of the child and family (Loffell, 1996; Sturgeon, 1998). For example, therapeutic approaches can be used in conjunction with research and social advocacy recognizing the impact of systemic issues, and ensuring that individual stories coalesce into collective testimony (Waldegrave, 2005).

By placing prevention at the center of child welfare activity, the meaning of statutory work shifts. As exemplified by the patch approach, where multidisciplinary teams—representing various agencies and based in a local office—utilize a community work approach, the barriers to service are broken down; families and communities become more cohesive; child protection concerns are understood systemically and holistically; and teams respond when families encounter minor difficulties, thus avoiding crises and the adoption of an adversarial, intrusive approach (Adams & Krauth, 1995; Smale, 1995). Even in instances where protective intervention is required holistic intervention results in a qualitatively different positive experience for the service user and community. This realignment results in fewer protection cases and different service responses, ultimately shifting the centrality and nature of statutory work.

When child welfare activities are defined mainly in preventive terms the system needs to be able to respond on a practical and policy level both to children who are made vulnerable through poverty, neglect, abuse, and exploitation, as well as those made vulnerable by HIV/AIDS (Proudlock, 2004; Ramsden, 2005; Streak, 2005; UNICEF & UNAIDS, 2004)—these often being the same children. Integrated efforts are easier to accomplish and more cost effective than separate services. A central pillar of a Developmental Child Welfare Model is therefore prevention.

Intra- and Intersectoral Collaboration

A further dimension of an integrated child welfare approach is intersectoral collaboration. Linkages in any child welfare sector are needed on a number of levels.

First, a unified child welfare sector is needed for effective lobbying and advocacy. Second, collaboration needs to occur within the welfare sector as a whole. Child protection organizations (which are usually standalone agencies) must build strong service delivery partnerships that can offer a palette of customized interventions (Cameron & Vanderwoerd, 1997; Waldfogel, 1998a, 1998b) and should ideally become integrated into general child and family welfare agencies. In resource-poor environments, such collaboration requires effective cooperation between social workers, child, and youth workers and other categories of social service personnel (Children First, 2005; Mohapi, 2005; Patel, 2005). Undoubtedly, interdisciplinary interaction will at points lead to role diffusion, though where a service team ensures that it is effectively engaging the community and delivering appropriate services, role distinctions become less important. Volunteers, typically women (Patel, 2010), play a critical role in child protection services. Comprehensive strategies to guide and support volunteers (Mbambo, 2005; September, 2006; Patel, 2010) are needed, particularly in contexts of poverty, Mkhabela (2007) cautioning that if this is not done, families are ultimately weakened further. A third level of collaboration facilitating comprehensive intervention is joint working between welfare and various fields such as health and education, as well as agencies focused on land, water, and housing issues (Green & Nieman, 2003). Finally, an integrated approach also necessitates collaboration between and with different levels and different departments of government.

In accordance with the idea of multidisciplinary teams and intersectoral work, integrated services are most easily delivered from a central hub. A range of facilities—schools (Mabetoa, 1999), residential facilities, early intervention centers (Swadener, Kabiru, & Njenga, 1997), clinics, and shelters for street children—can act as one-stop centers both in urban and rural areas. Mobile services may be needed in outlying areas where households are dispersed. Offering a diversity of services from one central venue facilitates community access to resources, eliminates duplication (Cape Town Child Welfare, 2005; Patel, 2005), and allows for a familiarity with neighborhood needs and matching of services with these needs (Adams & Krauth, 1995; Scheepers, 2006). In an integrated facility, generic and specialized services can be offered creatively and to maximum effect (Ehlers, 2004), as working in intersectoral teams allows specialist knowledge to be shared more broadly, blurring formal boundaries between fields, while teamwork allows for multiple service strategies to be utilized (Patel, 2005). Programs can be customized to meet individual family needs. Another advantage of a central hub is that it becomes possible to create a physically and emotionally safe space for community members, particularly in contexts where crime and violence impinge on daily life. To maximize the use of the one-stop service, programs should be offered universally.

Socioeconomic Integration

Socioeconomic integration is a further critical facet of an IDCW model achieved in part through social security mechanisms. An appropriate social safety net that is universal and non-stigmatizing removes the "poverty tax" poor families pay assisting relatives (De Swardt, 2003), supports children living with dying parents, offers long-term assistance to orphans, and allows for children's mobility between homes (Meintjes, Budlender, Giese, & Johnson, 2003).

In order for community-based alternatives to be successful, it is not only caregivers but also communities that need to be resourced. While it is important to draw on local assets, external community support is needed for stretched communities where families have over decades been dealing with issues of migration, poverty, and violence (Child Welfare South Africa, 2001; Salaam, 2005; UNICEF & UNAIDS, 2004).

Connecting income generation and job creation with child welfare initiatives is another strategy that allows for socioeconomic integration. Instead of offering such programs independently, child welfare organizations can work closely with agencies skilled in this area and with government.

Integrating the Knowledge of the Family Group and Service Providers

The democratization of welfare implicit in developmental social welfare implies that an integrated child welfare approach is family-driven rather than expert-led and presumes that the state and family work together raise children (Allsopp, 2005; Phiri & Webb, 2002; Organization of African Unity, 1999), the government thus providing a range of supports to families. This premise is fundamentally different from the idea that formal intervention occurs only when a family fails in its parenting obligations to its children.

An IDCW approach further assumes a collective position, noting that a child is inexorably intertwined with its kin and ancestors (Burman, 2003; Sefa Dei, Hall, & Rosenberg, 2000) and that a child's voice needs to be heard in conjunction with others in the family group. This view coincides with the orientations of many cultures (Love, 2006), and in South Africa, with the notion of *ubuntu*. Appreciating that a child's rights and best interests are inherently interlinked with the rights of those of the family network (Burman, 2003; Panter-Brick, 2002) requires an expanded definition of the family as the basic unit of intervention (Patel, 2005) (including immediate relatives, more distant relations, and friends); acknowledgment of the fluidity and boundary permeability within family constellations (Save the Children Alliance, 2003); and recognition that the child's connections with the family group result in greater protection from child abuse, both because relationships with relatives tend to endure over time and because there is a wider circle of people responding to the child's physical and emotional needs (Suda, 1999).

A collective, communal perspective shifts how decisions are made, requiring the use of planning and decision-making mechanisms that honor the collective voice of families, focus on their strengths, and devolve the decision making regarding the child from service providers back to the family group (Burford & Hudson, 2000; Mirsky, n.d.). Creating a space for the voice of families and community members requires the integration of the family circle's unique culture into the decision-making process. Service providers recognize that their knowledge base does not replace but rather complements that of the service user (Sturgeon, 1998). The collaborative approach needs to be extended to judicial processes, suggesting that through the use of ADR mechanisms consensual solutions be sought in the instances where court intervention is deemed necessary (Freymond, 2001; Waldegrave, 2006).

A collaborative participative approach transforms not only decision-making processes but also service delivery. Community members, rather than professionals decide the form and content of services needed, and the focus shifts to the circle around the child from only the child or the parent (mother). Noting complex power dynamics operative in various participatory models, recognizing the importance of facilitating inclusion, and appreciating that participation simultaneously means the exclusion of certain individuals (Cooke & Kothari, 2001; Lund, 1998), ostensibly participatory models, such as family involvement or family centered approaches (Katz & Pinkerton, 2003; Lohrbach et al., 2005) need to be scrutinized. These approaches tend to be expert-driven and are limited because they focus on the child's right (in this case to involve the family network because of the child's right to access kin in planning) rather than on the family group's right to be involved, thus maintaining an individual rather than a collective lens.

The integration of family group members' knowledge into child welfare processes implies the inclusion of local wisdoms, traditions, and perspectives. Ultimately, any child welfare approach will only be successful if it is an indigenous response, emerging from communities, and being connected into local discourses, though deciding what is indeed local is typically contested (Bar-On, 2003a, 2003b; Osei-Hwedie,1995).

By focusing on the collective in an integrated model, child welfare workers engage collaboratively with the family network, recognize the links between family troubles and structural issues, and involve family members (including children) in decision making, both in matters that affect them directly and in broader governance concerns. Further, such a model integrates cultural and spiritual perspectives into social work responses and builds on local knowledge.

Challenges in Applying Developmental Principles

A number of South African programs have adopted a developmental focus (Child Welfare South Africa, 2005; Mbambo, 2005; Patel, 2005; Sewpaul, 2001). Some of the programs fall into the trap of replicating and strengthening certain intrusive or instrumental aspects of child protection. However, the use of volunteers, the participation of community members, the focus on child well-being rather than malfunction or abuse, the strengthening of community networks, and integrated programming are all important. It is likely that in every country, province/state and neighborhood, there are successes that can be built upon in moving toward an integrated approach. The integrated model described above provides a framework for the application and operationalization of a developmental discourse in child welfare. Nevertheless, barriers exist:

- the state must significantly fund a developmental approach. No child welfare system, regardless of philosophical orientation, can operate effectively in a resource vacuum;
- service providers must be willing to utilize their expertise to support indigenous knowledge(s), rather than to silence or marginalize family and community voices;
- innovative thinking is required to shift the integration of services and policy development across sectors and level of government from simple networking to effective coordination;
- legislation and policies need to be fine-tuned to support an IDCW system. Because policy development typically is slow and dominant discourses resist the introduction of a developmentally oriented approach, agencies can initiate bottom-up operationalization; and
- joint socioeconomic development must become the vision of the state, because a welfare ministry and, in particular, a child welfare department cannot address this in an isolated fashion.

It may be suggested that these and other challenges to introducing an integrated developmental child welfare framework are not simply obstacles, but are fundamental limitations to this paradigm. Introducing such an anti-oppressive approach does indeed require broad-based commitment to honoring the voices of family and community members. However, in the tradition of Jane Adams, it is incumbent on social workers to seek ways of working that empower service users, rather than replicating the oppression with which they have dealt. In conclusion, it is not possible to change a system until one has visualized a potential alternative.

References

Adams, P. (2000). Bringing the community back in: Patch and family group decision making. In G. Burford & J. Hudson (Eds), *Family group conferencing: New directions in community-centered child and family practice* (pp. 105–119). New York: Aldine de Gruyter.

Adams, P., & Krauth, K. (1995). Working with families and communities: the patch approach. In P. Adams & K. Nelson (Eds), *Reinventing human services: Community centered and family centered practice* (pp. 87–108). New York: Aldine de Gruyter.

Agathonos-Georgopoulou, H. (1998). Future outlook for child protection policies in Europe. *Child Abuse and Neglect, 22*(4), 239–247.

Allsopp, M. (2005). Tracing our history: Contextualising child and youth care within a South African reality. *Child and Youth Care, 23*(7), 22–27.

Andersson, G. (2003). Evaluation of the contact family service in Sweden. In I. Katz & J. Pinkerton (Eds), *Evaluating family support: Thinking internationally, thinking critically* (pp. 291–306). West Sussex, England: Wiley and Sons.

———. (2006). Child and family welfare in Sweden. In N. Freymond & G. Cameron (Eds), *Towards positive systems of child and family welfare: International comparisons of child protection, family service and community caring systems* (pp. 171–190). Toronto: University of Toronto Press.

Bak, M. (2004). Can developmental social welfare change an unfair world—The South African experience. *International Social Work, 47*(1), 81–94. doi:10.1177/0020872804039385

Bar-On, A. (2003a). Indigenous practice: Some informed guesses—self-evident, but impossible. *Social Work/Maatskaplike Werk, 23*(1), 26–40.

———. (2003b). Culture: Social work's new deluge? *Social Work/Maatskaplike Werk, 39* (4), 299–311.

Bühler-Niederberger, D. (2007). *The power of innocence: Social politics for children between separation and integration.* Wellchi Working Paper, Series (WP no. 4/2007), Barcelona: Children's Well-Being International Documentation Centre.

Bunting, L., & Reid, C. (2005). Reviewing child deaths: Learning from the American experience. *Child Abuse Review, 14*(2), 82–96. doi:10.1002/car.886

Burford, G., & Hudson, J. (Eds). (2000). *Family group conferencing: New directions in community-centered child and family practice.* New York: Aldine de Gruyter.

Burman, S. (2003). The best interests of the South African child. *International Journal of Law, Policy and the Family, 17*(1), 28–40. doi:10.1093/lawfam/17.1.28

Cameron, G., Freymond, N., Cornfield, D., & Palmer, S. (2001). *Positive possibilities for child and family welfare: Options for expanding the Anglo-American child protection paradigm.* Department of Social Work: Wilfrid Laurier University.

Cameron, G., & Vanderwoerd, J. (1997). *Protecting children and supporting families: Promising programs and organizational realities.* New York: Aldine de Gruyter.

Cape Town Child Welfare. (2005). One-stop shops-the way forward for child welfare. *Children First, 61*(May/June). Retrieved from http://www.childrenfirst.org.za

Children First. (2005). Lifting the burden-and the standard-of care: Raising Africa's children. *Children First, 63*(September/October). Retrieved from http://www.childrenfirst.org.za

Child Welfare South Africa. (2001). Report on the national council and the structure of the child welfare movement (Unpublished document). Johannesburg.

———. (2005). South African council for child and family welfare: Triennial report, 2002–2004 (Unpublished document). Johannesburg.

Cooke, B., & Kothari, U. (2001). *Participation: The new tyranny.* London: Zed Books.

Department of Welfare (DW). (1997). Social Welfare White Paper. Retrieved from http://www.info.gov.za/view/DownloadFileAction?id=127937

Department of Welfare. (1997). White Paper for social welfare. DW: Pretoria. Retrieved from http://www.info.gov.za/view/DownloadFileAction?id=127937

De Swardt, C. (2003). *Unravelling chronic poverty in South Africa: Some food for thought.* Paper presented at the conference of Chronic Poverty Research Centre, Manchester, UK.

Dutschke, M. (2006). *Defining children's constitutional right to social services.* A Project 28 Working Paper. Cape Town: Children's Institute, University of Cape Town.

Ehlers, L. (2004). Legal reform: For better or for worse? *Children First, 54*(March/April). Retrieved from http://www.childrenfirst.org.za

Elliott, D. (1993). Social work and social development: Towards an integrative model for social work practice. *International Social Work, 36*(1), 21–37. doi:10.1177/002087289303600103

Follentine, S. (2004). *Towards a common conceptual understanding of developmental social welfare and its implication for practice.* Paper presented at the National Conference for Social Service Practitioners. Dialogue across Disciplines: Partnerships in Development. Pretoria, South Africa.

Freymond, N. (2001). *Using intermediary structures to support families: An international comparison of practice in child protection* (Monograph). Kitchener: Department of Social Work, Wilfrid Laurier University.

———. (2003). *Mothers and child welfare: Mothers' everyday realities and child placement experiences.* Presented at "Finding a Fit" Conference, Waterloo, Ontario: Wilfrid Laurier University.

Freymond, N., & Cameron, G. (Eds) (2006). *Towards positive systems of child and family welfare: International comparisons of child protection, family service and community caring systems.* Toronto, ON: University of Toronto Press.

Green, S., & Nieman, A. (2003). Social development: Good practice guidelines. *Social Work/Maatskaplike Werk, 39*(2), 161–181.

Hines, A., Lemon, K., Wyatt, P., & Merdinger, J. (2004). Factors related to the disproportionate involvement of children of colour in the child welfare system: A review and emerging themes. *Children and Youth Services Review, 26*(6), 507–527.

Jackson, S., Cleverly, S., Poland, B., Burman, D., Edwards, R., & Robertson, A. (2003). Working with Toronto neighbourhoods towards developing indicators of community capacity. *Health Promotion International, 18*(4), 339–350. doi:10.1093/heapro/dag415

Katz, I., & Pinkerton, J. (Eds). (2003) *Evaluating family support: Thinking internationally, thinking critically.* West Sussex, England: John Wiley and Sons.

Loffell, J. (1996). *Social work intervention in child sexual abuse.* (Unpublished doctoral dissertation). University of the Witwatersrand, Johannesburg, South Africa.

———. (2008). Developmental social welfare and the child protection challenge in South Africa. *Practice: Social Work in Action, 20*(2), 83–91. doi:10.1080/09503150802058889

Lohrbach, S., & Sawyer, R. (2004). Creating a constructive practice: Family and professional partnership in high-risk child protection case conferences. *Protecting Children, 19*(2), 26–35.

Lohrbach, S., Sawyer, R., Saugen, J., Astolfi, C., Schmitt, K., Worden, P., & Xaaji, M. (2005). Ways of working in child welfare: A perspective on practice. *Protecting Children, 20*(2, 3), 93–100.

Lonne, B., Parton, N., Thomson, J., & Harries, M. (2009). *Reforming child protection.* London: Routledge.

Love, C. (2006). Maori perspectives on collaboration and colonization in contemporary Aotearearoa/New Zealand and family welfare policies and practices. In N. Freymond & G. Cameron (Eds), *Towards positive systems of child and family welfare: International comparisons of child protection, family service and community caring systems* (pp. 237–268). Toronto, ON: University of Toronto Press.

Lund, F. (1998). *Who's in and who's out? The effects of poverty and inequality on participatory and institutional development.* South Africa: Olive.

Mabetoa, M. (1999). Indigenization of a school social work model for rural communities in South Africa. *Social Work/Maatskaplike Werk, 35*(1), 39–48.

Magongo, B. (2005). *Impact assessment survey on sustainable livelihoods and households for Goelama Project.* Johannesburg: Centre for AIDS Development, Research and Evaluation for Nelson Mandela Children's Fund.

Mbambo, B. (2005). Unpaid should not mean unsupported. *Children First, 63*(September/October). Retrieved from www.childrenfirst.org.za

Meintjes, H., Budlender, D., Giese, S., & Johnson, L. (2003). Children in "need of care" or in need of cash? Questioning social security provisions for orphans in the context of the South African AIDS pandemic. Retrieved from http://www.microlinks.org/ev02.php?ID=26138_201&ID2=DO_TOPIC

Merkel-Holguin, L. & Wilmot, L. (2005). Analyzing family involvement approaches and reviewing trends in FGDM. In J. Pennell & G. Anderson (Eds), *Widening the circle: the practice and evaluation of FGC with children, youths and their families* (pp. 183–202). Washington, DC: NASW Press.

Mirsky, L. (n.d.). Family group conferencing worldwide. Retrieved from http://www.iirp.org/article_detail.php?article_id=NDMz

Mkhabela, S. (2007). *Issues in South African foster care.* Presentation Conference hosted by Nelson Mandela Children's Fund, Johannesburg, South Africa.

Mohapi, B. (2005). Social service professionals as a response to the challenges in social development: "Together we can make it." *Child and Youth Care, 23*(4), 8.

Organization of African Unity. (1999). African charter on the rights and welfare of the child. Retrieved from www.african-union.org

Osei-Hwedie, K. (1995). *A search for legitimate social development education and practice models for Africa.* Lewiston: The Edwin Mellen Press.

Panter-Brick, C. (2002). Street children, human rights and public health: A critique and future directions. *Annual Review of Anthropology, 31,* 141–171.

Parada, H. (2004). Social work practices within the restructured child welfare system in Ontario: An institutional ethnography. *Canadian Social Work Review, 21*(1), 67–76.

Parton, N. (1998). Risk, advanced liberalism and child welfare: The need to rediscover uncertainty and ambiguity. *British Journal of Social Work, 28*(1), 5–27.

Patel, L. (1987). Towards a critical theory and practice in social work with special reference to South Africa. *International Journal of Social Work, 30,* 221–236.

———. (1992). *Restructuring social welfare: Options for South Africa.* Johannesburg: Ravan Press.

———. (2005). *Social welfare and social development in South Africa.* South Africa: Oxford University Press.

———. (2008). Overview of a decade of post apartheid social welfare. *Practice. Special Edition: South African Social Work.*

Patel, L. (2010). *Pointers for future research on gender and care in voluntary organisations in South Africa*. Paper presented at the South African-Swiss Joint Research Seminar University of Basel, Switzerland.

Pendlebury, S., Lake, L., & Smith, C. (2009). *South African child gauge 2008–9*. Children's Institute, University of Cape Town. Retrieved from www.ci.org.za/depts/ci/pubs/pdf/general/gauge2008/sa_child_gauge08.pdf

Phiri, S., & Webb, D. (2002). The impact of HIV/AIDS on orphans and program and policy responses. In G. Cornia (Ed.), *AIDS, public policy and child well-being*. Florence, Italy: UNICEF Innocenti Research Centre.

Pinkerton, J. (1994). *In care at home: Parenting, the state and civil society*. Aldershot, England: Avebury.

———. (2006). Developing a global approach to the theory and practice of young people leaving state care. *Child and Family Social Work, 11*(3), 191–198.

Pinkerton, J., & Campbell, J. (2002). Social work and social justice in Northern Ireland: Towards a new occupational space. *British Journal of Social Work, 32*(6), 723–737. doi:10.1093/bjsw/32.6.723

Proudlock, P. (2004). Ensure our call is heard. *Children First, 54*. Retrieved from www.childrenfirst.org.za

Quiery, N., McElhinney, S., Rafferty, H., Sheehy, N., & Trew, K. (2003). Empowering parents: A two-generation intervention in a community context in Northern Ireland. In I. Katz & J. Pinkerton (Eds), *Evaluating family support: Thinking internationally, thinking critically* (pp. 207–226). West Sussex, England: John Wiley and Sons.

Ramsden, N. (2005). Pay now or pay later. *Children First, 63*(September/October). Retrieved from www.childrenfirst.org.za

Richter, L., Manegold, J., Pather, R., & Mason, A. (2004). Harnessing our manpower. *Children First, 54*. Retrieved from www.childrenfirst.org.za

Salaam, T. (2005). *AIDS orphans and vulnerable children (OVC): Problems, responses and issues for Congress*. Baltimore, MD: Congressional Research Service.

Save the Children Alliance. (2003). The care and protection of children affected by armed conflict and disasters. *Child and Youth Care, 21*(8), 11–13.

Scheepers, L. (2006, January 27). The recipe for success. *Mail & Guardian*. Retrieved from http://mg.co.za/article/2006-01-27-the-recipe-for-success

Schmid, J. (2008). *The story of South African child welfare: A history of the present* (Unpublished doctoral dissertation), Faculty of Social Work, Wilfrid Laurier University, Canada.

Schmid, J., & Sieben, M. (2008). Help or hindrance: Family Group Conferencing as alternative dispute resolution in child welfare. *Protecting Children, 23*(4), 10–18.

Scourfield, J. (2003). *Gender and child protection*. United Kingdom: Palgrave Macmillan.

Sefa Dei, G., Hall, B., & Rosenberg, D. (Eds) (2000). *Indigenous knowledges in global contexts: Multiple readings of our world*. Toronto: University of Toronto Press.

September, R. (2005). Protecting children where it matters most: In their families and their neighbourhoods. *Social work/Maatskaplike werk, 41*(1), 27–37.

———. (2006). A review of child protection services in South Africa: State of the art policies in need of implementation. *Social Work/Maatskaplike Werk, 42*(1), 54–67.

Sewpaul, V. (2001). Models for intervention for children in difficult circumstances in South Africa. *Child Welfare, 80*(5), 571–86.

Smale, G. (1995). Integrating community and individual practice: A new paradigm for practice. In P. Adams & K. Nelson (Eds), *Reinventing human services: Community centered and family centered practice* (pp. 59–80). New York: Aldine de Gruyter.

Streak, J. (2005). *Government's social development response to children made vulnerable by HIV/AIDS: Identifying gaps in policy and budgeting*. Retrieved from http://www.sarpn.org.za/documents/d0001589/index.php

Sturgeon, S. (1998). The future of casework in South Africa. In M. Gray (Ed.), *Developmental social work in South Africa: Theory and practice* (pp.25–39). Cape Town: David Phillip Publishers.

Suda, C. (1999). African family and child welfare: Tradition in transition. *International Journal of Contemporary Sociology, 36*(1), 56–65.

Swadener, E., Kabiru, M., & Njenga, A. (1997). Does the village still raise the child? A collaborative study of changing child-rearing and community mobilization in Kenya. *Early Education and Development, 8*(2), 285–306.

Triegaardt, J. (2005). The Child Support Grant in South Africa: A social policy for poverty alleviation? *International Journal of Social Work, 14*(4), 249255. doi:10.1111/j.1369-6866.2005.00367.x

UNICEF & UNAIDS. (2004). *The framework for the protection, care and support of orphans and vulnerable children living in a world with HIV and AIDS.* Rome: World Food Programme. Retrieved from http://www.wfp.org/content/framework-protection-care-and-support-orphans-and-vulnerable-children-living-world-hiv-and-aids

Waldegrave, C. (2005). "Just therapy" with families on low incomes. *Child Welfare, 84*(2), 265–276.

———. (2006). Contrasting national jurisdictional and welfare responses to violence to children. *Social Policy Journal of New Zealand, 27*, 57–76.

Waldfogel, J. (1998a). Rethinking the paradigm for child protection. *Protecting Children from Abuse and Neglect, 8*(1), 104–119.

———. (1998b). *The future of child protection: How to break the cycle of abuse and neglect.* Cambridge: Harvard University Press.

SECTION 6

Interventions and Innovative Practices

14

Effect of Yoga on Mental Health in Children

Shirley Telles

Yoga for Children

There is an increasing interest in the use of yoga to calm the mind and increase overall health and well-being (White, 2009). Mental health in children has many dimensions such as having healthy interactions with peers and teachers and being able to show appropriate emotional responses while exerting control if necessary. Children can have mental, emotional, and behavioral problems which are real, painful, and costly (National Institute of Mental Health, 1999). Mental health disorders in children are caused by biological factors, the environment, or a combination of the two. Biological factors may include genetics, chemical imbalances in the body, and trauma. Environmental factors such as exposure to violence or abuse, acute or chronic stress, and conditions which increase feelings of insecurity in a child (e.g., loss of a parent) can contribute to mental disorders. Of course it does not follow, that children who have had such experiences would develop mental disorders or that all children who have developed mental disorders have had disturbing experiences.

Yoga is an ancient Indian way of life which includes the practice of certain postures (*asanas*), regulated breathing (*pranayamas*), and meditation (Taimini, 1986). Yoga practice has been shown to be beneficial for the physical and mental health of children. Given the fact that the brain is most susceptible to both external and internal influences early in life, especially during the brain growth spurt period (from the last three months before birth till the first two years of life), it is desirable to begin yoga practice as early as possible. This includes yoga during pregnancy, where clinical observations support the idea that the practice increases the chance of the infant being healthy and progressing well. A systematic study is underway to support these observations. Also, it is essential to mention here that there have been no studies which have shown that beginning to practice yoga early is really beneficial for children, though anecdotal reports from parents/caretakers and teachers suggest that children who learn yoga early on are physically healthier and mentally better adjusted. Some yoga enthusiasts have passively placed the limbs of infants in yoga postures, taking care to be gentle and not to use force. They observed (but there is no published report) that children attained certain milestones (e.g., standing, crawling, walking, and even talking) sooner than those who were not given the yoga postures passively. In the absence of a systematic study this remains an interesting but unproven report. Published research has shown that children as young as seven years of age can improve in attention, concentration, and coordination after learning yoga (Telles, Hanumanthaiah, Nagarathna, & Nagendra, 1993). One of the precautions suggested, again based on unpublished observations, is that prepubertal children should not be asked to practice inverted yoga postures as this is considered likely to result in precocious puberty. Also, those yoga breathing practices (pranayamas), which involve practicing physiological "locks" (*bandha*s) of the internal cavities (e.g., intrathoracic cavity), are also not advised to be practiced by children.

The benefits of yoga practice in children are evident from a study with a quasi-experimental design, in which 31 children (aged between 7 and 12 years) practiced yoga for seven weeks and the effects on their physical health were assessed (Chen, Mao, Lai, Li, & Kuo, 2009). Each 60-minute yoga session included 10 minutes of warm up and breathing exercises, 40 minutes of yoga postures, and 10 minutes of cool down exercises. There were significant improvements in their flexibility, muscle strength, and cardiopulmonary fitness. Since physical fitness and mental well-being are closely related, these results suggest that these children may have also had mental health benefits though the study was not intended to examine them. This study included both breathing exercises and physical postures. This is indeed considered the best approach. According to descriptions of the functioning of the body according to ancient yoga texts there are five levels of existence (*Taittreya Upanishad*). These are (*a*) physical, (*b*) a level of subtle energy (*prana* or *chi*), (*c*) the instinctual mental level, (*d*) the intellectual mental level, and (*e*) the fifth and ideal level, a state of optimal homeostasis and balance (Telles, 2010). Ideally a yoga practice session should include physical postures (asanas), breathing techniques (certain *kriya*s and pranayama practices), meditation, as well as knowledge of the philosophy of yoga. In children also, the ideal program should include all these practices.

Yoga practice has been shown to improve several aspects of mental health in normal children. Before discussing the use of yoga in the management of mental health disorders, the benefits of practicing yoga in promoting positive mental health will be discussed.

In a study by Telles et al. (1993), school children aged between 9 and 13 years, performed better on a hand steadiness test, suggestive of better attention and concentration, after yoga. There were two groups of 45 children each who were assessed using a standard test for static motor performance using a steadiness tester, at the beginning and end of a 10-day period during which one group practiced yoga while the other group continued with their regular routine. The yoga group showed a significant reduction in errors compared to the control group.

In a separate study of 135 school children aged between 9 and 13 years, those who practiced yoga for 10 days showed a significant improvement in spatial memory (Naveen, Nagarathna, Nagendra, & Telles, 1997). Spatial memory is principally a function of the right cerebral hemisphere and hence the results suggest that yoga practice facilitates right hemispheric functioning.

This was considered especially important as the educational system nowadays places a disproportionate emphasis on left brain skills such as logic and analysis, required to study science and mathematics. Another study further examined the degree to which yoga practice could influence performance in a spatial memory task when compared to time spent on fine arts, which are considered right hemispheric functions (Manjunath & Telles, 2004). There were two groups of children between 11 and 16 years of age, with 30 children in each group. One group attended a yoga camp, the other a fine arts camp which included drama, painting, and pottery. There was also a no-intervention control group. All three groups were assessed at the beginning and end of a 10-day period. The yoga group showed a significant increase in spatial memory scores. Memory is not the only mental faculty which improved with yoga practice, in the children. Strategic planning based on a Tower of London task, improved in ten girls between 10 and 13 years of age after yoga, compared to an equal number of girls who had a physical training program (Manjunath & Telles, 2001). The Tower of London task assesses the ability to plan by evaluating the number of moves required to complete a designated task. The yoga group showed a significant reduction in planning and execution time, as well as in the number of moves. More recently, a high frequency yoga breathing called *kapalabhati* where the breath rate ranged between 1.0 and 2.0 Hz, was shown to improve the ability to perform a cancellation task which requires both focused and selective attention (Telles, Raghuraj, Arankalle, & Naveen, 2008).

These examples show that yoga practice can promote certain higher mental functions in children with normal health. Girls in a community home, who were under legal custody as they had no responsible guardian to care for them also benefited by yoga practice (Raghuraj & Telles, 1997). Among these girls, a group who practiced yoga for six months had better visual perception (based on the critical flicker frequency test and a geometric optical illusion test) and better motor dexterity, than a group which was given physical training for the same period.

Apart from the examples mentioned above, yoga practice has also been shown to help children with diagnosed mental health problems. This includes anxiety, eating disorders, attention deficit hyperactivity disorder (ADHD), and post-traumatic stress disorder (PTSD) in children exposed to extreme violence or natural calamities. Childhood anxiety manifests in various ways, such as separation anxiety, phobias, somatic manifestations, which include undesirable habits and tics, nightmares, and in some cases extreme physical discomfort (as in panic disorder).

An hour of relaxation therapy was found beneficial in 40 hospitalized children and adolescents (Platania-Solazzo et al., 1992). Of course, while relaxation is an inherent part of yoga, yoga includes other components as well and hence is not the same as relaxation therapy. A randomized trial of yoga for adolescents aged 11 to 18 years with irritable bowel syndrome showed that yoga is effective in reducing anxiety as well (Kuttner et al., 2006). The yoga intervention consisted of a one hour instructional session, demonstration, and practice. This was followed by four weeks of daily practice at home guided by video. Those adolescents who were assigned to the yoga group reported lower levels of functional disability due to irritable bowel syndrome, as well as lower anxiety and less use of emotion-focused avoidance, which is an unhealthy coping strategy.

These results suggest that yoga practice can increase the likelihood of positive behavior patterns and reduce negative behaviors. These findings were further substantiated by a study conducted on fourth and fifth grade inner-city students in Bronx, New York (Berger, Silver, & Stein, 2009). There were 39 children who practiced yoga and 32 who did not. Both groups were assessed at the beginning and end of a 12-week period. Both yoga and non-yoga groups had similar pre-intervention levels of emotional well-being. After 12 weeks of yoga, children in the yoga group had better post-intervention negative behavior scores in response to stress. The results suggested a role for yoga as a preventive intervention as well as a means to improve children's perceived well-being.

When discussing stress coping strategies, it is essential that children develop positive and healthy coping strategies, rather than unhealthy strategies. Healthy strategies include communication with friends, relatives, teachers, or counselors, as well as deriving strength from philosophical and spiritual beliefs. Unhealthy strategies could include substance abuse, use of alcohol, sniffing volatile substances, and in younger children, eating disorders. When exposed to stress, children may overeat or eat less than usual. Nowadays this situation has been further worsened as children are over aware of their body image, and how they appear to their peers. This is probably related to the fact that a poor body image is associated with low self-esteem and children who are overweight are more often bullied and left out of group activities. Yoga has been useful in helping youth at risk for developing type 2 diabetes to lose weight (Benavides & Caballero, 2009). A 12-week prospective *Ashtanga* yoga program had 20 participants. Fourteen of them, aged 8 to 15 years, completed the program. The average weight loss in 12 weeks was two kilograms. Four out of five children who had low self-esteem to begin with improved, while two had decreased self-esteem.

Another 12-week program was evaluated in a separate study (Slawta, Bentley, Smith, Kelly, & Syman-Degler, 2008). This program was called *Be a Fit Kid* and included running, yoga, jumping, and strength exercises. There was also a nutrition component, which focused on a diet rich in vegetables, fruits, unsaturated fats, and whole grains, and was low in saturated fat and sugar. Following the 12-week intervention significant improvements were observed in body composition, fitness, nutrition knowledge, and dietary habits; in those who participated 75 percent of the time there were significant reductions in total cholesterol and triglyceride levels. Hence inclusion of yoga in a fitness program was helpful in improving the physical fitness of children.

The psychological impact of yoga practice was shown in another study which examined the possibility of reducing body dissatisfaction in fifth grade girls (Scime & Cook-Cottone, 2008). There were 75 yoga group participants and 69 in a control group. The yoga sessions consisted of interactive discourses, yoga practice, and relaxation. There was a significant decrease in body dissatisfaction and bulimia following yoga as well as an increase on the social scale of a multidimensional self-concept scale. Hence yoga practice appears to be useful in the management of eating disorders bringing about both physical and mental benefits.

Another disorder which has shown improvement with yoga practice is ADHD, one of the most common mental disorders that develop in children. It is a disabling condition if untreated, as children with ADHD have impaired functioning in multiple settings including their home, school, and in their relationship with peers. Symptoms of ADHD include impulsiveness, hyperactivity, and inattention. If ADHD is suspected, the diagnosis should be made by a professional with training in ADHD, which could include child psychiatrists, psychologists, developmental and behavioral pediatricians, behavioral neurologists, and clinical social workers. The medical treatment for ADHD is now considered best supplemented with behavior therapy.

Yoga may be considered a form of therapy intended to modify behavior. Boys diagnosed with ADHD by specialist pediatricians, and stabilized with medication, were the participants in one trial of yoga for ADHD. The boys were randomly assigned to two groups, a yoga group (n = 11) or a control group (n = 8). Assessments included the Conner's Parent and Teacher Rating Scales, the Test of Variables of Attention, and an actigraph which could detect and quantify movement. The result showed some benefits with yoga practice but could not be considered conclusive. The yoga group (but not the control group) showed significant improvement in five subscales of the Conner's Rating Scales, these were oppositional, and the global index for emotional lability, the global index total, global index restless/impulsive, and the ADHD index. However significant improvements were also found for the control group, but not the yoga group on three subscales, which were: hyperactivity, anxious/shy, and social problems. The improvements seen in the yoga group were increased for those who engaged in more home practice.

Another study also investigated the usefulness of yoga for children with a clinical diagnosis of ADHD (Haffner, Roos, Goldstein, Parzer, & Resch, 2006). There were 19 children with a clinical diagnosis of ADHD. They were randomized as two groups, a yoga group and a group given conventional motor training. The yoga group performed better than the control group in an attention task and in ratings of ADHD symptoms.

While ADHD is a diagnosed condition which requires treatment, many children nowadays are more active than would be expected. This has a number of repercussions, such as the inability to be attentive and perform well in school, apparent misbehavior, and in some children, sleep disorders, including restlessness. While polysomnograph recordings on adult experienced meditators have shown an increase in slow wave sleep with fewer arousals and overall lower sympathetic tone, compared to those who did not meditate, there have been no studies so far on the effect of yoga on children (Patra & Telles, 2009a, 2009b). However, it is reasonable to speculate that yoga practice may have similar effects on the sleep structure in children, which would have an impact on their functioning during the day.

The last mental health disorder mentioned in this chapter, which has been managed by yoga, is post traumatic stress disorder. Children may be exposed to different types of traumatic events and violence. While natural disorders such as floods or hurricanes have less chances of being personalized, direct confrontation with an assailant, or being a victim of sexual abuse, or torture is obviously more personalized and hence more traumatic. One hundred and thirty-six high school students were given a six-week intervention for PTSD in post-war Kosovo (Gordon, Staples, Blyta, & Bytyqi, 2004). The six-week program included meditation, biofeedback, drawings, autogenic training, guided imagery, genograms, movements, and breathing techniques. Three separate programs were held approximately two months apart. Posttraumatic stress scores significantly decreased after participation in the programs. The scores remained low in the two groups that took part in the follow-up study when compared to pretest measures. This is an example of PTSD following exposure to violence. In a separate study, spiritual hypnosis assisted therapy, which could be consisted as allied to yoga therapy was evaluated after the terrorist attack in Bali, in 2002 (Lesmana, Suryani, Jensen, & Tiliopoulos, 2009). There were 226 children between the ages of 6 and 12 years among whom 53 percent were females. All of them had experienced the terrorist bomb blasts in Bali in 2002 and were subsequently diagnosed with PTSD. Forty-eight of them received spiritual hypnosis assisted therapy, while 178 did not. Spiritual hypnosis assisted therapy produced a 77.1 percent improvement at a two-year follow-up compared to 24 percent in the control group.

These studies suggest that yoga and allied interventions are useful in the management of PTSD in children. In summary the present article shows that yoga improves physical and mental well-being in children. Specific faculties improve, such as spatial memory in a delayed recall task, performance in a strategic planning task and in a task for selective and sustained attention. There was also better performance in tasks for perception and motor skills.

Yoga also has beneficial effects in the management of anxiety, eating disorders, attention deficit hyperactivity disorder, and PTSD. Some of these studies were reasonably well designed, though further research is required to understand the mechanisms underlying the benefits seen with yoga practice. Other studies can be considered exploratory and form the basis for future more rigorous studies.

Challenges to Teaching Yoga and Testing Its Effects

There are several challenges in researching the effects of yoga in children. Some of the difficulties are related to carrying out assessments in children. Many studies use the easiest to measure objective tests (a standard example is the EUROFIT battery of tests). However many aspects of cognitive and emotional functioning require the use of complex psychological questionnaires. Depending on their age and comprehension, children may find it difficult to respond accurately to the questions asked. Other children may be hesitant to give responses which they would feel could possibly influence the way they are judged by their peers and teachers.

Apart from methodological issues related to assessing the children's response to yoga, there are certain issues related to teaching yoga to children. There are three main differences between yoga and physical activity. One of them is the fact that yoga practice is characterized by directing the attention to all sensations arising in the body and maintaining awareness without being distracted. This is often practically difficult. Therefore, to begin with, children are asked to sit still for brief periods and be aware of some sensation in their body which is easy to perceive, such as the movements associated with respiration. This also becomes a part of the training in learning to observe brief periods of silence.

The second difference is asking the children to remember to coordinate the phases of respiration with different body movements. For example they are asked to breathe in as they bend backwards and exhale with forward bending. These instructions about accompanying specific movements with phases of respiration are the second distinguishing feature between yoga and physical activity.

The third distinguishing feature between yoga and physical exercise is that during the practice of yoga the instructor continually reminds the children to relax. This also is often challenging as children would prefer to be actively engaged in physical activity. Nonetheless training in relaxation is both important and feasible to do with children.

While teaching yoga to children poses a set of challenges, there are different difficulties associated with carrying out research on the effects of yoga in children. One of the difficulties is making the test interesting for the child so that the child would feel like performing the test. In many cases long or involved questionnaires cause a child to be disinterested and careless in responding. The other difficulty is ensuring that the child understands what is required to be done or what exactly a question means, and the kind of response expected.

This situation in which the results may be modified by the fact that children may either not understand or not perform the tests with complete interest and understanding would be particularly relevant for younger children. Apart from this when attempting to understand the effects of yoga practice it is interesting to understand how the practices impact the behavior of children, particularly their interaction with their peers and teachers at school and their siblings and parents at home. Questionnaires may often give misleading results. In these cases observing the actual behavior of the children in a school setting using a structured observational method may be far more useful than attempting to answer these questions through questionnaires even if they are proven to be reliable and valid for children of a particular age group. Hence a combination of research methods would to be the best way to understand the impact of yoga on the physical, mental, emotional, and social health and behavior of children.

Acknowledgments

The author gratefully acknowledges the help of Mr Abhishek Bhardwaj and Ms Arti Yadav in compiling the manuscript.

References

Benavides, S., & Caballero, J. (2009). Ashtanga yoga for children and adolescents for weight management and psychological well being: An uncontrolled open pilot study. *Complementary Therapies in Clinical Practice, 15*(2), 110–14. doi:10.1016/j.ctcp.2008.12.004

Berger, D., Silver, E., & Stein, R. (2009). Effects of yoga on inner-city children's well-being: A pilot study. *Alternative Therapies in Health and Medicine, 15*(5), 36–42.

Chen, T., Mao, H., Lai, C., Li, C., & Kuo, C. (2009). The effect of yoga exercise intervention on health related physical fitness in school-age asthmatic children. *Chinese Journal of Nursing-Zhonghua Huli Zazhi, 56*(2), 42–52.

Gordon, J., Staples, J., Blyta, A., & Bytyqi, M. (2004). Treatment of posttraumatic stress disorder in postwar Kosovo high school students using mind-body skills groups: A pilot study. *Journal of Traumatic Stress, 17*(2), 143–147. doi:10.1023/B:JOTS.0000022620.13209.a0

Haffner, J., Roos, J., Goldstein, N., Parzer, P., & Resch, F. (2006). The effectiveness of body-oriented methods of therapy in the treatment of attention-deficit hyperactivity disorder (ADHD): Results of a controlled pilot study. *Zeitschrift fur Kinder und Jugendpsychiatrie und Psychotherapie, 34*(1), 37–47.

Kuttner, L., Chambers, C., Hardial, J., Israel, D., Jacobson, K., & Evans, K. (2006). A randomized trial of yoga for adolescents with irritable bowel syndrome. *Pain Research Management, 11*(4), 217–223.

Lesmana, C., Suryani, L., Jensen, G., & Tiliopoulos, N. (2009). A spiritual-hypnosis assisted treatment of children with PTSD after the 2002 Bali terrorist attack. *American Journal of Clinical Hypnosis, 52*(1), 23–34.

Manjunath, N., & Telles, S. (2001). Improved performance in the Tower of London Test following yoga. *Indian Journal of Physiology and Pharmacology, 45*(3), 351–354.

———. (2004). Spatial and verbal memory test scores following yoga and fine arts camps for school children. *Indian Journal of Physiology and Pharmacology, 48*(3), 353–356.

National Institute of Mental Health. (1999). *Brief notes on the mental health of children and adolescents*. Bethesda, MD: Author. Retrieved from http://www.ncbi.nlm.nih.gov/pubmed/12540145

Naveen, K., Nagarathna, R., Nagendra, H., & Telles, S. (1997). Yoga breathing through a particular nostril increases spatial memory scores without lateralized effects. *Psychological Reports, 81*(2), 555–561.

Patra S., & Telles, S. (2009a). Heart rate variability during sleep following the practice of cyclic meditation and supine rest. *Applied Psychophysiology and Biofeedback, 35*(2), 135–140. doi:10.1007/s10484-009-9114-1

———. (2009b). Positive impact of cyclic meditation on subsequent sleep. *Medical Science Monitor, 15*(7), 375–381.

Platania-Solazzo, A., Field, T., Blank, J., Seligman, F., Kuhn, C., Schanberg, S., & Saab, P. (1992). Relaxation therapy reduces anxiety in child and adolescent psychiatricpatients. *Acta Paedopsychiatrica, 55*(2), 115–120.

Raghuraj, P., & Telles, S. (1997). Muscle power, dexterity skill and visual perception in community home girls trained in yoga or sports and in regular school girls. *Indian Journal of Physiology and Pharmacology, 41*(4), 409–415.

Scime, M., & Cook-Cottone, C. (2008). Primary prevention of eating disorders: A constructivist integration of mind and body strategies. *International Journal of Eating Disorders, 41*(2), 134–142.

Slawta, J., Bentley, J., Smith, J., Kelly, J., & Syman-Degler, L. (2008). Promoting healthy lifestyles in children: A pilot program of be a fit kid. *Health Promotion Practice, 9*(3), 305–312. doi:10.1177/1524839906289221

Taimini, I. K. (1986). *The science of yoga*. Madras, India: The Theosophical Publishing House.

Telles, S. (2010). A theory of disease from ancient yoga texts. *Medical Science Monitor, 16*(6), LE9.

Telles, S., Hanumanthaiah, B., Nagarathna, R., & Nagendra, H. (1993). Improvement in static motor performance following yogic training of school children. *Perceptual and Motor Skills, 76*(3), 1264–1266.

Telles, S., Raghuraj, P., Arankalle, D., & Naveen, K. (2008). Immediate effect of high-frequency yoga breathing on attention. *Indian Journal of Medical Sciences, 62*(1), 20–22.

White, L. S. (2009). Yoga for children. *Pediatric Nursing, 35*(5), 277–283.

15

Raga Therapy: Power of Music to Alleviate Academic Stress in Adolescents

Vandana Sharma
Mamta Sharma

Children and adolescents today face a plethora of stressful problems, including family and relationship conflict, death of close family members or friends, and academic and social pressures. The effects of stress in a student's life can have a serious impact on his/her ability to perform, progress, or succeed in school. The degree of stress experienced by an individual in a given situation depends not only on the objective properties of the stressor (e.g., intensity, frequency, duration), the individual's perception and processing of the event, and one's personal coping resources and strategies in transacting with environmental stressors, but also on the specific context and period of one's life cycle in which environmental demands are experienced.

Academic stress is a common issue that everyone has to cope with at some time in their lives and not knowing how to cope with stress can affect other areas in a persons' life. Academic stress is the product of a combination of academic related demands that exceed the adaptive resources available to an individual. The extent of academic stress appears to be similar across the cultures. Research indicates that higher levels of stress can predict later academic failure which has serious implications on several levels (Needham, Crosnoe, & Muller, 2004). If a student is unable to cope effectively with academic stress, then serious psychosocial-emotional health consequences may result (Arthur, 1998; MacGeorge, Samter, & Gillihan, 2005; Tennant, 2002). These include academic failure, social misbehavior, interpersonal problems, depression, and psychological distress (Steinhardt & Dolbier, 2008).

Adolescents are often ill-equipped to cope with stress during transitions from childhood to preadolescence and from preadolescence to adolescence phases. For adolescents, identity crisis; the perils of peer interaction; acceptance and rejection of situations, persons, and ideas; and academic pressures are a constant source of stress and depression. Life for many young people is a painful tug of war filled with mixed messages and conflicting demands from parents, teachers, friends, and one's own self. Adolescents today face greater hazards to their physical and mental well-being than did their counterparts in earlier years (Peterson, Maier, & Seligman, 1995). Adolescents lack self-reliance, confidence, and ability to plan for themselves (Erickson, 1963). Research has given enough explanation for this; the most prominent is the age itself and the characteristics associated with it. An adolescent is faced with rapid physiological changes and a sudden drive to behave like an adult, but lacks the experience for the same. Theories of stress are useful in explaining and understanding the dynamics of behaviors, the processes for changing behaviors, and the effects of external influences on behaviors (Glanz, Rimer, & Lewis, 2002).

Theoretical Approaches to Stress

Hans Selye, the first major stress researcher, defined stress as essentially the rate of wear and tear on body. Selye found that any problem, real or imagined, results in the cerebral cortex (the thinking part of the brain) to send an alarm to the hypothalamus (the main switch for stress response). The hypothalamus then stimulates the sympathetic nervous system to make changes in the body. Heart rate, breathing rate, muscle tension, and blood pressure all increase. Hands and feet get cold as blood is directed away from extremities. Pupils dilate to sharpen vision and hearing also becomes more acute. At one time in the lives of the human race, these changes were an alarm system that prepared our body stay and fight or to flee from the stressful situation. Stress and its psychological manifestations are inherent in human life and are a major source of concern in modern day society (Selye, 1956).

The Cognitive Approach

This approach to stress is based on a mental process of how the individual appraises the situation, and its sources include physical resources, such as how healthy one is, how much energy one has; social resources, such as the family or friends one has to depend on for support in the immediate surroundings; psychological resources, such as self-esteem and self-efficacy; and material resources, such as how much money one has or what kind of equipment is available for use. Environmental stress occurs when environmental stimuli or demands are perceived by an individual to tax or exceed his or her resources to handle them (Lazarus & Launier, 1978). The level of appraisal determines the level of stress and the unique coping strategies that the individual partakes (Lazarus & Folkman, 1984). There are two types of appraisals, the primary and the secondary. A primary appraisal is made when the individual makes a conscious evaluation of the matter at hand of whether it is harm or a loss, a threat or a challenge. Then a secondary appraisal takes place when the individual asks him/herself, "What can I do?" by evaluating the coping resources around him/her.

The Diathesis-Stress Model

A psychological theory that explains behavior as both a result of biological and genetic factors (nature) and life experiences (nurture), this model assumes that a disposition toward a certain disorder may result from a combination of one's genetics and early learning. The term "diathesis" is used to refer to a genetic predisposition toward an abnormal or diseased condition. According to the model, this predisposition, in combination with certain kinds of environmental stress, results in abnormal behavior.

Academic stress is a mental stress with respect to some anticipated frustration associated with academic failure or even an awareness of possibility of such failure (Gupta & Khan, 1987). The academic setting is facing a major trend of high levels of student stress. The changes affecting students are, being away from parents and home for the first time, handling financial matters, and competition for grades (Fisher, 1994). Children are constantly under the stress of studies and examinations; they are entangled in the web of "academic stress." Academic stress means a pervasive sense of urgency to learn all those things which are prescribed by the school (Shah, 1988).

What Are Academic Stress Points?

Academic stress points normally occur at certain developmental periods in education. When expectations for academic performance increase, adolescents feel stress. All adolescents have to make adjustments at times of transition. The key is to see if the child can adapt to these challenges and learn new strategies within a normal period of time. Expectations change in school at different grade levels when significantly new and different requirements are placed on learning (see Table 15.1).

Table 15.1 Learning Expectations at Different Grade Levels

Grade Level	Expectations
Preschool/Kindergarten	Learning to learn
Grade 1	Learning to read
Grade 4	Reading to learn
Middle School	Learning to organize your learning
High School	Learning to read, organize, and learn on your own
College	Doing it on your own

Source: Jan Baumel (2008).

Academic stress is on rise, partly because the "information age" now provides the students with vast information at their fingertips and because of that students are expected to synthesize such information at a more accelerated rate than when their parents attended school. It is of concern because of its negative effect on the physical, emotional, social, psychological development of the children (Omizo, Omizo, & Suzuki, 1988). Adolescents under stress experience a variety of serious problems (Chandler, 1982). It leaves the overburdened students listless and often feeling suicidal (Gurung, 2005) Thus with the mounting standard, rising stress on intellectual context and sharpening competition, it is adding to the numbers who show the symptoms of academic stress.

Children are often ill equipped to deal with life's pressures, resulting in angry outbursts, defiant behaviors, and long-lasting negative impacts on their learning and development (Honig, 2010), but little systematic research has been conducted on the issue. Social scientists term such a tendency as "rational disaster" which is not curable but preventable (Fr. Norby Vithayathil, 2009). Studies on mental health, well-being, and behavior problems among the adolescents remain limited. The data suggest the need for curative, preventive, and promotive measures dealing with mental health problems among the adolescents (Malhotra et al., 2002; Bijlani, 2000; Verma & Saraswathi, 2002).

The efforts to treat this psychosocial-biological stage of adolescence have led to the introduction of complementary therapies, which take care of the often unmet psychological and social needs of the clients and patients. In a country like India, known for its rich cultural heritage and traditions, many traditional healing systems like Yoga, Meditation, and Ayurveda have been welcomed globally and have been given scientific endorsements for their therapeutic values. Music therapy (Sundar, 2005) is one such approach which can be useful in preventing rational disaster.

Music therapy is the use of music by health care professionals to promote healing and enhance quality of life. Numerous studies have shown that music therapy can inhibit stress, reducing the neurohormonal responses to psychological stress as well as preoperative anxiety and postoperative pain (David, Wun, & Stern, 2011; Leardi et al., 2007; Ulrica, 2009). Many experts suggest that it is the rhythm of the music or the beat that has the calming effect, although one may not be very conscious about it. A distinction can be made between music therapy and music *as* therapy. The former is practiced by trained music therapists, whilst the latter may be used in a more informal manner to achieve significant improvements in health and well-being (Biley, 2001).

Indian music therapy is an integration of ancient healing practices and musical traditions coupled with the recent modifications derived based on modern day practice. Indian music therapy is based on long empirical traditions not proven in the western sense of empiricism, but it is unique and cultural. It is an aesthetic process which contains qualities such as creativity, intuition, inspiration, intention, and spiritual elements (Amir, 1993). These qualities are connected to the inner state of the living being.

Music therapy has a long history dating back to ancient Greece. King David's curing an illness by playing the harp would count for the same in the Old Testament. Hippocrates, the father of modern medicine, is said to have used it extensively. In ancient Egypt, pain of childbirth was reduced thus. In Indian legends, Thyagaraja, the famous South Indian musician is believed to have sung back life into the dead. And in 1729 Richard Browne compiled the well-known *Medicina Musica*.

Hindustani Classical Music

The North Indian style of Indian classical music is known as Hindustani music. Originating in the Vedic period, it is a tradition that has been evolving from the 12th century AD, in what are now northern India, Bangladesh, and Pakistan, and also Nepal and Afghanistan. It is one of the two kinds of Indian classical music, the other being Carnatic music, which represents the music of South India.

One of the unique characteristics of Hindustani music is the assignment of definite times of the day and night for performing and listening to *raga* (melody). It is believed that only in this period the raga appears to be at the height of its melodic beauty and majestic splendor. There are ragas and *ragini*s which can be distinguished as root-ragas and their derivatives. Raginis are considered to be minor and graceful and abbreviated forms of ragas reflecting the character of the ragas (Sharma, 2000). The ragas and raginis derived their names from seasons, religion cults, flowers, birds, geographical area, names of musicians, and particular times of the day when they are supposed to be sung. Although the total number of ragas in Hindustani classical music was as large as 300, several of them have been lost over the centuries. About 100 ragas are known and performed these days. Some of the popular ragas are *asavari, bhairavi, bahar, darbari, desh, jai-jaiwanti, malhar, piloo, todi, yaman*, etc. Raga is the sequence of selected *swara*s (notes) that lend appropriate mood or emotion. Depending on their nature, a raga could induce or intensify joy or sorrow, violence, or peace and it is this quality which forms the basis for musical application. Thus, a whole range of emotions and their nuances could be captured and communicated within certain rhythms and melodies. Playing, performing, and even listening to appropriate ragas can work as a medicine (Bagchi, 2003). Various ragas have since been recognized to have a definite impact on certain ailments.

Each of the *shuddha* (pure) swaras (viz., *Sa, Re/Ri, Ga, Ma, Pa, Dha/Da*, and *Ni*) is associated with one of the seven *chakras*[1] of the body. The chakras regulate the flow of vital energies into and from the body and are exercised to facilitate health, happiness, and spiritual growth. These seven chakras are: Root Chakra, Spleen Chakra, Solar Plexus Chakra, Heart Chakra, Throat Chakra, Third Eye Chakra, and Crown Chakra. The seven basic swaras of the musical octave have a one-to-one correspondence with these chakras (Seaward, 2011). Just as the swaras ascend through the *saptak* (seven chakras), so they are mapped onto the chakras in the body in ascending order. *Komal* (soft) notes are associated with the left side of each chakra; the left channel, *Ida Nadi*, is the

---
[1] The seven invisible portals that lie within the human electromagnetic field; in Sanskrit, *chakra* means wheel.

side of emotion and intuition. Shuddha and *tivra* (fast) notes are associated with the right side; the right channel, *Pingala Nadi*, is the side of logic. Ragas, therefore, have more or less of an effect on a given chakra depending on the notes they contain.

How Music Therapy Does Wonders

To understand the basic mechanism how music therapy works, one needs to understand its two approaches.

Physiological Approach

The neuron endocrine system is responsible for the maintenance of the body through the proper secretion of hormones and chemicals into the bloodstream. Music affects this system in three principal ways. First, endorphins the body's natural opiates—are released from the pituitary gland, thereby relieving pain and influencing mood state and memory (Cook, 1986). Second, there is a decrease in the secretion of catecholamines, such as epinephrine and norepinephrine, from the adrenal medulla associated with reductions in heart rate, metabolic rate, blood pressure, free fatty acids, and oxygen consumption. In addition, the chances of having a migraine, experiencing coronary heart disease, gastrointestinal ulcers, and cerebral vascular accident decreases (O'Sullivan, 1991). Third, there is a decrease in levels of adrenal corticosteroids as well as corticotrophin-releasing hormone (CRH) and adrenocorticotrophic hormone (ACTH), which are secreted during stress (Kaminski & Hall, 1996).

On the other hand, music is thought to activate biochemical and electrical memory material across the corpus callosum, thus enhancing the ability of the two hemispheres to work in unity, rather than in opposition (Updike, 1990). After reaching the corpus callosum, music stimuli go down toward the regions of the autonomic nervous system and neuroendocrine system. In the autonomic nervous system, music allows the parasympathetic system to override the sympathetic system, resulting in a relaxed response state (Cook, 1986; Coughlan, 1994; O'Sullivan, 1991). Another approach which attempts to explain how music might affect physiological response is by Asha (1991) who says that the sound waves touch certain sets of neurons in the brain that get activated and increase the amount of ethanol in the body. The level of the ethanol in the body is related to the emotional health of the individual.

Psychological Approach

Music pertains to the perception and expression of the infinite spectrum of the rhythmic flow of the *ahata nada* (perceivable sonic currents) pervading in nature. Music has direct impact on the seven major chakras hidden along the endocrine column and hence affects our physical as well as subtle bodies. The ancient system of *Nada yoga*,[2] which dates back to the times of *Tantras*,[3] has fully acknowledged the impact of music on body and mind and put into practice the vibrations emanating from sounds to uplift one's level of consciousness (Bagchi, 2003). According to Yati (1987), music can change the lifestyle of an individual if he listens to it with concentration.

Research in energy medicine (*pranic* healing) and classical music shows that specific *shahtriya* ragas enhance the level of vital energy. It is the deficiencies and disorders in the vital energy distribution in the mind–body system, which is the root cause of its ailing state. The smooth and increased flow of vital energy rejuvenates the mind and empowers the immune system as well as the auto-regulatory healing mechanism of the body. This is how classical music generates new hope, joy, and enthusiasm in the otherwise dull or depressed mind and removes the disorders and relieves one of the untoward pressures and excitements of inferiority, despair, fear, anger, and so on. Music in itself activates and brings joy and belief in oneself and can help people to feel that they can manage (Orth & Verburgt, 1998).

Research has shown that music therapy in any form, be it Indian or Western, has yielded beneficial effects for the modification of emotional, behavioral, and psychological problems. More recent studies which have recognized the therapeutic effect of music on health and education as an alternative therapy are primarily based on western viewpoint and have been carried out in western countries (Davy, 2001; Pouliot, 1998; Roth, 2011) but its effect is almost negligibly investigated in context to academic stress among adolescents in the Indian setting. The therapeutic benefits of music have been known and harnessed since ancient times. However, music is considered the best tranquilizer in modern days of anxiety, tension, and stress.

The need of the hour is to scientifically explore the curative power of music of certain ragas on hormonal or glandular functions which produce secretions that keep the body balanced and infection free, and to ameliorate stress and especially chronic stress to improve everyday functioning.

Studying the Effect of Raga Darbari Kanada on Stress

Objective of the Study

Research in neurological functioning supports the association between music and cognitive development. Music functions to ease stress responses psychologically, physiologically, and endocrinologically. It is well known that listening to music eases uneasiness (Gerdner & Swanson, 1993),

---

[2]The ancient yoga of sound, both audible and inaudible. Yoga means union with the divine.
[3]The varied scriptures pertaining to secret traditions rooted in Hindu and Buddhist philosophy. It represents the practical aspect of the Vedic tradition.

depression, and fatigue (Hanser & Thompson, 1994; Field, Quintino, Henteleff, Wells-Keife, & Delvecchio-Feinberg, 1997). The aim of the study was to facilitate change in the behavior of adolescents with an emphasis on lowering their academic stress, through the therapeutic use of music in general and raga Darbari Kanada[4] in particular.

In the present study, four forms of academic stress were assessed using the Bisht Battery of Stress Scale (1987): academic pressure, academic anxiety, academic conflict, and academic frustration. Academic anxiety is wherein the anxiety gets in the way of the person's performance in school, to the extent of it affecting his/her ability to learn even outside school. It is the apprehension one feels about the overall picture of academic evaluation including test taking, test preparation, assignment completion, and so forth. It generally includes disruptive thought patterns and physiological responses and behaviors that follow from concern about the possibility of an unacceptably poor performance on an academic task. At school there is a range of academic pressure that is felt, derived from a need for perfection; worry over grades; and parental pressure—whether about obtaining marks or making career choices, competition, sports, or a tough class load. Sometimes it is the pressure from peers when friends in groups continuously compare marks and discuss the extent of revisions done. Academic frustration is the quality or state of being frustrated or thoroughly upset by one or multiple things either directly or indirectly related to school, classes, homework, or other academic aspects. In academic conflict, when students do not share common experiences or hold common beliefs with their parents and teachers in terms of their career choices, experience differences between the norms and attitudes which operate in practice and the norms and attitudes characteristics of the academic setting. Conflicts between home and school may occur over how children have been taught to view the world, the qualities of interpersonal relationships, standards of behavior, and the goals and objectives of education.

Raga Darbari Kanada was chosen because of its somber and majestic appeal which makes a profound emotional impact on the human mind. We hypothesized that adolescents experiencing academic stress will benefit by listening to raga Darbari. Post-intervention scores on all four dimensions of academic stress would be significantly less as compared to pre-intervention scores.

Design and Procedure

A pre- and post-assessment design was adopted for the study. Music therapy was used with fifty adolescents who had high scores on four parameters of academic stress identified with the help of

---

[4]Raga Darbari Kanada, one of the most popular ragas, has been described as the Emperor of Ragas. This raga is associated with the Moghul Emperor Akbar's court (darbar) and is considered to have been brought into North Indian music by Tansen, Akbar's court musician. Several prominent musicians have even stated that Darbari Kanada is the raga they would choose to sing before passing away!

the Bisht Battery of Stress scale. As per availability of participants, the subjects were divided into six groups. Each group comprised 5 participants. Raga Darbari was used to evaluate the efficacy of music therapy program on academic stress. According to Halpern and Savary (1985), the music played should be without lyrics (only instrument); if there are lyrics, attention is focused on the lyrics, not the music. The time duration should be between 25 and 60 minutes (the longer the music is played it would become an "attention catcher") and the beat per minute should be in the range of 50–60 beats because it can bring the audience from the beta waves (14–20Hz) to alpha waves (9–13 Hz) (Campbell, 1997). The timing of therapy should be according to the timings of the ragas. All the above mentioned parameters were taken care of while selecting the particular piece of music for this intervention.

The intervention phase took around two months to complete. The participants were exposed to the raga Darbari for fifteen days. These sessions were conducted in the school premises after obtaining permission from the respective Principals. The sessions were conducted in a separate classroom of each school in which they were seated in a semicircle facing outwards so that they could not look at each other and were instructed to enjoy the music through headphones till the music continued. Each session lasted 30–40 minutes and was conducted five times a week. After two weeks, the same Academic stress Scale was given to see the effect of raga Darbari on academic stress.

According to Sharma (2000), music with its roots in rhythm is related to the Id and the unconscious as well as to the emotional elements and sensual experiences within the ego. Therefore, music is perceived on the subcortical level, that is, in the thalamus which is the seat of emotions, feelings, and sensation and has an almost magical effect on the students who are suffering from high anxiety levels at school (Sharma, 2006). Instrumental music can help to focus because there are no lyrics and loud sound effects to distract, especially when reading or writing.

Results

Post-intervention mean scores on subscales of frequency dimension of the academic stress scale are comparatively less than pre-intervention scores (Table 15.2). There is a significant difference between pre- and post-scores on frequency dimension of academic frustration (t = 5.24**, p < .01), academic pressure (t = 4.32**, p < .01), academic anxiety (t = 2.56*, p < .05) and academic stress (t = 5.45**, p < .01). No significant difference is observed on academic conflict.

Table 15.3 depicts post-intervention mean scores on subscales of quantity dimension of the academic stress scale, which were less compared to pre-intervention scores. Significant difference is seen between pre- and post-scores on quantity dimension of academic frustration (t = 4.65**, p < .01), academic pressure (t = 3.84**, p < .01), academic anxiety (t = 4.27, p < .01) and academic stress (t = 5.52**, p < .01). There is no significant difference on academic conflict scores.

Table 15.2 Pre- and Post-scores on Subscales of Frequency Dimension of the Academic Stress Scale

Variables	Pre-intervention Means	SDs	Post-intervention Means	SDs	t-values
AA	25.11	6.68	22.09	5.24	2.56*
AP	38.02	9.23	30.9	7.14	4.32**
AF	45.21	8.55	36.34	8.10	5.24**
AC	24.24	7.97	22.69	6.20	0.72
Academic Stress Total	132.58	21.82	112.02	15.44	5.45**

Notes: AA = Academic anxiety, AP = Academic pressure, AF = Academic frustration, AC = Academic conflict, *Significant at .05 level, **Significant at .01 level.

Table 15.3 Pre- and Post-scores on Subscales of Quantity Dimension of the Academic Stress Scale

Variables	Pre-intervention Means	SDs	Post-intervention Means	SDs	t-values
AA	25.28	6.80	20.66	3.51	4.27**
AP	45.35	6.38	40.7	5.80	3.84**
AF	52.90	6.15	46.80	6.99	4.65**
AC	16.90	5.92	16.80	4.03	0.10
Academic Stress Total	134.42	14.79	119.83	11.37	5.52**

Note: AA = Academic anxiety, AP = Academic pressure, AF = Academic frustration, AC = Academic conflict.

Discussion

The findings of the study showed significant decrease in participants' academic stress in terms of academic anxiety, academic pressure, and academic frustration but no statistically significant difference was found between pre- and post-scores of academic conflict scores following music therapy intervention. It depicts the efficacy of music therapy in reducing academic stress among adolescents. The findings can be explained within the framework of physiological basis of music therapy and academic stress. Music allows the parasympathetic system to override the sympathetic system, resulting in a relaxed response state. Music can stimulate the production of endorphins, the body's natural opiates, as well as reduce levels of cortisol and nor adrenaline, hormones related to stress (Watkins, 1997). Music therapy helps in decreasing the levels of adrenal corticosteroids as well as CRH and ACTH which are secreted during stress (Kaminski & Hall, 1996).

Another explanation may be that music provides a mood enhancing effect. Music can be used to bring a more positive state of mind, helping to keep depression and anxiety at bay. This can help prevent the stress response from wreaking havoc on the body, and can help keep creativity and optimism levels higher, bringing many other benefits. Music has been found to obscure peripheral environmental stimuli in cognitive and motor tasks (Poulton, 1979). As a result, potential sources of frustration, anger, and threat are less likely to be noticed.

Music has been found to reduce stress, anger, frustration, agitation, and arousal due, in part, to distraction (McCaffery, 1990; Wiesenthal, Hennessy, & Totten, 2000; Wostratzky, Braun, & Roth, 1988). Music therapy can be supplied to allay anxiety in patients receiving mechanical ventilation (Korhan, Khorshid, & Uyar, 2011). Creative arts therapies share a commitment to an expressive action that engages emotions in a direct and physical way. It is believed that music has an ability to generate creative energy as a healing force for mind, body, and spirit; which can find its way through out most perplexing and complex problems and conflicts (McNiff, 2005).

The results also fall in line with Sharma's (2006) findings which state that music therapy has an almost magical effect on the students who are suffering from high anxiety levels at school. The results are also aligned with the findings of Leardi et al. (2007) who concluded that music therapy could reduce stress and the stress response, and Brennan & Charnetski (2000) who studied the effect of music on self-reported stress levels and the immune system and found that music reduces participants' perceived level of stress.

Conclusion

Indian music therapy is an integration of ancient healing practices and musical traditions coupled with the recent modifications derived based on the modern day practice and the knowledge gained by current clinical studies undertaken. Therapeutic music therapy service in form of Raga Darbari is found desirable by academically stressed adolescents and a vital tool in reduction of stress. Since significant differences have been found between pre- and post-therapy sessions, one can conclude that the usefulness of music as therapy has been proven to be valid and should be included as part of their daily routine.

References

Amir, D. (1993). Research in music therapy: Quantitative or qualitative? *Nordic Journal of Music Therapy, 2*(2), 3–10.
Arthur, N. (1998). The effects of stress, depression, and anxiety on postsecondary students's coping strategies. *Journal of College Student Development, 39*(1), 11–22.
Asha. (1991). Sangeet Dhara. *Vaidya Shastrm, 20,* 42–43.
Bagchi, K. (Ed.). (2003). *Music, mind and mental health.* New Delhi: Society for Gerontological Research.
Bijlani, S. (2000, October). Why do children commit suicide? *Reader's Digest,* 137–142.

Biley, F. C. (2001). Music as therapy. In D. Rankin-Box (Ed.), *The nurse's handbook of complementary therapies* (pp. 223–228). Edinburgh: Baillière Tindall.

Bisht, R. A. (1987). *Bisht battery of stress scale*. National Psychological Corporation, Agra, UP, India.

Brennan, F. X., & Charnetski, C. J. (2000). Stress and immune system function in a newspaper's newsroom. *Psychological Reports, 87*, 218–222.

Campbell, D. (1997). *The Mozart effect: Tapping the power of music to heal the body, strengthen the mind, and unlock the creative spirit*. New York: HarperCollins.

Chandler, L. A. (1982). *Children under stress: Understanding emotional adjustment reactions*. Springfield, IL: Charles C. Thomas Publishing.

Cook, J. D. (1986). *Music as an intervention in the oncology setting. Cancer Nursing, 9*(1), 23–28.

Coughlan, A. (1994). *Music therapy in ICU. Nursing Times, 90*(17), 35.

David, H., Wun, E., & Stern, A. (2011). Current treatments and advances in pain and anxiety management. *Dental Clinics of North America, 55*(3), 609–618. doi:10.1016/j.cden.2011.02.014

Davy, E. (2001). The relationship between background music in the classroom, attitudes toward nursing research and academic achievement. *Current Science, 87*(7), 10–11.

Erickson, E. (1963). *Childhood and society*, New York: W.W. Norton.

Fr. Norby Vithayathil, V. (2009). *Delving into adolescent suicides in Kerala and suggesting measures to prevent. De Paul Tomes, E-Journal*. www.depaul.edu.in/depaultimes

Field, T., Quintino, O., Henteleff, O., Wells-Keife, L., & Delvecchio-Feinberg, G. (1997). Job stress reduction therapies. *Alternative Therapies in Health and Medicine, 3*(4), 54–56.

Fisher, S. (1994). *Stress in academic life: The mental assembly line*. Bristol, UK: Open University Press.

Gerdner, L. A., & Swanson, E. A. (1993). Effects of individualized music on confused and agitated elderly patients. *Archives of Psychiatric Nursing, 7*(5), 284–291.

Glanz, K., Rimer, B. K. & Lewis, F. M. (Eds). (2002). *Health behavior and health education: Theory, research and practice*. San Francisco: John Wiley & Sons.

Gupta, K., & Khan, B. N. (1987). Anxiety level as factor in concept formation. *Journal of Psychological Reports, 31*(3), 187–192.

Gurung, R. A. R. (2005). How do students really study (and does it matter)? *Teaching of Psychology, 32*, 367–372.

Halpern, S., & Savary, L. (1985). *Sound health: The music and sounds that make us whole*. London: HarperCollins.

Hanser, S. B., & Thompson, L. W. (1994). Effects of a music therapy strategy on depressed older adults. *Journal of Gerontology, 49*(6), 265–269. doi:10.1093/geronj/49.6.P265

Honig, A. S. (2010). *Little kids, big worries: Stress-busting tips for early childhood classrooms*. Baltimore, MD: Brookes Publishing, ISBN 978-1-59857-061-8.

Jan Baumel, M. S. (2008). How changing grade levels causes academic stress. Great Schools Inc. Schwab Learning.org. http://www.schwablearning.org/print_resources.asp?

Kaminski, J., & Hall, W. (1996). The effect of soothing music on neonatal behavioral states in the hospital newborn nursery. *Neonatal Network, 15*(1), 45–54.

Korhan, E. A., Khorshid, L., & Uyar, M. (2011). The effect of music therapy on physiological signs of anxiety in patients receiving mechanical support. *Journal of Clinical Nursing, 20*(7–8), 1026–1034. doi:10.1111/j.1365-2702.2010.03434.x

Lazarus, R. S., & Folkman, S. (1984). *Stress, appraisal, and coping*. New York: Springer.

Lazarus, R. S., & Launier, R. (1978). Stress-related transactions between person and environment. In L. A. Pervin & M. Lewis (Eds), *Perspectives in interactional psychology* (pp. 287–327). New York: Plenum.

Leardi, S., Pietroletti, R., Angeloni, G., Necozione, S., Ranalletta, G., Del Gusto, B. (2007). Randomized clinical trial examining the effect of music therapy in stress response to day surgery. *The British Journal of Surgery, 94*(8), 943–947. doi:10.1002/bjs.5914

MacGeorge, E. L., Samter, W., & Gillihan, S. J. (2005). Academic stress, supportive communication, and health. *Communication Education, 54*(4), 365–372. doi:10.1080/03634520500442236

Malhotra, S., Kohli, A., & Arun, P. (2002). Prevalence of psychiatric disorders in school children in India. *Indian Journal of Medical Research, 116*, 21–28.

McCaffery, M. (1990). Nursing approaches to nonpharmacological pain control. *International Journal of Nursing Studies, 27*(1), 1–5. doi:10.1016/0020-7489(90)90018-E

McNiff, S. (2005). In C. Malchiodi (Ed.), *Expressive therapies*. New York: Guilford Press.

Needham, F. J., Crosnoe, R., & Muller, C. (2004). Academic failure in secondary school: The inter-related role of health problems and educational context. *Social Problems, 51*(4), 569–586. doi:10.1525/sp.2004.51.4.569

Omizo, M. M., Omizo, S. A., & Suzuki, L. A. (1988). Children and stress: An exploratory study of stressors and symptoms. *The School Counselor, 35*(4), 267–274.

Orth, J., & Verburgt, J. (1998). One step beyond: Music therapy with traumatised refugees in a psychiatric clinic. In D. Dokter (Ed.), *Arts therapists, refugees and migrants: Reaching across borders* (pp. 80–93). London: Jessica Kingsley Publishers.

O'Sullivan, R. (1991). A musical road to recovery: Music in intensive care. *Intensive Care Nursing, 7*(3), 160–163. doi:10.1016/0266-612X(91)90004-B

Peterson, C., Maier, S. F., & Seligman, M. E. P. (1995). *Learned helplessness: A theory for the age of personal control*. New York: Oxford University Press.

Pouliot, J. S. (1998, May). The power of music. *The World and I*. Retrieved from http://www.highbeam.com/doc/1G1-21161353.html

Poulton, E. C. (1979). Composite model for human performance in continuous noise. *Psychological Review, 86*(4), 361–375.

Roth, E. (2011). *Neurologic music therapy*. Retrieved from http://homepages.wmich.edu/~eroth/NMT%20Overview.pdf

Seaward, B. L. (2011). *Essentials of managing stress* (2nd ed.). Sudbury, MA: Jones & Bartlett Publishers.

Selye, H. (1956). *The stress of life*. New York: McGraw-Hill.

Shah, M. L. (1988). Academic climates and its concept. *Progress of Education, 62*(1), 13–15.

Sharma, M. (2000). *Mental relaxation: Music therapy, extraversion and neuroticism*. Chandigarh, India: Arun Publishing House.

Sharma, P. (2006, August 22). Worried over children's stress? Try music therapy. *The Tribune*.

Steinhardt, M. A., & Dolbier, C. L. (2008). Evaluation of a resilience intervention to enhance coping strategies and protective factors and decrease symptomatology. *Journal of American College Health, 56*(4), 445–453.

Sunder, S. (2005). Can traditional healing systems integrate with music therapy-Sumathy Sundar interviews T. V. Sairam. *Voices: A World Forum of Music Therapy, 5*(2).

Tennant, C. (2002). Life events, stress, and depression. *Australian and New Zealand Journal of Psychiatry, 36*, 173–182.

Ulrica, N. (2009). The effect of music intervention in stress response to cardiac surgery in a randomized clinical trial. *Heart & Lung: The Journal of Acute and Critical Care, 38*(3), 201–207. doi:10.1016/j.hrtlng.2008.07.008

Updike, P. (1990). Music therapy results for ICU patients. *Dimensions of Critical Care Nursing, 9*(1), 39–45.

Verma, S., & Saraswathi, T. S. (2002). *Adolescence in India: An annotated bibliography*. New Delhi: Rawat Publications.

Watkins, G. R. (1997). Music therapy: Proposed physiological mechanisms and clinical implications. *Clinical Nurse Specialists, 11*(2), 43–50.

Wiesenthal, D. L., Hennessy, D. A., & Totten, B. (2000). The influence of music on driver stress. *Journal of Applied Social Psychology, 30*(8), 1709–1719. doi:10.1111/j.1559-1816.2000.tb02463.x

Wostratzky, S., Braun, E., & Roth, N. (1988). The influence of distraction on coping with stress in dentistry. *Activitas Nervosa Superior, 30*, 120–121

Yati, N. C. (1987). *The psychology of darsanmala*. Verkala, Kerala: Narayana Gurukula Sri Niwasapuram.

16

Cultivating the Capacity to Care in Children and Youth: Implications from EI Theory, EI Self, and BEVI

Craig N. Shealy
Devi Bhuyan
Lee G. Sternberger

Introduction

Around the globe, we face two great challenges—and opportunities—as we seek to raise ourselves with greater wisdom and skill. First, how do we inculcate in our children not only a set of attributes that are associated with mental health, broadly defined, but the associated capacity to experience a sense of caring for oneself, others, and the larger world? Second, what are the implications of the empirically demonstrable fact that our capacity for caring—and our concomitant beliefs about "the other"—are highly correlated with how we ourselves were cared for and experienced by others during our own developmental process? Our ability to apprehend these fundamental realities about the human condition is directly proportional to the amount of suffering that is subsequently alleviated or perpetuated by these same children when they become adults.

But how possibly can we apprehend the complex and idiographic interactions among formative variables (e.g., culture, context, development, and language) and core human needs (e.g., attachment and affiliation) that culminate in our capacity and inclination to care for ourselves and others while translating such understanding into pragmatic form? In full recognition of their complexity, this chapter demonstrates how such big picture questions may productively be explored by examining theory and data from a 20-year national project that seeks to understand (*a*) how, why, and under what circumstances human beings develop their relative capacities to care for self, others, and the larger world, (*b*) the concomitant beliefs, values, attitudes, and worldviews that accompany such capacities, and (*c*) the implications of such findings for the development and well-being of children as well as the functioning of the adults whom they become.

Drawing upon the Forum BEVI Project,[1] a national and multi-site research and assessment initiative which uses the Beliefs, Events, and Values Inventory (BEVI) and its accompanying "Equilintegration" or EI theoretical framework, we highlight how the acquisition of beliefs and values is partly influenced by formative (e.g., developmental life history) and contextual (e.g., ethnic background) variables that interact with affective and attributional processes to produce a tendency to "see" self, others, and the world in particular ways.

Beliefs, Values, and the Capacity to Care

Lacey is a 15-year-old girl with a history of interpersonal problems at home, school, and in her community, which have resulted in a number of suspensions, detentions, foster care placements, and psychiatric hospitalizations. Lacey often is described as irritable, aggressive, defiant, oppositional, and emotionally labile. She also reports having intrusive thoughts and nightmares and demonstrates self-injurious behaviors such as cutting her wrists. Lacey's background is characterized by a history of domestic violence, neglect, abandonment, and sexual abuse. Lacey often focuses on deep and persistent feelings of being unloved, rejected, and abandoned. From the standpoint of research and practice, Lacey's serious clinical presentation almost certainly is causally related to the abuse and chaotic life history that she has experienced.

Lacey's story is prototypical of many children and adolescents who occupy mental health settings and juvenile detention centers. Clinicians of all stripes immediately will recognize this all-too-familiar pattern of symptoms, behaviors, and interpersonal problems in the children and youth whom they have encountered during their careers. Lacey's background history and attendant problems illustrate dynamics that mental health professionals universally agree are highly unfavorable for the psychological and emotional well-being of children and youth. However, these formative variables (e.g., background and life history) affect not only our mental health and well-being in the traditional sense, but also our basic capacity and inclination to experience and express caring for self, others, and the world at large. As such, in this chapter, we eschew artificial delineations between behavioral, emotional, and psychological processes that typically are encompassed by diagnostic and other categorical frameworks, illustrating instead—through theory and data—that these processes affect all aspects of human experience, from our capacity to feel emotions through our inclination to care for the natural world.

At the outset, it should be emphasized that presentations like Lacey's notwithstanding, complex interactions among biology, development, affect, cognition, behavior, life experiences, and sociocultural processes affect all aspects of human functioning, including why we believe and

---

[1] www.ibavi.org/content/featured-projects

value that which we do (Shealy, 1995, 2004, Forthcoming). Because it is beyond the scope of this chapter to provide such an all-inclusive and wide ranging overview of these complex issues (cf. Cummings, Davies, & Campbell, 2000), we restrict our examination to selected findings and literature from the field of developmental psychopathology to underscore the role of children's developmental pathways that result in outcomes of adaptation and maladaptation, which consecutively influence the cultivation of a set of beliefs and values that are associated with caring about self, others, and the larger world.

Within developmental psychopathology and the psychotherapy process and outcome literature is a central contention, if not truism, that how we come to experience ourselves, and respond to others, is largely determined by the way in which we were experienced and responded to during our own processes of development (see Davies & Cummings, 1994; Kohut & Wolfe, 1978; Norcross, 2004). Implicit to this perspective is a corollary process by which we come to explain our relationship and conduct to ourselves, and others, largely through our stated "beliefs" about why we think, feel, or behave as we do. The phenomenology of such processes is so ubiquitous and non conscious, it often goes unrecognized. For example, the developing child has neither the means nor the motivation to reflect on processes of emotional regulation that are being inculcated within him or her as they are happening in real time. Instead, children acquire specific capacities and inclinations *vis-à-vis* the regulation of affect without knowing how, or even that such tendencies were developed, much less an appreciation that entirely different capacities and inclinations might have emerged under different circumstances.

The interrelationship among affect, behavior, beliefs, and values has been considered at varying levels of analysis and via a range of complementary perspectives (cf. Frijda, Mastead, & Bem, 2000; Inglehart, Basanez, Díez-Medrano, Halman, & Luijkx, 2004; Newberg & Waldman, 2006; Rokeach, 1979; Shealy, 2004, 2005). Despite a lack of definitional and conceptual clarity among related concepts (e.g., beliefs, values, and attitudes)—and inherent difficulties with measurement—beliefs and values are implicit if not central to many dominant theories within psychology regarding the development, psychological functioning, and behavior of human beings, although such centrality may not be recognized explicitly (Shealy, Forthcoming).

Moreover, in everyday life, beliefs are perhaps most readily apparent in what we say about ourselves, others, and the world at large. For example, in reflecting upon our own experience, we may comment to ourselves or others, "I feel things more deeply than others." Such a contention is a "belief," which may be defined as "an internalized and discrete version of reality that can influence and mediate the experience and expression of needs, feelings, thoughts, and behaviors" (Shealy, in press). Irrespective of whether such a belief is objectively "true," the fact that it is felt to be true is all that is typically necessary for it to be true to the individual expressing this belief. What is most interesting about these processes is that seldom are declarations of belief accompanied by concomitant reflection about their origins. Such apparent indifference is striking given how central beliefs and values are to what we hold to be true and good or false and bad, especially since such contentions affect every aspect of existence, from the friends we keep to the politicians we elect to the religious faith—or lack thereof—that we call our own. How do we explain such ingenuousness about these fundamental matters that ought to be of deep personal interest? Specifically, what are the implications of the degree to which we do—or do not—cultivate such awareness and the concomitant capacity to care in children and youth? In an attempt to address these questions, we next highlight Equilintegration (EI) Theory, the EI Self, and the Beliefs, Events, and Values Inventory (BEVI), an interrelated model, framework, and method that have been in development since the early 1990s, to examine and apprehend the processes by which beliefs and values—including our attendant inclination and capacity to care for self, others, and the larger world—are acquired, maintained, and transformed.

EI Theory, the EI Self, and the BEVI

The first four hypotheses and principles of EI Theory (Shealy, 2004) "explain the processes by which beliefs, values, and 'world views' are acquired and maintained, why their alteration is typically resisted, and how and under what circumstances their modification occurs" (p. 1075). They are:

1. Beliefs and values are central mediating processes for behavior at individual and societal levels, but they may or may not be "known" (i.e., may be implicit or nonconscious), and are not necessarily rational or logically grounded.
2. Beliefs and values are determined by an individual's history, larger culture, and unique Zeitgeist, inculcated over time, and may or may not transcend a specific time and place. Although that which is believed and valued may be relative to a given time or place, the human capacity and need for an organizing worldview is an etic derivative of the self; thus, although the content of our beliefs and values may vary as a function of what is available for acquisition, the processes (e.g., developmental, affective, and attributional) by which beliefs and values are acquired are determined by constitutive aspects of the self.
3. When combined with sufficient knowledge about important life experiences and events, belief and value statements often provide (*a*) a great deal of information about the hypothetical structure and organization of personality or "self"; and (*b*) a relatively accessible point of entry to issues and phenomena that are meaningful in a wide range of settings and contexts.
4. Beliefs and values are not easily modified because they represent, for each individual, the unique culmination of an interaction among these affective and attributional processes and developmental/life experiences, which are codified (ultimately at a physiological level) in personality and "self." Because human beings balance the desire for equilibrium and stasis against the inevitable internal and external pressures for development and growth,

changing beliefs, and values often means changing underlying structure (and vice versa); this process of understanding how structure came to be inevitably involves an emotionally charged and not-always-conscious examination of what one believes and values about self, others, and the world at large.

Derivative of EI Theory, the Equilintegration or EI Self represents in pictographic form (see Figure 16.1) the integrative and synergistic processes by which beliefs and values are acquired, maintained, and transformed as well as how and why these are linked to the formative variables, core needs, and adaptive potential of the self (Shealy, in press). Informed by scholarship in a range of key areas (e.g., "needs-based" research and theory, developmental psychopathology, social cognition, affect regulation, theories and models of "self"), the EI Self seeks to illustrate how the interaction between our core needs (e.g., for attachment and affiliation) and formative variables (e.g., caregiver and culture) results in beliefs and values about self, others, and the world at large that we all internalize over the course of development and across the life span.

Concomitant with EI Theory and the EI Self, the BEVI is a comprehensive analytic tool that examines how and why we come to see ourselves, others, and the larger world as we do (e.g., how life experiences, culture, and context affect our beliefs, values, and worldview) as well as the influence of such processes on multiple aspects of human functioning (e.g., learning processes, relationships, personal growth, the pursuit of life goals). For example, the BEVI assesses processes such as: basic openness; the tendency to (or not to) stereotype in particular ways; self- and emotional awareness; preferred strategies for making sense of why "other" people and cultures "do what they do"; global engagement (e.g., receptivity to different cultures, religions, and social practices); and, worldview shift (e.g., to what degree do beliefs and values change as a result of specific experiences). BEVI results are translated automatically into reports at the individual, group, and organizational levels which include a range of scores, indexes, and narratives. Individuals, groups, institutions, and organizations use the BEVI and its report system in a wide range of contexts (e.g., education, mental health, organizational) for a variety of applied and research purposes (e.g., to track and examine changes in worldviews over time; evaluate and improve educational programs or experiences; cultivate growth and awareness in individuals, couples, and groups; develop leadership capacity and enhance organizational functioning).

The BEVI consists of four interrelated components: (*a*) a comprehensive set of demographic/background items that may be modified for particular projects (65 on the Exploratory Factor Analysis [EFA] version of the BEVI), (*b*) a life history questionnaire, which is built into the measure, (*c*) two validity and eighteen "process scales" (comprised of 336 items total), and (*d*) three qualitative "experiential reflection" items. As a Web-based and Likert-type inventory with four response options (Strongly Agree, Agree, Disagree, Strongly Disagree), the EFA version of the BEVI typically requires between 35 and 45 minutes to complete. Items are deliberately balanced to minimize social desirability and other response-set confounds (e.g., Robinson, Shaver, &

Figure 16.1 EI Self

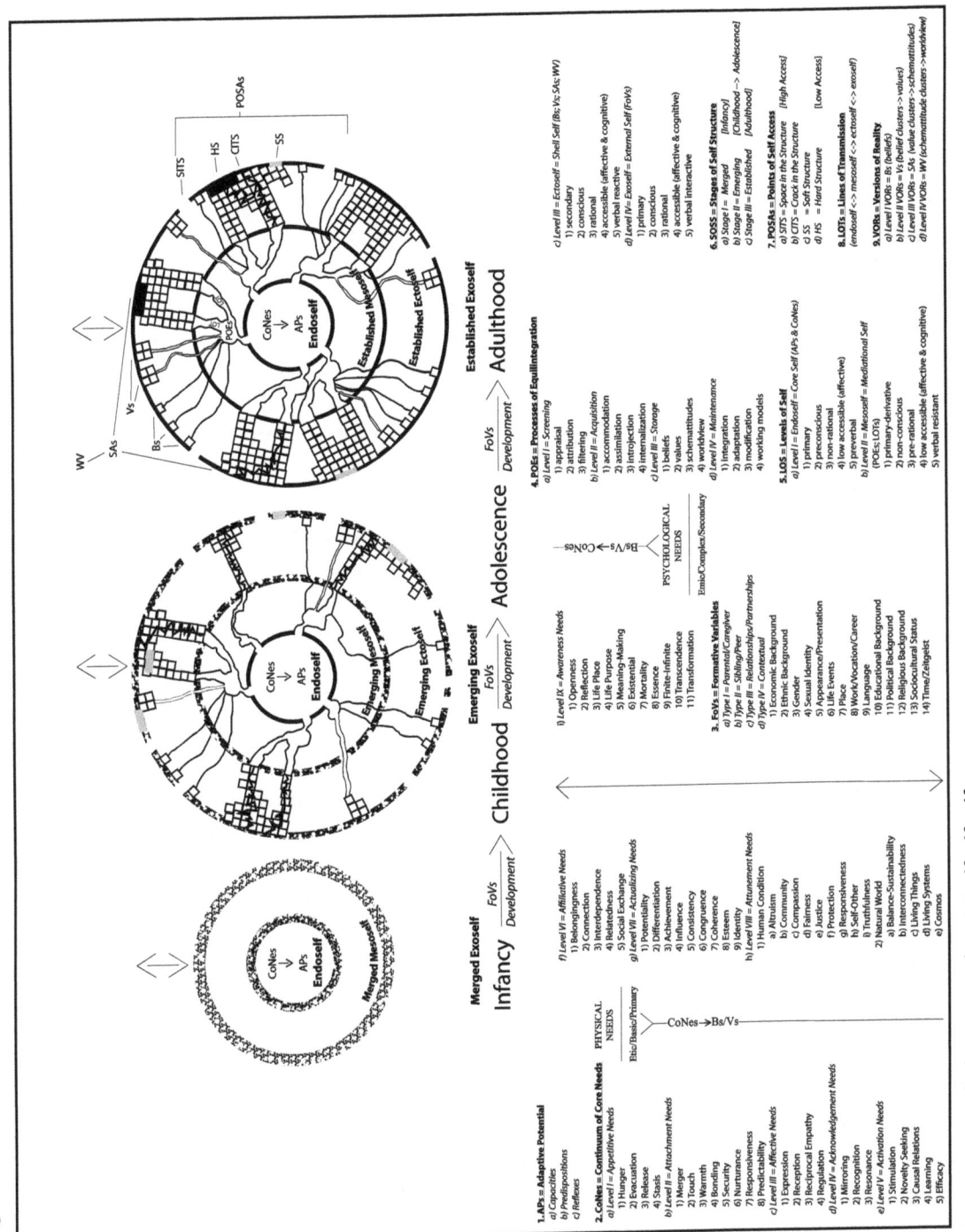

Source: www.thebevi.com/docs/eiselfpdf.pdf.

Wrightsman, 1991, 1999). Most importantly, the BEVI is not designed to appraise the debatable correctness or incorrectness of individual responses, but rather to investigate how overall response patterns predict various processes and outcomes, from the beliefs and values associated with ethnocentrism, religious tolerance, partisanship, and gender-based practices and policies, to issues of openness, self-access, and emotional attunement.

Evidence of validity is indicated by a number of studies demonstrating that the BEVI is able to predict group membership across a wide range of demographic variables, including gender, ethnic background, parental income, political orientation, and religious orientation as well as other categorical variables (cf. Hayes, Shealy, Sivo, & Weinstein, 1999; Isley, Shealy, Crandall, Sivo, & Reifsteck, 1999; Shealy, 2000a, 2000b, 2004, 2005, 2006, in press). Furthermore, EI theory, the EI Self, and the BEVI offer an integrative framework and method for predicting and explaining characteristics that are linked to other global issues such as environment concerns (Patel, 2008) and intercultural awareness (Reisweber, 2008).

Since 2007, the Forum BEVI Project—a joint partnership between the Forum on Education Abroad (www.forumea.org) and International Beliefs and Values Institute (www.ibavi.org)—has been investigating the processes and outcomes of international, multicultural, and transformative learning through the BEVI (see www.forumea.org/research-bevi-project.cfm). During the "pilot phase" of the Forum BEVI Project, a range of colleges, universities, and study abroad providers administered the BEVI to nearly 2,000 participants in the US and internationally. Statistical analysis narrowed the original number of factors on the BEVI from 40 to 18; nearly 60 items also were eliminated during the subsequent review process. Norms are now established for each of these "scales" (i.e., factors) with most reliabilities above 0.80 or 0.90 (no scale has a reliability of less than 0.75). Three new qualitative items were integrated into the BEVI prior to the pilot phase, which allow for complementary types of analyses.

Based upon factor analytic and correlation matrix data, the 18 scales of the EFA version of BEVI are organized in a manner that corresponds with the basic EI theoretical framework of this measure.[2] Reliabilities for each scale are listed in parentheses; "PF" (Primary Factor) and "SF" (Secondary Factor) designations and the accompanying numbers refer to whether the scale was extracted as a "primary" or "secondary" factor, and in which order of extraction (primary factors were derived via a Schmid–Leiman transformation (Schmid & Leiman, 1957), which essentially is a factor analysis of a factor analysis). The descriptive information listed for each scale corresponds to the type of content assessed by the items which load on each scale. The scales that are listed underneath each numbered scale are presented in descending order of magnitude from correlation matrix findings (e.g., the correlation of each scale by all other scales). For present purposes, we will focus on two scales, "Needs Closure" (Scale 2) and "Emotional Attunement" (Scale 10), which have the following characteristics:

---

[2] More information about the BEVI is available at www.thebevi.com

Scale 2. Needs Closure (0.88, PF 1)
(bad childhood, unhappy, disturbed thinking, odd explanations for why things are the way they are)

Socioemotional Convergence (–0.93)
Sociocultural Openness (–0.90)
Emotional Attunement (–0.85)
Identity Closure (0.84)
Negative Life Events (0.81)
Basic Closedness (0.78)
Ecological Resonance (–0.72)
Divergent Determinism (0.65)
Hard Structure (0.53)
Socioreligious Traditionalism (0.31)

Scale 10. Emotional Attunement (0.87, SF 17)
(highly emotional, highly sensitive, highly social, needy, affiliative, undifferentiated, values emotional expression)

Needs Closure (–0.85)
Socioemotional Convergence (0.84)
Basic Closedness (–0.77)
Sociocultural Openness (0.77)
Ecological Resonance (0.64)
Identity Closure (–0.63)
Negative Life Events (–0.62)
Hard Structure (–0.59)
Divergent Determinism (–0.58)
Socioreligious Traditionalism (–0.20)

Cultivating the Capacity to Care: The Role of Formative Variables

Against the above backdrop of theory and data, how might an EI perspective help illuminate processes by which the capacity to care is cultivated in children and youth? We consider the above two BEVI scales—Needs Closure and Emotional Attunement—along with relevant correlation matrix data to examine how: (*a*) the degree to which we believe our core needs were met is associated with how we experience ourselves, others, and the larger world; and (*b*) how such processes are associated with our capacity to resonate emotionally with self and others. Needs Closure (the first of the "primary factors") is comprised of items that indicate whether a respondent reports that his/her childhood was "happy," the degree to which basic needs were or were not met in a "good enough" way, and subjectively held explanations for why people or the world work as they do. In considering the interrelationship among Needs Closure and its three most highly correlated scales, note that the relationship between the reported experience of a "bad childhood" is associated with: (*a*) relative difficulty holding complex, equally plausible, and sometimes contradictory realities simultaneously in the mind (i.e., socioemotional convergence); (*b*) a relative lack of openness to beliefs and practices that are different from one's own (i.e., sociocultural openness); and (*c*) a relative difficulty with, or indifference toward, the "emotional world" of self or others (i.e., emotional attunement). How do we understand and interpret such findings?

Abundant evidence suggests that what we believe and value as good or true is a partly a function of our unique formative variables (family, culture, context, life, and contextual experiences), which interact with powerful core needs (such as attachment, affiliation, actualization etc.) and mediate our affective and attributional processes of which we often have little awareness (Shealy, 2004, 2005, in press). Along these lines, the field of developmental psychopathology provides important insights about the variables that shape pathways to adaptation or maladaptation, by examining the interactions among genetic, biological, psychosocial, and familial domains in order to understand developmental processes and outcomes from infancy to adulthood. More specifically, this interdisciplinary field of inquiry examines the etiology and interactions among a wide range of processes that are causally associated with variation in human conduct and functioning, ranging from "disturbed" or "maladaptive" to "healthy" or "optimal" (e.g., Carlson & Sroufe, 1995; Cicchetti & Toth, 1998; Cummings, Davies, & Campbell, 2000; Rutter & Sroufe, 2000; Shealy, 1995; Sroufe & Rutter, 1984). Given the complexity of understanding the etiology of human functioning, developmental psychopathology provides perhaps the most encompassing framework through which such complexity can be accounted (Carlson & Sroufe, 1995). Thus, informed by BEVI data above, and seen through an EI lens, we highlight selected findings from developmental psychopathology to understand the variables that promote or impede the capacity to experience a sense of care for self, others, and the larger world.

As a logical point of departure, we focus first on attachment theory. Essentially, attachment theory posits that the foundation of personality development and socio emotional relationships is based on "an affective bond" between an infant and caregiver, which begins to develop in the first year of life (Bowlby, 1969, 1982). This dyadic, emotional bond is conceptualized as a cognitive, emotional, and behavioral control system that mediates the diverse ways in which children handle and maintain their relationships. Forming the basis of the infant's sense of emotional security, this bond is associated with the nature and quality of care received, which interacts further with a range of developmental and maturational processes such as biological organization, neural fine tuning, schema development, affective exchanges, and emotional regulation (Carlson & Sroufe, 1995).

Cicchetti, Toth, & Maughan (2000) and Crittenden (1992) have found that approximately two-thirds of maltreated children develop insecure attachments as compared to a third of children who do not. As a result of maltreatment, it is thought that children adopt internal working models of self and other that are based on doubt and mistrust. A small segment of maltreated children also have been found to have a disorganized pattern of attachment (Main, Kaplan, & Cassidy, 1985). Likewise, children who are severely neglected (e.g., denial of core appetitive, attachment, affective, or acknowledgment needs as specified in the EI Self), may be at a high risk of developing Reactive Attachment Disorder (RAD), which is characterized by extreme patterns of attachment behavior (e.g., highly aloof or indiscriminately affectionate with strangers). Moreover, children diagnosed with RAD demonstrated higher incidences of a disorganized pattern of insecure attachment (Minnis et al., 2009). Many of these children also may suffer from a range of deficits in cognitive and other domains. For example, Becker-Weidman (2009) found significant developmental delays in communication, daily living skills, and socialization with children diagnosed with RAD as well as continued behavioral and interpersonal problems in adulthood. Conversely, adults who experienced relatively secure relationships in childhood typically establish and maintain relationships that are characterized as relatively coherent, emotionally open, and autonomous with simultaneous valuation of their relationships (Bretherton & Mullholand, 2008). In short, a lack of sufficiently secure attachment can be a substantial risk factor for children's mental and emotional health causing significant disruptions in the development of their own capacity to care for self and others across the lifespan.

Allied literature demonstrates robust correlational relationships among parental neglect, rejection, impoverishment, sexual abuse, physical abuse, and the corresponding development of emotional and conduct problems in children. The global repercussions of such processes have been recognized by various international bodies, such as the United Nations, which has documented the scope of child maltreatment around the world along with attendant and substantial social, legal, and economic implications (Pinheiro, 2006). Maltreated youth are more likely to have lower academic and professional achievements, and greater disruptive behavior problems, often resulting in diagnoses of Oppositional Defiant Disorder and Conduct Disorder (Weis, 2008). Such diagnoses are typically assigned because of negativistic tendencies, hostility, and contempt for prescribed rules and norms. Furthermore, interpersonal relationships of such minors often are characterized by both proactive and reactive aggression (Koenig, Cicchetti, & Rogosch, 2004), which may be exacerbated in socially ambiguous situations (Price & Glad, 2003). In addition to neglect, abuse, and impoverishment, antisocial tendencies also appear to be mediated by moral disengagement (Hyde, Shaw, & Moilanen, 2010; Malley-Morrison, Oh, Wu, & Zaveri, 2009), which may be associated with theft, cheating, physical aggression, truancy, and school suspensions in addition to more serious and violent crime. Abused and neglected girls also are more likely to be underemployed and resort to prostitution in adulthood (Koenig et al., 2004; Luntz & Widom, 1994). Antisocial behaviors also occur with neglected children where caregivers provide inadequate and inconsistent monitoring (Knutson, DeGarmo, Koeppl, & Reid, 2005). Mood and anxiety disorders, in addition to substance use and abuse, are likewise positively associated with child maltreatment (Kilpatrick et al., 2003). For example, Post-traumatic Stress Disorder (PTSD) is observed in 16 percent to 36 percent of children who have been physically abused (Danielson, de Arellano, Kilpatrick, Saunders, & Resnick, 2005). Physically abused and neglected children also are at a high risk for developing cognitive delays and impairment in areas of executive functioning, language, and working memory, typically underperform academically, and are more likely to receive special education services due to learning and behavior problems (e.g., Eigsti & Cicchetti, 2004).

Highly consistent with the Needs Closure intercorrelations from the BEVI, findings cited above demonstrate that poor parenting, insecure attachment, abuse, and neglect are negatively associated with the capacity in children and youth to experience care for self and others (cf. Shealy, 1995). Among related explanations for such outcomes, perhaps the most parsimonious is that children and youth who were not well cared for themselves tend to be preoccupied by their own emotional, cognitive, and behavioral struggles, which are compounded by an impaired capacity for self-care as well as poor or inadequate support from caregivers. Clearly, in addition to preventing and ameliorating such conditions for children, youth, and their families, it behooves us also to understand better those processes that facilitate altruism and empathy or pro-social behavior—an allied construct to which we turn next.

Cultivating the Capacity to Care: The Role of Socioemotional Processes

Pro-social behavior is defined by actions that are experienced as favorable by and towards other individuals (Eisenberg, 1982). Although there is disagreement regarding the parameters of pro-social behavior (e.g., whether only those behaviors resulting in positive outcomes should be defined as pro-social), this construct encompasses behaviors such as helping, sharing, cooperating, and comforting (Hay, 1994). Experts often contend that "moral" cognitive and emotional processes underlie the expression of pro-social behavior by children and youth. While moral judgments may be derived on the basis of social standards such as justice and concern (Nussbaum, 1992), moral emotions such as sympathy or empathy often are seen to mediate moral behavior (Eisenberg, 1986; Hoffman 2000). Even so, moral judgment and moral emotion have robust intercorrelations as well (Arsenio, Gold, & Adams, 2004). Moral motivation, or the inclination to stand up for "right" and against "wrong" in the face of competing desires and motives (cf. Nunner-Winkler, 2007) is inversely related to aggressive behavior by children towards others (Arsenio, Gold, & Adams, 2006; Krettenauer & Eichler, 2006) and is an underlying factor in moral emotions such as sympathy and pro-social behavior (Malti, Gummerman, Keller, & Buchmann (2009). As emotions play a crucial role in moral behavior, the socialization of such emotions is an important factor in pro-social behavior. Therefore, as noted above, consider the definitional and intercorrelational implications of another BEVI scale, Emotional Attunement (Scale 10).

Note from the correlation matrix data, given earlier, that Needs Closure is the most highly negatively correlated scale with Emotional Attunement. How might such findings be interpreted? Essentially, it appears that the degree to which individuals report that their core needs were *not* met in a "good enough" manner is associated with a *lack* of capacity and inclination to attend to emotional processes in self and other, and vice versa. Such findings do receive support from extant literature. For example, Garner, Dunsmore, and Southam-Gerrow (2008) examined the conversations of mothers regarding the explanation of emotion and emotional knowledge *vis-à-vis* the relational and physical aggression and pro-social behavior in their children. Essentially, children with mothers who explained emotion were more likely to engage in pro-social behavior. The authors hypothesize that such discussions facilitate the development of emotional capacity and skill, by validating their children's emotions and helping them to be aware of and sensitive to emotional cues in self and in others. Grounded in attachment theory, emotional security is mediated by the relative capacity to regulate one's own emotions (Cummings & Davies, 1996). Children living in homes characterized by domestic violence have significant challenges in safeguarding their security in the presence of unpredictable and volatile behaviors posing considerable challenges to their adjustment (Davies, Winter, & Cicchetti, 2006; Shealy, 1995). Furthermore, McCoy, Cummings, and Davies (2009) found that how parents handled conflict (constructively or destructively) was associated with their children's emotional security and their relative likelihood to engage in pro-social behavior. Such findings have rightly influenced a wide range of interventions, such as values-based curricula, which emphasizes the importance of attending to emotional experiences in self and others as well as other prosocial behaviors, all of which are designed to enhance a capacity and inclination to care (cf., Singh, 2009; Toomey & Lovat, 2009). In short, the above findings suggest that warm parenting is an important variable in positive mental health outcomes for children, which in turn yields a higher likelihood that children will engage in pro-social behaviors. Likewise, as the above BEVI correlational matrix data illustrate, the degree to which we report the experience of "warm parenting" is highly associated with our attendant capacity and inclination toward "emotional attunement" in self and other.

In Summary

In this chapter, we first described the Forum BEVI Project (www.ibavi.org/content/featured-projects), a multiyear, multi-institution project that has been using the Beliefs, Events, and Values Inventory (BEVI), which examines a wide range of interrelated processes including the following: (*a*) how, why, and under what circumstances human beings develop their relative capacities to care for self, others, and the larger world; (*b*) the concomitant beliefs, values, attitudes, and worldviews that accompany such capacities; and (c) the implications of such findings for the development and well-being of children as well as the functioning of the adults whom they become. More specifically, we have emphasized two scales—Needs Closure and Emotional Attunement—to illustrate how life experience is associated with the fundamental capacity and inclination to experience and express "caring" for self, others, and the larger world.

Although the above analysis highlighted the "negative" aspects of such interactive processes (e.g., a greater degree of reported abuse or neglect is associated with a lesser degree of reported interest in or capacity for emotional expression or access), it may be helpful to conclude on a more hopeful note. For example, just as we observe the negative associations of unhappy childhood experiences on beliefs about self, others, and the larger world, observe from the above correlation matrix data that a lower degree of Needs Closure is strongly associated with a higher degree of Sociocultural Openness (0.90) as well as Ecological Resonance (0.72). How do we interpret these findings? From the needs-based perspective of the EI Self, such results suggest that children and youth who believe that their core needs were met in a "good enough" manner appear much more likely to express care for cultures that are different as well as the relative health of the natural world. In other words, the way we experience how we were regarded and treated in childhood and adolescence appears to be directly associated with our capacity and inclination to express "care" toward the self (e.g., our emotional world), the other (e.g., people from different cultural backgrounds), and the world at large (e.g., environmental systems necessary to sustain life). In the final analysis, these are not small matters, as the "wicked issues" of our day (Coffman, Hopkins, Ali, 2009), such as cultural conflict and climate change, call upon us to cultivate a capacity for caring not only to promote mental health, but global well-being in the broadest and most meaningful sense. That is because the way children and youth were cared for during their formative years appears to be directly associated with their capacity and inclination to care for self, others, and the larger world when they become adults. Such a conclusion seems concurrently hopeful and bleak since it appears that our future and fate are in our own hands, and of our own making, for better or for worse.

References

Arsenio, W., Gold, J., & Adams, E. (2004). Adolescents' emotion expectancies regarding aggressive and nonaggressive events: Connections with behavior problems. *Journal of Experimental Child Psychology, 89*(4), 338–355. doi:10.1016/j.jecp.2004.08.001

———. (2006). Children's conceptions and displays of moral emotions. In M. Killen & J. Smetana (Eds), *Handbook of moral development*. Mahwah, NJ: Erlbaum.

Becker-Weidman, A. (2009). Effects on early maltreatment on development: A descriptive study using the Vineland Adaptive Behavior Scales—II. *Child Welfare, 88* (2), 137–161.

Bowlby, J. (1969). *Attachment and loss: Vol. 1. Attachment*. New York: Basic Books.

Bowlby, J. (1982). *Attachment and loss: Vol. 1. Attachment* (2nd Ed.). New York: Basic Books.
Bretherton, I., & Mulholland, K. A. (2008). Internal working models in attachment relationships: Elaborating a central construct in attachment theory. In J. Cassidy & P. R. Shaver (Eds), *Handbook of attachment: Theory, research, and clinical applications* (2nd ed., pp. 102–130). New York: The Guilford Press.
Carlson, E. A., & Sroufe, L. A. (1995). Contribution of attachment theory to developmental psychopathology. In D. Cicchetti & D. Cohen (Eds), *Developmental psychopathology: Vol. 1. Theory and methods* (pp. 581–617). Oxford, England: Wiley.
Cicchetti, D., & Toth, S. L. (1998). The development of depression in children and adolescents. *American Psychologist, 53*(2), 221–241.
Cicchetti, D., Toth, S. L., & Maughan, A. (2000). An ecological-transactional model of child maltreatment. In A. J. Sameroff, M. Lewis, & S. M. Miller (Eds), *Handbook of Developmental Psychopathology* (2nd ed., pp. 689–722). New York: Kluwer Academic.
Coffman, J. E., Hopkins, C., & Ali, I. M. (2009). Education for sustainable development: Halfway through the decade of ESD and a long way from sustainability. *Beliefs and Values, 1*(2), 142–150. doi:10.1891/1942-0617.1.2.142
Crittenden, P. (1992). Children's strategies in coping with adverse home environments: An interpretation using attachment theory. *Child Abuse & Neglect, 16*(3), 329–343. doi:10.1016/0145-2134(92)90043-Q
Cummings, E. M., & Davies, P. (1996). Emotional security as a regulatory process in normal development and the development of psychopathology. *Development and Psychopathology, 8*, 123–139. doi:10.1017/S0954579400007008
Cummings, E., Davies, P., & Campbell, S. (2000). *Developmental psychopathology and family process.* New York: Guilford Press.
Danielson, C. K., de Arellano, M. A., Kilpatrick, D. G., Saunders, B. E., & Resnick, H. S. (2005). Child maltreatment in depressed adolescents: Differences in symptomatology based on history of abuse. *Child Maltreatment, 10*(1), 37–48. doi:10.1177/1077559504271630
Davies, P., & Cummings, E. M. (1994). Marital conflict and child adjustment: An emotional security hypothesis. *Psychological Bulletin, 116*(3), 387–411. doi:10.1037/0033-2909.116.3.387
Davies, P. T., Winter, M. A., & Cicchetti, D. (2006). The implications of emotional security theory for understanding and treating childhood psychopathology. *Development and Psychopathology, 18*(3), 707–735. doi:10.1017/S0954579406060354
Eigsti, I., & Cicchetti, D. (2004). The impact of child maltreatment on expressive syntax at 60 months. *Developmental Science, 7*(1), 88–102. doi:10.1111/j.1467-7687.2004.00325.x
Eisenberg, N. (Ed.). (1982). *The development of prosocial behavior.* New York: Academic Press.
———. (1986). *Altruistic emotion, cognition and behavior.* Hillsdale, NJ: Erlbaum.
Frijda, N., Mastead, A., & Bem, S. (Eds). (2000). *Emotions and beliefs: How feelings influence thoughts.* Cambridge: Cambridge University Press.
Garner, P. W., Dunsmore, J. C., & Southam-Gerrow, M. (2008). Mother-child conversations about emotions: Linkages to child aggression and prosocial behavior. *Social Development, 17*(2), 259–277. doi:10.1111/j.1467-9507.2007.00424.x
Hay, D. (1994). Prosocial development. *Journal of Child Psychology and Psychiatry, 35*(1), 29–71. doi:10.1111/j.1469-7610.1994.tb01132.x
Hayes, D. J., Shealy, C. N., Sivo, S. A., & Weinstein, Z. C. (1999, August). *Psychology, religion, and Scale 5 (Religious Traditionalism) of the "BEVI."* Poster session presented at the meeting of the American Psychological Association, Boston, MA.
Hoffman, M. L. (2000). *Empathy and moral development: Implications for caring and justice.* New York: Cambridge University Press.

Hyde, L.W., Shaw, D. S., & Moilanen, K. L. (2010). Developmental precursors of moral disengagement and the role of moral disengagement in the development of antisocial behavior. *Journal of Abnormal Child Psychology, 38*(2), 197–209. doi:10.1007/s10802-009-9358-5

Inglehart, R., Basanez, M., Díez-Medrano, J., Halman, L., & Luijkx, R. (2004). *Human beliefs and values: A cross-cultural sourcebook based on the 1999-2002 values survey.* Mexico: Siglo XXI Editores.

Isley, E. B., Shealy, C. N., Crandall, K. S., Sivo, S. A., & Reifsteck, J. B. (1999, August). *Relevance of the "BEVI" for research in developmental psychopathology.* Poster session presented at the meeting of the American Psychological Association, Boston, MA.

Kilpatrick, D. G., Rugierro, K. J., Acierno, R., Saunders, B. E., Resnick, H. S., & Best, C. (2003). Violence and risk of PTSD, major depression, substance abuse/dependence, and comorbidity: Results from the national survey of adolescents. *Journal of Consulting and Clinical Psychology, 71*(4), 692–700.

Knutson, J. F., DeGarmo, D., Koeppl, G., & Reid, J. B. (2005). Care neglect, supervisory neglect, and harsh parenting in the development of children's aggression: A replication and extension. *Child Maltreatment, 10*(2), 92–107. doi:10.1177/1077559504273684

Koenig, A. L., Cicchetti, D., & Rogosch, F. A. (2004). Moral development: The association between maltreatment and young children's prosocial behaviors and moral transgressions. *Social Development, 13*(1), 87–106. doi:10.1111/j.1467-9507.2004.00258.x

Kohut, H., & Wolfe, E. S. (1978). The disorders of the self and their treatment: An outline. *International Journal of Psychoanalysis, 59,* 413–425.

Krettenauer, T., & Eichler, D. (2006). Adolescents self-attributed moral emotions following a moral transgression: Relations with delinquency, confidence in moral judgment and age. *British Journal of Developmental Psychology, 24*(3), 489–506. doi:10.1348/026151005X50825

Luntz, B., & Widom, C. S. (1994). Anti-social personality disorder in abused and neglected children grown up. *American Journal of Psychiatry, 151*(5), 670–674.

Main, M., Kaplan, N., & Cassidy, J. (1985). Security in infancy, childhood, and adulthood: A move to the level of representation. *Monographs of the Society for Research in Child Development, 50*(1/2), 66–104.

Malley-Morrison, K., Oh, D. Y., Wu, T., & Zaveri, T. (2009). Moral disengagement and engagement. *Beliefs and Values, 1*(2), 151–167. doi:10.1891/1942-0617.1.2.151

Malti, T., Gummerman, M., Keller, M., & Buchmann, M. (2009). Children's moral motivation, sympathy, and prosocial behavior. *Child Development, 80*(2), 442–460. doi:10.1111/j.1467-8624.2009.01271.x

McCoy, K., Cummings, E. M., & Davies, P. T. (2009). Constructive and destructive marital conflict, emotional security and children's prosocial behavior. *The Journal of Child Psychology and Psychiatry, 50*(3), 270–279. doi:10.1111/j.1469-7610.2008.01945.x

Minnis, H., Green, J., O'Connor, T. G., Liew, A., Glaser, D., Taylor, E., & Sadiq, F. A. (2009). An exploratory study of the association between reactive attachment disorder and attachment narratives in early school-age children. *Journal of Child Psychology and Psychiatry, 50*(8), 931–942. doi:10.1111/j.1469-7610.2009.02075.x

Newberg, A., & Waldman, M. R. (2006). *Why we believe what we believe.* New York: Free Press.

Norcross, J. (Ed.). (2004). *Psychotherapy relations that work.* Oxford: Oxford University Press.

Nunner-Winkler, G. (2007). Development of moral motivation from childhood to early adulthood. *Journal of Moral Education, 36*(4), 399–414. doi:10.1080/03057240701687970

Nussbaum, M. (1992). Human functioning and social justice. In defense of Aristotelian essentialism. *Political Theory, 20*(2), 202–246. doi:10.1177/0090591792020002002

Patel, R. (2008). *Environmental beliefs, values, and worldviews: Etiology, maintenance, and transformation.* Unpublished doctoral dissertation, James Madison University.

Pinheiro, P. S. (2006). *World report on violence against children.* Geneva: United Nations.

Price, J. M., & Glad, K. A. (2003). Hostile attributional tendencies in maltreated children. *Journal of Abnormal Child Psychology, 31*(3), 329–343. doi:10.1023/A:1023237731683

Reisweber, J. (2008). *Beliefs, values, and the development of intercultural awareness.* Unpublished doctoral dissertation. James Madison University.

Robinson, J. P., Shaver, P. R., & Wrightsman, L. S. (Eds.) (1991). *Measures of personality and social psychological attitudes.* San Diego, CA: Academic Press.

———. (Eds). (1999). *Measures of political attitudes.* San Diego, CA: Academic Press.

Rokeach, M. (1979). Some unresolved issues in theories of beliefs, attitudes and values. *Nebraska Symposium on Motivation, 27,* 261–304.

Rutter, M., & Stroufe, L. A. (2000). Developmental psychopathology: Concepts and challenges. *Development and Psychopathology, 12,* 265–296.

Schmid, J., & Leiman, J. N. (1957). The development of hierarchical factor solutions. *Psychometrika, 22,* 53–61.

Shealy, C. N. (1995). From *Boys Town* to *Oliver Twist*: Separating fact from fiction in welfare reform and out-of-home placement of children and youth. *American Psychologist, 50*(8), 565–580.

———. (2000a, July). *The Beliefs, Events, and Values Inventory (BEVI): Implications for cross-cultural research and practice.* Paper presented at the meeting of the International Congress of Psychology, Stockholm, Sweden.

———. (2000b, July). *The Beliefs, Events, and Values Inventory (BEVI): Implications for research and theory in social psychology.* Paper presented at the meeting of the International Congress of Psychology, Stockholm, Sweden.

———. (2004). A model and method for "making" a combined-integrated psychologist: Equilintegration (EI) theory and the beliefs, events, and values inventory (BEVI) [Special Series]. *Journal of Clinical Psychology, 60*(10), 1065–1090. doi:10.1002/jclp.20035

———. (Forthcoming). Justifying the justification hypothesis: Scientific-humanism, equilintegration (EI) theory, and the beliefs, events and values inventory (BEVI). *Journal of Clinical Psychology 61*(1), 81–106. doi:10.1002/jclp.20092

———. (2006). *The beliefs, events, and values inventory (BEVI): Overview, implications, and guidelines.* Harrisonburg, VA.

———. (in press). *Making sense of beliefs and values.* New York: Springer Publishing.

Singh, K. (2009). Learning values for living together. *Beliefs and Values 1*(1), 90–93. doi:10.1891/1942-0617.1.1.90

Sroufe, L. A., & Rutter, M. (1984). The domain of developmental psychopathology. *Child Development, 55,* 17–29.

Toomey, R., & Lovat, T. (2009). Values education, quality teaching, and service learning: The harmony of a new pedagogy? *Beliefs and Values, 1*(2), 220–229. doi:10.1891/1942-0617.1.2.220

Weis, R. (2008). *Introduction to abnormal child psychology adolescent psychology.* Thousand Oaks, CA: SAGE.

17

Research on Child Poverty and Development from a Cognitive Neuroscience Perspective: Examples of Studies in Argentina

Sebastián Javier Lipina
María Soledad Segretin
María Julia Hermida
Jorge Augusto Colombo

Introduction

Child poverty and child development are complex and multidimensional phenomena. The study of their interaction involves the analysis of different biological and psychosocial components within a continuous, dynamic, and growing interaction (Bradley & Corwyn, 2002; Evans, 2004; Lipina & Colombo, 2009). Hence, their study requires the involvement of multidisciplinary frameworks that consider different epistemological, conceptual, methodological, cultural, and ethical issues.

Specifically, over the last decade, neuroscientists have begun to join collaborative efforts with developmental and social scientists to contribute, both conceptually and methodologically, to the study of the effects of poverty on basic cognitive processes (Hackman, Farah, & Meany, 2010; Lipina & Colombo, 2009; Raizada & Kishiyama, 2010).

Considering the neurobiological mechanisms underlying cognitive, emotional, and learning competences, new exploratory avenues aimed at understanding the socioeconomic gaps affecting them could be opened. In addition, neurocognitive analysis may reveal different socioeconomic-related factors, playing several mediating roles across neurocognitive systems. In turn, examining which underlying factors are associated with cognitive, emotional, and/or learning competences allows the design of testing interventions with increased specificity.

Brain Plasticity

In experimental settings, rodents and non-human primates that are exposed to motor, sensory, and social stimulation in complex environments show several structural and functional changes in different neuronal and non-neuronal components, in comparison with those subjects reared in deprived environments (Lipina & Colombo, 2009; Mohammed et al., 2002). Specifically, exposure of different species to complex environments, in comparison with either standard or deprived environments, has been associated with several structural changes such as synaptic number and morphology, dendritic arborization, cell morphology, the number of astrocytes and glial–synaptic contacts, myelination, glial cell morphology, brain vasculature, brain cortex weight and thickness, rate of hippocampal neurogenesis, availability and metabolism of both neurotrophic factors and neurotransmitters in different brain areas, and neurotrophic and neurotransmitter gene expression as well. In turn, these multiple changes in neural structure have been repeatedly correlated with functional changes at motor, cognitive, and emotional outcomes (Lipina & Colombo, 2009; Mohammed et al., 2002).

Neural plasticity in humans may also lead to use-dependent brain structural adaptation in response to environmental demands (Bavelier & Neville, 2002). At the level of imaging studies, there is evidence that the brain may adapt dynamically to reflect environmental cognitive requirements. For instance, neuroimaging studies show structural changes in specific areas after training in difficult motor tasks, such as the increased activation of motor, auditory, and visual–spatial brain areas and white matter tracts, as well in professional players (Imfeld, Oechslin, Meyer, Loenneker, & Jancke, 2009). The insights stemming from neural plasticity research may also be potentially relevant to the design of neuroprotective and neurorestorative strategies applicable to the optimization of cognitive, emotional, and learning skills in biological and social vulnerable populations.

Brain Development

Neural development is modulated by neural activity that in turn is mediated by experience. Therefore, cognitive and emotional processing and learning shape the neural networks that are responsible for this processing. In turn, this activity changes the nature of neural representations and their processing, which leads to new experiences and further changes in the neural systems. So, the basis of cognitive, emotional, and learning development can be characterized by mutually induced changes between the neural, cognitive, emotional, and learning levels, in a complex ecological context involving social interactions with cultural specificities. Therefore, researchers have to be aware about this complexity when trying to study each one of these dimensions in isolation. By taking into account constraints on all levels from the gene to the cultural environment, current conceptual approaches tend to integrate different views of brain and cognitive development (Sirois et al., 2008).

Impact of Poverty on Brain and Cognitive Development

The effects of poverty on child development may be mediated by the impact of multiple environmental risk or protective factors, present in nearly all the contexts where children grow up. This involves several pre- and perinatal health factors, home and school environments, availability of community resources, and culture. Research has also identified different patterns of modulation of poverty impacts, depending on the accumulation of factors, the length of poverty exposure, and children individual susceptibility (Lipina & Colombo, 2009; Najman et al., 2009).

The exploration of mediating mechanisms is also important for a better understanding of the basic processes involved in poverty influences on cognitive and brain development. Such research could contribute to the identification of key features for more effective intervention programs and policies. In general, the mediators included in western literature reviews are: (*a*) peri- and postnatal physical health and nutrition, (*b*) home environment, (*c*) parent–children interactions, (*d*) parental mental health, and (*e*) neighborhoods' social and material resources. Complementary, in many studies on impacts of poverty on cognitive outcomes, family income, material hardship, maternal education, marital status, and the number of children in the household were uniquely associated with children performances, suggesting a mediating role for such factors too (Bradley & Corwyn, 2002; Hackman et al., 2010).

Regarding cognitive development, the most commonly described impacts of poverty have been Developmental Quotients, children's verbal and achievement Intelligence Quotients (IQ), incidence of learning disorders, rates of school absence and retention, and completed school years (Bradley & Corwyn, 2002). Current language development studies also show different patterns of socioeconomic modulation on several outcomes, such as vocabulary, spontaneous speech, grammatical development, and communication styles and skills (Hoff, 2006).

With respect to the progression of these effects in later stages of development, some studies show a decrease in the negative impact of poverty on adolescents' IQ (Najman et al., 2009). However, the same trend is not necessarily verified with other measures, such as arithmetic and reading abilities. For instance, a recent study with more than 1,000 adolescents from different ethnic groups and socioeconomic status (SES) backgrounds in the US showed that poverty was indirectly related to lower achievement, through its associations with less cognitively stimulating and emotionally supportive home environments (Eamon, 2005). Also, recent evidence suggests a long-term impact of childhood poverty on working memory processing in adults, mediated by elevated chronic stress experienced during childhood (Evans & Schamberg, 2009).

Viewing cognition as consisting of component codes, computed in different ways and programmed to perform complex tasks, leads to new ways of thinking about how the brain might organize thought and emotional processes (Posner & Raichle, 1994). Specifically, basic processes involved in early cognitive control and language development, such as the different subsystems of attention, working memory, and flexibility are fundamental to all forms of cognitive activity and social behavior throughout the lifespan in most cultural systems worldwide (Sperber & Hirschfeld, 2004). Given the multiplicity of factors that influence and modulate brain development, it is most likely that the impact of poverty on cognition would have a neurocognitive basis, and those more basic cognitive functions would also be modulated by socioeconomic backgrounds.

Only recently, studies that began to evaluate associations between different factors usually associated with poverty and its impact on basic cognitive processing have been reported. Among them are: (*a*) studies that verify deficits on cognitive control skills after prenatal and postnatal exposure to toxic agents, such as PCB and methyl mercury, or legal and illegal drugs such as alcohol and cocaine, in neonates, infants, children, and adolescents (Hubbs-Tait, Nation, Krebs, & Bellinger, 2005); (*b*) studies that found associations between alterations in several bio-behavioral markers, such as salivary cortisol, heart rate and vagal tone, and self-regulatory skills and early school adjustment in children from low-income homes (Lupien, McEwen, Gunnar, & Heim, 2009); and (*c*) studies that verify the modulation of socioeconomic characteristics on different attentional, inhibitory control, working memory, flexibility, planning, phonological awareness, self-regulatory, and theory of mind processes related to different neurocognitive systems, in infants, preschoolers, and school and middle school age-children (D'Angiulli, Herdman, Stapells, & Hertzman, 2008; Farah et al., 2006, 2008; Kishiyama, Boyce, Jimenez, Perry, & Knight, 2009; Lipina, Martelli, Vuelta, Injoque-Ricle, & Colombo, 2004; Lipina, Martelli, Vuelta, & Colombo, 2005; Noble, Norman, & Farah, 2005; Noble, Wolmetz, Ochs, Farah, & McCandliss, 2006; Noble, McCandliss, & Farah, 2007; Raizada, Richards, Meltzoff, & Kuhl, 2008).

Regarding the role of poverty in neural language processing, Noble et al. (2005, 2006, 2007) studied children aged six to nine who had been selected for having below-average phonological awareness scores, and found a complex modulator role for poverty, in which the higher the SES, the less typical were the children's brain–behavior relationships. In a recent study of normal five-year-old children performing an auditory rhyme–judgment task, Raizada et al. (2008) found a more direct relation: the higher the SES, the greater the degree of hemispheric specialization in Broca's area, as measured by the left-minus-right fMRI activation during rhyming tasks. This suggests that the maturation of Broca's area in children may be governed by the complexity of the linguistic environments in which they grow up.

One of the most explored neurocognitive systems, particularly by Farah et al. (2006, 2008), is the prefrontal/executive system, which includes subsystems such as the lateral prefrontal cortex and the anterior cingulate cortex related to working memory and cognitive control processing, respectively. In studies of preschoolers, first graders, and middle-school children, low-SES children had reduced performance on these tasks compared to middle-SES children (Farah et al., 2006; Noble et al., 2005). These findings suggest that the prefrontal/executive system is one of the primary neurocognitive systems associated with social inequalities in early experience.

Similar results have been observed in studies using specific paradigms designed to measure aspects of both executive function and attention. For example, Lipina et al. (2005) examined performance of low- and middle-SES infants from Buenos Aires (Argentina) using the A-not-B task. This task is a variant of a delayed-response paradigm, which incorporates the evaluation of processes such as working memory and inhibitory control. Findings showed that low-SES infants had more errors associated with impairments of inhibitory control and spatial working memory and errors associated with attention and search strategies.

The effects of socioeconomic disparities on attention have been examined in several studies. For example, Mezzacappa (2004) used the Attention Network Test to investigate the effects of socioeconomic disparity on attentional processes in children of 6 years of age. This task can be used to assess levels of attention related to the capacity to maintain alertness, to shift the focus of attention from one stimulus to another, and processes involved in goal-directed behaviors. Results showed that low-SES children had reduced measures of both speed and accuracy on measures of alerting and executive attention. This result indicates that low-SES children were less able to manage response conflict and inhibit distracting information than high-SES children.

The medial temporal/memory system was assessed by Farah et al. (2006) using an incidental learning paradigm in which subjects are not aware that memory will be tested during the learning phase of the task and both verbal and non verbal stimuli (for example, pictures and faces) can be employed. In studies of first grade and middle-school children, low-SES children showed reduced performance. This difference was not initially found in kindergarten children, but after adding a delay interval, it was observed in the older groups.

The findings from the mentioned behavioral studies indicate that SES disparities adversely affect cognitive processes, such as executive function, attention, and memory. In addition, these findings suggest that specific brain regions are associated with these cognitive functions, and that the employed techniques represent advancement beyond those techniques from traditional frameworks of general cognitive ability. However, these tests are still behavioral in nature and as such they are subject to a number of limitations. For instance, researchers can make only indirect inferences about brain function from behavioral tests. In addition, many of these tests are multifactorial and performance could be disrupted for reasons other than those resulting from a specific dysfunction. Moreover, correlations among these tests are low, which means that two tasks can engage the same system in different ways. So a deep examination of the impact of SES on the relationship between cognitive processes and brain function is needed.

In this sense, the mentioned fMRI studies are good examples of the administration of combined behavioral–neuroimaging techniques for a better understanding of these relationships. In addition, recent studies of socioeconomic disparities have used electrophysiological techniques to obtain direct measures of brain activity. For example, D'Angiulli et al. (2008) examined the influence of socioeconomic disparities on attention, using an auditory selective attention task and event related potential (ERP) techniques. In this study, low- and high-SES children had to respond to target tones in an attended channel while withholding responses to all other tones in the attended and unattended channels. A negative difference waveform, reflecting selective attention, was observed for high-SES but not low-SES children. These results suggest that high-SES children selectively attended to relevant information whereas low-SES children attended equally to relevant and irrelevant information.

In a similar study, the effects of SES on attention were investigated by Stevens, Lauinger, & Neville (2009) using an adapted version of the selective auditory attention paradigm. In this case, children were instructed to attend to one of two narratives played simultaneously in speakers located to their left or right. They also observed that low-SES children showed reduced ERP measures of selective attention, suggesting that low-SES children have a reduced ability to filter or suppress irrelevant information.

In a recent study using a visual novelty oddball paradigm, Kishiyama et al. (2009) examined the impact of socioeconomic disparity on prefrontal-dependent ERP components. This task involves detecting target stimuli embedded in streams of repetitive standard stimuli. In addition to the target stimuli, task-irrelevant novel events occurred on 15 percent of the trials. Behavioral differences were not observed between low- and high-SES children on measures of reaction time and accuracy, and no differences were observed in target ERP responses. The behavioral results indicate that both groups could perform the task with a high degree of accuracy. In addition, group differences were predicted in prefrontal-dependent ERP components. Specifically, researchers found that low-SES children had reduced amplitudes for early, attention-sensitive, visual ERP components and novelty ERP responses.

In general, the findings from the ERP studies are consistent with those of behavioral studies of attention and executive function. However, specifically, the results of these studies provide a characterization of these processes that are not necessarily observable from behavioral studies alone. And once again, these findings strongly suggest that the prefrontal cortex may be particularly vulnerable to SES disparities.

Intervention Efforts from Neurocognitive Perspectives

Recently, growing interest has been observed regarding the potential contributions of developmental cognitive neuroscience to intervention efforts. This interest is based on results from different laboratory studies on behavioral training and remediation of basic cognitive process in healthy, attention deficit hyperactivity disordered (ADHD), dyslexic, and dyscalculic children. At present time, there are evidences of moderate improvements on performance, in some cases a generalization effect on others tasks and changes in the pattern of brain activations measured with different techniques, in those children participating in the intervention groups (Klingberg, 2010; McCandliss, Beck, Sandak, & Perfetti, 2003; Rueda, Rothbart, McCandliss, Saccomanno, & Posner, 2005; Shaywitz et al., 2004; Temple et al., 2003; Wilson et al., 2006).

Specifically, the application of developmental cognitive neuroscience frameworks to intervention programs aimed at improving the cognitive development of low-income children is even more preliminary than the mentioned studies. Based on previous studies (Lipina et al., 1999; Lipina, Vuelta, Martelli, Bisio, & Colombo, 2000; Lipina et al., 2004; Lipina et al., 2005) Colombo, Lipina and colleagues designed two multimodular intervention programs, which were carried out with samples of healthy three- to five-year-olds from low-income homes in two districts in Argentina: *Programa de Intervención Escolar* (Program 1) and *Programa Piloto de Estimulación Cognitiva* (Program 2). Both were aimed at promoting the development of basic neurocognitive processing (see Table 17.1 for a detailed description of both programs) and were implemented between the years 2002 and 2005 (Colombo & Lipina, 2005; Martelli et al., 2007; Segretin et al., 2007).

Program 1 sample comprised 237 healthy three- to five-year-old children recruited from three public schools in the city of Buenos Aires, between the years 2002 and 2004. Program 2 sample comprised 382 healthy three- to five-year-old children recruited from 16 official childcare centers in the city of Salta, in the year 2005.

In both programs, the following recruitment criteria were applied: Spanish as mother language, absence of records of serious medical conditions, and no history of significant head injury or neurological diseases. Children showed no symptoms of acute disease at the time of initial and final cognitive evaluations, and came from Unsatisfied Basic Needs homes (UBN, poverty criteria). This information was obtained through maternal report, direct medical examination, and school records.

Programa de Intervención Escolar (Program 1)

Program 1 was designed as a randomized controlled cognitive exercising program, which involved the following intervention modules:

Module 1: Cognitive Exercising (Individual Approach)

Before the cognitive intervention, children were individually evaluated with a battery of cognitive tasks (attention, inhibitory control, working memory, flexibility, and planning processes) (see Table 17.2 for details on the administered cognitive battery) (*Stage 1*).

Table 17.1 Description of Programs 1 and 2

Item	Program 1	Program 2
Design	Controlled, randomized (longitudinal)	Quasi-experimental (longitudinal)
Groups	Intervention (individual)/Control	Intervention 1 (individual)
		Intervention 2 (group)
Intervention		
Modules (M)	M 1: Exercising (Stage 2)	M 1: Training (Stage 2)
	M 2: Iron and folic acid supplementation (Stage 2)	M 2: Iron and folic acid supplementation (Stage 2)
	M 3: Teacher counseling (Stage 1 to 3)	M 3: Teacher counseling (Stage 1 to 3)*
	M 4: Parent counseling (Stage 1 to 3)	M 4: Parent counseling (Stage 1 to 3)*
Stages (S)	S 1: Baseline (individual evaluation)**	S 1: Baseline (individual evaluation)***
	S 2: Modules 1 and 2 implementation	S 2: Modules 1 and 2 implementation
	S 3: Impact evaluation (individual evaluation)**	S 3: Impact evaluation (individual evaluation)***
Schedules	16 sessions (once a week - 4 months in 1 year)	32 sessions (twice a week - 4 months in 1 year)
	25 sessions (twice a week - 4 months in 1 year)	
	32 sessions (once a week - 2 periods of 4 months in 2 years)	
Cognitive demands	Inhibitory control	Attention
	Working memory	Working memory
	Planning	Planning
	Flexibility	Flexibility
Activities	Exercising on laboratory tasks** using novel trials	Extra-curricular classroom activities based on the exercising framework implemented in Program 1
Session stage	S 1: Motivation evaluation	S 1: Motivation evaluation
	S 2: Instruction comprehension	S 2: Instruction comprehension
	S 3: Exercising	S 3: Training
Exercising/Training demands increment Criteria	One level after reaching 80% of efficiency	One level after reaching 80% of efficiency

Sources: Colombo & Lipina (2005) and Segretin et al. (2007).
Note: M: Module; S: Stage; *Implemented by government agency; **see Table 17.2; ***see Table 17.3.

Table 17.2 Cognitive Battery Administered at Stages 1 and 3 in Program 1

Task	Cognitive Process
Tower of London (TOL)	Planning
Corsi Blocks	Spatial working memory
Three and Four Colors	Spatial working memory
Digit Span	Verbal working memory
Day/Night like Stroop	Inhibitory control
Flexible Item Selection Task (FIST)	Flexibility

Sources: Colombo & Lipina (2005) and Segretin et al. (2007).

After that, children were randomly assigned to one of two study groups: exercising and control. Exercising group was administered tasks with cognitive demands (see Box 17.1 for a description of the activities); while control group was involved in tasks with no cognitive control demands (same schedules as in exercising group). Three schedules were applied according to the frequency of sessions: (*a*) 16 sessions once a week during four months, (*b*) 25 sessions twice a week during four months, and (*c*) 32 sessions once a week during two periods of four months (*Stage 2*). Sessions were run outside the classroom in a quiet room. Tasks were divided into levels, with 5 to 10 exercises in each level, and children progressing to the next level by solving a number of correct responses (80%) in one block. Each session, of about 30 to 40 minutes, comprised two different tasks with two or three blocks of exercises each one, according to children's performance.

Box 17.1 Program 1 Exercise Examples

Planning

Tower of London. Each block of exercises consisted of five trials in which children were required to reach a goal configuration of three colored balls, moving one ball at a time, in a minimum number of moves generating an appropriate action sequence. Levels of difficulty comprised exercises from one to nine movements. For example, two movements are required to reach the goal configuration in this example:

Example:

1st
2nd

Start configuration   Goal configuration

(Box 17.1 contd.)

(Box 17.1 contd.)

Working Memory
Corsi Blocks. A sequence of lights (from two to eight) was turned on, and children were required to remember and point the boxes following the light sequences. Levels of difficulty increased with the number of lights children had to remember.

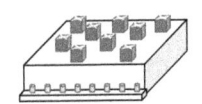

Three and four colors. After the experimenter told the children a sequence of colors (between two and six), the child was required to reproduce the sequence, pressing the same colored buttons.

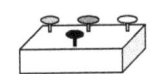

Digit Span: Children were required to listen, remember and reproduce a sequence of numbers (between two and nine).

Inhibitory Control
Stroop-like Day-Night: Children were asked 16 times to say the opposite of what they saw in a series of cards (e.g., when a picture of a sun was presented, they had to say "night," and when the picture showed was a moon, they had to say "day"). Difficulty was increased adding different cards (from one to three opposite pairs).

Say "night"   Say "day"

Categorization and Flexibility
Flexible Item Selection Task (FIST). A set of cards were used in this task, conformed with items according to four dimensions: shape, color, size, and number. In each trial children were required to select two cards sharing the same criteria. In the easier level, children were required to make one selection (selecting two cards), but in the second selection and level, the child was required to make two selections: first, select two cards equals in one way, and then select another other two cards in a different way. Example: (1) Cards "A" and "B" are equals because they have **two** fish with the same color; (2) Cards "A" and "C" are equals because they have **big** fishes with the same color. Shape and color are equals in all cards; number and size are common in two cards.

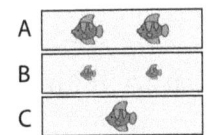

Source: Colombo & Lipina, 2005.

The initial level for each child in each activity was determined in the *Stage 1* (higher level completed with at least the 80 percent of efficiency or correct responses). The exercising schedule applied in each session was organized in the following four consecutive steps:

1. Experimenters evaluated children's motivational state and instruction comprehension. A Likert scale, including six pairs of opposite constructs was administered (willing/not willing to collaborate, extroversion/introversion, talkative/quiet, active/passive, impulsive/thoughtful, and trustful/distrustful). If children were not adequately motivated, trainers made interventions in order to modify this condition.
2. Experimenters presented the materials and tasks instructions.
3. In order to evaluate instruction comprehension, two pretest exercises were administered. Only when children solved these exercises properly, the experimenters continued with the next step.
4. Two blocks of exercises of each task (from five to ten) were presented. After the first block of exercises, experimenters evaluated children's performance, and determine the level of difficulty of the next block of exercises. When children reached the efficiency criterion (80 percent of correct responses), the second block was presented with a higher level of difficulty. Otherwise, experimenters made interventions according to the performance difficulties observed before presenting the second block of exercises with the same level of difficulty.

The performance corresponding to the last group of exercises determined the initial level of difficulty of next session exercises in each task. Children in the control group participated in activities with no cognitive control demands but same frequency and conditions as in the training group. They were asked to make drawings in a specific sequence and with specific contents (e.g., free content, him/herself, house, tree, school, family, animals, street, land, transportation, park, kitchen, toys, and what he/she would like to be as an adult). Finally, cognitive performance was reevaluated with the same battery of tasks used in Stage 1 (*Stage 3*).

Module 2: Nutritional Supplementation

Each child (control and intervention groups) received a pill containing 60mg of elementary iron and 0.4mg of folic acid provided by UNICEF-Argentina, once a week for 16 weeks, to maintain stability of iron levels during training period.

Module 3: Teacher Training

Twice a month teachers from both groups (control and intervention) participated in workshops on child development, poverty impacts on child development, and the use and implementation of play activities inside classrooms to promote cognitive development.

Module 4: Social and Health Counseling

This was for parents (from control and intervention groups) with a frequency according to parental demand (approximately once a week).

Programa Piloto de Estimulación Cognitiva (Program 2)

Based on the Program 1 framework, the same team of researchers designed a new cognitive training module for a new cohort of children, which was implemented in the year 2005 in the city of Salta as part of a quasi-experimental prospective study (Program 2). The general aim of this second program was to train cognitive control processes in children from UBN homes—as in Program 1—and to reduce the number of human resources necessary to run this type of activities (in comparison with Program 1 that needed one adult per child for cognitive stimulation). Program 2 was designed to compare two training modalities: individual and group approaches (Table 17.1) and comprised the following four intervention modules for both groups:

Module 1: Cognitive Training (Individual and Group Approaches)

Before the intervention, children were individually evaluated with a battery of cognitive tasks (attention, working memory, flexibility, and planning processes) (see Table 17.3 for details on the administered cognitive battery) (*Stage 1*).

Table 17.3 Cognitive Battery Administered at Stages 1 and 3 in Program 2

Task	Cognitive Process
Tower of London (TOL)	Planning
Corsi' Block	Spatial working memory
Selective Attention	Attention
Flexible Item Selection Task (FIST)	Flexibility

Sources: Colombo & Lipina (2005) and Segretin et al. (2007).

After that, four-year-old children were randomly assigned to one of two study groups (individual and group training). Three- and five-year-old children were only assigned to the latter condition. In both training modalities, activities were implemented during 16 weeks with the same schedule in both groups (32 training sessions, twice a week) (*Stage 2*) (see Box 17.2 for a description of the activities). In the individual training modality, between five to seven children were assigned to each experimenter, while in the group training modality, two experimenters worked together with two groups of about 20 children each (one adult per 10 children).

Box 17.2 Program 2 Training Examples

Attention

Search the same drawing as a target. Children were required to select identical stimuli as the target (10 identical stimuli and 15 distractors). Difficulty was increased with number of distractors and its similarity with the target.

Freeze game. Children had to move/dance until music stopped, and they had to stay like a sculpture. In the group training modality, children had to reproduce the position of a picture (e.g., a child opening his arms), while in the Individual modality; they have to put their hands according to a model (picture). Easier trials demanded the reproduction of what represented in a picture (congruent condition). Trials that are more difficult consisted in reproducing the opposite of what a picture represented (incongruent condition).

Searching for differences. Children had to search and identify ten differences between two similar pictures. Difficulty was increased with designs that are more complex.

Working Memory

Peer recognition. After observing a set of cards for few seconds children were asked to remember them. Levels of difficulty involved remembering from 3-to-7 cards from a set of 10-to-20 cards.

Grid location. Children were required to remember and indicate the spatial location (grid) of a set of cards (2-to-6 with different pictures) after observing them for few seconds. Grids had 9 (3×3), 16 (4×4) or 20 (4×5) squares. Difficulty was increased with adding more cards and places in the grid.

Sequences. Children were required to remember and reproduce the spatial order of a set of cards (3-to-5). In the easier

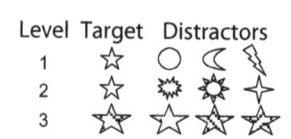

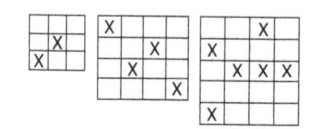

(Box 17.2 contd.)

(Box 17.2 contd.)

levels of difficulty, the stimuli was visual (cards were displayed on a board). In the more difficult levels verbal cues were administered (experimenters named the drawings in the order that children had to put them).

Planning
Construction. Children had to build a geometric array by assembling a set of pieces following a model (between 2 and 6 according to the level of difficulty). At the first levels of difficulty, children were helped with shape and color information through pre-designed drawings.

Dog, cat, mouse. Children had to match in a certain number of movements (2-to-7), three animals with their corresponding food (dog-bone; mouse-cheese; cat-fish), applying two rules: (1) only one animal can be moved at a time; and (2) it is not possible to put two animals in the same place.

Mazes.

Categorization and Flexibility
Lottery. Children were required to mark on their cards those items corresponding to different target categories: shape, color, or their combination. Difficulty was increased adding more categories or category combinations.

Flower. Children were required to select cards according to four dimensions: shape, color, number, and size. Two versions were implemented: In the first one, one card was placed in the centre of the flower and children had to select its components from each petal. Between 2 (easier levels) and 4 (in more difficult levels) dimensions were required in each trial. In the second version, based on some cards selected from the petals (between 2 and 4), children were required to select the target card that combined with those dimensions.

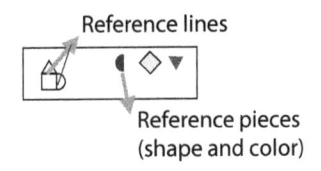

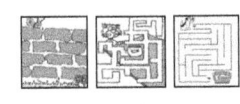

Source: Segretin et al. (2007).

The schedule followed in each session for both modalities was structured in the following four consecutive steps:

1. Experimenters evaluated children's motivational state and instruction comprehension (following the same procedures described for Program 1).
2. Experimenters presented the materials and tasks instructions.
3. Two pretest exercises were administered.
4. Two blocks of exercises (5 to 10) were presented to children in each activity following the same criteria as in Program 1. After training, all children were evaluated with the same battery used in Stage 1 (*Stage 3*).

Module 2: Nutritional Supplementation

Each child received a pill containing 60 mg of elementary iron and 0.4 mg of folic acid provided by UNICEF-Argentina, once a week for 16 weeks.

Module 3: Counseling for Teachers and Caregivers

Module 4: Counseling for Parents in Health and Social Issues

The last two modules were implemented by the government agency and were not coordinated by researchers.

Summary of Results

In Program 1, results showed a positive effect of cognitive training combined with iron and folic acid supplementation on children in cognitive performance. Children in schedule-2 (32 sessions in two periods) had the highest performance, followed by children in schedule-3 (25 sessions in one period) and finally the children in schedule-1 (16 sessions in one period) (Colombo & Lipina, 2005).

In Program 2, results suggested that four-year-old children from UBN homes, both individual and group trained significantly improved their initial cognitive performance. They also suggested that group modality was as effective as the individual modality in incrementing children's initial cognitive performance (Martelli et al., 2007; Segretin et al., 2007). With regard to three- to five-year-old children from UBN homes group trained, results were similar: age variations depending on the cognitive process were observed, what suggests the need for further studies (Segretin et al., 2007). For details see Colombo and Lipina (2005); Martelli et al. (2007); and Segretin et al. (2007).

Conclusion

Cognitive neuroscience studies have been useful to identify effects of poverty on specific basic cognitive processes strongly associated with early development of crucial literacy and numeracy competences. For instance, comparison of different ways of learning novel arithmetic operations—specifically memorizing math facts versus learning to compute them—suggests a significant role of spatial working memory during execution of algorithms and revealed that different learning conditions are associated with different neural networks (Delazer et al., 2005). Another recent neuroimaging study revealed that the continuous improvement in speed to solve simple arithmetic problems was the result of a transition from domain-general processing to domain-specific processing (Ischebeck et al., 2006). Specifically, younger children recruited general memory and reasoning brain areas, while older children used visual and verbal areas. These studies raise the possibility of designing activities that help children shift between modes of thought. Moreover, the same type of cognitive processes were subjected to the design and implementation of intervention programs or trials, whose promising results with different population of children encourage researchers to transfer them to the poverty field of study (see the previous section, *Intervention Efforts from Neurocognitive Perspectives*). Beyond this, Neuroscience has still little to say about the social construction of inequity.

It is necessary to design and carry out more basic and applied studies to adjust multiple conceptual and methodological issues from laboratory to community settings. These multidisciplinary efforts will have to bear in mind different methodological, epistemological, and practical concerns and opportunities that just recently neuroscience began to consider (Lipina & Colombo, 2009; Shonkoff, 2010). In this context, it would be important to support efforts aimed at promoting collaborations focused on the integration of different levels of analysis. Some examples of this type of efforts from a neurocognitive perspective are: (*a*) the modulation of parenting on the development of self-regulatory competences; (*b*) the analysis of the associations between teaching styles and the development of executive control competences; (*c*) the integration of cognitive, emotional, and social competences stimulation in the design of school curricula; and (*d*) the inclusion of art in community interventions as a tool for social and health transformations.

Given the multidimensional nature of both complex phenomena of poverty and child development, any intervention intended to optimize or improve poor children opportunities, requires the design of programs and policies with actions at different levels. To establish an interdisciplinary research agenda focused on child development and its biological and social determinants involves the need to start from a wide conceptualization that allows approaching the multiple dimensions and interactive mechanisms of complexity in a systemic, comprehensive, and coherent way. However, bridging neuroscience and other disciplines also requires bridging academic communities and improving their communications and collaborations. Since each discipline addresses a broad range of research questions using a variety of methods, one important challenge is to identify the questions and methods that overlap the most to build complementary research agendas. This would be necessary to promote the visualization of child development and its determinants as complex phenomena at different government, academic, and civil organization levels.

References

Bavelier, D. & Neville, H. J. (2002). Cross-modal plasticity: Where and how? *Nature Reviews Neuroscience, 3*(6), 443–452. doi:10.1038/nrn848

Bradley, R. H., & Corwyn, R. F. (2002). Socioeconomic status and child development. *Annual Review of Psychology*, 53, 371–399. doi:10.1146/annurev.psych.53.100901.135233

Colombo, J. A., & Lipina, S. J. (2005). *Hacia un programa público de estimulación cognitiva infantil: Fundamentos, métodos y resultados de una experiencia de intervención preescolar controlada (Towards a public program of child cognitive stimulation: Foundations, methods, and results of a controlled randomized intervention)*. Buenos Aires: Paidós.

D'Angiulli, A., Herdman, A., Stapells, D., & Hertzman, C. (2008). Children´s event related potentials of auditory selective attention vary with their socioeconomic status. *Neuropsychology, 22*, 293–300.

Delazer, M., Ischebeck, A., Domahs, F., Zamarian, L., Koppelstaetter, F., Siedentopf, C.M., & Felber, S. (2005). Learning by strategies and learning by drill-evidence from an fMRI study. *NeuroImage, 25*(3), 838–849. doi:10.1016/j.neuroimage.2004.12.009

Eamon, M. K. (2005). Social-demographic, school, neighborhood, and parenting influences on the academic achievement of Latino young adolescents. *Journal of Youth and Adolescence, 34*(2), 163–174. doi:10.1007/s10964-005-3214-x

Evans, G. W. (2004). The environment of childhood poverty. *American Psychologist, 59*(2), 77–92. doi:10.1037/0003-066X.59.2.77

Evans, G. W., & Schamberg, M. A. (2009). Childhood poverty, chronic stress, and adult working memory. *Proceedings of the National Academy of Sciences (PNAS), 106*(16), 6545–6549. doi:10.1073/pnas.0811910106

Farah, M. J., Shera, D. M., Savage, J. H., Betancourt, L., Giannetta, J. M., Brodsky, N. L., & Hurth, H. (2006). Childhood poverty: Specific associations with neurocognitive development. *Brain Research, 1110*(1), 166–174. doi:10.1016/j.brainres.2006.06.072

Farah, M. J., Betancourt, L., Shera, D. M., Savage, J. H., Giannetta, J. M., Brodsky, N. L., & Hurt, H. (2008). Environmental stimulation, parental nurturance and cognitive development in humans. *Developmental Science, 11*(5), 793–801. doi:10.1111/j.1467-7687.2008.00688.x

Hackman, D. A., Farah, M. J., & Meany, M. H. (2010). Socioeconomic status and the brain: Mechanistic insights from human and animal research. *Nature Reviews Neuroscience, 11*(9), 651–659. doi:10.1038/nrn2897

Hoff, E. (2006). How social contexts support and shape language development. *Developmental Review, 26*(1), 55–88. doi:10.1016/j.dr.2005.11.002

Hubbs-Tait, L., Nation, J. R., Krebs, N. F., & Bellinger, D. C. (2005). Neurotoxicants, micronutrients, and social environments: Individual and combined effects on children's development. *Psychological Science in the Public Interest, 6*(3), 57–121.

Imfeld, A., Oechslin, M. S., Meyer, M., Loenneker, T., & Jancke, L. (2009). White matter plasticity in the corticospinal tract of musicians: A diffusion tensor imaging study. *NeuroImage, 46*(3), 600–607. doi:10.1016/j.neuroimage.2009.02.025

Ischebeck, A., Zamarian, L., Siedentopf, C., Koppelstätter, Benke, T., Felber, S., & Delazer, M. (2006). How specifically do we learn? Imaging the learning of multiplication and subtraction. *NeuroImage, 30*(4), 1365–1375. doi:10.1016/j.neuroimage.2005.11.016

Kishiyama, M. M., Boyce, W. T., Jimenez, A. M., Perry, L. M., & Knight, R. T. (2009). Socioeconomic disparities affect prefrontal function in children. *Journal of Cognitive Neuroscience, 21*(6), 1106–115. doi:10.1162/jocn.2009.21101

Klingberg, T. (2010). Training and plasticity of working memory. *Trends in Cognitive Sciences, 14*(7), 317–324. doi:10.1016/j.tics.2010.05.002

Lipina, S. J., Bisio, N., Martelli, M. I., Penela, V., Back, B., Yáñez, A., & Colombo, J. A. (1999). Influencias ambientales sobre el desempeño cognitivo en la prueba A no B deuna población de niños argentinos de entre 6 y 14 meses [Environmental influences on cognitive performance in the A not B task in a sample of Argentine infants of 6-to-14 months old]. *Investigaciones en Psicología, 4*(2), 73–88.

Lipina, S. J., & Colombo, J. A. (2009). *Poverty and brain development during childhood: An approach from cognitive psychology and neuroscience.* Washington, DC: American Psychological Association.

Lipina, S. J., Martelli, M. I., Vuelta, B. L., & Colombo, J. A. (2005). Performance on the A-not-B task of Argentinean infants from unsatisfied and satisfied basic needs homes. *Interamerican Journal of Psychology, 39*(1), 49–60.

Lipina, S. J., Martelli, M. I., Vuelta, B., Injoque-Ricle, I., & Colombo, J. A. (2004). Pobreza y desempeño ejecutivo en alumnos preescolares de la ciudad de Buenos Aires (Argentina) [Poverty and executive performance in preschoolers from the City of Buenos Aires (Argentina)]. *Interdisciplinaria, 21*(2),153–193.

Lipina, S. J., Vuelta, B., Martelli, M. I., Bisio, N., & Colombo, J. A. (2000). Planificación enniños de edad preescolar: Efectos de la pertenencia a hogares con Necesidades Básicas Insatisfechas (NBI) [Planning in preschool children: Effects of belonging to households with unsatisfied basic needs (UBN).] *Anuario de Investigaciones, 8,* 436–454.

Lupien, S. J., McEwen, B. S., Gunnar, M. R., & Heim, C. (2009). Effects of stress throughout the lifespan on the brain, behaviour and cognition. *Nature Reviews Neuroscience, 10,* 434–445.

Martelli, M. I., Vuelta, B. L., Blanco, M., Cristiani, V., Segretin, M. S., Lipina, S. J., & Colombo, J. A. (Eds). (2007). Programas de intervención temprana en nuestro país. Experiencia de una aplicación individual de estimulación cognitiva. En *Pobreza y desarrollo infantil: Una contribución multidisciplinaria.* [Early intervention programmes in our country. Experience of an individual application of cognitive stimulation. In *Poverty and child development: A multidisciplinary contribution.*] (Colombo Eds.), Buenos Aires: Editorial Paidós.

McCandliss, B. D., Beck, I. L., Sandak, R., & Perfetti, C. (2003). Focusing attention on decoding for children with poor reading skills: Design and preliminary tests of the Word Building Intervention. *Scientific Studies of Reading, 7*(1), 75–104. doi:10.1207/S1532799XSSR0701_05

Mezzacappa, E. (2004). Alerting, orienting, and executive attention: Developmental properties and sociodemographic correlates in an epidemiological sample of young, urban children. *Child Development, 75*(5),1373–1386. doi:10.1111/j.1467-8624.2004.00746.x

Mohammed, A. H., Zhu, S. W., Darmopil, S., Hjerling-Leffler, J., Ernfors, P., Winblad, B., & Bogdanovic, N. (2002). Environmental enrichment and the brain. *Progress in Brain Research, 138,* 109–133. doi:10.1016/S0079-6123(02)38074-9

Najman, J. M., Mohammad, R., Hayatbakhsh, M. D., Heron, M. A., Bor, W., O'Callaghan, M. J., & Williams, G. M. (2009). The impact of episodic and chronic poverty on child cognitive development. *Journal of Pediatrics, 154*(2), 284–289.

Noble, K. G., McCandliss, B. D., & Farah, M. J. (2007). Socioeconomic gradients predict individual differences in neurocognitive abilities. *Developmental Science, 10*(4), 464–480. doi:10.1111/j.1467-7687.2007.00600.x

Noble, K. G., Norman, M. F., & Farah, M. J. (2005). Neurocognitive correlates of socioeconomic status in kindergarten children. *Developmental Science, 8*(1), 74–87. doi:10.1111/j.1467-7687.2005.00394.x

Noble, K. G., Wolmetz, M. E., Ochs, L. G., Farah, M. J., & McCandliss, B. D. (2006). Brain-behavior relationships in reading acquisition are modulated by socioeconomic factors. *Developmental Science, 9*(6), 642–651. doi:10.1111/j.1467-7687.2006.00542.x

Posner, M. I., & Raichle, M. E. (1994). *Images of mind*. Washington, DC: American Psychological Association.

Raizada, R. D., & Kishiyama, M. M. (2010). Effects on socioeconomic status on brain development and how cognitive neuroscience may contribute to leveling the playing field. *Frontiers in Human Neuroscience, 4*(3), 1–18. doi:10.3389/neuro.09.003.2010

Raizada, R. D., Richards, T. L., Meltzoff, A., & Kuhl, P. (2008). Socioeconomic status predicts hemispheric specialization of the left inferior frontal gyrus in young children. *NeuroImage, 40*, 1932–1401.

Rueda, M. R., Rothbart, M. K., McCandliss, B. D., Saccomanno, L., & Posner, M. I. (2005). Training, maturation, and genetic influences on the development of executive attention. *Proceedings of the National Academy of Sciences USA, 102*(41), 14931–14936. doi:10.1073/pnas.0506897102

Segretin, M. S., Martelli M. I., Cristiani V. A., Blanco M., Vuelta B., Lipina S. J., & Colombo, J. A. (2007). Programas de intervención temprana en nuestro país. Experiencia de aplicaciones grupales de estimulación cognitiva. En J. A. Colombo (Ed.), *Pobreza y desarrollo infantil: Una contribución multidisciplinaria*. [Early intervention programmes in our country. Experience of group application of cognitive stimulation, In J. A. Colombo (Ed.), *Poverty and child development: A multidisciplinary contribution*.] Buenos Aires: Editorial Paidós.

Shaywitz, B. A., Shaywitz, S. E., Blachman, B. A., Pugh, K. R., Fullbright, R. K., Skudlarski, P., & Gore, J. C. (2004). Developments of left occipitotemporal systems for skilled reading in children alter a phonologically-based intervention. *Biological Psychiatry, 55*(9), 926–933. doi:10.1016/j.biopsych.2003.12.019

Shonkoff, J. P. (2010). Building a new biodevelopmental framework to guide the future of early childhood policy. *Child Develpoment, 81*(1), 357–367. doi:10.1111/j.1467-8624.2009.01399.x

Sirois, S., Spratling, M., Thomas, M. S. C., Westermann, G., Mareschal, D., & Johnson, M. H. (2008). Précis of neuroconstructivism: How the brain constructs cognition. *Behavioral and Brain Sciences, 31*(3), 321–356. doi:10.1017/S0140525X0800407X

Sperber, D., & Hirschfeld, L. A. (2004). The cognitive foundations of cultural stability and diversity. *Trends in Cognitive Sciences, 8*(1), 40–46. doi:10.1016/j.tics.2003.11.002

Stevens, C., Lauinger, B., & Neville, H. (2009). Differences in the neural mechanisms of selective attention in children from different socioeconomic backgrounds: An event-related brain potential study. *Developmental Science, 12*(4), 634–646. doi:10.1111/j.1467-7687.2009.00807.x

Temple, E., Deutsch, G. K., Poldrack, R. A., Miller, S. L., Tallal, P., Merzenich, M. M., & Gabrieli, J. D. (2003). Neural deficits in children with dyslexia ameliorated by behavioral remediation: evidence from functional MRI. *Proceedings of the National Academy of Sciences, 100*(5), 2860–2865. doi:10.1073/pnas.0030098100

Wilson, A. J., Dehaene, S., Pinel, P., Revkin, S. K., Cohen, L., & Cohen, D. (2006). Principles underlying the design of "The Number Race," an adaptive computer game for remediation of dyscalculia. *Behavioral and Brain Functions, 2*(19). doi:10.1186/1744-9081-2-19

18

Countering the Rush to Medication: Psychodynamic, Intergenerational, and Cultural Considerations in Understanding Children's Psychic Distress

Michael O'Loughlin

How to bring relief to the lives of children who suffer is a question that has long preoccupied me. The sheer complexity of the contexts in which children have to live their lives and the sheer overwhelming forces arrayed against children in difficult circumstances can defy the efforts of even the best theorists, policy makers, and community workers. Poverty, lack of educational opportunity, wars, genocides and displacements, despotism, classism, racism, sexism, and other forms of institutional violence can profoundly constrain children's life chances. In such a complex realm the contribution of any single discipline is likely to be meager and promising solutions will only emerge from the kind of integrative efforts that this book embodies. My own disciplines are psychoanalysis, child psychology, and childhood education and in what follows I intend to focus on the contribution of psychoanalysis to an understanding of children's mental health issues and particularly to interventions that can advance the psychic wellness of children. The choice of psychoanalysis as a vehicle for addressing children's mental health issues in a critical and grounded way may surprise some readers, so perhaps a little background is in order.

The Case for a Liberatory Psychoanalysis

When I became a student of psychoanalysis I anticipated that it would give me benefits in terms of self-insight and that it would equip me with clinical skills that would allow me to develop new career opportunities. I did not anticipate that it would give me new tools for understanding the relationship between individual suffering and larger sociopolitical systems, nor did I expect to gain new insights into social justice and oppression. My training at a conventional psychoanalytic institute reinforced many of my stereotypes of psychoanalysis as a field developed by bourgeois intellectuals to alleviate the neuroses of bourgeois fee-paying clients. With the exception of a course on gender, issues of difference were not explored. No mention was made of economic inequality. Transcultural differences in manifestations of suffering and potential modes of treatment were not examined. Indigenous modes of healing were not examined. And, of course, my training was silent on the embeddedness of people's psychic suffering in larger sociopolitical and postcolonial contexts of the kind discussed by Good and colleagues (2008) under the rubric "postcolonial disorders." As Derrida (1998) noted, while psychoanalysts established selective outposts around the world they did so without ever examining the European gaze on which their work was founded:

> [T]here is practically no psychoanalysis in Asia, or in the South Seas. These are among those parts of "the rest of the world" where psychoanalysis has never set foot, or in any case where it has never taken off its European shoes. (p. 69)

Psychoanalysis began with radical intentions but, sadly, contemporary psychoanalysis in North America and elsewhere—particularly psychoanalysis as clinical practice—suffers from what Jaccoby (1975) terms *social amnesia*. Danto's (2005) book, *Freud's Free Clinics,* however, documents the early aspirations of some psychoanalysts to develop praxis of social justice. Watkins and Shulman (2008) noted that

> prominent members of the early psychoanalytic movement who were Marxists included Erich Fromm, Otto Fenichel, Gustave Landauer, Annie Reich; socialists included Bruno Bettelheim, Greta Bibring, Helene Deutsche, Ernst Simmel, and Siegfried Bernfeld; communists included Edith Jacobson, Marie Langer, and Wilhem Reich; and social democrats included Karen Horney, Paul Federn, and Sigmund Freud. (p. 58)

With its recognition of symptoms only as surface manifestations of psychic distress and with an acknowledgment that all actions are embedded in contexts, Watkins & Shulman (2008) observe that depth psychology is ideally suited for developing rich conceptualizations of the embeddedness of human subjectivity and human action in cultural, historical, and institutional contexts. Early psychoanalysis also had a strong focus on praxis—on the carrying over of analytic ideas into analysis of and intervention in the inequalities of everyday life:

> In the early period of psychoanalysis forged in Red Vienna, psychoanalysts were personally involved in initiatives for free clinics for psychoanalytic treatment, free clinics for reproductive health care and education for women, experimental schools for children of the poor, the kindergarten movement, school-based treatment centers for children traumatized by war and poverty, settlement house psychology classes for workers, the first child guidance clinics, and suicide prevention centers. They paid attention to building conditions for peace and stability in Austria and Europe, put forward initiatives to help women struggle against various forms of domination and control, and suggested

architectural changes for public housing that would help build urban families' sense of community, understood to undergird psychological health. (p. 56)

Freud, himself, tackled larger societal questions in works such as *Civilization and its Discontents* (1930*)* and *The Future of an Illusion* (1927)*,* and he was chagrined at the way in which American psychiatrists gained exclusive control of psychoanalytic training in the US and used it to advance their own self-interest by excluding lay analysts and narrowing the mission of the field to private treatment of individuals. Many of the Jewish analysts who fled Austria and Germany during World War II sought refuge in the US, and, as Altman (1995) shows in *The Analyst in the Inner City*, anxious about their outsider status as Jews, many of these émigré analysts worked hard to earn a place in the mainstream white profession of American psychoanalysis, The price they paid for this assimilation, Altman notes, was to turn a blind eye to racism and inequality in the profession, and to abandon any interest in social justice or praxis.

Shibboleths such as the notion that certain classes of marginal people—notably persons of limited means and those with serious psychotic disorders or complex social suffering—were *unanalyzable*, and mendacious and self-serving arguments about the need for rigidity in schedules, fees, and so on, served to further perpetuate the image of psychoanalysis as elite, out-of-touch, racist, classist, and so forth. Obendorf (1953) noted: "Psychoanalysis has finally become legitimate and respectable, perhaps paying the price in becoming sluggish and smug, hence attractive to an increasing number of minds which find security in conformity and prosperity" (quoted in Moskowitz, 1996, p. 29). Stepansky (2009) recently noted that American psychoanalysis has been profoundly myopic about the long-term consequences of creating an exclusive privileged white club of well-remunerated analysts working for the power elite.

My purpose here is to show that it need not be so. In this chapter I am seeking to address what Moskowitz (1996) speaks of as the radical and liberatory potential of psychoanalysis both as a means of treatment and as a tool of social analysis. More precisely, I hope to offer some illustrations of the power of psychoanalysis as a means of treatment *through* social analysis, taking as a particular case in point enhancement of the psychic wellness of children. In addressing the suffering of children, I will focus on some insights from psychoanalysis that have important implications for how societies and agencies might intervene therapeutically and educationally to enhance children's life chances in the area of mental health and wellness.

Negative Consequences of the Globalization of Western Medical Models of Mental Health

The Western psychiatric notion that mental health issues are biologically based and perhaps even genetic in origin has its roots in the struggle by Western psychiatry to gain hegemony over defining the parameters and treatment of mental disorders (see Andre, 2009; Bentall, 2009; Breggin, 1991; Read, Mosher, & Bentall, 2005; Whitaker, 2001). A key strategy in this process has been the propagation and dissemination of the Diagnostic and Statistical Manual (DSM) of Mental Disorders (American Psychiatric Association, 1952). There has been a palpable shift in emphasis over time such that the most recent edition, DSM-IV (2000), has moved away from a contextualization of the origins of distress to an agnostic listing of clusters of symptoms which supposedly constitute various mental disorders. The next revision of DSM, to be published in 2013, is likely to continue this trend. Watters (2010) noted that the DSM is increasingly influential in the classification of mental disorders throughout the world. Watters and others (see also Kirk & Kutchins, 1992; Kutchins & Kirk, 2003) explore the hegemonic and capitalist pretensions behind the attempt to create a single global discourse to categorize mental distress. The DSM is constructed around medicalizing and pathologizing assumptions that mental health issues are diseases and their etiology is necessarily biological and perhaps even genetic. Disorders such as depression, schizophrenia, obsessive compulsive disorder, bipolar disorder, and so on are glossed as the result of "chemical imbalance"[1] and this of course opens the door to the pharmaceuticalization of distress, often with the kind of devastating consequences Biehl (2005) illustrated so deftly in his study of marginal peoples in Brazil.

This ostensibly neutral medical stance denies the possibility that forms of mental distress can be precipitated by sociohistorical circumstance, sociopolitical context, or institutional forms of violence such as poverty, forced migration, lack of adequate health and educational infrastructure, or even lack of hope arising from the foreclosure of people's futures by totalitarian and despotic regimes. Instead of *suffering* that might be understood in terms of the circumstances of people's lives, we are presented instead with *disease*—afflictions that people supposedly acquire through ill luck in the genetic lottery. Later I will explore the catastrophic consequence of excluding from consideration indigenous and folk ways of understanding psychic distress, as well as the potentially catastrophic consequences of an amnesiac medical approach that is blind to history, blind to circumstance, and even blind to personal narrative.

There is, however, a more pressing issue. As Bentall (2009), Breggin (1995), Whitaker (2001) and others have noted, the shift toward the medicalization of mental disorders not only advanced the professional aspirations of psychiatrists, but it also provided a beachhead for the pharmaceutical industry to define psychic distress as mental *illness* and thereby to offer an increasing array of expensive and often dangerous pharmaceuticals as the *only* acceptable approach to treatment. I use the word "only" advisedly here since the legal standard of care for virtually all forms of serious

---

[1]Daniel Mackler's documentary *Take These Broken Wings: Recovery from Schizophrenia Without Medication* offers illustration and critique of the chemical imbalance hypothesis. Available from http://www.iraresoul.com/dvd1.html.

mental distress in the US is currently defined as requiring medication. With the globalization of dominant psychiatric discourses we can expect this standard of care to gain increasing acceptance across the globe.

The consequences for children are particularly nefarious. Whitaker devotes two chapters of his recent book, *Anatomy of an Epidemic* (2010), to detailing how the treatment of children in the US has been reconceptualized as a result of a strategic alliance between the pharmaceutical industry (Big Pharma) and the psychiatric profession (see also Breggin, 2000; Breggin & Breggin, 2002). Whitaker (2010) sums up the issue this way:

> However, once psychiatry began treating children with psychotropic medications, it rethought the view of childhood. The story that psychiatry now tells is that during the past fifty years it *discovered* that children regularly suffer from mental illnesses, which are said to be biological in kind. First psychiatry fleshed out ADHD as an identifiable disease, and then it determined that major depression and bipolar illness regularly struck children and adolescents. (p. 217)

Whitaker reports that by 1990, the number of children in the US diagnosed with Attention Deficit Hyperactivity Disorder (ADHD) had reached one million. This number had doubled by 1995 and he estimates that today 3.5 million children are taking ADHD medications—all of this despite mounting concerns about the side-effects of such medications. With respect to depression in children, Whitaker says that the percentage of children medicated with selective serotonin reuptake inhibitors (SSRIs) in the US "tripled between 1988 and 1994, and by 2002 one in every 40 children under 19 years of age in the US was taking an antidepressant" (p. 229), despite considerable concern that such medications may elevate suicidal potentiality in some children. The epidemic has gone so far that even two-year-olds and three-year-olds are now being prescribed SSRIs. SSRI prescriptions to children below six years of age have tripled in the US between 2000 and 2007 (Whitaker, 2010, p. 245).

The psychiatric and pharmaceutical establishments have now turned to bipolar as the disorder of the moment in children, or, perhaps, more precisely, as the latest untapped market for their products. Whitaker (2010) reports "a fortyfold increase" in bipolar diagnosis from 1995 to 2003 in the US (p. 233). Joseph Biederman, Chief of the Program in Pediatric Psychopharmacology at Harvard University, who has accepted funding for his research from 15 pharmaceutical companies, has been instrumental in gaining widespread acceptance for diagnosing even preschoolers with bipolar disorder, and for gaining concomitant acceptance of the alleviation of supposed bipolar symptoms by means of antipsychotic medications. The Citizens Commission on Human Rights International (CCHR, 2010) explains Biederman's problematic influence this way:

> *The New York Times* exposed how Biederman earned $1.6 million in consulting fees from drug makers between 2000 and 2007 but did not report all of this income to Harvard University officials. His marketing of the theory that children have "bipolar" was attributed to the increase in antipsychotic

drug sales for pediatric use in the US—today 2.5 million children. Following exposure of his conflicts, he stepped down from a number of industry-funded clinical trials. In March 2009, in newly released court documents, Biederman was reported to have promised drug maker Johnson & Johnson *in advance* that his studies on the antipsychotic drug Risperidone would prove the drug to be effective when used on preschool age children.

A thicket of complex issues surrounds the labeling and treatment of children as bipolar. Among the most troubling are not only the known side-effects of the potent antipsychotic medications that are used, but also the fact that the prescription of antipsychotic medications to children is generally off-label, and no systematic, independent testing program has been instituted to assess the risk to children's developing bodies and minds posed by such potent drugs. Whitaker also raises the troubling question of whether, if indeed childhood bipolar disorder exists, it may be produced as an iatrogenic effect of the prior prescription of SSRIs to children. What if children are indeed developing bipolar symptoms but that it is occurring as a byproduct of their prolonged prior consumption of SSRIs? Finally, Breggin and Breggin (2002) and Whitaker (2010) raise very troubling questions about the overuse of psychotropic medications among vulnerable groups of children in the US including ethnic minority children, children who are poor, and children who are in foster care.

In presenting the foregoing argument I am not arguing against the potential benefits of psychotropic medications in assisting children who are experiencing significant psychic distress such as, for example, temporary florid episodes of psychosis. I am, however, profoundly concerned with the proliferation of pharmacology as a frontline response to children's difficulties, and I am deeply concerned too about the rush to dispense medications to children over long periods of time without careful and systematic study of potential side-effects. The overprescription of psychotropic medications to marginal children such as those who are poor, those in foster care, and those who are ethnic minorities raises in very concrete ways the concern expressed by Paulo Freire (1969, 1970) that one of the most powerful weapons the dominant power structure uses against the oppressed is anesthetization. If people are asleep or numbed they are a lot less likely to express potentially odious criticisms of the status quo, as Scanlon and Adlam (2011) note pointedly in their discussion of refusal of such disciplining mechanisms by marginal groups such as homeless persons (see also O'Loughlin, 2011a).

I will use the remainder of this chapter to explore how psychoanalysis can contribute to re-conceptualization of mental health treatment for children. While policy makers and legislators may balk at the expense of providing therapeutic support for children, we have an obligation to raise questions about the enormous social costs, as well as the likely long-term health-care costs, associated with pharmacological solutions that have the potential to entrap children and their families in long-term dependence on untested and dangerous medications as a solution to life's challenge.

Imagining Children Otherwise: Exploring the Origins of Psychic Distress

A core principle of psychoanalytic work is that overt behavior needs to be understood in terms of its deeper significance. Using medical terminology, this is often characterized as the journey from naming a symptom—for example a DSM diagnosis—to uncovering the origins of the observed actions or feelings. More formally, in Lacanian terms[2] there is a recognition that surface level manifestations represent signifiers for unresolved issues in the unconscious. Surface level manifestations include the panoply of disorders that come under the pejorative assessment rubric of terms such as addiction disorders, eating disorders, oppositional defiant disorder, obsessive compulsive disorder, conduct disorder, psychosomatic complaints, anxiety, depression, phobias, psychosis, and so on. The working assumption of psychoanalysis and psychodynamic clinical psychology is that as surely as smoke suggests the presence of fire, childhood disorders have origins; that long-term relief is more likely if we work back from symptoms to uncover and address the sources of psychic distress.

Some children experience impasses or difficulties from early on in life. Cyrulnik (2009) notes that resilience is a gift, and children who either possess resilience or who have their resilience fostered through loving existential encounters with caring others, will weather difficulties more ably than children whose resilience is sapped by adversity. In research into adult psychosis with my colleague Marilyn Charles of Austen Riggs Center, we have discovered that the difficulties that result in adolescent/adult onset psychosis often have their origins in unaddressed early trauma or dysregulation (O'Loughlin & Charles, 2012), a fact borne out by the literature on the strong relationship between early trauma and adolescent or early adult onset psychosis (Herman, 1997; Hammersley, Burston, & Reid, 2004; Read et al., 2005).

In addition to the Lacanian work noted above, there is a long tradition of psychodynamic work with children emanating from the Tavistock Clinic in London. Clinicians at this publicly funded clinic have worked with children with all kinds of complex psychological difficulties. Over the years they have published extensive literature detailing the uses of Kleinian psychoanalytic theory in addressing the most recalcitrant difficulties children face.[3] This work illustrates the exquisite complexity of resolving psychic distress in children. While some conditions—such as developmental disorders—may be present since birth, many of the conditions from which children

---

[2]For a general introduction to Lacanian theory, see Apollon, Bergeron, & Cantin (2002); Fink (1995, 1997). For illustrative clinical examples in work with children, see Danon-Boileau (2001); Dolto (1999); Mannoni (1970, 1999); Mathelin (1999); Rogers (2006).

[3]See Alvarez (1992); Alvarez & Edwards (2001); Alvarez & Reid (1999); Briggs, (2002); Rhode & Klauber (2004); Rustin, Rhode, Dubinsky, & Dubinsky (1997); Tustin (1990, 1992).

suffer are produced by circumstance. I have noted repeatedly in my own clinical work that children suffer considerably when, as Lacanians would put it, adult *demand* supplants a child's own desire (O'Loughlin, 2009a; O'Loughlin & Charles, 2012). How can a child become free from anxiety and free from the burden of excess responsibility under such circumstances? Is the response to such anxiety best conceptualized through medication of symptoms or through opportunities for such a child to engage in the process analysts know as the *working through* of emotions? What of children's imagination? Surely, children in therapy for distress, particularly those in circumstances where institutional violence has constrained their lives, need opportunities to imagine themselves otherwise (cf. O'Loughlin & Johnson, 2010). This raises a difficult political question. Can governments and societies that distribute resources to families and communities inequitably, and that cause many families to live foreclosed lives, ever allow their children the luxury of imagination, feeling, and possibility?[4] This is one of those political questions that Scanlon & Adlam (2011) explore so ably in their work and practice and that serves as subtext to clinical work with children who are poor or subject to any of a variety of other oppressions.

While part of the solution lies in the provision of individual and group therapy to children in distress by mental health professionals, the possibility of building capacity for emotional work among childcare workers, teachers, community workers, and parents should not be underestimated as a means of extending emotional support and caring to large numbers of children. As part of my work with beginning teachers, for example, I offer a course on classroom management that focuses on psychoanalytic understandings of the experiences of children who present with complex emotional issues. For over twenty years, I have also taught a class entitled *The Emotional Lives of Children and the Possibility of Classroom as Community.*[5] This course offers in-depth inquiry into the origins of childhood suffering to teachers and school psychologists. Both courses are designed to build capacity among teachers and school personnel around understanding and responding to children's emotional vulnerabilities. There is a long tradition of psychoanalytic intervention with teachers and with children in schools (e.g., Cohen 2001, 2007; Field, Cohler, & Wool, 1989; Freud, 1935/1979; Jersild, 1955/2000; Mayes, 2007; O'Loughlin, 2009a; O'Loughlin, Forthcoming a, b). The humanization of schooling by increasing the social competence and sensitivity of teachers and other child professionals as frontline workers with children can greatly enhance the psychic well-being of children and serve as a critical adjunct to more formal mental health services. The same, of course, could be said for increasing opportunities for parents to understand how to respond sensitively to their children's psychic distress (cf. Ginott, 2003). It cannot happen, however, unless, following Cyrulnik (2009) and Van Manen (1986) we view every life as worth living, and every child as meriting recognition and a chance to live a full life unconstrained by psychic burdens.

---

[4] Joanna Lipper's film *Inside Out: Portraits of Children* (1996) offers compelling portraits of children across diverse cultural backgrounds sharing their emotions and using imagination and fantasy both to protect themselves from pain and to imagine their futures. See http://joannalipper.com/films_insideout.html for further detail.

[5] Syllabi for both courses are available in the author's website: michaelolougelinphhd.com.

Recreating Social Links between Children and Their Histories

Davoine and Gaudillière (2004) point out the appalling reductionism involved in articulating an intrapsychic notion of clinical practice that takes no account of history, ancestry, and intergenerationally transmitted or buried trauma. Instead of seeing the difficulties of an individual as reflecting individual pathology, Davoine and Gaudillière argue that we must pay attention to the gaps and ruptures of individual experience because these are symptoms pointing us precisely to the moments of history that have been erased. They suggest that we should recognize severe symptoms such as psychosis and major depression as signifiers pointing to lack or rupture arising from historical crises or trauma. Persons with such symptoms, therefore, need our assistance to bring "into existence zones of nonexistence wiped out by a powerful blow that actually took place" (2004, p. xxvii). Here, Davoine and Gaudillière are referring not only to actually experienced traumatic events in people's lives, such as, for example, sexual abuse, forced relocation, or war trauma, but also to symptoms of severe psychic distress reflected in the spectral presences of restless ghosts and unsymbolized, archaic, and ancestral experiences. For Davoine and Gaudillière, therefore, a manifestation such as psychosis is a welcome messenger, a signifier, pointing us to untold and seemingly untellable stories. History is spoken through the symptom: "Sometimes a fit of madness tells us more than all the news dispatches about the leftover facts that have no right to exist" (2004, p. xxvii).[6]

The analyst, therefore, might be considered an "annalist," in that an important healing component of our work is to serve as recuperators of memory and history. The analyst becomes "the chronicler who keeps the records of a gesture that has been silenced" (2004, p. 28). Severe psychic suffering of this type can best be conceptualized as severance of social linkages between living individuals and ancestral epistemologies, spiritual practices, and ways of being. The destruction of social cohesion produces collective trauma and severe individual suffering across generations. As Lear (2006) noted in *Radical Hope*, the consequence of the westward expansion in the US produced cultural devastation for the indigenous peoples of what became North America. Forced relocation, genocide, deliberate destruction of tribal bonds to eradicate social cohesion, and coercion of tribal children into residential schools designed to eliminate cultural and familial continuity, all contributed to the devastation of a way of life. Symptoms of this devastation today, in some indigenous communities, include alcohol dependence, elevated rates of domestic violence, and depression emanating from a sense of a foreclosed future and severance from ancestral ways

---

[6]Notable writers addressing the issue of ancestral inheritances, spectral memory, and what Fraiberg, Adelson, & Shapiro (1975) referred to as "ghosts in the nursery," and Judy Atkinson (2002) calls "trauma trails", include Abraham & Torok (1994); Faimberg (2005); Ferenczi (1988); Garon (2004); Gordon (1997); and Kaplan (1996). For overview and further discussion see O'Loughlin (2008, 2009b, 2010, Forthcoming c).

of knowing and being. Erikson (1976) speaks similarly of the cultural devastation experienced by residents of the mining community of Buffalo Creek in West Virginia when pollution from the local mining industry caused a community to be broken up and located to disparate places, causing a catastrophic loss of social cohesion and the development of severe social dysfunction. I have applied similar arguments to the analysis of the suffering of Aboriginal Australians caused by intentional strategies of cultural annihilation pursued by successive colonizing Australian governments (O'Loughlin, 2008, 2009a, 2009b).

Addressing the Cultural Unconscious in Children's Lives

Recently, addressing the issue of the educational and mental health needs of indigenous children, I wrote:

> My approach begins with the assumptions that each indigenous child has a culturally constituted unconscious and is thereby a bearer of the collective history of their people. Trauma in the unconscious may be unspeakable because of the severance of social links through devices such as residential schooling, fosterage, language prohibition and cultural genocide. This severance may continue to occur in the present or may be located in history. Teachers of indigenous children need to be thoroughly familiar with the history and customs of the groups with whom they work—and ideally they should be members of those groups—and they should also be trained, as Judy Atkinson is doing at Gnibi College,[7] in understanding the workings of intergenerationally transmitted trauma so that they know how to recognize and address trauma symptoms.

> Psychoanalysts have long recognized that a powerful agent of change in therapy is the presence of the analyst as witness and receiver of unconscious knowledge. Teachers, too, ought to be prepared to receive such knowledge, and should understand how to evoke the unconscious in children through their own evocative presences. A teacher with a passion for myth, storytelling, drama, memory, and the wisdom of elders will draw these evocative knowledges into the classroom, and will elicit evocative responses from students that allow students to experience their own inner knowledge as namable and addressable (O'Loughlin, 2009a, p. 160).

There is a considerable literature both from transcultural writings on trauma (e.g., Drožđek, & Wilson, 2007) and from indigenous psychology (e.g., Duran & Duran, 1995; Duran, Duran, Yellow Horse Brave Heart, & Yellow Horse-Davis, 1998; Rezentes, 1996) and related scholarship (e.g., Battiste, 2000) recognizing the importance of locating mental health services and educational services in local cultural contexts, and drawing upon unconscious knowledges as an important aspect of healing. These knowledges include ancestral wisdom and lineage that may have been

---

[7]For details of Judy Atkinson's work at Gnibi College in Australia, see http://www.scu.edu.au/schools/gnibi/index.php/25/

severed through war, relocation, erasure of indigenous languages, and so on. It also includes intergenerationally transmitted trauma, often conveyed by means of silence, gaps, and ruptures. Psychoanalysts who value the socially constituted origins of the unconscious can do this work well and they are also well equipped to assist caregivers, educators, and health-care providers in bringing this kind of acutely attuned sensitivity to memory, history, and buried trauma to their work with children who suffer psychic distress.

Postscript: The Need to Feed

In a recent paper (O'Loughlin, 2011b) I presented the story of Irish-American journalist, Carolyn Ramsay. She offers a visceral account of the workings of hungry ghosts in her daily life. Having discussed how her grandmother, a child of famine survivors, developed an obsession for feeding sandwiches to imaginary people in her old age, Ramsay (1997) begins to ruminate on her own "need to feed":

> I don't know another working mother who worries about feeding people the way I do.... It has taken me years, on the other hand, to focus on just feeding my family—not the whole world. On late nights when I've pounded chicken and chopped vegetables alone in my kitchen while my family sleeps, I've wondered precisely what my problem is… Part of me passes off the feeding urge as a slightly embarrassing compulsion, although its emotional depth and power indicate otherwise. After dropping food at a soup kitchen for the first time a decade ago, I had to steer my car to the side of the street because I was sobbing so hard I couldn't see. There's such unremitting sadness at the root of this drive to feed people that I've come to assume that it links me somehow to the dark events in Ireland in the mid 1800s. I can't know this. No famine stories made their way from my migrating great-grandparents to me, or even to my parents. "The Irish aren't real talkers," my mother once said. When I consider how my grandmother's need to feed imagined ghosts has followed me for thirty years though, it seems likely her famine-surviving parents' attitudes towards food made a deep impression on her. How could they not? (p. 138)

References

Abraham, N., & Torok, M. (1994). *The shell and the kernel: Renewals of psychoanalysis*. Chicago: University of Chicago Press.
Altman, N. (1995). *The analyst in the inner city: Race, class and color through a psychoanalytic lens*. Hillsdale, NJ: Analytic Press.
Alvarez, A. (1992). *Live company: Psychoanalytic psychotherapy with autistic, borderline, deprived and abused children*. New York: Routledge.
Alvarez, A., & Edwards, J. (2001). *Being alive: Building on the work of Anne Alvarez*. New York: Routledge.
Alvarez, A., & Reid, S. (1999). *Autism and personality: Findings from the Tavistock autism workshop*. New York: Routledge.
American Psychiatric Association. (1952). *Diagnostic and statistical manual of mental disorders*. Washington, DC: American Psychiatric Association.

Andre, L. (2009). *Doctors of deception: What they don't want you to know about shock treatment*. New Brunswick, NJ: Rutgers University Press.

Apollon, W., Bergeron, D., & Cantin, L. (2002). *After Lacan: Clinical Practice and the subject of the unconscious*. Albany, NY: SUNY Press.

Atkinson, J. (2002). *Trauma trails: Recreating song lines: The transgenerational effects of trauma in indigenous Australia*. North Melbourne, Australia: Spinifex Press.

Battiste, M. (Ed.). (2000). *Reclaiming indigenous voice and vision*. Vancouver: UBC Press.

Bentall, R. (2009). *Doctoring the mind: Is our current treatment of mental illness really any good?* New York: New York University Press.

Biehl, J. (2005). *Vita: Life in a zone of social abandonment*. Berkeley: University of California Press.

Breggin, P. (1991). *Toxic psychiatry: Why therapy, empathy and love must replace the drugs, electric Shock and biochemcial theories of the "New Psychiatry."* New York: St. Martin's Press.

———. (1995). *Talking back to Prozac: What doctors aren't telling you about today's most controversial drug*. New York: St. Martin's Press.

———. (2000). *Reclaiming our children: A healing plan for a nation in crisis*. New York: Da Capo Press.

Breggin, P., & Breggin, G. (2002). *The war against children of color: Psychiatry targets inner city youth*. Monroe, ME: Common Courage Press.

Briggs, A. (Ed.). (2002). *Surviving space: Papers on infant observation*. London: Karnac Books.

CCHR (Citizens Commission on Human Rights International). (2010). *The corrupt alliance of the psychiatric pharmaceutical industry*. Retrieved from http://www.cchrint.org/cchr-issues/the-corrupt-alliance-of-the-psychiatric-pharmaceutical-industry/

Cohen, J. (Ed.). (2001). *Caring classrooms/intelligent schools: The social emotional education of young children*. New York: Teachers College Press.

———. (2007). Interdisciplinary psychoanalysis and the education of children: Psychoanalytic and educational partnerships. *Psychoanalytic Study of the Child*, 62, 180–207.

Cyrulnik, B. (2009). *The whispering of ghosts*. New York: Other Press.

Danon-Boileau, L. (2001). *The silent child: Bringing language to children who cannot speak*. New York: Oxford University.

Danto, E. (2005). *Freud's free clinics: Psychoanalysis and social justice* (pp. 1918–1938). New York: Columbia University Press.

Davoine, F., & Gaudillière, J. (2004). *History beyond trauma*. New York: Other Press.

Derrida, J. (1998). Geopsychoanalysis: "…and the rest of the world." In C. Lane (Ed.), *The Psychoanalysis of Race*. New York: Columbia University Press.

Dolto, F. (1999). *Françoise Dolto, c'est la parole qui fait vivre: Une theorie corporelle du langage*. Paris: Gallimard.

Drožđek, B., & Wilson, J. (Eds). (2007). *Voices of trauma: Treating psychological trauma across cultures*. New York: Springer Science.

Duran, E., & Duran, B. (1995). *Native American post-colonial psychology*. Albany, NY: SUNY Press.

Duran, E., Duran, B., Yellow Horse Brave Heart, M., & Yellow Horse-Davis, S. (1998). Healing the American Indian soul wound. In Y. Danieli (Ed.), *International handbook of multigenerational legacies of trauma* (pp. 341–354). New York: Plenum Press.

Erikson, K. (1976). Disaster at Buffalo Creek: Loss of communality at Buffalo Creek. *American Journal of Psychiatry*, 133(3), 302–305.

Faimberg, H. (2005). *The telescoping of generations: Listening to the narcissistic links between generations*. New York: Routledge.

Ferenczi, S. (Ed.). (1988). *The clinical diary of Sandor Ferenczi*. [J. Dupont. (Ed.). M. Balint & N. Zarday Jackson, (Trans.)] Cambridge, MA: Harvard University Press.

Field, K., Cohler, B., & Wool, G. (Eds). (1989). *Learning and education: Psychoanalytic perspectives.* Madison, CT: International Universities Press.
Fink, B. (1995). *The Lacanian subject.* Princeton: Princeton University Press.
———. (1997). *A clinical introduction to Lacanian psychoanalysis.* Cambridge, MA: Harvard University Press.
Fraiberg, S., Adelson, E., & Shapiro, V. (1975). Ghosts in the nursery: A psychoanalytic approach to the problems of impaired infant-mother relationships. *Journal of the American Academy of Child Psychiatry, 14*(3), 387–421. doi:10.1016/S0002-7138(09)61442-4
Freire, P. (1969). *Education for critical consciousness.* New York: Continuum.
———. (1970). *Pedagogy of the oppressed.* New York: Continuum.
Freud, S. (1927). *The future of an illusion.* New York: W.W. Norton & Company.
———. (1930). *Civilization and its discontents.* New York: W.W. Norton & Company.
———. (1935/1979). *Psychoanalysis for teachers and parents.* New York: W.W. Norton & Company.
Garon, J. (2004). Skeletons in the closet. *International Forum of Psychoanalysis, 13*(1–2), 84–92. doi:10.1080/08037060410031142
Ginott, H. (2003). *Between parent and child.* New York: Three Rivers Press.
Good, M. J. DelVecchio, Hyde, S., Pinto, S., & Good, B. (Eds). (2008). *Postcolonial disorders.* Berkeley, CA: University of California Press.
Gordon, A. (1997). *Ghostly matters: Haunting and the sociological imagination.* Minneapolis: University of Minnesota Press.
Herman, J. (1997). *Trauma and recovery.* New York: Basic Books.
Hammersley, P., Burston, D., & Read, J. (2004). Learning to listen: Childhood trauma and psychosis. *Mental Health Practice, 7*(6), 18–21.
Jaccoby, R. (1975). *Social amnesia: A critique of contemporary psychology from Adler to Laing.* Boston: Beacon Press.
Jersild, A. (1955/2000). *When teachers face themselves.* New York: Teachers College Press.
Kaplan, L. (1996). *No voice is ever wholly lost: An exploration of the everlasting attachment between parent and child.* New York: Simon & Schuster.
Kirk, S., & Kutchins, H. (1992). *The selling of DSM: The rhetoric of science in psychiatry.* Boston, MA: Aldine de Gruyter.
Kutchins, H., & Kirk, S. (2003). *Making us crazy: DSM: The psychiatric Bible and the creation of mental disorders.* New York: Free Press.
Lear, J. (2006). *Radical hope: Ethics in the face of cultural devastation.* Cambridge, MA: Harvard University Press.
Mannoni, M. (1970). *The child, his "illness" and the others.* London: Karnac Books.
———. (1999). *Separation and creativity: Refinding the lost language of childhood.* New York: Other Press.
Mathelin, C. (1999). *The broken piano: Lacanian psychotherapy with children.* New York: Other Press.
Mayes, C. (2007). *Inside education: Depth psychology in teaching and learning.* Madison, WI: Atwood Publishing.
Moskowitz, M. (1996). The social conscience of psychoanalysis. In R. Perez Foster, M. Moskowitz, & R. Javier (Eds), *Reaching across boundaries of culture and class: Widening the scope of psychoanalysis* (pp. 21–46). Lanham, MD: Jason Aronson.
Obendorf, C. P. (1953). *History of psychoanalysis in America.* New York: Harper & Row.
O'Loughlin, M. (Ed.). (Forthcoming). *Rethinking children's emotions: Psychodynamic perspectives on children and schools* [Manuscript submitted for publication].
O'Loughlin, M. (2008). Radical hope, or death by a thousand cuts? The future for Indigenous Australians. *Arena Journal, 29/30,* 175–202.
———. (2009a). *The subject of childhood.* New York: Peter Lang.
———. (2009b). A psychoanalytic exploration of collective trauma among indigenous Australians and a suggestion for intervention. *Australasian Psychiatry, 17*(S1), S33–S36.

O'Loughlin, M. (2010). Ghostly presences in children's lives: Toward a psychoanalysis of the social. In M. O'Loughlin & R. Johnson (Eds), *Imagining children otherwise: Theoretical and critical perspectives on childhood subjectivity* (pp. 49–74). New York: Peter Lang.

———. (2011a). Commentary on Scanlan & Adlam: [Anti?] social critics: Mangy curs or pesky gadflies? *Group Analysis, 44*(2), 149–154. doi:10.1177/0533316411398805

———. (2011b). Trauma trails from Ireland's great hunger: A psychoanalytic inquiry. In L. Bohm, R. Curtis, & B. Willock (Eds), *Loneliness & longings: Psychoanalytic reflections* [Manuscript submitted for publication]. New York: Routledge.

O'Loughlin, M. (Ed.) (Forthcoming, a). *Psychodynamic perspectives on working children, families and schools*. Lanham, Maryland: Jason Aronson.

———. (Ed.) (Forthcoming, b). *The uses of psychoanalysis in working with children's emotional lives*. Lanham, Maryland: Jason Aronson.

———. (Forthcoming, c). Reclaiming genealogy, memory and history: The psychodynamic potential for reparative therapy in contemporary South Africa. In G. Lobban, M. O'Loughlin, & C. Smith (Eds), *Psychodynamic psychotherapy in contemporary South Africa: Theory, practive, and policy perspectives*. Johannesburg: University of Witwatersrand Press.

O'Loughlin, M., & Johnson, R. (Eds). (2010). *Imagining children otherwise: Theoretical and critical perspectives on childhood subjectivity*. New York: Peter Lang.

O'Loughlin, M. & Charles, M. (2012). Psychiatric survivors, psychiatric treatments, and societal prejudice: An inquiry into the experience of an extremely marginal group. In G. Cannella & S. Steinberg (Eds), *Critical qualitative research reader*. New York: Peter Lang.

O'Loughlin, M. & Merchant, A. (2012). Working obliquely with children. *Journal of Infant, Child and Adolescent Psychotherapy*, 11, 149–159.

Ramsay, C. (1997). The need to feed. In T. Hayden (Ed.), *Irish hunger: Personal reflections on the legacy of the famine* (pp. 137–142). Boulder, CO: Roberts Rinehart Publishers.

Read, J., Mosher, L., & Bentall, R. (2005). *Models of madness: Psychological, social and biological approaches to schizophrenia*. New York: Brunner-Routledge

Rezentes, W. (1996). *Ka lama kukui—Hawaiian psychology: An introduction*. Honolulu: A'ali'i Books.

Rhode, M., & Klauber, T. (2004). *The many faces of Asperger's Syndrome*. London: Karnac Books.

Rogers, A. (2006). *The unsayable: The hidden language of trauma*. New York: Random House.

Rustin, M., Rhode, M., Dubinsky, A., & Dubinsky, H. (Eds). (1997). *Psychotic states in children*. New York: Routledge.

Scanlon, C., & Adlam, J. (2011). "Defacing the currency?" A group-analytic appreciation of homelessness, dangerousness, disorder and other inarticulate speech of the heart. *Group Analysis, 44*(2), 131–148. doi:10.1177/0533316410397697

Stepansky, P. (2009). *Psychoanalysis at the margins*. New York: Other Press Professional.

Tustin, F. (1990). *The protective shell in children and adults*. London: Karnac Books

———. (1992). *Autistic states in children,* London: Routledge.

Van Manen, M. (1986). *The tone of teaching*. Portsmouth, NH: Heinemann.

Watkins, M., & Shulman, H. (2008). *Toward psychologies of liberation*. New York: Palgrave Macmillan.

Watters, E. (2010). *Crazy like us? The globalization of the American psyche*. New York: Free Press.

Whitaker, R. (2001). *Mad in America: Bad science, bad medicine, and the enduring mistreatment of the mentally ill.* New York: Basic Books.

———. (2010). *Anatomy of an epidemic: Magic bullets, psychiatric drugs, and the astonishing rise of mental illness in America*. New York: Crown.

SECTION 7

Country Focus—Status, Policies, and Children's Voices

19

Family Structure in Ireland and Child Emotional and Behavioral Outcomes

Maeve Thornton

Introduction

The family form has undoubtedly changed dramatically in a relatively short period of time and these changes have posed challenges for traditional social theories, where the two-parent family is still often seen as the ideal family form. It is necessary therefore to explore the complex mechanisms involved in children's adjustment and coping in the context of various family structures, including those that are associated with risk. The nature of some key family variables (such as poverty, depression, and family conflict) often mediate the effects of both—the type of family the child belongs to as well as the sociocultural context within which the family exists (Sanson & Lewis, 2001).

The Family in Ireland

The traditional family unit headed by a husband and wife is still the most common structure for children living in Ireland today. Eighteen percent of all families in Ireland are now lone parent families (Central Statistics Office, 2006). Recent years have also seen a decrease in the overall marriage rate although there are indications that people may be postponing marriage rather than choosing not to marry at all, and may be using cohabitation as a precursor to marriage (Kennedy, 2004).

Divorce became possible in Ireland only in 1997 and since then numbers availing of it have grown steadily. Between 2002 and 2005, 35,100 divorces were granted compared to 59,500 in 2006 (an increase of 69.8 percent). The number of legal separations has also increased but at a much lower rate. Clearly both separation and divorce have major implications for Irish children (Hogan, Halpenny, & Greene, 2002). Remarriage was not an Irish phenomenon on any scale until recently although some children would certainly have lived in informally constituted blended families. Unlike previous Census information, 2006 was the first year that the number of reconstituted families could be identified representing 1.7 percent of all family units, although there are over 3 percent in the current sample. The experience of children living in such households is an important area for further exploration, given that second marriages have a higher breakdown rate than first marriages (Bramlett & Mosher, 2001) and that the reconstituted family structure is probably the least researched in the Irish context.

Changes in the family are also associated with the decline in the influence of the Catholic Church on Irish family life. The traditional family in Ireland has long been characterized as highly conservative, reflecting the dominant value system of the Catholic Church. Although religious practice continues to be relatively high, evidence shows that the influence of Catholic teaching on family life has greatly diminished, accelerated to some extent by recent controversies within the Catholic Church (Paseta, 2003). This is evidenced, for example, with the widespread use of contraception and the extent of sexual activity outside marriage (Fahey & Layte, 2008), and was accompanied by the introduction of extensive new legislation on family matters in the 1980s and 1990s, including the introduction of no-fault divorce.

Despite these immense social changes, the marital family has remained until recently the only officially recognized unit in Irish law. In the 1937 Constitution, the family was recognized in Article 41 as the "natural primary and fundamental unit group of society," and generally interpreted to mean only the marital family, suggesting that the non-marital family lacked any constitutional status or legal protection. Lack of legal recognition has created fundamental problems for unmarried cohabiting partners on a whole range of critical issues: child custody, adoption, health care, taxation, maintenance, citizenship, property, and inheritance rights. This was the case for the respondents in the current study, although it should be noted that from January 2011, The Civil Partnership and Certain Rights and Obligations of Cohabitants Act 2010 not only gave same-sex couples extended rights but also provided increased rights for participants in long-term cohabiting relationships and not in a civil partnership or marriage.

Literature Review—Family Structure

Research in the UK shows that while more than 70 percent of children whose parents divorce are under 10 years of age, most studies to date have tended to focus on children over this age (Wade & Smart, 2002). It is important for researchers to try to understand why some children can be resilient to the seemingly negative event of separation, while others experience various levels of stress. For example, international research (e.g., Amato, 2001; Pryor & Rodgers, 2001) has generally found that children who have experienced their parents' separation have lower well-being and school achievement. Kerr and Michalski (2004) found that living in an intact family was advantageous while living in a stepfamily was associated with greater risks in terms of hyperactivity in children. Several studies also suggest that family reconstitution and the formation of stepfamilies can have a negative impact on children's well-being (e.g., Jonsson & Gähler, 1997; Bhrolcháin, Campbell, Diamond, & Jameson, 2000), although it should be noted from the resilience research that some children may show less obvious effects, and often escape disturbance (Amato, 2001; Kelly & Emery, 2003).

Some research points to the fact that longer spells in a single parent or divorced family lead to more detrimental outcomes for children, possibly because of the prolonged lack of a positive role model for healthy relationships (Cavanagh, 2008; Heard, 2007). On the other hand, the amount of time spent living in a single-parent home has been found by some to have no influence on child outcomes (Albrecht & Teachman, 2003). Moving from a cohabiting stepfamily to a single mother family was found to be associated with improvements in school engagement, although adolescent well-being was found to decrease when the move was from a single mother family to a cohabiting stepfamily (Brown, 2006).

While family structure is clearly very important there are clearly other salient factors which may mediate the relationship between family structure and child outcomes.

Socioeconomic Factors

Lack of resources is a huge issue for many families but this is especially true of single-parent families, divorced, or otherwise. Mothers who are separated are often forced to divide limited time resources between childcare, housework, and paid labor without a partner to rely on. This has been described as the "negative child effect," but it is also a function of the institutional support available to these parents (Uunk, Kalmijn, & Muffels, 2005).

Some research suggests that economic instability accounts for half of the disadvantage that accompanies being raised by a single parent (McLanahan, 1999). Figures for 2007 from UNICEF in relation to Ireland report that 22 percent of children aged less than 15 years are living in relative income poverty (set at 60 percent of median income per adult equivalent). This is one of the highest rates in the EU. Figures for 2005 from the Central Statistics Office EU-SILC survey (European Union Survey on Income and Living Conditions in Ireland) indicate that one in nine children under the age of 14 is living in consistent poverty (Central Statistics Office, 2006).

The unprecedented economic boom in Ireland which began in the mid-1990s brought high employment and new prosperity but there remained high levels of income inequality. The economic boom was accompanied by an increased participation of women in the workforce, including mothers of young children (Collins & Wickham, 2001). While these women tend to be more educated they still tend to have primary responsibility for childcare (Sayer, 2005), meaning that there may be implications for children's social, cognitive, and psychological outcomes.

Some children do well despite living in poverty although the fact remains that poverty is associated with multiple risks and a higher level of negative outcomes for children in their current functioning and in the longer term (Evans, 2004; Nolan, Layte, Whelan, & Maître, 2006).

Family Environment

Family relationships, both parental and parent–child relationships play important roles which are no longer seen as discrete entities but rather as being affected by and affecting each other (Fauchier & Margolin, 2004). The intimate and influential nature of family relationships means that the manner in which parents interact is crucial for child outcomes (Wilson & Gottman, 2002). Exposure to marital hostility is associated with behavioral and emotional problems in children (Davies, Harold, Goeke-Morey, & Cummings, 2002).

Social learning theory suggests that children's friendships are modeled on the behaviors and relationships they observe in the home (Bandura, 1989), therefore family instability experienced during this period could be crucial, given that middle childhood is when children begin to understand the relationship dynamics between parents and understand feelings of stress.

The relationship that parents have with their child is often a function of family structure, with single parenthood linked to lower levels of parental involvement with the child and less emotional and cognitive stimulation (Carlson & Corcoran, 2001). O'Connor et al. (2001) found that a child's relationship with their single parent was likely to be more conflicted than if they were living with two biological parents; others have suggested that differences in mother–child relationships may depend on whether the mother has parented alone since the pregnancy or following a relationship breakdown. MacCallum and Golombok (2004) report positive interactions between mothers and children in families who have always been fatherless, a trend echoed by doctoral research undertaken in the Irish context (Nixon, 2007). Positive and supportive interactions between parents and children encourage appropriate social behavior, and have been shown to raise school grades and decrease externalizing behaviors (O'Connor, Hetherington, & Clingempeel, 1997).

Parental depression is another family factor widely reported as one of the most important negative influences on child outcomes (Martins & Gaffan, 2000). It is associated with early developmental outcomes and identified as a risk factor for poorer socio-emotional and cognitive development (Cummings & Davies, 1994; McLeod & Kaiser, 2004). It has been noted that one third of children born to parents with a mental illness are likely to suffer persistent emotional and behavioral disturbance (Rutter & Quinton, 1984). Other studies have noted much higher rates of child psychiatric diagnosis among offspring of a parent with mental illness compared to those in the general population (Oyserman, Mowbray, Meares, & Firminger, 2000). However, while the research is unequivocal that parental mental health is linked to poorer child outcomes, it often interacts with or is associated with other variables or processes (e.g., poverty) that can either increase risk or generate resilience in children (Goodman & Gotlib, 1999).

Female depression has been extensively researched (e.g., Field, 2000; Martins & Gaffan, 2000; Campbell et al., 2004) based on the assumption there is a risk that babies and children might be affected if their primary carer suffers from depression. Paternal depression on the other hand has not received as much attention (Phares, Duhig, & Watkins, 2002), although research to date shows mixed results (see Kane & Garber, 2004; Mezulis, Hyde, & Clark 2004; Meadows, McLanahan, & Brooks-Gunn, 2007).

Growing Up in Ireland—The National Longitudinal Study of Children[1]

This study is the first study of its kind ever to be carried out in Ireland and its principal objective is to describe the lives of Irish children, to establish what is typical and normal as well as what is atypical and problematic.

Being longitudinal in nature the study addresses developmental trajectories over time and explores the factors which most impact on those trajectories and on the life chances of children as they grow up. One cohort follows children from nine months to early childhood (the infant cohort) and another from nine years to thirteen years (the child cohort). The current chapter uses data from the first phase of the child cohort, which was selected through the primary school network throughout Ireland. A random sample of schools was drawn and subject to the school's participation age-eligible children and their families in that school were invited to participate in the study. A total of 8,568 interviews were completed between September 2007 and March 2008. A wide range of perspectives were included in the study, including health (of parents and children), the family structure, and environment, socioeconomic factors, education, neighborhood, and so forth, so as to encompass all aspects of the ecological systems theory (Bronfenbrenner, 1979) which provides the conceptual framework for the study. Information was recorded from parents, teachers, principals, and carers, as well as the study-child him- or herself.

What Is Being Measured

Social, emotional, and behavioral well-being contributes significantly to the quality of children's lives. Children who generally feel good about themselves tend to exhibit more enthusiasm for life and welcome opportunities to develop and learn. However, experiencing social, emotional, or behavioral difficulties can be associated with depression (e.g., Meagher, Arnold, Doctoroff, Dobbs, & Fisher, 2009), educational underachievement (e.g., McClelland, Morrison, & Holmes, 2000),

---

[1]The *Growing Up in Ireland* data have been funded by the Government of Ireland through the Office of the Minister for Children and Youth Affairs; have been collected under the Statistics Act, 1993, of the Central Statistics Office. The project has been designed and implemented by the joint ESRI-TCD *Growing Up in Ireland* Study Team. © Department of Health and Children

poor peer relations in childhood (e.g., Newcomb, Bukowski, & Pattee, 1993) and physical illness, mental health difficulties, and impaired relationships with partners and family in adulthood (e.g., Buchanan, 1999). Thus, understanding the factors that help or hinder children's social, emotional, and behavioral development and functioning at home, at school, and in the wider community is of considerable consequence to both policy and practice.

Methodology

The Strengths and Difficulties Questionnaire (SDQ; Goodman, 1997) is a brief (25 items) behavioral screening questionnaire designed to assess emotional health and problem behaviors and was completed by the primary caregiver of the study child. The instrument has five subscales: (*a*) Emotional symptoms; (*b*) Conduct problems; (*c*) Hyperactivity/inattention; (*d*) Peer relationship problems; and (*e*) Pro-social behavior, each comprising 5 items. A Total Difficulties score is obtained by summing scores across the four deficit-focused scales (i.e., all except the pro-social behavior scale). Respondents are required to indicate their level of agreement for each item on a three-point scale of "Certainly true," "Somewhat true," or "Not true." The subscale scores range from 0–10 and the total difficulties score ranges from 0–40. Scores can also be grouped into normal, borderline, or abnormal according to the level of emotional and behavioral difficulties experienced by the child. The authors recommend that 80 percent will normally fall into the normal category with 10 percent each in the borderline and abnormal categories. In the current study the sample was divided into two groups—abnormal and normal/borderline, the focus of interest being on those with an abnormal total score on the SDQ.

After running some initial bivariate analyses to ascertain factors of interest, logistic regression models were developed to run with two different samples so that different aspects of the family structure data could be explored. The models were run in forward stepwise manner using SPSS.[2] The models were run in three steps, first with child gender and household type, then with socio-economic variables, and finally with family environment variables. Child gender was controlled for in the models because boys are significantly more likely than girls to fall into the "abnormal" category on the SDQ.

Evidence from previous research, as well as our own exploratory analyses using the current data (not shown) indicated that maternal factors such as education, emotional health, and (conflicted) relationship with the child were important factors in terms of child emotional and behavioral outcomes. It was therefore deemed appropriate to include these in the analysis. In order to do this, Sample 1 in the analysis included only families where the mother was the primary caregiver,

---

[2]Computer program, originally known as the Statistical Package for the Social Sciences, but is usually referred to as SPSS.

thereby excluding the small number (n = 187) of male headed families. In this analysis, the focus was on the effects of family structure, socioeconomic factors, and some family variables relating to the mother—maternal depression and mother–child conflict.

Since paternal factors are relatively under-researched and could not be explored in the context of lone parent families (of which mothers are the majority), Sample 2 included children who were living in two parent families at the time of the interviews, that is those living with both biological parents and those living in reconstituted families. This model included effects of family structure, socioeconomic factors, and family variables relating to both the mother and father such as marital distress, parental depression, and parent–child conflict.

Four socioeconomic indicators were used in the analysis. *Welfare receipt* was based on one question in the primary caregiver main questionnaire which asked about receipt of welfare benefits. Benefits in this instance included any state benefits.

Social class of primary and secondary caregiver was derived from their occupation. In the course of the survey, both caregivers, where relevant, were asked to provide details on their occupation; current or—where the respondent was economically inactive at the time of interview—previous employment outside the home. On this basis a household social class was generated and the following categories were used in the current analyses: Professional/managerial; Non-manual/skilled manual; Semiskilled/unskilled manual; Validly no social class (i.e., not working or have never worked outside the home). *Household tenure* was based on whether the home was owned or being bought, as opposed to being rented or rent free. Highest level of *maternal education* was included as both the literature and our own analysis have shown this to have more of an impact on child outcomes than father's education. Educational attainment was grouped into three categories: primary education or no education, secondary education, degree or posgraduate degree.

Family factors included *maternal and paternal depression, marital distress* (maternal and paternal) and *parent–child conflict* (maternal and paternal). Depression was measured using an 8-item version of the Center for Epidemiological Studies Depression Scale (CES-D; originally developed by Radloff, 1977), a widely used self-report measure that was developed specifically as a screening instrument for depression in the general population as opposed to being a diagnostic tool that measures the presence of clinical depression. A composite score is calculated by summing item responses (range: 0–24) and respondents are categorized according to the recommended criterion for depression, with composite scores of ≥ 7 being classified as depressed and scores <7 defined as not depressed.

The seven-item version of the Dyadic Adjustment Scale (DAS) (Spanier, 1976; Hunsley, Best, Levebvre, & Vito, 2001) was used to assess the marital relationship. Marriages were classified as distressed (<1 S.D. from the mean) or non-distressed (>1 S.D. from the mean).

The parent–child relationship was assessed using the Pianta Child–Parent Relationship Scale (Pianta, 1992). The measure includes three subscales: closeness, conflict, and dependency. In the current analyses we used the conflict subscale (12 items) to assess the impact of this construct on the child's emotional and behavioral difficulties. Scores greater than one S.D. from the mean were regarded as highly conflicted.

In total, data were collected from 8,568 households. Most of the information on family structure, socioeconomic, and family context was collected from the primary caregiver (usually the mother) using CAPI (Computer Assisted Personal Interview) in face-to-face interviews, while important information was also collected from the secondary caregiver (usually the father or father figure).

Results

Sample 1

The first sample accounted for families where the mother was the primary caregiver so that specific maternal factors could be included in the logistic regression model. Looking at the effect of family structure in Table 19.1 shows that being in any other type of family than two parent biological (i.e., lone mother or reconstituted) resulted in a twofold increase in the chance of high SDQ scores.

When socioeconomic variables were added to the model, the influence of family type was generally weakened, but being in a lone mother household (never married) became non-significant in terms of child outcomes. However, children in reconstituted families were still 90 percent more likely to have psychological difficulties than those with two natural parents. Mother's education had the strongest effect on outcomes (OR 2.04, CI 1.42–2.93 for those with no or primary education compared to those with a degree or above). Being in receipt of welfare or being in the lowest social class both increased the chances of an abnormal SDQ score by a factor of 0.7. Housing tenure did not have a significant effect on SDQ scores, although it had been significant when included on its own in the model.

The effects of other family context variables (maternal depression and mother–child conflict) when added to the model can be seen in Table 19.1. While the effect of being in a reconstituted family remained virtually unchanged, the significant effect of being in a lone mother household (previously married) was removed at this point. The effects of mother's education and welfare receipt were reduced slightly but remained significant, children with a mother with no or primary education remained twice as likely to have more psychological problems than those with a parent educated to degree or above.

High levels of parent–child conflict were shown to have the largest effect on SDQ scores in this model (OR 8.29, CI 7.05–9.74). The addition of mother–child conflict decreased the effect of depression (when included in a stepwise fashion) considerably from a factor of 2.5 to one of 0.8, although the effects of family type, mother's education, welfare receipt, and social class on child SDQ scores remained fairly stable when conflict was added.

Table 19.1 Effects of Family Type, Socioeconomic Factors, and Family Environment on Emotional and Behavioral Outcomes in Families with a Female Primary Caregiver

	Bases	Family Type OR	95% CI	Family Type + Socioeconomic OR	95% CI	Family Type + Socioeconomic + Family Environment OR	95% CI
Gender							
Girl*	3,762						
Boy	3,948	1.18	1.03–1.35	1.16	1.00–1.34	1.23	1.05–1.44
Family Type							
Two parent families*	6,633						
Reconstituted families	259	1.95	1.41–2.71	1.88	1.32–2.66	1.94	1.32–2.85
Lone mother_prev married	417	2.23	1.81–2.73	1.37	1.04–1.80	1.15	0.85–1.55
Lone mother_nev married	401	1.94	1.57–2.39	1.05	0.80–1.40	0.95	0.70–1.29
Welfare							
No*	6,208						
Yes	1,502			1.71	1.43–2.04	1.65	1.36–2.01
Household class							
Prof/man*	4,167						
Semi/non-man	2,586			1.31	1.09–1.58	1.37	1.13–1.67
Man/unskilled	616			1.26	0.97–1.64	1.30	0.98–1.74
Validly no soc class	341			1.68	1.25–2.25	1.62	1.18–2.24
Housing tenure							
Own/buying*	6,594						
Rent/rent free	1,116			1.06	0.86–1.29	0.84	0.68–1.05
Mother education							
Degree or above*	2,092						
Secondary	5,416			1.57	1.23–2.00	1.45	1.12–1.88
Primary or none	202			2.04	1.42–2.93	1.98	1.34–2.92
Mother depressed							
No*	7,097						
Yes	613					1.84	1.48–2.28
Mother–child conflict							
Low conflict*	6,553						
High conflict	1,157					8.29	7.05–9.74

Note: * = reference category.

Sample 2

Sample 2 was a smaller group which included only those children in two parent families, that is, households with two biological parents or reconstituted families. This meant that because two parents were present in these households, both maternal and paternal factors could be explored. Table 19.2 first shows the base model with just two family type variables plus child gender. The effect of living in a reconstituted family was still significant in this subsample, the effect size on SDQ scores almost twice that for reconstituted families (OR 1.91) compared to families with two natural parents.

Table 19.2 Effects of Family Type and Socioeconomic Factors and Family Environment on Emotional and Behavioral Outcomes in Families Headed by Two Parents

	Bases	Family Type OR	95% CI	Family Type + Socioeconomic + Family Environment OR	95% CI	Family Type + Socioeconomic + Family Environment OR	95% CI
Gender							
Girl*	3,024						
Boy	3,029	1.17	1.00–1.37	1.06	0.88–1.27	1.13	0.92–1.38
Family Type							
Two natural parents*	5,873						
Reconstituted	180	1.91	1.38–2.65	1.59	1.01–2.49	1.64	0.98–2.73
Welfare							
No*	5,220						
Yes	833			1.68	1.33–2.12	1.63	1.26–2.10
Household class							
Prof/man*	3,612						
Semi/non-man	1,977			1.15	0.93–1.42	1.20	0.95–1.51
Man/unskilled	402			1.10	0.79–1.53	1.14	0.79–1.65
Validly no soc class	62			2.00	1.24–3.23	1.49	0.85–2.59
Housing tenure							
Own/buying*	5,541						
Rent/rent free	512			1.34	1.01–1.79	1.12	0.81–1.54

(Table 19.2 contd.)

(Table 19.2 contd.)

	Bases	Family Type OR	95% CI	Family Type + Socioeconomic + Family Environment OR	95% CI	Family Type + Socioeconomic + Family Environment OR	95% CI
Mother education							
Degree or above*	1,759						
Secondary	4,180			1.71	1.27–2.30	1.77	1.29–2.45
Primary or none	114			2.36	1.44–3.87	2.57	1.49–4.44
Marital distress moth							
No*	5,387						
Yes	666					1.40	1.06–1.86
Marital distress fath							
No*	5,407						
Yes	646					0.89	0.64–1.24
Mother depressed							
No*	5,701						
Yes	352					1.92	1.40–2.63
Father depressed							
No*	5,820						
Yes	233					1.09	0.69–1.72
Mother–child conflict							
Low conflict*	5,083						
High conflict	852					6.42	5.18–7.95
Father–child conflict							
Low conflict*	5,083						
High conflict	970					3.00	2.41–3.73

Note: * = reference category.

When socioeconomic factors were accounted for, the effect of family type was reduced somewhat, but belonging to a reconstituted family remained significant, with about a 60% greater likelihood of scoring highly on the SDQ (OR 1.59, CI 1.01–2.49). Mother's education remained important in this model with a more than twofold chance of poorer outcomes for children of mothers with no or primary education (OR 2.36, CI 1.44–3.87), while social class (OR 2.00, CI 1.24–3.23) and being in receipt of benefits (OR 1.68, CI 1.33–2.12) were also significantly influential in this model. Children living in rented accommodation were also about 30 percent more likely to have a high SDQ score as those living in accommodation that is owned or being bought (OR 1.34, CI 1.01–1.79).

When family context variables such as marital relationship, parental depression, and parent–child conflict were added to the model, as can be seen in Table 19.2, the effects of welfare receipt and mother's education were not attenuated, but the effects of family type, social class, and housing tenure fell away at this point. Although belonging to a reconstituted family is associated with around a 60% increase in the likelihood of a higher SDQ score, it falls just below significance ($p = 0.06$) when these other family variables were included in the model.

The effect of maternal mental health remained strong in this model (OR 1.92, CI 1.40–2.63). Maternal marital distress was also significantly associated with child psychological problems, increasing it by a factor of 0.4, although neither paternal marital distress nor depression was significantly associated with child SDQ scores.

Parent–child conflict (for both parents) had the strongest effect on child outcomes when other factors were accounted for in the model (OR 6.4—mothers; OR 3.0—fathers). Stepwise creation of the model showed that it was only when conflict with the secondary caregiver was added to the model that the effect of family type was removed. From our initial analyses (not shown here) it was noted that while there were no significant differences for primary caregivers, conflict with a secondary caregiver was significantly higher in reconstituted families than in families with two natural parents ($p < 0.01$).

Discussion

Reconstituted Families

The fact that the risk associated with belonging to a lone mother household (where the mother has previously been married) is accounted for in the first model by socioeconomic and family variables (namely maternal depression), but that family type effects were not accounted for in reconstituted families, may reinforce the notion that recoupling or remarriage may not always be beneficial to the child (e.g., Brown, 2006). Parent–child conflict with the secondary caregiver (usually the father) is much higher in reconstituted families compared to families with two biological parents, possibly adding credence to this notion. Most, though, would recognize this as a complex process which can begin before a divorce or separation and continue long afterwards, in the case of previously partnered parents (Emery, 1999; Hetherington & Stanley-Hagan, 1999).

The fact that being in a reconstituted family still has a relatively large impact on child psychological outcomes, when socioeconomic and other factors have been accounted for (Model 1), highlights how complicated this issue is. Even in the cross-sectional models there still appears to be evidence of *possible* different processes in the way in which family structure can impact on child outcomes, especially through relationships within the family and maternal mental health. That said, it remains difficult to determine what the precise dynamics behind this finding are, or indeed what effect a previous separation or divorce has had on the child (if any), or tell us what effect a new partner coming into the home has had.

The findings are still important though, given that in countries like the US, most children live with both biological parents, which is true of children in the current study, but life course estimates suggest that more than half of children will spend some time in an alternative family structure by the time they are 18 (Bumpass & Lu 2000; Teachman, 2003). Although Ireland lags behind other countries in this respect, there remains a clear need for understanding the implications of family transitions for child psychological development.

Lone Parent Families

The findings showed that being from a lone mother household did not on its own account for high levels of emotional and behavioral problems in nine-year-old children. Socioeconomic factors seemed to remove the effect of being from a lone mother household where the mother has never been married, although they did not entirely account for the risk of being in a lone mother household (previously married) as indicated by the fact that this family type was still associated with having a higher risk of emotional and behavioral problems. However, when depression was added to the model, the risk was removed. This was in keeping with exploratory analysis indicating that depression was more prevalent in (previously married) lone mother households ($p < 0.01$). Since it is known that these parents have experienced divorce, separation, or (in a very small number of cases) widowhood, the well-documented stress that often coexists with these transitions may offer some explanation as to why this group is more likely to experience depression, although in the context of cross-sectional work it is nearly impossible to ascertain the exact reasons why this may be the case.

Family Environment

In the current research, family constructs such as maternal depression and parent–child conflict emerged as very influential. Depression in particular has been widely discussed in the literature and it was found here to be strongly associated with child well-being, independent of socioeconomic factors or family structure. Lone mothers were more likely to be depressed, however the fact that they are more likely to be living in poverty—they are more likely to be receipt of welfare benefits—suggests that lacking financial resources may impact on the child through the mother's psychological distress. Family change itself can produce feelings of depression and financial stress as parents (usually mothers) deal with a whole new set of demands, including the emotional needs of household members and changes in parenting and other responsibilities (Amato, 2005).

Parent–child conflict was also strongly correlated with the psychological well-being of the nine-year-olds, and there was also a significant positive association between parent–child conflict and parental depression in the current sample ($p < 0.001$)—possibly a function of a bidirectional relationship where parent mental health both affects, and is affected by, the parent–child relationship. It should be noted, however, that the parent–child relationship is assessed by the parents themselves and may be a function of their state of mind when responding to those particular questions. For example, depressed parents are more likely to have a negative view of their relationships with others, including their child (Moore et al., 2006).

Conclusions

This chapter has demonstrated that some of the main family related factors associated with psychological difficulties in children include family type (living in a reconstituted family), mother's education (no or primary education), social class (parents who have never worked outside the home), and being in receipt of welfare. It has also demonstrated the importance of other family context factors, such as maternal depression as well as parental, and parent–child relationships. It should be recognized, however, that causation is multifactorial and although cross-sectional research using correlations between predictors often points to "vicious circle" processes where poor outcomes are predetermined, longitudinal research offers a cautionary note that multiple and cumulative disadvantage is a good deal less common than some research suggests (Layte & Whelan, 2002).

Finally, the principle of equifinality emphasizes that there can be heterogeneous pathways to the same outcomes (Cicchetti & Rogosch, 1996). The existence of turning points and the role of chance events in deflecting children from either positive or negative pathways emphasize the unpredictable nature of developmental pathways (Rutter, 1989). The implication is that relationships between variables can only be understood probabilistically and that understanding possible developmental pathways and crucial points of transition is more important than understanding the correlation between dependent and independent variables. It should also be noted that problems or dysfunctionality are only some of the possible outcomes from a wide range of potential outcomes in any interaction between individual characteristics and the environment in which they develop (Lerner, 2006).

References

Albrecht, C., & Teachman, J. D. (2003). Childhood living arrangements and the risk of premarital intercourse. *Journal of Family Issues, 24*(7), 867–894. doi:10.1177/0192513X03252731

Amato, P. R. (2001). Children of divorce in the 1990s: An update of the Amato and Keith (1991) meta-analysis. *Journal of Family Psychology, 15*(3), 355–370. doi:10.1037/0893-3200.15.3.355

———. (2005). The impact of family formation change on the cognitive, social, and emotional well-being of the next generation. *Future of Children 15*(2), 75–96.

Bandura, A. (1989). Social cognitive theory. In R.Vasta (Ed.), *Annals of child development* (Vol. 6, pp. 1–60). Greenwich, CT: JAI Press.

Bhrolcháin, M. N., Chappell, R., Diamond, I., & Jameson, C. (2000). Parental divorce and outcomes for children: Evidence and interpretation. *European Sociological Review, 16*(1), 67–91. doi:10.1093/esr/16.1.67

Bramlett, M. D., & Mosher, W. D. (2001). *First marriage dissolution, divorce and remarriage: United States* (Advance data 323). Hyattsville, MD: National Center for Health Statistics.

———. (2002). Cohabitation, marriage, divorce and remarriage in the United States: Data from the national survey of family growth. *Vital Health Statistics* (Series 23, Number 22). National Center for Health Statistics.

Bronfenbrenner, U. (1979). *The ecology of human development: Experiment by nature and design.* Cambridge: Harvard University Press.

Brown, S. L. (2006). Family structure transitions and adolescent well-being. *Demography, 43*(3), 447–461. doi:10.1353/dem.2006.0021

Buchanan, A. (1999). *What works for troubled children? Family support for children with emotional and behavioral problems.* London: Barnardo's.

Bumpass, L. L., & Lu, H. (2000). Trends in cohabitation and implications for children's family contexts in the United States. *Population Studies, 54*(1), 29–41.

Campbell, S. B., Brownell, C. A., Hungerford, A., Spieker, S., Mohan, R., & Blessing, J. (2004). The course of maternal depressive symptoms and maternal sensitivity as predictors of attachment security at 36 months. *Development and Psychopathology, 16*, 231–252. doi: 10.1017/S0954579404044499

Carlson, M., & Corcoran, M. (2001). Family structure and children's behavioral and cognitive outcomes. *Journal of Marriage and Family, 63*(3), 779–792. doi:10.1111/j.1741-3737.2001.00779.x

Cavanagh, S. E. (2008). Family structure history and adolescent adjustment. *Journal of Family Issues, 29*(7), 944–980. doi:10.1177/0192513X07311232

Central Statistics Office. (2006). *Quarterly national household survey—Childcare Quarter 1 2005.* Dublin: Central Statistics Office.

Cicchetti, D., & Rogosch, F. A. (1996). Equifinality and multifinality in developmental psychopathology. *Development and Psychopathology, 8*(4), 597–600. doi:10.1017/S0954579400007318

Collins, J., & Wickham, G. (2001). *What childcare crisis? Irish mothers entering the labour force.* Report for ERC Labour Market Observatory.

Cummings, E. M., & Davies, P. T. (1994). Maternal depression and child development. *Journal of Child Psychology & Psychiatry, 35*(1), 73–112. doi:10.1111/j.1469-7610.1994.tb01133.x

Davies, P. T., Harold, G. T., Goeke-Morey, M. C., & Cummings, E. M. (2002). Children's emotional security and interparental conflict. *Monographs of the Society for Research in Child Development, 67*(3), 1–115.

Emery, R. E. (1999). *Marriage, divorce, and children's adjustment* (2nd ed.). Thousand Oaks, CA: SAGE.

Evans, G. (2004). The environment of childhood poverty. *American Psychologist, 59*(2), 77–92. doi:10.1037/0003-066X.59.2.77

Fahey, T., & Layte, R. (2008). Family and sexuality. In T. Fahey, H. Russell, & C. T. Whelan (Eds), *Quality of life in Ireland: Social impact of economic boom* (Vol. 32, pp. 155–174). Dordrecht, NL: Springer. doi:10.1007/978-1-4020-6981-9

Fauchier, A., & Margolin, G. (2004). Affection and conflict in marital and parent-child relationships. *Journal of Marital and Family Therapy, 30*(2), 197–211. doi:10.1111/j.1752-0606.2004.tb01234.x

Field, T. M. (2000). Infants of depressed mothers. In S. L. Johnson, A. M. Hayes, T. M. Field, M. N. Schneiderman, & P. McCabe (Eds), *Stress, coping and depression* (pp. 51–67). Mahwah, NJ: Lawrence Erlbaum.

Goodman, R. (1997). The strengths and difficulties questionnaire: A research note. *Journal of Child Psychology and Psychiatry, 38*(5), 581–586. doi:10.1111/j.1469-7610.1997.tb01545.x

Goodman, S. H., & Gotlib, I. H. (1999). Risk for psychopathology in the children of depressed mothers: A developmental model for understanding mechanisms of transmission. *Psychological Review, 106*(3), 458–490.

Heard, H. (2007). Fathers, mothers, and family structure: Family trajectories, parent gender, and adolescent schooling. *Journal of Marriage and Family, 69*(2), 435–450. doi:10.1111/j.1741-3737.2007.00375.x

Hetherington, E. M., & Stanley-Hagan, M. (1999). The adjustment of children with divorced parents: A risk and resiliency perspective. *Journal of Child Psychology and Psychiatry, 40*(1), 129–140. doi:10.1111/1469-7610.00427

Hogan, D., Halpenny, A., & Greene, S. (2002). *Children's experiences of parental separation.* Dublin: Children's Research Centre.

Hunsley, J., Best, M., Levebvre, M., & Vito, D. (2001). The seven-item short form of the Dyadic Adjustment Scale: Further evidence for construct validity. *American Journal of Family Therapy, 29*(4), 325–335. doi: 10.1080/01926180126501

Jonsson, J. O., & Gähler, M. (1997). Family dissolution, family reconstitution, and children's educational careers: Recent evidence for Sweden. *Demography, 34*(2), 277–293. doi:10.2307/2061705

Kane, P., & Garber, J. (2004). The relations among depression in fathers, children's psychopathology, and father–child conflict: A meta-analysis. *Clinical Psychology Review, 24*(3), 339–360. doi:10.1016/j.cpr.2004.03.004

Kelly, J. B., & Emery, R. E. (2003). Children's adjustment following divorce: Risk and resilience perspectives. *Family Relations, 52(4),* 352–362. doi:10.1111/j.1741-3729.2003.00352.x

Kennedy, F. (2004). *Cottage to crèche: Family change in Ireland.* Dublin: Institute of Public Administration.

Kerr, D., & Michalski, J. (2004). Family structures and children's behavioral problems: A latent growth curve analysis. *PSC Discussion Papers Series, 18*(11). Retrieved from http://ir.lib.uwo.ca/pscpapers/vol18/iss11/1

Layte, R., & Whelan, C. (2002). *Moving in and out of poverty: The impact of welfare regimes on poverty dynamics in the EU* (EPAG Working Paper 2002-30) Colchester: University of Essex.

Lerner, R. M. (2006). Developmental science, developmental systems, and contemporary theories of human development. In W. Damon, & R. M. Lerner (Eds), *Handbook of child psychology: Theoretical models of human development* (Vol. 1, pp. 1–17*)*. Hoboken, NJ: John Wiley.

MacCallum, F., & Golombok, S. (2004). Children raised in fatherless families from infancy: A follow-up of children of lesbian and single heterosexual mothers at early adolescence. *Journal of Child Psychology and Psychiatry, 45*(7), 1407–1419.

Martins, C., & Gaffan, E. A. (2000). Effects of early maternal depression on patterns of infant-mother attachment: A meta-analytic investigation. *Journal of Child Psychology and Psychiatry, 41*(6), 737–746. doi:10.1111/1469-7610.00661

McClelland, M. M., Morrison, E. J., & Holmes, D. H. (2000). Children at risk for early academic problems: The role of learning related social skills. *Early Childhood Research Quarterly, 15*(3), 307–329.

McLanahan, S. S. (1999). Parent absence or poverty: Which matters more?. In G. Duncan & J. Brooks-Gunn (Eds), *Consequences of growing up poor* (pp. 35–48). New York: Russell Sage Foundation.

McLeod, J. D., & Kaiser, K. (2004). Childhood emotional and behavioral problems and educational attainment *American Sociological Review, 69*(5), 636–658. doi:10.1177/000312240406900502

Meadows, S. O., McLanahan, S., & Brooks-Gunn, J. (2007). Parental depression and anxiety and early childhood behavior problems across family types. *Journal of Marriage and Family, 69,* 1162–1177.

Meagher, S. M., Arnold, D. H., Doctoroff, G. L., Dobbs, J., & Fisher, P. H. (2009). Social-emotional problems in early childhood and the development of depressive symptoms in school-age children. *Early Education and Development, 20*(1), 1–24. doi:10.1080/10409280801947114

Mezulis, A., Hyde, J. S., & Clark, R. (2004). Father involvement moderates the effect of maternal depression during a child's infancy on child behavior problems in kindergarten. *Journal of Family Psychology, 18*(4), 575–588.

Moore, K. A., Hair, E. C., Vandivere, S., McPhee, C., McNamara, M., and Ling, T. (2006). Depression among moms: Prevalence, predictors, and acting out among third grade children. *Child Trends* (Publication #2006-19). Retrieved from http://www.childtrends.org/Files//Child_Trends 2006_03_31_RB_MomDepression.pdf

Newcomb, A. F., Bukowski, W. M., & Pattee, L. (1993). Children's peer relations: A meta-analytic review of popular, rejected, neglected, controversial, and average sociometric status. *Psychological Bulletin, 113*(1), 99–128.

Nixon, E. (2007). *Children's and mothers' experiences of parenting and parent–child relationships in lone mother households* (Unpublished doctoral thesis). University of Dublin, Ireland.

Nolan, B., Layte, R., Whelan, C. T., & Maiitre, B. (2006). *Day in, day out: Understanding the dynamics of child poverty in Ireland.* Dublin: Institute for Public Administration/Combat Poverty Agency.

O'Connor, T. G., Dunn, J., Jenkins, J. M., Pickering, K., & Rasbash, J. (2001) Family settings and children's adjustment: Differential adjustment within and across families. *British Journal of Psychiatry, 179*, 110–115.

O'Connor, T. G., Hetherington, E. M., & Clingempeel, W. G. (1997). Systems and bidirectional influences in families. *Journal of Social & Personal Relationships, 14*(4), 491–504. doi:10.1177/0265407597144005

Oyserman, D., Mowbray, C. T., Meares, P. A., & Firminger, K. B. (2000). Parenting among mothers with a serious mental illness. *American Journal of Orthopsychiatry, 70*(3), 296–315. doi:10.1037/h0087733

Paseta, S. (2003). *Modern Ireland: A very short introduction.* Oxford: Oxford University Press.

Phares, V., Duhig, A. M., & Watkins, M. M. (2002). Family context: Fathers and other supports. In S. H. Goodman & I. H. Gotlib (Eds), *Children of depressed parents: Alternative pathways to risk for psychopathology* (pp. 203–225). Washington, DC: American Psychological Association.

Pianta, R. C. (1992). *Child-parent relationship scale.* Unpublished instrument. University of Virginia.

Pryor, J., & Rodgers, B. (2001). *Children in changing families: Life after parental separation.* Oxford: Blackwell.

Radloff, L. S. (1977). The CES-D Scale: A self-report depression scale for research in the general population. *Applied Psychological Measurement, 1*(3), 385–401. doi:10.1177/014662167700100306

Rutter, M., & Quinton, D. (1984). Parental psychiatric disorder: Effects on children. *Psychological Medicine, 14*(4), 853-880. doi:10.1017/S0033291700019838

Rutter, M. (1989). Pathways from childhood to adult life. *Journal of Child Psychology & Psychiatry, 30*(1), 23–51. doi:10.1111/j.14697610.1989.tb00768.x

Sanson, A., & Lewis, V. (2001). Children and their family contexts. *Family Matters, 59*, 4–9.

Sayer, L. C. (2005). Gender, time and inequality: Trends in women's and men's paid work, unpaid work, and free time. *Social Forces, 84*(1), 285–303. doi: 10.1353/sof.2005.0126

Spanier, G. B. (1976). Measuring dyadic adjustment: New scales for assessing quality of marriage and similar dyads. *Journal of Marriage and the Family, 38*(1), 15–28.

Teachman, J. (2003). Premarital sex, premarital cohabitation, and the risk of subsequent marital dissolution among women. *Journal of Marriage and Family, 65*(2), 444–455. doi:10.1111/j.1741-3737.2003.00444.x

Uunk, W., Kalmijn, M., & Muffels, R. (2005). The impact of young children on women's labour supply: A reassessment of institutional effects in Europe. *Acta Sociologica, 48*(1), 41–62. doi:10.1177/0001699305050986

Wade, A., & Smart, C. (2002). *Facing family change: Children's circumstances, strategies and resources.* York: Joseph Rowntree Foundation.

Wilson, B., & Gottman, J. (2002). Marital conflict, repair, and parenting. In M. H. Bornstein (Ed.), *Handbook of parenting* (Vol. 4, pp. 227–258). Mahwah, NJ: Lawrence Erlbaum Associates.

20

Child and Adolescent Mental Health in Chile and Latin America

Helia Molina
Paula Bedregal
Maria Paz Guzman

Introduction

Mental health can be defined as the state of well-being that enables individuals to improve their abilities, to manage their normal stress of life, work productively and fruitfully, and to make a significant contribution to their communities. The concept includes the idea of subjective well-being, autonomy, competence, and acknowledging and developing the ability to self-fulfill both emotionally and intellectually. These concepts apply to the individual, family, and the community and offer an overview of the context where people develop (World Health Organization [WHO], 2004b).

Physical and mental health are inextricably linked, yet child mental health is not given the importance needed, despite alarming figures in this matter (Pan American Health Organization [PAHO], 2009). There is no true health without mental health. Mental disorders increase the risk of communicable and noncommunicable diseases, and contribute to intentional and unintentional injuries. Many pathological conditions also increase the risk of mental disorders and that comorbidity not only makes help-seeking and treatment more difficult, but it also influences the prognosis (Prince et al., 2007).

When the mental health issue is circumscribed to the child level, the subject becomes even more complex. For decades, child health policies have focused on reducing infectious diseases and infant mortality for under-five children (Kohn et al., 2005). A WHO report (2005) on mental health resources for children and adolescents highlighted the lack of mental health services for this population, although most countries are signatories on the Convention on the Rights of the Child. Well-structured programs for promoting and preventing mental health are few or have not been given the appropriate attention in the region of the Americas. Furthermore, they are not always well-articulated with other sectors of particular relevance, such as education (PAHO, 2009).

Developing public policies on child mental health must highlight the complex set of determinants (biological, social, and psychological) that affect children and their communities. Consequently, it is assumed that developing effective programs requires intervening in many aspects which are subject to change: economic and social conditions that affect the families, monitoring pregnancy, rearing practices, social and cognitive stimulation, day care availability, and preschool education (Molina & Silva, 2010).

The emphasis on the social determinants of mental health highlights the concept of intersectoral action and has revitalized promotional and preventive interventions. This has resulted in a variety of early intervention programs geared toward a comprehensive development of children in developed and developing countries (Ministerio de Salud de Chile, 2007; WHO, 2005).

There is a growing body of knowledge and evidence showing the neurobiological and environmental bases for the comprehensive development of children, which is a major factor in the emergence of emotional and behavioral disorders and a key element in most mental health problems in childhood, adolescence, and adulthood. There is evidence that children's program and early childhood interventions are effective (Anderson et al., 2003; MINSAL, 2006).

This chapter discusses the epidemiology of child mental health in Latin America and two strategies implemented in Chile to promote early childhood development and mental health: the Social Protection Subsystem *Chile Crece Contigo* (Chile Grows Along With You) for children between 0 and 4 years, and the Skills for Life Program for school-going children between 4 and 9 years.

Epidemiological Situation in Child and Adolescent Mental Health in Latin America

The information available on development and mental illnesses in Latin America and Chile is limited and difficult to compare. On the one hand, the information comes from specific studies with no national representation, and on the other hand, from research using different instruments and classifications. Additionally, the interpretation of results has created controversy in terms of the cross-cultural validity of the definitions (Rutter & Stevenson, 2008). An additional difficulty involves the assessment of children under five years, especially those below two. The information available for these groups is primarily directed to cognitive, socioemotional, and motor development or to assess the prevalence of some diseases, such as autism.

0–3-year-olds

Recently, research on mental health has been gaining legitimacy for the age group 0–3 years. Research in neurobiology and early child development allows this age group to be regarded as sensitive to mental illnesses (Osofsky & Fitzgerald, 2000). Studies on this group have reported prevalence ranges from 6 percent to 24 percent caused by some kind of disorder. The most common are sleep, eating, and adjustment disorders (Skovgaard, Houmann, Christiansen, & Andreasen, 2005). In Buenos Aires, a study reported a prevalence of 39 percent of sleep disorders in children aged 2–3 years with dyssomnia as the most common disorder. Resistance to sleep, fear of sleeping alone, followed by nightmares and night terrors were some of the other common disorders (Convertini, Krupitzky, Tripodi, & Carusso, 2003). A Chilean study on eating disorders in children aged 4–24 months reported a prevalence of 23 percent with selective rejection of food as the most common (46.5 percent) (Salas & Pizarro, 1998).

Forty percent of the children in this age group may show a delay in psychomotor development. For instance, through the Ages and Stages Questionnaire (ASQ), children aged 3–23 months in Ecuador showed a prevalence of developmental delay from 15.5 percent (social) to 36 percent (language) (Handal, Lozoff, Breilh, & Harlow, 2007). This study also reported a high prevalence of anaemia (up to 60 percent) and undernutrition (53 percent). In the case of Chile, a national survey on the quality of life and health, the *Encuesta Nacional de Calidad de Vida y Salud 2006* showed that the prevalence of developmental delays in the group aged 6–23 months was 6 percent while the prevalence of risk to delay in the group aged 2–23 months was 35 percent with higher rates for male children and in rural areas (Bedregal, Cumsille, Guederlini, & García, 2007).

4–5-year-olds

The information on mental disorders for children aged 4–5 years is also limited. Several studies have shown a prevalence rate around 25 percent with oppositional defiant disorder as the main problem. In Chile, a recent study which included a sample of 216 preschoolers showed that the overall prevalence of behavioral and emotional problems was 16 percent (Lecannelier, Hoffmann, Flores, & Ascanio, 2008).

In child development, the study from Ecuador reported a prevalence of developmental delay in children aged 24–61 months ranging from 40.9 percent (problem-solving area) to 12.5 percent (gross motor development) per area (Handal et al., 2007). In the Chilean study, the developmental assessment in the national survey *Encuesta Nacional de Calidad de Vida y Salud 2006* reported a 16 percent prevalence of delays as well as a 42 percent prevalence of risk, in children aged 24–59 months (Bedregal et al., 2007).

School-aged Population

More information is available about school-aged children than preschool children in Latin America. The mental health of the school-aged population has been a matter of concern since 1980. For example, Giel et al. (1981) showed that the prevalence of mental disorders in Colombia accounted for 29 percent of the population aged 5–15 years. Canino et al. (2004) used the DISC-IV interview[1] (Shaffer, Fisher, Lucas, Dulcan, & Schwab-Stone, 2000) and the Children's Global Assessment Scale[2] to report prevalence rates of 19.8 percent (excluding impairment), 16.4 percent (specific impairment), and 6.9 percent (total disability) in children aged 4–17 years in Puerto Rico. Only 49.6 percent of the latter group had used health services. The most common disease with a rate of 3.7 percent was Attention Deficit Hyperactivity Disorder (ADHD) followed by oppositional defiant disorder (3.4 percent), anxiety disorders (2.9 percent), depression (1.7 percent), and behavioral disorders (1.3 percent). Another study in Brazil (Fleitlich-Bilyk & Goodman, 2004), based on the Development and Well-Being Assessment (DAWBA) which is a package of integrated questionnaires for parents, teachers and self-report, reported a prevalence rate of 12.7 percent in children aged 7–14 years, in which the most common problems were: disruptive disorders (7 percent), anxiety disorders (5.2 percent), ADHD (1.8 percent), and depressive disorders (1 percent). A study on adolescents aged 12–17 years in Mexico City (Benjet, Borges, Medina-Mora, Zambrano, & Aguilar-Gaxiola, 2009) based on a CIDI-A interview,[3] found annual prevalence rates of 39.4 percent. The most common disorders were: anxiety disorders (29.8 percent), impulse control disorders (15.3 percent), mood disorders (7.2 percent), and substance abuse disorders (3.3 percent).

In the case of Chile, the first study based on the Child Behavior Checklist reported a prevalence rate of 15 percent for behavioral and affective problems in the population aged 6–11 years, living in the Metropolitan Region (Bralic, Seguel, & Montenegro, 1984). In another recent study, a 10 percent prevalence of behavioral and affective problems was reported in schoolers from seven low socioeconomic schools, based on the Pediatric Symptom Checklist. Currently, the first national study in the population aged 4–18 years is being conducted (Vicente et al., 2009). Preliminary information for the city of Iquique reported a prevalence rate of 36 percent in 2008–2009 (twelve months before the structured interview) with anxiety disorders accounting for 16 percent and affective disorders accounting for 5.6 percent. The Province of Cautín—which has a high rate of poor and indigenous population—reported a prevalence rate of 24.1 percent during the same period, with a prevalence rate of 10.1 percent for anxiety disorders and 7.1 percent for affective disorders (Vicente et al., 2010).

Table 20.1 shows the situation of the region and some selected countries on some health determinants.

---

[1]National Institute of Mental Health Diagnostic Interview Schedule for Children Version IV (NIMH DISC-IV) is a highly structured diagnostic interview, designed to assess more than 30 psychiatric disorders occurring in children and adolescents. It can be administered by "lay" interviewers after a minimal training period. The interview is available in both English and Spanish.

[2]The Children's Global Assessment Scale (CGAS) is one of the most widely used measures of the overall severity of disturbance in children. It measures social and psychiatric functioning for children ages 4–16 years and can be used as an indicator of need for clinical services, a marker for the impact of treatment, or a single index of impairment in epidemiological studies.

[3]Composite International Diagnostic Interview-Automated (CIDI-A) is a structured interview which generates both DSM-III-R and ICD-10 psychiatric diagnosis.

Table 20.1 Determinants of Health in Selected Latin-American Countries

	Percentage of Children Living in Conditions of …				Percentage of Children That …						Resources Available	
Country	Poverty*	Bad Housing*	Literacy*	Attend Preschool*	Have a Health Insurance*	Have Received an MMR Vaccine or a Measles Vaccine (2007)	Are Low-birth Weight Babies*	Die (Infant Mortality)	Are Breast-fed Exclusive (<4 Months)*	Health Spending*	Mental Health Spending (% of Health Spending)**
Argentina	15	9	98	72	53	99	7	13	nd	5	2
Bolivia	45	62	91	76	13	86	10	54	63	3	0
Brazil	32	5	90	40	nd	100	8	20	nd	4	3
Chile	8	12	97	41	96	92	6	8	77	4	2
Colombia	31	14	93	91	nd	95	8	15.5	34	4	0
Costa Rica	11	7	96	71	87	90	7	10	47	5	8
Dominican Republic	14	35	89	76	nd	96	11	30	25	2	1
Ecuador	32	nd	84	91	9	100	nd	18	42	2	nd
El Salvador	49	35	82	41	17	100	9	22	30	3	nd
Guatemala	44	nd	73	nd	nd	93	5	39	56	2	1
Honduras	39	17	84	43	nd	89	10	23	nd	4	2
Mexico	24	nd	93	94	nd	96	8	16	52	5	1
Nicaragua	51	17	78	26	15	100	9	33	40	5	1
Panama	24	nd	93	79	43	89	9	15	32	4	nd
Paraguay	31	17	95	74	22	80	nd	17	7	2	0
Peru	49	25	90	60	64	95	8	21	73	2	2
Uruguay	19	1	98	55	45	97	8	11	63	9	8
Venezuela	40	15	95	68	nd	53	8	16	nd	3	nd

Sources: 1) Pan American Health Organization (2010).
2) WHO (2005) Mental Health Atlas 2005. Available at http://www.who.int/mental_health/evidence/mhatlas05/en/

Although the results show great heterogeneity, they are marked by a context of global disadvantage, thus posing a risk to the mental health of the children and adolescent population. As seen, while information is sparse and there is an urgent need for better information systems, the evidence of an unfavorable environment, and a very variable expenditure on mental health programs in the region, makes it imperative to develop effective and efficient policies and programs to promote mental health. In addition, the development of mental health services geared toward primary, secondary, and tertiary prevention will be required along with an improvement in the information addressing the magnitude of the problem in the region.

Early Child Development Subsystem of Social Protection

Recognizing the importance of early childhood development as a health determinant through the lifespan and the evidence provided by neurosciences, behavioral sciences, social, and economic sciences has enabled Chile to build a public policy for children to promote biopsychosocial development of children (Anderson et al., 2003).

Through a process of diagnosis, which includes evidence review; systematization of existing policies, plans and programs; and multidisciplinary and multisectoral involvement from experts and organizations, a national proposal—driven by political will—was developed and implemented from 2006 (Molina & Silva, 2010). The available evidence on child development problems shows about 30% risks of delay and around 10% delay rates (MINSAL, 2006). These rates are not homogeneous in the population as the highest figures focus on the lowest income quintiles. This inequity has served as the focus for developing policies for children in Chile. The proposed policy is part of the System of Social Protection, a law promulgated in 2009. Known as the "Subsystem of Social Protection of Children: Chile Grows Along with You," it has the following guiding principles and approaches:

- Child and adolescent rights
- Promoting comprehensive biological, psychological, and social development
- Acknowledging family as a key element in the comprehensive development of children, respecting their preferences, choices, labor and/or educational needs
- Importance of the social and community environment for child development
- Protection and one-on-one support of every child (according to their needs) throughout their life cycle, based on development goals
- The State as guarantor of rights that must emphasize investment in children by the time the resource planning is done

The main objective of this program is to enable children to reach their optimum health potential and development, irrespective of their socioeconomic status, place of residence, or ethnicity.

Interventions are selected based on available evidence (Bedregal, Margozzini, & Molina, 2001) and the awareness of the importance of the environments responsible for fostering nurturant conditions for comprehensive development, which range from the intimate realm of the family and community, to the characteristics of government, society, income distribution, and cultural aspects as more distal determinants (Molina, Cordero, & Silva, 2008).

Structure and Delivery of Chile Crece Contigo

The program is coordinated by the Ministry of Social Planning, which also coordinates the entire national social protection system. The main implementers of this program are health and education sectors, although at the local level (municipalities), the network is extended to housing, labor, justice, social welfare, public works, and so on. The focus of this program is to develop legislative frameworks that protect the family and provide appropriate parenting, as well as offering quality solutions based on the needs for care and early education when the mother has to resume work or studies.

The main entry to Chile Crece Contigo for children is through the health sector, particularly primary care, which is free and provides national coverage. This occurs in the first prenatal control, during which the mother is informed about her entry into the social protection system and her rights. Then, a vulnerability assessment is made according to pre-established and standardized protocols so that the mother receives a special form, which activates the entire municipal network if vulnerability factors are identified (for example, late entry into antenatal care, mental health problems, substance abuse, history of domestic violence, being an adolescent, being poor, among others). The following outline shows what are known as universal actions, actions for mothers and children in the public health system, actions focused on the poorest 60 percent of the population, and specific actions geared toward children with special needs.

Universal Actions

In order to build an environment and a social context that enables families and communities to promote early childhood development, the following strategies were developed:

A Mass Educational Program

Through radio and closed-circuit television and social communication activities such as educational and awareness-raising campaigns on child development; enabling environments; children's rights and the supply of social services; educational cartoon series for parents, children, and the community in general; famous leaders' testimony; good practices; and successful experiences from the program are broadcast. Awareness-raising and information campaigns are held in the subway (Metro) too.

Web Portal

It serves as a resource center for parents, caregivers, children, and professionals. The main services offered are:

- Information on child development
- Expert consultations
- Learning material for download
- Interactive forums
- Exchange among relevant actors.

Children's Phone Service (Fono Infancia)

It offers free confidential consultation to parents for their children's health or behavior problems.

Laws Protecting Children and the Family

Some specifical laws are part of the social protection system, such as, one year of postnatal leave with salary for mothers who have children with special needs; two hours per day from the working activity for breastfeeding (with salary); paid leave for 42 days before delivery and 84 days after delivery; medical licence for mothers whose children less than a year old are sick. These legal rights apply to adopted children as well.

The Support Program on Biopsychosocial Development

It consists of quality psychosocial interventions, which also complement antenatal care, childbirth care, and child health checkups, and hospital care for children. This is a program for children and their families belonging to the public health system (80 percent of the population) and offers a range of services that were defined according to the best available evidence of effectiveness, and respecting cultural relevance. Support materials are delivered to every family speaking Spanish and the main indigenous languages of the country. Financial resources, management skills, and necessary conditions have been provided. A lot of support material for health teams and families has been developed and disseminated. The programme provides different services to women during pregnancy and the delivery process as well as children in the age group 0–4 years.

Pregnancy

Antenatal care is provided by a midwife and it focuses on detecting biopsychosocial risks and developing careplans with an emphasis on family, education for childbirth, and child-raising preparation. If one or more vulnerability factors exist, a multidisciplinary and comprehensive home visit is made. In such cases, the mother's mental health is the primary concern in the diagnosis and treatment. During the period January 2008 to December 2009, it was found that 45.8 percent of pregnant women with one or more risk factors showed symptoms of depression.

Delivery Process

Childbirth is a crucial moment for bonding between mother and child. It is encouraged that the father or any other adult closely connected to the mother should be present with her during the delivery process. After childbirth, the baby is placed for at least 20 minutes in skin-to-skin contact with the mother before being sent to the nursery room. If necessary, a psychosocial team supports the mother during postpartum period. Management of pain during labor and delivery is also considered. Every mother receives individual or group postpartum counseling.

Newborn Support Program

In order to support the development possibilities from the moment of birth and ensure that all children have the optimal conditions of care, all mothers and children in public health hospitals receive a set of elements, such as, portable cribs, nursing pillow, shoulder strap, massage oil, cleaning supplies, and educational material before going home.

First Four Years

Primary care facilities perform the newborn screening and later checkups during the first four years. Chile Crece Contigo strengthens actions promoting the comprehensive development and the early detection of any problem that may threaten the process. Similarly, the program aims at detecting maternal depression and mother–child bonding problems. Parental education is the core of the program, consisting of standardized activities with quality support material. The Canadian parenting program *Nobody's Perfect* was adapted to the Latin American culture. The principle of the program is to promote the empowerment of the family to improve what they already know and develop parenting skills, and consists of six sessions (90 minutes each) with a problem-based methodology. The pediatric hospital where children may spend transcendental periods of their life for their development (especially if they are chronic patients requiring more days of stay) undertakes serious interventions. The main initiatives implemented are adapting physical spaces to facilitate parental company and child play; integrating family care by facilitating access to parents for at least 10 hours per day; providing multidisciplinary and comprehensive care by incorporating psychosocial professionals into the clinical staff to support families and children (keeping company during crises, bereavements, or other traumatic events); and avoiding harmful stimuli for development, such as noise, intense light, and excessive manipulation to premature newborns. Standardized technical guidelines for neonatal and paediatric wards have been developed as basic services for promoting child development.

Vulnerable Children and Families

Vulnerable children, that is, children who may be poor, abused, neglected, disabled, belonging to dysfunctional families, or institutionalized because of legal problems of parents represent a priority for the program as it offers a range of services and benefits for the child and family, on a case-to-case basis. What have proved to be more cost-effective are: comprehensive home visits (Sweet & Appelbaum, 2004; Barlow & Coren, 2004) education workshops and enrolling children into some early stimulation program. To each child and family the following services are made available:

- A personalized plan for the child and family
- Access to peer education and family counseling
- Comprehensive home visits
- Assisted referrals to different child development support resources/services
- Preferential access to allowances and benefits for the family, depending on their needs
- Free access to quality nursery and kindergarten, according to schedules compatible with the working hours of the mother
- Children with special needs or disabilities.

Implementation

Typically, the primary health care team in Chile is composed of physicians, midwives, nurses nutritionists, and social workers. With the implementation of new services it is possible to find psychologists, preschool teachers, phonoaudiologists, and occupational therapists to include in the team. The national program was implemented in 2008 for the entire country. At present there is no assessment of its impact on child development, although assessment models have been developed and baselines to measure the population results have been established. The structure and the process of implementation, together with the expected coverage improvements have been assessed. Special emphasis has been given to monitoring the quality of the interventions that are being implemented. The degree of satisfaction among users and health workers involved has also been assessed. The health workers perceive that the program is very useful and important as it facilitates the childraising process. They feel that this system greets and protects them as a family and accompanies them in the child development process.

Currently, Chile Crece Contigo program applies only to children between 0 to 4 years; from 2013, it will probably extend to children up to eight years.

Skills for Life Program

Chile has established very high goals at the national level in regard to the quality of and access to education. The National Board of School Assistance and Scholarships (Junta Nacional de Auxilio Escolar y Becas [JUNAEB]) has identified student health as a priority element of this effort in view of the fact that an adequate bio-psychosocial environment is critical to the attainment of high levels of human development and academic performance.

It has been proven that early and ongoing implementation of intervention programs for at-risk groups at the primary school level contributes to children's biological, emotional, and social development. JUNAEB's Student Health Program focuses on public and subsidized schools in municipalities that are considered to be high-risk, offering the Skills for Life program (SFL) to students in prekindergarten, kindergarten, first, second, and third grades.

The development of the SFL program began during the 1990s. SFL has validated an intervention strategy and model that has been implemented in the educational community and has allowed for the accumulation of experience in this field. International studies have found that 10–20% of children in the age group 3–15 years present persistent and socially incapacitating problems (US Public Health Service, 2000; President's New Freedom Commission on Mental Health, 2003; Haggerty, 2006). Kellam's research (1980–1997) in the field of applied epidemiology in the US. outlines early indicators for adolescent psychiatric problems such as depression, criminal behavior and addiction including aggressiveness, shyness and low levels of academic achievement. Some data suggest that early, continuous intervention (before the ages of six to eight) can improve the biological, emotional, and social development of children in at-risk groups (Werthamer-Larsson, Kellam, & Wheeler, 1991; Zins, Weissberg, Wang, & Walberg, 2004).

This results in better health and social skills and well-being that can be observed throughout their life (Berrueta-Clement, Schweinhart, Steven Barnett, Epstein, & Weikart, 1984). Psychosocial problems at the beginning of elementary school translate into maladaptive behaviors that can be observed in the classroom by teachers and in the home by parents. In Chile, studies of students in the first cycle of elementary school have shown a prevalence of around 24.2 percent of psychiatric disorders, 6.2 percent of which involve attention and activity disorders. Limitations in school performance were detected in 17.2 percent of these children. Aggressive behaviors with hyperactivity are the most frequent risk factors of the children included in the study along with family variables that have a significant correlation to risk for psychiatric disorders in children (Wasserman et al., 1999).

Research conducted as part of the process of validating the SFL program shows a significant decrease in at-risk psychosocial behavior in children who participated in the intervention compared to the control group. In other words, those who took part in the program were able to overcome behaviors related to aggressiveness, hyperactivity, concentration and attention problems, social inhibitions, and shyness. These changes resulted in more favorable and positive perceptions of the children by their parents and teachers once they had finished the intervention cycle.

Program Objectives and Beneficiaries

The general objective of SFL is to develop a structured sector-specific response that contributes to successful educational performance and leads to high levels of learning and low repetition and dropout rates in educational communities that present high rates of socioeconomic vulnerability and psychosocial risk. The long-term goal of SFL is to increase psychosocial well-being and personal skills (relational, emotional, and social) and decrease behaviors or conditions that are harmful to individuals' health (depression, suicide, alcohol and drug abuse, and violent behavior).

SFL focuses on public and subsidized private schools in municipalities with high levels of psychosocial risk (based on UNICEF data and the School Risk Index). It includes children who are transitioning out of preschool and first, second, and third graders (boys and girls ages four through nine). Program beneficiaries are students, their parents, and teachers, and the school community in general. SFL is applied in schools that meet the JUNAEB criteria outlined above.

Program Management

The SFL program is executed at the municipal level by psychosocial teams that are included in the executing agencies. The team is designed to meet a profile based on experience and knowledge of psychosocial development, the promotion of good mental health, and prevention of psychological problems—skills related to educational strategies and learning within schools, and community and inter-sectoral work.

In order to implement the SFL program at the local level, JUNAEB calls on public and private legal entities (municipalities, municipal corporations, universities, etc.) located in the target area to present proposals to the technical and administrative foundations of SFL, which are responsible for ensuring the sustainability and inclusion of the program. A shared execution and funding modality has been developed between JUNAEB and the entity responsible for the program at the municipal level.

SFL management involves three levels with complementary functions: national follow-up and monitoring by JUNAEB's national office, regional supervision and accompaniment by JUNAEB's regional office, and municipal level execution.

Program Structure

The SFL program units are as follows:

1. Promotion of psychosocial wellbeing and development within the educational community (for all)

    The goal of this unit is to promote mental health by reinforcing protective factors in teachers, parents, and children. Its staff members develop activities that allow for the acquisition of skills, attitudes, and behaviors that protect mental health such as decision-making and problem-solving skills, creative and critical thinking, effective communication skills and the ability to establish healthy interpersonal relationships. All of these favor self-esteem, self-image, and autonomy. The priorities for the teacher in this area are to focus on self-care, create a positive emotional climate in the classroom, and achieve positive interaction between parents and educators (Satcher, Kaczorowski, & Topa, 2005; US Department of Health and Human Services, 2000; Huang et al., 2005).

    The main activities of this unit include:

    - Organizing workshops for parents and preschool teachers
    - Organizing teacher self-care workshops
    - Providing advice to teachers for classroom work (healthy behaviors)
    - Providing advice to teachers for parent/caregiver meetings

2. Early detection of risky behavior

    A key action of the program is detection of risky behaviors in first graders. The risk detection instruments used in the SFL program by JUNAEB are: (*a*) Teacher Observation of Classroom Adaptation (TOCA; Kellam, Branch, Agrawal, & Ensminger, 1975); (*b*) TOCA-R adapted to Chile (George, Siraquian, & Mores, 1995); and (*c*) Pediatric Symptom Checklist (Jellinek, Murphy, & Burns, 1986). These instruments evaluate the children's classroom performance according to the teacher and their behavior at home according to their parents (Murphy et al., 1996; Mores & Siraquyan, 1993).

3. Prevention of psychosocial problems and risky behaviors (for some)

    The preventive intervention of SFL looks to reduce the negative impact of risk factors (aggressiveness, low cognitive achievements, hyperactivity, and shyness) and the promotion of protective factors (communication, sociability, and expression of feelings) in order to stimulate the development of skills and abilities in children in a comprehensive manner that is adaptive to the school environment (Jellinek, Bishop-Joseph, Murphy, & Zigler, 2005).

The preventive activity is selective (it includes children with risks that have been detected) and focused, that is, the instruments detect specific risks. The various risk factors are grouped into color profiles. The preventive actions (workshops) are held during second grade. They are attended by children in whom risk factors were detected using the TOCA-R and PSC that were applied in first grade.

4. Referrals to care providers and monitoring of children with mental health issues (for few)
5. Development of networks that can provide local support for the program
The objective of this unit is to coordinate and develop the Community Support for Mental Health Network within the school by promoting greater commitment on the part of local authorities in decision making, resource allocation, and technical advising at the municipal level with the program.
6. Program evaluation and monitoring
The objective of this unit is to regularly evaluate the progress of the program and effectiveness of the proposed intervention model. This evaluative work is supported by the application of user satisfaction surveys and systematic self-evaluation by each executing team. We know that there is a 64.7%, decrease of risk in girls and boys who participate in preventive program activities. Psychosocial risk detected early predicts outcomes in SIMCE (Chilean National Performance in School Test).

The evaluation is currently complemented by support indicators (general information on performance, satisfaction, and management of SFL teams) proposed by JUNAEB, which are designed to contribute to a more global evaluation of the SFL program.

Future of SFL in Chile

SFL represent a valuable contribution to public health policies in our country. There is the ability to interrupt the vicious circle of: vulnerability—psychosocial risk—poor school performance—poverty. The program's impact on school performance is particularly important to our country. We are aware that achieving greater development and equity will be accomplished while improving education results.

In most countries of Latin America, the issue of child mental heath has not been given the necessary importance in terms of extent and its consequences. We believe that improving comprehensive support policies for early childhood development is major step in preventing and detecting early mental health problems and risk factors. It is imperative to make progress in terms of information systems, records, services, specific plans, and comprehensive actions. The experience of these two Chilean policies can contribute to the Latin America region.

Acknowledgment

To Miss Viviana Hernández Llewellyn for her kindness and support in editing.

References

Anderson, L., Shinn, C., Fullilove, M., Scrimshaw, S., Fielding, J., Normand, J., Carande-Kullis, V. & The Task Force on Community Preventive Services. (2003). The effectiveness of early childhood developments programs: A systematic review. *American Journal of Preventive Medicine 24*(3S), 32–46. doi:10.1016/S0749-3797-(02)00655-4

Barlow, J., & Coren, E. (2004). Parent-training programmes for improving maternal psychosocial health. Cochrane Database of Systematic Reviews, Issue 2, Art. No. CD002020. doi:10.1002/14651858

Berrueta-Clement, John, R., Schweinhart, L. J., Steven Barnett, W., Epstein, A. S., & Weikart, D. P. (1984). Changed lives: The effects of the Perry Preschool Program on youths through age 19 (Monograph No. 8). Ypsilanti, MI: High/Scope Educational Research Foundation.

Bedregal, P., Cumsille, P., Guederlini, P., & García, M. (2007). Informe Final. Análisis módulo de infancia Encuesta Nacional de Calidad de Vida y Salud Chile 2006.

Bedregal, P., Margozzini, P., & Molina, H. (2001). Revisión sistemática de evidencias costoefectivas para el desarrollo biopsicosocial en la infancia. Publicación OPS.

Benjet, C., Borges, G., Medina-Mora, M., Zambrano, J., & Aguilar-Gaxiola, S. (2009). Youth mental health in a populous city of the developing world: Results from the Mexican adolescent mental health survey. *Journal of Child Psychology and Psychiatry, 50*(4), 386–395.

Bralic, S., Seguel, X., & Montenegro, H. (1984). *Prevalencia de trastornos psíquicos en la población escolar de Santiago.* Santiago, Chile: CEDEP-UNICEF.

Canino, G., Shrout, P., Rubio-Stipec, M., Bird, H., Bravo, M., Ramirez R. et al. (2004). The DSM IV rates of child and adolescent disorders in Puerto Rico. *Arch Gen Psychiatry, 61*, 85–93.

Convertini, G., Krupitzky, S., Tripodi, M., & Carusso, L. (2003). Trastornos del sueño en niños sanos. *Arch Argent Pediatr, 101*, 99–105.

Fleitlich-Bilyk, B., & Goodman, R. (2004). Prevalence of child and adolescent psychiatric disorders in southeast Brazil. *Journal of the American Academy of Child and Adolescent Psychiatry, 43*(6), 727–34.

George, M., Siraquian, X., & Mores, R. (1995). Adaptaci´on y validaci´on de dos instrumentos de pesquisa de problemas de salud mental en escolares de 1o¯ b´ asico. Revista de Psicolog´ýa 5, 17–25.

Giel, R., Arango, M., Climent, C., Harding, T., Ibrahim, H., Ladrido-Ignacio, L., Srinivasa Murthy, R., & Younis, V. (1981). Childhood mental disorders in primary health care: Results of observations in four developing countries. *Pediatrics, 68*(5), 677–683.

Haggerty, R. (2006). Some steps needed to ensure the health of America's children: Lessons learned from 50 years in pediatrics. *Ambulatory Pediatrics, 6*(3), 123--29.

Handal, A., Lozoff, B., Breilh, J., & Harlow, S. (2007). Sociodemographic and nutritional correlates of neurobehavioral development: A study of young children in a rural region of Ecuador. *Revista Panamericana de Salud Pública, 2*(5), 292–300.

Huang, L., Stroul, B., Friedman, R., Mrazek, P., Friesen, B., Pires, S., & Mayberg, S. (2005). Transforming mental health care for children and their families. *American Psychologist, 60*(6), 615--627.

Ishizaki, Y., Ishizaki, T., Ozawa, K., Fukai, Y., Hattori, Y., Taniuchi, S., & Kobayashi, Y. (2005). Psychosocial problems among siblings of children with disabilities in Japan: Psychosocial association between mothers and siblings. *Journal of Developmental and Physical Disabilities, 17*(2), 119–132. doi:10.1007/s10882-005-3684-5

Jellinek, M., Bishop-Joseph, S., Murphy, M., & Zigler, E. (2005). Mental health in Head Start, Leave no child behind. *NHSA Dialog, 8*(1), 25–35.

Jellinek, M., Murphy, J., & Burns, B. (1986). Brief psychosocial screening in outpatient pediatric practice. *Journal of Pediatrics, 109*(2), 371–378.

Kellam, S., Branch, J., Agrawal, K., & Ensminger, M. (1975). *Mental health and going to school: The Woodlawn program of assessment, early intervention, and evaluation.* Chicago, IL: University of Chicago Press.

Kohn, R., Levav. I., Caldas de Almeida, J., Vicente, B., Andrade, L., Caraveo-Anduaga, J., & Saraceno, B. (2005). Los trastornos mentales en América Latina y el Caribe: Asunto prioritario para la salud péblica (Mental health in Latin America and the Caribbean: A primary subject for public health). *Rev. Panam Salud Publica, 18*(4/5), 229–240.

Lecannelier, F., Hoffmann, M., Flores, F., & Ascanio, L. (2008). Problemas, proyecciones y desafíos en la salud mental infantil: La necesidad de reformular el rol profesional. *Horiz Enferm, 19*, 1–9.

Ministerio de Salud de Chile. (2006). Quality of life survey.

———. (2007). Intervenciones basadas en evidencia en el ámbito de prevención de la salud mental en familias con niños de 0-6 años, Revisión sistemática de la literatura.

Molina, H., Cordero, M., & Silva, V. (2008). From survival to early child development: Steps in developing a comprehensive social protection system for children. *Revista Chilena de Pediatría, 1*,11–17.

Molina, H., & Silva, V. (2010). *Four years growing together.* Ministry of Health Chile. Retrieved from http://www.crececontigo.cl

Mores, R., & Siraquyan, X. (1993). Adaptación de la Prueba PSC en Universidad de Chile. Estudio Fondecyt.

Murphy, J., Ichinose, C., Hicks, R., Kingdon, D., Crist-Whitzel, J., Jordan, P., & Jellinek, M. (1996). Utility of the Pediatric Symptom Checklist as a psychosocial screen to meet the federal Early and Periodic Screening, Diagnosis, and Treatment (EPSDT) standards: A pilot study. *Journal of Pediatrics, 129*(6), 864–869.

Osofsky, J., & Fitzgerald, H. (2000). *WAIMH Handbook of infant mental health, I-IV.* Madrid: John Wiley & Sons.

Pan American Health Organization. (2009). Estrategia y plan de acción sobre salud mental. 49º Consejo Directivo OPS WDC.

———. (2010). Regional core health data initiative. Table generator system. Retrieved from http://www.paho.org/English/SHA/coredata/tabulator/newTabulator.htm

President's New Freedom Commission on Mental Health. (2003). *Achieving the promise: Transforming mental health care in America.* Rockville, MD: US Department of Health and Human Services.

Prince, M., Patel, V., Saxena, S., Maj, M., Maselko, J., Phillips, M., & Rehman, A. (2007). No health without mental health. *The Lancet, 370* (9590), 859–877. doi:10.1016/S0140-6736(07)61238-0

Rutter, M., & Stevenson, J. (2008). Using epidemiology to plan services: A conceptual approach. In Rutter et al. (Eds), *Rutter's child and adolescent psychiatry* (5th ed., pp. 71–80). Hoboken, NJ: Wiley-Blackwell.

Salas, M., & Pizarro, F. (1998). Problemas de rechazo alimentario en lactantes. *Revista Chilena de Nutrición, 25*, 45–50.

Satcher, D., Kaczorowski, J., & Topa, D. (2005). The expanding role of the pediatrician in improving child health in the 21st century. *Pediatrics, 115*, 1124–1128.

Shaffer, D., Fisher, P., Lucas, C., Dulcan, M., & Schwab-Stone, M. (2000). NIMH Diagnostic interview schedule for children, version IV: Description, differences from previous versions, and reliability of some common diagnoses. *Journal of the American Academy of Child and Adolescent Psychiatry, 39*, 28–38.

Skovgaard, A., Houmann, T., Christiansen, E., & Andreasen, A. (2005). The reliabitiy of the ICD-10 and the DC 0-3 in an epidemiological sample of children 1.5 years of age. *Infant Mental Health Journal, 26,* 470–480.

Sweet, M., & Appelbaum, M. (2004). Is home visiting an effective strategy? A meta-analytic review of home visiting programs for families with young children. *Child Development, 75*(5), 1435–1456.

U. S. Department of Health and Human Services. (2000). *Healthy People 2010: Understanding and improving health* (Vols. 1&2). Washington, DC: U. S. Department of Health and Human Services.

U. S. Public Health Service. (2000). *Report of the surgeon general's conference on children's mental health: A national action agenda.* Washington, DC: Department of Health and Human Services.

Vicente, B., Saldivia, S., Rioseco, P., De la Barra, F., Pihan, R., Capella, C., & Zúñiga, M. (2009). Epidemiología de trastornos mentales infanto juveniles en la Provincia de Iquique. *Revista Chilena de Psiquiatría y Neurología de la Infancia y Adolescencia* 1S, 75.

Vicente, B., Saldivia, S., Rioseco, P., De la Barra, F., Valdivia, M., Melipillán, R., & Pihan, R. (2010). Epidemiología de trastornos mentales infanto juveniles en la Provincia de Cautín. *Revista Médica de Chile 138*(8), 965–973. doi: 10.4067/S0034-98872010000800004

Wasserman, R., Kelleher, K., Bocian, A., Baker, A., Childs, G., Indacochea, F., & Gardner, W. (1999). Identification of attentional and hyperactivity problems in primary care: A report from Pediatric Research in Office Settings and the Ambulatory Sentinel Practice Network. *Pediatrics, 103*(3), E38. doi:10.1542/peds.103.3.e38

Werthamer-Larsson, L., Kellam, S., & Wheeler, L. (1991). Effect of first-grade classroom environment on shy behavior, aggressive behavior, and concentration problems. *American Journal of Community Psychology, 19*(4), 585–602.

World Health Organization. (2004a). *Invertir en salud mental.* Geneva: WHO.

———. (2004b). *Promoting mental health: Concepts, emerging evidence, practice.* Geneva: WHO.

———. (2005). *Atlas: Child and adolescent mental health resources: Global concerns: Implications for the future.* Geneva: WHO.

Zins, J., Weissberg, R., Wang, M., & Walberg, H. (2004). *Building academic success on social and emotional learning: What does the research say?* New York: Teachers College Press.

21

Children's Voices in the Psychologist's Office: Contributions about Mental Health from Peru

Beatriz Oré
Martín Benavides

Introduction

Since 1978 many professionals have tried to implement a comprehensive definition of health that includes physical, mental, and social welfare.[1] A more specific point of view of mental health shows that it is the welfare state through which the individuals realize their abilities, are able to face up to the common stress of life, work in a productive and fruitful way, and contribute to their communities. This has to do with the possibility of increasing the competence of individuals and communities to reach their own objectives (OMS, 2004). With this perspective, the focus on mental health moved from mental disorders only to incorporating different aspects related to the living conditions of people in their sociocultural environment.

These definitions suggest that the approach to mental health is explained from the perspective of adults. Although children are not intended to be excluded, the conceptual frames in the majority of documents refer to the characteristics of a person in stages of development that correspond to adulthood. To analyze what happens in the case of children, it is necessary to adapt the concepts. We wonder if this is already a sign of the vulnerability to which the minors are exposed.

In developing countries like Peru, the principal challenge that mental health faces is poverty (Ministry of Health [MINSA], 2004), a condition in which around 30 percent of the Peruvian population lives. Though there is not a unique definition of poverty, various authors agree on considering it as a multidimensional phenomenon (Herrera, 2001; Roca Rey & Rojas, 2002; Niños del Milenio, 2003) related to the lack of financial resources, the quality of life, and the access to

---

[1]International Conference about Primary Health Attention. Alma-Ata, URSS, September, 1978, WHO.

basic services, as well as to vulnerability and insecurity (Roca Rey, 2003). From our perspective, these last two have to do with the right to speak, the feelings of risk, insecurity, of being defenseless, the lack of means to solve problems, and marginalization.

Poverty is, above all, a phenomenon that affects people and like Minujin (2005, 2010) points out, child poverty is different from adult poverty, in particular by the impact that it generates in the long term in the lives of children. The evidence that comes from various studies in different countries shows that poverty restricts the child opportunities to develop his/her intellectual potential. Those children who live in contexts of poverty not only show poor performance at school, but also in different cognitive tests (Pollitt, 2002). It is not only the main cause of child morbidity and mortality, but it also has a negative influence on the subsequent psychobiological development (Grantham-McGregor et al., 2007). The efforts to define child poverty and understand its consequences in the long term have been focused. There has not been a here-and-now perspective which has to do with children in a specific stage of development, that is, before they grow up.

For Minujin (2010), the traditional measurements of poverty do not allow the inclusion of dimensions such as insecurity, lack of freedom, maltreatment, negligence, and social exclusion. The author himself points out that in the child population, poverty covers three mutually related domains: the deprivation of basic needs for development; the vulnerability that implies growing up in a society that is incapable of avoiding diverse threats for the security of minors; and the exclusion as a result of processes in which the right to speak, as well as other children's rights are denied or threatened.

It's in the field of vulnerability and violence where we can better study the consequences of poverty on children's mental health. The violence against children who live in contexts of poverty is a reality that severely affects the child population in Peru. According to Dughi (2002), more than a third of the population hit their children to try to discipline them. Bardales and Huallpa (Ministry of Women and Social Development [MIMDES], 2005), who carried out a study in three different districts of Peru, point out that 89.3 percent of the children interviewed admitted suffering some kind of psychological and/or physical maltreatment in their homes. The National Mental Health Strategy and Culture of Peace General Plan 2005–2010 (MINSA, 2005) holds evidence that indicates that one in three people from Lima (36.2 percent) maltreats his/her children psychologically, and two in four or five people (43.2 percent) maltreat their children physically. On the other hand, another government study (MIMDES, 2006) points out that eight out of ten boys, girls, and teenagers refer to having experienced some kind of domestic abuse in the last year, that the most common form of aggression against children are insults, and that school is also a space of violence against them. One in ten children admits that he/she should report the maltreatment but does not know where to do it. This way, although the statistical information around the problem of violence against children is new and not abundant, there's evidence that allows us to show the magnitude and seriousness of it.

Objectives of the Study

In this study we were interested in the way poor children express their vulnerability and experience of violence. The starting points are the topics which emerged from children, expressed in their own voices, drawings, and through their play/games. In most studies related to this topic, it is adults who pose the questions and propose the supposedly relevant topics. Few exceptions in Peru are Bardales and Huallpa (MIMDES 2005), and Salazar, Arias, Pareja, and Aramburú (2006). The present study's contribution is to explore those issues which are considered relevant by children.

The project took place in the context of a psychologist's office in San Juan de Lurigancho. This is the most populated district of Lima and Peru (Alva, 2000; Municipal Council of San Juan de Lurigancho, 2011), where 24.3 percent of the population lives in conditions of poverty.[2] The children were brought by their mothers[3] to the psychologist's office between the years 2000 and 2007. When a mother wanted to consult a psychologist for her child, the first appointment was attended by the mother alone. Thereafter, the child in question was taken to meet the psychologist. Usually, each child attended a minimum of three sessions, following which, the mother met the psychologist again—with, if possible, the father. Some of the children were suggested to continue with psychotherapeutic treatment for some months. In the office, toys[4] and material for graphical expression were made available to the children The psychologist asked the children if they knew why they were there, and if not, explained the concern of their parents. After that, children were told the number of times he/she would visit the office, the duration of the sessions, and that he/she could play freely with the material that was available.

The play/games, stories, and drawings discussed in this document took place in this context. Four cases, which showed in a synthetic way some type of common problem observed in the population of children that attended the psychologist's office and had more complete transcriptions, were selected. We present some fragments of the sessions with a four-year-old girl and one boy of the same age, as well as a couple of seven-year-olds. Thereafter we discuss some relevant issues on violence as perceived by children.

---

[2] 2007 National Census, poverty indicators. Instituto Nacional de Estadística e Informática del Perú (National Institute of Statistics and Informatics).

[3] The age of the women ranged between 24 and 30 years. All of them participated in research projects related to nutrition or health topics from a NGO. They had free access to the psychology, nutrition, and pediatric services that the NGO in that area offered.

[4] The toys available at the office were: a Barbie, a Ken, animals, pots, cars, trucks, a gun, and a little kitchen, among others.

Encounters with Children

He Is Going to Kill Them because He's Angry

Nelly's mother was worried and consulted the psychologist and asked for a psychological evaluation because her four-year-old daughter "*has become very fresh and grumpy.*" She also said that Nelly appeared to be too mature for her age, and spoke in a way that older girls do. When Nelly attends the office, she plays with the tricycle, drives around the table, and repeats this action: she gets on the tricycle, drives around the table, instructs the psychologist about making a drawing or cutting something with the scissors, and then drives around the table again. Each time she returns to the point she started from, she asks if the psychologist has "finished the work" and this "play" is repeated for several times. On some occasions, she gets off the tricycle and sits down to draw or cut too. In the context of this play, Nelly said:

> I'm going to go for a walk, if you are not finished by the time I come back, I'll hit you… [she drives away with the tricycle, comes back, and sits down to cut]. Do you know what my mother does?… my mother is seeing another man, and my father knows about it… and he says he's going to give her a terrible beating. [Keeps drawing]. Take this paper, you have to draw some circles there. I'm going to go for a walk, if you haven't finished by the time I come back, I'll hit you… I'll be back at eight. [She drives around the table.] I'm back, if you haven't finished… I told you I was coming back at eight, so you know… let's see… [with a face that showed surprise and seriousness]. Look what you have done! There's nothing… I'm going to help you with the half, only the half… you do the rest. [She doodles on the paper and then doodles on another one. She takes out a third paper.] Now you are going to work here.

In another visit, Nelly grabs a Barbie that is not well-dressed and spends several minutes trying to fix the Barbie's dress which is too small. Nelly says: "You can see her breasts" and then hands the doll to the psychologist for her to put it to sleep. Then Nelly says:

> My mother wants to go to bed without clothes… to sleep with her husband… Put the doll there, this is her husband, lie him down, next to her. Nelly grabs a soldier he's going to kill them because he's angry… lie him down too because he wants to sleep with them.

He's Sad

Juan Andrés, a four-year-old boy, was taken by his parents to the office for a psychological evaluation because they discovered that he had been practicing sexual games with his cousins. Both parents attend every session with the child. In one of the meetings, the psychologist asks the boy to draw a person. Spontaneously, while he's drawing, Juan Andrés mentions he's sad (referring to the drawing). However, when he gets to the mouth, he changes it: "I prefer it happy." When he finishes, the psychologist asks him to draw a woman, and while he's doing that, he comments that the lady from the drawing is crying because her son died. When he was asked about the cause of the death, Juan Andrés said that the son jumped off the roof, and then the mother had another child.

My Mom Tells Me to Keep Coming until You Can't Stand Me Anymore

Mary's mother was worried because her seven-year-old daughter didn't speak very well, but it only happened at home, not at school: "When she gets nervous, it seems that words can't come out of her mouth." She wanted Mary to have a psychological evaluation; however, she took her only for the first two appointments. Thereafter, the mother's sister, Mary's aunt, was the one taking her to the office. When the evaluation process finished, neither the mother, nor the father went to the interview to know the results. Mary continued meeting the psychologist once a week; her aunt said that Mary's mother had started to work all day, and that Mary's father was never at home, but the child insisted on being taken to the office. The reason Mary visited the psychologist's office for the next five months was because, in Mary's words: "My mother tells me to keep coming until you can't stand me anymore."

A note in the personal register of the psychologist who was in charge of Mary states:

> It's strange because the evaluation is over, but the mother and the father never came for the results. The aunt of the girl says that the mother is working all day and that the father doesn't come despite the fact I called him. The aunt is sick, she has tuberculosis and it seems that Mary is the one that arranges everything to come. Everything is very strange; I could get an appointment with a pneumologist for the aunt, but she never went. There are many things I don't understand; the only thing that is clear is that Mary wants to keep coming and she makes it. Maybe I'm wrong, but I'm not going to be the one that tells her not to come.

Mary tends to play soccer, pretends she is a hairdresser, and likes to draw. She seldom plays with dolls, but she once grabbed a doll and made her "drink" something from a glass. "Can you guess what this is?" she asked, and immediately gave a clue to the psychologist: "Li…." When the psychologist tried to complete the word by saying, "lime juice," Mary laughed and corrected her: "No…, it's liquor." She kept laughing and grabbed a clockwork ship, to which she said: "Stop," slapping it. She was laughing while doing this and, finally, she said: "Did you see? It stopped moving the third time I slapped it."

Three months later, Mary tried to draw her mother, but it seemed she couldn't draw her just like she wanted; she erased the drawing several times and expressed her irritation and concern because one arm didn't look like the other one, one hand didn't look like the other one, and the same happened with the shoes. Finally, she ended up asking the psychologist to draw for her while she describes the drawing:

> My dad is tall, blond, he has a nice shirt, a new pair of pants, and old underwear, (she laughs and continues) he wears a clean tie, he likes to smoke and drink beer… He doesn't work, but my mom is the opposite, she works all day… I prefer that because, this way, she doesn't hit me that much.

Father Was Taken to the Hospital and the Machine Emitted a Peee-Peee Sound

Carlos' mother was worried because her seven-year-old son was very aggressive at school. She said that he sometimes reacted violently at home too.

> The other day, he threw a stone at his dad and, luckily, it didn't hit him. It was because his dad and I were arguing, and Carlos was nervous, he got agitated and threw a stone at his dad.

Besides this concern, she also said that he was very absentminded, he couldn't concentrate and it seemed he was not learning. When she asks him, he knows the answers, but sometimes he doesn't answer any question in the exam. His mother says that when he comes home, it turns out that he knew the answers. Carlos attended three meetings with the psychologist. This is an excerpt from the psychologist's notes:

> In every encounter with Carlos, he takes the toys out of the box and plays, narrating a story that, to me, seems never-ending, in which the characters kill each other, they crash their cars, they destroy themselves, they have nightmares and wake up in the middle of the night, etc. For example: "… the parents of the baby elephants went to sleep, leaving them in their cribs, but at night, he a human character got into the woods, left his truck far from the place to avoid waking the animals up and stole a baby elephant. He took it to his house and cut the baby elephant with a knife; he cut it into pieces and cooked it. He ate it and then he went back to the woods to leave the little bones in the crib of the baby elephant. When the parents woke up, they just saw the little bones…" This content shocks me at first, then I am weighed down by the amount of destruction, deaths, violence, horror, and fear in it. The first time I was with Carlos, I had the fantasy that his dad or some other relative was a robber or criminal. Towards the end of that hour with him, I felt I couldn't stand the contents anymore and I started to doze.

> In another game, Carlos uses a father, a mother, and two kids that are brothers. These characters do different daily activities, like eating or going out for a walk and, as part of the game, certain things are said. For example: "…The father got sick, he was taken to the hospital and the machine emitted a peee, peee, peee, peee sound, until it emitted a peeeeeeeeeeeeeeeeee sound and a line appeared." After that, the activity of the dolls continues in a regular way, as if nothing has

happened. The psychologist who was in charge of Carlos constantly expressed her consternation and difficulty to face the content that arose in the meetings with him.

Reflections around Certain Evidences

Childcare

All the encounters with these children have been possible because their parent(s), or other close relative took them to the office. This suggests that the adults in charge of them worry about them and are interested in the welfare of the children, being able to ask for help when they have access to it. The majority of the minors who visited the psychologist were taken by their mothers. Some fathers, and other relatives like grandmothers and aunts, attended the sessions too.

In these four case excerpts, what concerns the adults is the observed behavior of their child which is interpreted as being inappropriate. This suggests that parents have criteria to analyze or evaluate the behavior of their children and direct their actions accordingly. Therefore, the necessity to explore the social representations of parents—as well as other agents of child development—about childhood and care assumes importance.

Social representations are systems of values, ideas, and practices that allow individuals to establish an order to locate themselves in their material and social world. On the other hand, they facilitate the communication among the members of a community, offering them a code for social exchange, to name and classify different aspects of their world, their history (Moscovici, 1976). Social representations have different dimensions of symbol, activity, knowledge, and practice, because all of them are demonstrations of our social life (Moscovici, 2001). Palacios and Moreno (1994) point out that the social representations are cultural premises that direct the raising and educational practices. Childhood is a reality that can be observed and, at the same time, represented by each individual and by the communities (Casas, 2006); it is not something static. We believe that it is necessary to consider not only the perspective of children, but also of the mothers, fathers, and other adults in charge of the children. They are the co-protagonists, next to the children themselves and, therefore, they are responsible for changes observed in children. We, as researchers, are forced to find new, flexible, and complex methodological strategies that give adults room to express their own issues.

Violence and Aggression

Different dimensions of the adult world emerge in the children's fantasy plays and stories: violence and aggression, illness, alcohol, and drug abuse. The children show that the care and the violence are not distinctly separate, but are part of a complex dynamic between children and parents. Nelly perceives the threats, the fear, and physical maltreatment as part of the daily relationship with her mother. However, care is also shown: Nelly's mother is also trying to make her daughter do her homework and learn, she is also the person who brought Nelly to the office for the first two times.

In the case of Carlos, we observed through his play that adults are preparing food for the children and do different activities in which care is observed. However, the violence, aggression, and destruction come to life in his game in a dramatic way. Failures are observed in the care tasks ("he stole the baby elephant") as well as concrete physical violence ("and he cut the baby elephant with a knife; he cut it into pieces and cooked it. He ate it…") and symbolic violence ("he went back to the woods to leave the little bones in the crib of the baby elephant. When the parents woke up, they just saw the little bones….")

The complex dynamic between care and violence in childcare represents a challenge for professionals who work for the welfare of childhood, particularly in the field of mental health in Peru where traditional methods of caring exist along with child-centered practices. Ames and Rojas (2010) point out that at national level, violence prevention and detection campaigns, whose emphasis is placed in the accusation, have been carried out over the past years. After seven years of work, listening to girls, boys, and their parents in the psychologist's office, we believe it is necessary to question these kinds of strategies as principal ways to face domestic violence. Any intervention planned in that way is required to consider that care and violence are related in the link of the adult–child relationship. For face up domestic violence, it is very important to develop an integrated system. When the approach is only legal this can increase violence and damages against the children (Oré, 2009).

Children and Adult Topics

Along with violence, sexuality, alcohol consumption, work, and health problems are noticeably present in the games and fantasies of the boys and girls. In their stories, the mothers and fathers take their clothes off and lie down, they have intimate encounters; they also consume alcohol, get sick, suffer, and attack each other. The psychologists who were in charge of them not only expressed their surprise, but also their confusion and difficulty to act when they were faced with these kinds of expressions. One of them wrote the following:

> I could only ask: what happened? Why did that character do that? But I didn't know what else to do. For me, an adult, it was very difficult to process what I felt when I was faced with the contents that the children explained: a mix of surprise, confusion, sorrow, and anguish, sometimes fear which, in concrete, was expressed as a "don't know what to do," "don't know what to say," and simply let the stories and games go by. I would calm myself down by thinking that the mere emergence of such content could be therapeutic.

We can say that children are growing in a familial environment where the indicated problems are not only a part of the adult world, but they go beyond that and invade the children's world. We believe that these aspects of violence are becoming part of the lives of many children although they operate in an indirect way.

In a multinational study about domestic violence carried out in ten countries,[5] they found that Peru has the highest levels of violence against women who have been linked to a man in the past. The percentage shown in the study varies according to the location, and ranges between 40 percent and 60 percent. On the other hand, in one of the few studies about child maltreatment in which boys and girls from three districts of the country were surveyed (MIMDES, 2005), it was found that 38.9 percent of the children said that there exists psychological and/or physical aggression between their parents. It is also revealed that the children who presented school backwardness mentioned violence between their parents in a higher proportion.

The few statistical indicators are relatively coincident and show that a great number of children are witness to the violence between the adults in their families.[6] Our findings are not quantitative, but they lead us to include some additional elements; violence between adults is not the only factor that impacts children, but also other phenomena related to the consumption of alcohol, diseases, and sexuality. In the games and stories that they narrate in the office, these topics emerge raw and starkly; they were difficult even for the psychologists to elaborate. In such a situation, we wonder what other spaces are available for children to reflect about their experiences, who do they talk to, and who is the person to whom they can talk about their worries and fears?

Final Reflections

There are studies about violence that have shown that children express their exposure to and experience of violence in the environment in different ways (Osofsky, 1995). They also show that there exist certain protective factors, such as the education level of the mother and the social support that she offers (Goodman and Lawrence, 2010). It has also been found that there are some factors that can protect minors, such as, if the child has at least one person that offers him/her support in his/her environment, if the child has access to a safe place to protect him/herself and has the individual resources such as intelligence, adaptation capacity (Osofsky, 1995). As risk factors, Goodman and Lawrence (2010) find that maternal depression and the fact that the mother didn't

---

[5] Bangladesh, Brazil, Ethiopia, Japan, Namibia, Peru, Samoa, Serbia and Montenegro, Thailand, and the United Republic of Tanzania (WHO, 2005).

[6] The are different surveys that show that at least one-third of the mothers with children 0 to 5-year-olds had experienced violence.

live with her mother since the day she was born, are significantly related to the representations of aggression in their children.

Drawing upon the ecological perspective proposed by different authors (Bronfenbrenner, 2001; Belsky, 1993; Heise, 1998) violence and poverty are phenomena that affect children at different levels: (*a*) individual level; (*b*) family level which includes the characteristics of the parents/adults who take care of them, the dynamics of the couple, and the family relationships in which the children are immersed; (*c*) characteristics of the community and the health and educational institutions to which they have access; and (*d*) the sociocultural context that comes to life in a particular way for every child and his/her family.

In the field of mental health, effort is made to know and understand a lot of these variables. That is, how the education, the social support, and the mental health of the mother seem to be key elements in the protection of boys and girls. In a country like Peru, where psychological instruments adapted for our complex reality are scarce, and there is also a cultural diversity that makes the generalization of any result difficult—if not impossible—it is very important to observe and listen to the children, as well as to their parents.

Despite the problems that the mothers face daily, we observe their initiative to take their children to the psychologist's office. Some of them are even able to recognize and accept that they hit their own children. These elements are fundamental for any program that attends to the welfare of children and their families. On the other hand, the boys and girls show a great capacity to express and share their experiences and fears. They are the protagonists and agents of their own change; they also need adults to be interested in their development, to listen, and to offer them spaces in their own communities to express themselves. It is fundamental to understand and consider that the boys and girls can't be excluded from the alternatives in favor of their own welfare. They are a powerful resource for social change.

From the children themselves we found that they are protected and at the same time abused by their main caretakers; also, that the children are participating in adult dynamics related to sexuality, diseases, and financial problems. They are also witnesses to and part of the problems present in the couple and in the family, such as aggression and violence between adults, the consumption of alcohol and drugs, as well as delinquency. All this has a direct impact on children, but they also have a few spaces to talk and share their experiences, ask some questions, and explain their fears and concerns. Their symptoms, games, and stories reflect that their behavior and actions are a way to express their unease. Such expression is effective because mothers are concerned by it and they take the children to the psychologist's office. However, the use of words is minimal which raises the question whether it is difficult for children to express themselves verbally? Or, is it that the adult caretakers are not responding to this way of communication and the children are therefore forced to "act out" or "talk with their bodies?"

Domestic violence corresponds to a private field and does not always reach the ear of public knowledge (Narayan, 2000; Mannarelli, 2002). However, people have been trying to reverse this situation with massive prevention campaigns, and like Ames and Rojas (2010) point out, nowadays, there are many organizations in Peru that contribute to the detection of domestic violence, but there are only a few that offer psychological treatment to the victims. For Dughi (2002) and Ames and Rojas (2010), this reflects the invisibility of the problem of violence against children and the lack of political will or the capacity of the government to provide the services that are needed in the solution of the problem. This is evident although the regulatory proposal of the Peruvian government holds the same views with the Convention on the Rights of the Child and other international agreements about childhood. The Political Constitution of Peru, the Children's and Adolescents' Code[7], and the National Plan of Action for Children and Adolescents 2002–2010 (NPAIA, 2002–2010) are some of the documents that the country's legal framework offers in relation to childhood. They explain that childhood should be protected and treated with care but, unfortunately, the reality is very different from what regulations indicate. This is also a topic for future studies. This topic is closely related to violence, and it pertains not only to children but is also observed in adults. If we take the concerns of children as a starting point, more questions than answers emerge. Perhaps that would be their best way to communicate how they are feeling: with questions that don't have a place to be asked or a person to answer them. From here on, a way to contribute to their welfare will be to open safe spaces for dialogue and expression.

References

Alva, J. (2000). *Una experiencia local de salud para tod@s*. Lima. Organismo de Coordinación Permanente en Salud OCP San Juan de Lurigancho.

Ames, P., & Rojas, V. (2010). *Infancia, transiciones y bienestar en el Perú: Una revisión bibliográfica*. Lima: GRADE, Niños del Milenio.

Bardales, O., & Huallpa, E. (2005). *Maltrato y Abuso Sexual en Niñas, Niños y Adolescentes: Estudio realizado en los distritos de San Martín de Porres, Cusco e Iquitos*. Ministerio de la Mujer y Desarrollo Social (MIMDES). Programa Nacional contra la Violencia Familiar y Sexual.

Belsky, J. (1993). Etiology of child maltreatment: A developmental-ecological analysis. *Psychological Bulletin, 114*(3), 413–434.

Bronfenbrenner, U. (2001). *The bioecological theory of human development*. In U. Bronfenbrenner (Ed.), *Making human beings human: Bioecological perspectives on human development* (pp. 3–15). Thousand Oaks, CA: SAGE.

Casas, F. (2006). Infancia y representaciones sociales. *Política y Sociedad, 43* (1), 27–42.

Dughi, P. (2002). *Estigmas y Silencios: Salud mental y violencia contra la infancia en el Perú*. En: Políticas Públicas e Infancia en el Perú. Save the Children—UK. Lima, Perú. Marzo del 2002.

Goodman, G., & Lawrence, J. (2010). Predictors of representational aggression in preschool children of low-income urban African American adolescent mothers. *Infant Mental Health Journal, 31*(1), 33–57. doi:10.1002/imhj.20241

---

[7]Enacted on December 24, 1992.

Grantham-McGregor, S., Cheung, Y. B., Cueto, S., Glewwe, P., Richter, L., Strupp, B., and the International Child Development Steering Group. (2007). Child development in developing countries: Developmental potential in the first 5 years for children in developing countries. *Lancet, 369*, 60–70.

Heise, L. (1998). Violence against women: An integrated, ecological framework. *Violence against Women, 4*, 262–290.

Herrera, J. (2001). *Nuevas Estimaciones de la Pobreza en el Perú, 1997–2000*. Lima: INEI, IRD

Manarelli, M. (2002). *La infancia y la configuración de los vínculos en el Perú. Un enfoque histórico*. En: Políticas Públicas e Infancia en el Perú. Recomendaciones de Política. Niños del Milenio y Save the Children.

MIMDES. (2005). *Maltrato y abuso sexual en niños, niñas y adolescentes. Una aproximación desde los casos atendidos en los Centros de Emergencia Mujer*. Programa Nacional contra la Violencia Familiar y Sexual.

———. (2006). *Estado de las investigaciones sobre violencia familiar y sexual en el Perú. Período 2001-2005*. Olga Bardales. Ministerio de la Mujer y Desarrollo Social (MIMDES). Lima.

MINSA. (2004). *Lineamientos para la acción en salud mental*. Ministerio de Salud del Perú, Consejo Nacional de Salud, Comité Nacional de Salud Mental. Lima, Perú.

———. (2005). *Estrategia Sanitaria Nacional de Salud Mental y Cultura de Paz*. Plan General 2005–2010. Lima, Perú.

Minujin, A. (2005). *Children living in poverty. A review of child poverty definitions, measurements, and policies*. UNICEF'S conference on children and poverty: Global context, local solutions. New School. April 25–27.

———. (2010). *¿Por qué se diferencia la pobreza infantil de la pobreza que afecta a los adultos?* Desafíos, Boletín de la Infancia y adolescencia sobre el avance de los objetivos de desarrollo del Milenio. N°10, mayo. Naciones Unidas, CEPAL y UNICEF.

Moscovici, S. (1976). *Social influence and social change*. Londres. Academic Press.

———. (2001). *Social representations: Explorations in social psychology*. New York: New York University Press.

Municipal Council of San Juan de Lurigancho. (2011). Retrieved from http://www.munisjl.gob.pe/

Narayan, D. (2000). *Voices of the poor: Can anyone hear us?* Washington, DC: Oxford University Press.

Niños del Milenio. (2003). *Estudio internacional sobre pobreza infantil, Perú. Informe Nacional Preliminar 2003*. Versión 31 julio 2003. IIN, GRADE, SC UK.

OMS. (2004). *Invertir en salud mental*. Impreso en Suiza.

Oré, B. (2009). *Habla mujer: Narrativas íntimas de un grupo de mujeres que acude a un consultorio psicológico en San Juan de Lurigancho*. Revista Ius Et Veritas N°39, PUCP, año 2009.

Osofsky, J. D. (1995). The effects of exposure to violence on young children. *American Psychologist*, 50, 782–788.

Palacois, J., & Moreno, C. (1994). Contexto familiar y desarrollo social. En M. J. Rodrigo (Ed.), *Contexto y desarrollo social*. Madrid: Sintesis.

Pollitt, E. (2002). *Consecuencias de la desnutrición en el escolar peruano*. Lima: Fondo Editorial de la Pontificia Universidad Católica del Perú.

Roca Rey, B. (2003). *¿Por qué y cómo escuchar la opinión de los pobres?* En: Buscando el bienestar de los pobres. ¿Cuán lejos estamos? Editores: Enrique.

Roca Rey, I., & Rojas, B. (2002). *Pobreza y exclusión social: una aproximación al caso peruano*. En J. Herrera (Ed.), Pobreza y desigualdad en el área andina. Elementos para un nuevoparadigma. fIFEA: Bulletin de l'Institut Francais d'Etudes Andines *31*(3). Vásquez y Diego Winkelried. Lima, Universidad del Pacífico.

Salazar, X., Arias, R., Pareja, V., & Aramburú, C. (2006). *Dando voz a los niños*. Lima, Redess Jovenes y Niños del Milenio. 2 de Marzo del 2006.

WHO. (2005). *WHO multi-country study on women's health and domestic violence against women*. Geneva: World Health Organization.

22

Mental Health of Children and Adolescents in Contemporary India

Usha S. Nayar
Shankar Das

Context

India is one of the world's most populous regions with a population of 1.21 billion. India is home to 400 million children below the age of 18 years which constitute approximately 40 percent of its population. India is home to almost 19 percent of the world's children. The children in India face a multifaceted exclusion from birth to adulthood because of a number of factors. The problems for many Indian children begin antenatally either due to lack of care or poor maternal nutrition or poor physical health. The problems continue after birth as well. Nearly one-third of newly born children weigh less than 2.5 kilograms. Around half the child populace under 3 years of age is undernourished. Physical illness like diarrhea and fever are widespread. Sadly, one-tenth of the children die before they reach five years of age (Drèze, Khera, & Narayanan, 2007). The performance on education, another key indicator of development, is also poor. The literacy percentage of population above 7 years of age is 65, of which the share of girls is much less (54 percent) than that of boys (76 percent) (GOI, 2002). India is struggling to improve the basic indicators of child development and ranks 100 out of 137 countries on the Child Development Index (Save the Children, 2008). (The Child Development Index is made up of three indicators of three areas of child wellbeing: health, nutrition, and education.)

One of major reasons for missing out on developmental opportunities is poverty. The World Bank (2010) opines that poverty is still a major challenge for India. The revised estimates reveal that 37.2 percent of the population (about 410 million people) remains poor, making India home to one third of the world's poor people. There have been a number of studies to prove a relationship between poverty and child development in India (e.g., Rose-Jacobs et al., 2008; Black et al., 2004). In addition to the lack of basic services like education and health, the vulnerabilities come in other forms like child labor, trafficking, physical, mental and sexual abuse, child marriages, and social exclusion and discrimination. The vulnerabilities cited here and related difficult circumstances, as well as children suffering due to natural disasters and sociopolitical conflicts render the children and adolescents to risks of mental health problems. Moreover, the considerable stigma attached to mental disorders, lack of information regarding mental illness and available help and treatment (Indian Council of Medical Research [ICMR], 2005) further complicate the situation in India.

Despite the strong commitment to child protection enshrined in the Indian Constitution and child related policies, the country's progeny is at profound risk. The mental health problems cause great suffering to the child, their families, and communities and great loss to the society and nation. Although there has been a paradigm shift in construction of childhood, where a child is now considered an individual in his/her own right, we need to examine how far this has been put to practice in the everyday life of children in India. A healthy childhood lays the foundation for a healthy adulthood. Children and adolescents are valuable assets to families and nations and thus their overall well-being is a matter of grave concern. This chapter shall elucidate the context of Indian children, the policy, and practices of mental health development and theorize the process of effective service delivery which is a real challenge in terms of the large young population in need.

Scenario

It is estimated that 10 percent of children in the 5–15 age group have a diagnosable mental health disorder. There are 50 million children under 18 years who could benefit from specialist services. As regards adolescents, 20 million are projected to have a severe mental disorder. Unfortunately, 90 percent of children with a mental health disorder are not receiving any specialist services (Shastri, 2009).

The prevalence rates of psychiatric disorders among children range from 2.6 percent to 35.6 percent (Ahmad, Khalique, Khan, & Amir, 2007; Anita, Gaur, Vohra, Subash, & Khurana, 2003; Hackett, Hackett, Bhakta, & Gowers, 1999; Deivasigamini, 1990; Lal & Sethi, 1977). Bansal and Burman (2011) have reported a prevalence rate of 20.2 percent with most children in the age group of 13–14 years, belonging to middle income group and second in birth order. ICMR (2001) reports a prevalence rate of 12.8 percent among children and adolescents in the age group of 1 to 16 years. Another study by ICMR (2005) indicates that 33 percent in the 0–5 age group suffered from hyperkinetic syndrome. In the 6–11 years age group the common diagnoses included hysterical neurosis, hyperkinetic syndrome, and conduct disorders; in the 12–16 age group, psychosis, hysterical neurosis, and conduct disorders. While psychoses and conduct disorder cases were more common in males, hysterical neurosis cases were more common among female children. Amongst children attending psychiatric/child guidance clinics, 22 percent children in the 0–5 age group, 19 percent in the 6–11 age group, and 6 percent in children of 12–16 years age group suffered from mild mental retardation. Keeping in mind that almost half of India's billion are children and adolescents (Sen, 2003), it makes it imperative for the state to look into their mental health needs for securing a bright future for them, their families, and nation.

Status of Mental Health Services

The divergence of child and adolescent mental health services from the adult mental health services is relatively a recent development. Historically, there is no evidence of any specialized services to children and adolescents. Nonetheless, it may be interesting to note the evolution of mental health services in the country.

Tuli and Alam (2004) have traced the mental health service provision to the colonial period. Though mental hospitals were erected since 1787 at various places, it was not until 1817 that efforts were made to improve the living conditions by Sergeant Bredmore in Kolkata. Other major developments included enactment of Lunacy Act in 1858 where the procedures for establishment of mental hospitals and admitting patients were laid out. The next two decades witnessed an increasing growth in the number of these hospitals. However, these institutions attracted considerable criticism for their living conditions and treatment modalities of the inpatients. Thus, in 1906 central supervision was contemplated for these hospitals and the charge was shifted from the Inspector General of Prisons to Civil Surgeons of the Indian Medical Services.

At the time of India's Independence, psychiatrists were appointed as fulltime medical officers to these hospitals; for a population of 300 million there were 10,000 psychiatric beds. The real difference came with the initiation of community psychiatry in 1,975 (Murthy, 2011). The National Mental Health Program has been a milestone in the history of mental health services. There were three major objectives of the program: ensuring availability and accessibility to minimum mental health care for all, encouraging mental health knowledge and skills in the general health stream, and promoting community participation and mobilizing community resources in mental health service development (National Institute of Health and Family Welfare, 2009). Barua (2009) contends that though the implementation of NMHP was good initially, over time the efforts reduced resulting in limited expansion. Thara and Patel (2010) reason out this poor outreach of the program to its innate nature, which is biomedical—medicines were prescribed only at the health centers.

Mental health services for child and adolescent are very limited in India. It is reported that such services are restricted to urban areas, accessible only to tiny proportion of children and adolescents, not provided early enough, and are substandard in nature (Shastri, 2009). The first child guidance clinic (later named *Muskaan* meaning smile) in the country was started in 1937 at the Tata Institute of Social Sciences, Mumbai. However, such clinics could not spread uniformly across the country. Of the reported 100 CGCs in the country, most are concentrated in the large cities of certain states. The largest service provision for child mental health is at the National Institute of Mental Health and Neuro Sciences (NIMHANS) in Bengaluru (Kapur, 2005). The child and adolescent psychiatry services began in 1950s at NIMHANS with a threefold aim of catering to the mental health needs of children and adolescents, training professionals, and facilitating research in the area. The clientele is from the age group of 0–16 years which get clinical treatment for common developmental disorders (e.g., autism, mental retardation, and learning disorders) and mental health disorders (e.g., ADHD, mood disorders, obsessive-compulsive disorders, emotional, and behavioral problems). All inpatient, outpatient, and emergency services are available in the hospital. In addition, advocacy for the cause of child and adolescent mental health in partnership with NGOs, Child Welfare Committee, and Childline India Network is also a major activity.

There are however various views regarding the history of child mental health services in India. Apart from the account that we have presented, some authors contend (see Shah & Sheth, 1998) that child mental health services began in the late 1950s when indigenous knowledge developed after independence from colonial rule. Regardless of when these services were initiated, even the present reality is not very satisfying.

Presently, the services are provided at tertiary care centers where a clinical model is followed. There is a huge gap in areas of prevention, promotion, and early intervention (Shastri, 2009). There is a great urban–rural divide when it comes to sharing of health infrastructure, trained personnel, and other health resources. The urban areas get a massive share of 75 percent even when only 27 percent of the population lives there. In terms of mental health resources, India has 0.25 beds per 10,000 population (0.2 in mental hospitals and 0.05 in general hospitals). There are only 0.2 psychiatrists per 100,000 population which amounts to an acute shortage (WHO, 2006).

Contributions of School in Mental Health Program

Schools play a pivotal role in identifying and meeting the mental health needs of students (Substance Abuse Mental Health Services Administration, 2003). In several states in India, school mental health programs have proved to be effective in terms of its preventative and promotive value. The programs have mainly dealt with emotional and behavioral problems of students before they advance into diagnosable disorders. Many experts believe that school mental health programs help in detecting early symptoms and treating the psychological problems in school children. However, the significance of mental health promotion in schools is not uniformly recognized in the mental health arena as many consider that meager financial resources could instead be effectively utilized to provide treatment to people with mental disorders. Due to paucity as well as absence of earmarked funds for school mental health programs in the country, such initiatives are scanty and sporadic in nature. Often implementers experience challenges and difficulties in maintaining the stability of such initiatives. For example, the Maharashtra Institute of Mental

Health reported that the school mental health program was discontinued due to lack of funds and no budgetary provision from the government (Isalkar, 2010). It has been observed that the department of psychiatry in public hospitals generously extended resources and initiated school mental health programs as part of community outreach in several states. However, several factors such as overcrowding of patients in the hospital, heavy workload, and lack of human/material resources have made it cumbersome to maintain continuity of school mental health programs in the community.

Many Indian schools also promote traditional practices, such as yoga and meditation in the promotion of mental and physical well-being of children, although there are no clear statistics. These century-old practices are now being recognized within the school program as being effective in promoting overall growth and development of children. However, these have certainly not been used universally as an important measure for the promotion of mental health of children in all schools.

In addition to treatment and care of mental disorders, the national mental health programs and policies in India should recognize and address the broader issues that promote mental health. School mental health programs may be considered as a cost-effective intersectoral strategy and intervention that may be implemented in all school settings in the country.

Traditional Mental Health Resources

In many cultures, people turn to neo-spiritual and alternative healing practices for physical and mental well-being in keeping with the belief that the human being is the unity of mind, body, and spirit as espoused by our Indian society (Das, 2003). From time immemorial people of all faiths turned to religious and sacred places for help and relief in emotional distress and various mental health problems.

Interestingly, it is believed in India that the place of worship provides an alternative to psychiatric treatment for mental illnesses. The alternative approaches to mental disorders that are prevalent may be a result of a traditional set of beliefs and paucity of public mental health services. Raguram, Venkateswaran, Ramakrishna, and Weiss (2002) indicated that the therapeutic value recognized with "temple healing" may be present in the location itself, and not because of any treatment or charisma of any religious priest in the site. The healing process may be a result of supportive, non-threatening, and reassuring environment within the temple, as compared to the treatment provided in psychiatric settings. Notable improvements reported by people with mental illness without any psychopharmacological and other somatic interventions calls for research to explore merits of temple healing.

In recent years, mental health professionals have adopted multimethod based practice which has a spiritual component as well. This newer approach is becoming popular in various mental health settings in the country such as schools, child and adolescent guidance centers, correctional settings, community health centers, vocational/career guidance centers, de-addiction centers, and crisis interventions centers. The edifice of such a system of therapeutic interventions encompasses a whole range of practices that may include alternative healing, yoga, meditation, and so on. As an example, children can be introduced to yoga, a psycho-physiologic technique developed during ancient time in India. Yoga has been recognized in numerous behavioral and clinical studies; recent research has focused on the adaptive effects of yoga on the brain (Ganesan, 2010). The participatory experience of yoga through a variety of techniques such as *asanas* (body positions), *mudras* (hand positions), meditation, *kriyas* (internal cleansing processes) such as *pranayama* (breathing exercise), and exploration of bodily sensations and impulses are employed in the treatment (Das, 2003). The Advanced Center for Yoga—Mental Health and Neuro Sciences at NIMHANS integrates yoga as a complementary therapy in the treatment and care of mental patients including children and their caregivers admitted to the Child and Adolescent Psychiatry Unit. Yoga therapy is particularly provided to patients with depression and caregivers of patients with schizophrenia.

There are some factors within Indian culture which play a positive role in mental health. For instance, prayers and religious rituals play a significant role in socializing its members; during various family occasions and the school assembly, children are taught inspiring prayers and motivational songs. In all faiths, prayer is believed to be powerful and effective in achieving mental peace.

Along with the spiritual belief and healing of mental health disorders, there are other alternative systems for treatment which are quite popular. India has developed and retained diverse systems of health services delivery over a period of time. These alternate systems of health coexist with the general health system. A considerable population both in urban and rural areas believes in and visits the religious, Ayurvedic, Unani, traditional healers, and homeopaths for general and mental health problems of children and adolescents. The Department of AYUSH (Ayurveda, Yoga and Naturopathy, Unani, Siddha, and Homoeopathy) was created by the central government's Ministry of Health and Family Welfare in 2003 with the aim to provide concerted attention to development of education, research and upgradation in these alternative systems.

Contribution of Nongovernmental Organizations in Mental Health Service Delivery

In the context of service provision, the contribution of the nongovernmental organizations cannot be overlooked. Thara and Patel (2010) highlight the role of NGOs in providing mental health services which are clubbed in four major areas: treatment, care and rehabilitation; community-based activities and prevention; research and training; and advocacy and empowerment. Though the action of NGOs is more localized and cannot match the reach of the government programs, their quality of care and dedication toward the cause is unparalleled. They submit that most likely the oldest NGOs are those which are working in the area of child mental health and more specifically in the field of mental retardation. However, the concept of child mental health has broadened to include more common problems such as autism, hyperactivity, and conduct disorders.

There is noteworthy contribution from the NGO sector in the areas of school mental health. For instance, the School Health Annual Report Program (SHARP) is a nongovernmental organization with the largest school health network in India. It promotes healthy lifestyle among school going children through school health awareness and checkup programs in public and private schools in Delhi, Mumbai, Chennai, Bengaluru, Hyderabad, and other metropolitan cities as well as some rural areas of the country. Importantly, psychological counseling provided by its qualified professionals helps school children with various psychological problems such as depression, adjustment problems, scholastic difficulties, problems of daily living, and in curtailing the school dropouts. The Promise Foundation in Bengaluru provides counseling services to underprivileged school going children with a special focus on career guidance and training teachers in career guidance. There are many popular and innovative telephonic helpline services that have been initiatives in the country; Childline brought hope to millions of children in distress that deserves special mention. It is a toll-free round-the-clock emergency phone number service for the children in need of aid and assistance. The program is supported by the Government of India, NGOs, the corporate sector, and UNICEF. This service also liaises with other community services for their long-term care and rehabilitation.

Another area that NGOs have significantly contributed in is preparation of training materials, training human resource personnel, service providers, as well as organizing direct services to children and adolescents during disasters. Trauma, fear, anxiety, sadness, repetitive thoughts, flashback about the events, stress, depression, other emotional reactions, and psychosocial adverse impacts are experienced by child and adolescent survivors during and post-disaster situations when they witness the loss of their near and dear ones. The sudden onset of unanticipated natural disasters, political conflicts, or war situations create psychological stress amongst young people. Rescue, relief, rehabilitation, and rebuilding are the key phases of disasters during which psychosocial care is to be provided to survivors. Sekar (2006), in his report on psychosocial support following the tsunami in 2005, stated that disasters are abnormal situations and the responses of survivors can be considered normal. Consequently, the approach of interventions should be to normalize coping patterns and encourage the survivors to gain control of the situation—rather than one of mental illness.

Mental Health Policy

India is amongst the nations which do not have a mental health policy for children and adolescents. However, there are a number of policy commitments for overall development and wellbeing of children. Some major ones include National Policy for Children, 1974; National Policy on Education,1986; National Policy on Child Labour, 1987; National Nutrition Policy, 1993;

National Health Policy, 2002; National Charter for Children, 2004; and National Plan of Action for Children, 2005. It is pacifying to find direct reference of mental health issues in the National Health Policy which envisages a network of decentralized mental health services involving the diagnosis of common disorders, and the prescription of common therapeutic drugs, by general duty medical staff. The policy also focuses on upgrading the physical infrastructure of mental health institutions for securing the human rights of people with mental health problems (National Health Policy, 2002).

The National Policy for Children lays down that all children are a "supremely important asset" and the State shall provide all adequate services for their complete physical, mental, and social development. The relatively recent plan of action for children includes goals, objectives, strategies, and activities for overall well-being of Indian children aimed at improving nutritional status, reducing infant mortality rate, increasing enrollment ratio, reducing dropout rates, universalization of primary education, and increasing coverage for immunization.

The Integrated Child Protection Scheme (ICPS) was approved by the government in 2009 translates the vision of a protective environment into practice putting together existing dispersed initiatives under one umbrella of ICPS. Various initiatives related to child protection aspects were brought under one umbrella of ICPS. The significant change in this scheme is that it focuses on quality care and capacity building of all stakeholders.

Additionally discussions are underway for formulation of a comprehensive mental health policy. Recently, the Ministry of Health and Family Welfare has constituted a policy group to prepare a National Mental Health Policy and Plan (Mental Health Policy Group, 2011). The broad objectives include preparing a situational analysis of the mental health care and service provision of the country, draft a National Mental Health Care Policy and Plan which is in consonance with the existing National Mental Health Program and the District Mental Health Program, and take into consideration the draft Mental Health Care Act in order to make the two complementary. It would also take into account the varying mental health needs of children and adolescents and lay out clear guidelines for action.

There is also a need to refer to the guidance package (WHO, 2005) with a call for nations to develop a comprehensive mental health policy for children and adolescents. National governments are urged to develop adequate policies in order to make the mental health care systems effective, affordable, and accessible. Figure 22.1 illustrates the various steps for developing an effective mental health policy for children and adolescents. The initial step involves gathering specific data for policy development, which encompasses the prevalence of mental health disorders and psychological issues among children and adolescents infected/affected by the disease. The second step involves critically examining the literature on pilot projects and programs which may provide useful guidelines for developing the policy. The policy must also define the various areas for action like financing, organization of services, promotion, prevention, treatment and rehabilitation, intersectorial collaboration, advocacy, legislation and human rights, human resources and training, quality improvement, information systems, research, and evaluation of policies and

Figure 22.1 Steps for Developing an Effective National Child and Adolescent Mental Health Policy

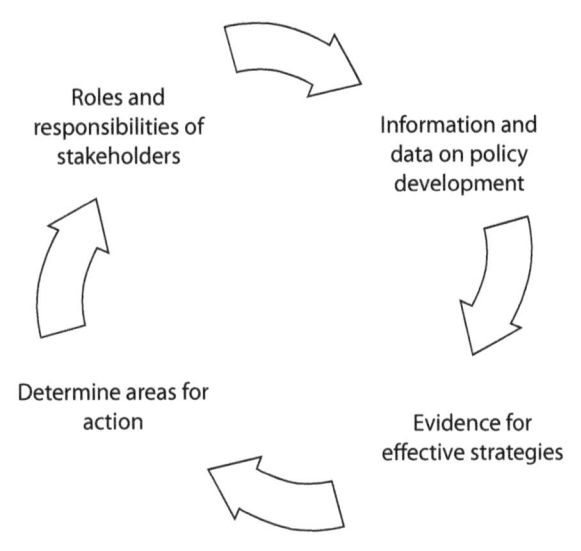

Source: Adapted from WHO (2005).

services. Finally, the roles and responsibilities of all the stakeholders must be clearly delineated for successful implementation.

Legislations

Mental health legislation is concerned with (*a*) rights of the mentally ill (right to care and human rights), (*b*) quality of care, (*c*) the use of administrative and budget control measures, and (*d*) consumer participation and involvement in the organization and management of mental health care services (Bertolote, 1995). In India there are a few legislations which encompass aspects of mental health (Math & Nagaraja, 2008):

- Narcotic Drugs & Psychotropic Substances Act, 1985 (NDPS, 1985)
- Mental Health Act, 1987(MHA, 1987)
- Rehabilitation Council of India Act, 1992 (RCI, 1992)
- Persons with Disabilities (Equal Opportunities, Protection of Rights and Full Participation) Act, 1995 (PWD, 1995)
- Juvenile Justice (Care and Protection of Children) Act, 2000 (JJA, 2000)
- National Trust for Welfare of Persons with Autism, Cerebral Palsy, Mental Retardation and Multiple Disabilities Act, 1999 (NTA, 1999)
- Protection of Women from Domestic Violence Act, 2005 (DMV, 2005)

We focus on few primary Acts which are more relevant for the paper and would help in building the discourse. India had enacted the Mental Health Act in 1987 with an aim to simplify admission and discharge procedures, providing separate facilities to children (>16 years) and drug users, and upholding the rights of the mentally ill. The Act attracted a number of criticisms, the principal being the emphasis on inpatient care in licensed institutions. Murthy (2010) has critiqued the Act and pointed out its: (*a*) omission of mental retardation and personality disorders altogether, (*b*) retention of the traditional belief that persons with mental illness are dangerous and mental illness is incurable, (*c*) complete neglect of community based health care, and (*d*) failure to address the issues of social stigma.

The PWD Act 1995 defined mental retardation and mental illness amongst the seven disabilities. Though there has been a misconception of mental illness as a disability among policy makers, the scenario is gradually changing (Math & Nagaraja, 2008). This Act was promulgated to ensure equal opportunities for all people with disabilities in areas of education, employment, vocational training, job reservation, and research and manpower development. Unfortunately, there are a number of pitfalls in the Act (see Sinha, 2009); a significant one being the complete silence on the aftercare management of vulnerable groups like children.

The Juvenile Justice Act (2000) is a comprehensive law relating to juveniles in conflict with law and children in need of care and protection by providing for proper care, protection, and treatment by catering to their development needs in a child-friendly approach. It aims towards social integration of all children coming under the purview of this Act through restoration (re-integration with families), adoption, foster care, sponsorships, and after-care homes. The Act also advocates for the collaborative functioning of various stakeholder groups like governmental and nongovernmental agencies and families. However, there are apparent weaknesses like relying on same custodial institutions which have been accused of maltreatment and abuse of children (Math & Nagaraja, 2008).

As pointed out, that there are a number of legislations which directly or indirectly protect the rights of the children and adolescents and lay guidelines for service delivery. Nonetheless, there are unaddressed loopholes, hurdles in getting them fully implemented, and interpreting them for the benefit of children and adolescents with mental health problems.

Child and Adolescent Mental Health: Implications for Policy

A vast majority children and adolescents in India lack basic amenities of education and health and are susceptible to adverse circumstances. In addition, in many cases the familial influences and life events like parental divorce, crisis and bereavement, disability, and so on, significantly affect mental health of children and adolescents. These adverse events assume etiological importance in particular sociocultural contexts (Bansal & Barman, 2011). Patel, Flisher, Hetrick, & McGorry (2007) narrate that poor mental health and development concerns like lower educational achievements, substance abuse, and violence in young people are strongly correlated. They also report suicide as the leading cause of death in young people along with self-harm tendencies.

The mental health policies in the country are not getting implemented effectively due to lack of sensitivity regarding mental health issues in India and shortage of adequate resources and trained personnel to carry out the provisions of such policies. Moreover, the availability of counseling and psychiatric services is inadequate (Das & Leibowitz, 2011). Thus, we need a comprehensive policy and services for prevention and promotion of mental health and treatment of mental illness among children and adolescents in India.

Figure 22.2 illustrates the integration of three main elements for formulation of a mental health policy. These elements ensure the basic rights of survival, development, protection, and participation of all children thereby reducing vulnerability and promoting mental health. In addition to

Figure 22.2   Elements for a Mental Health Policy for Children and Adolescents in India

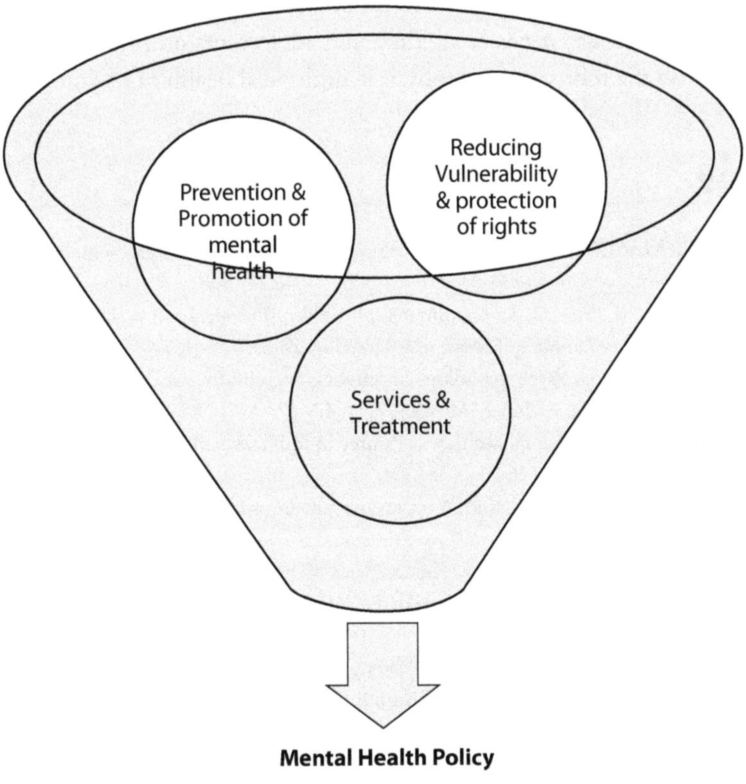

Source: Authors.

providing treatment and services to children and adolescents, it is equally important to undertake prevention and promotion activities in order to mitigate harm. There is also a need to shift focus from the biomedical model to community based approaches which offer better outreach. Shastri (2009) has highlighted the importance of five sectors for good child and adolescent mental health services: early years, school years, community based needs, additional and support needs, and children in need of special care. Thus, the policy must offer coverage to the listed components and there must be strong mechanisms for effective implementation.

Conclusion

Keeping in mind the diversity and disparity of children and adolescents in the country due to their family background, the mental health services are to be provided accordingly. For school-going children, the provision of quality mental health services, preventive and promotive, may be more effectively arranged through schools. For out-of-school children in urban areas as well as children living in rural areas, community-outreach quality mental health services may be organized using both modern and traditional methodologies. The current mental health policy under development, must address the mental health needs of children and adolescents on priority basis as the country's future is dependent on the robust mental, physical, and social health of its young generation.

References

Ahmad, A., Khalique, N., Khan, Z., & Amir, A. (2007). Prevalence of psychosocial problems among school going male adolescents. *Indian Journal of Community Medicine, 32*(3), 219–221. doi:10.4103/0970-0218.36836

Anita, Gaur, D. R., Vohra, A. K., Subash, S., & Khurana, H. (2003). Prevalence of psychiatric morbidity among 6 to 14 years old children. *Indian Journal of Community Medicine, 28*(3), 133–137.

Bansal, P. D., & Barman, R. (2011). Psychopathology of school going children in the age group of 10-15 years. *International Journal of Applied & Basic Medical Research, 1*(1), 43–47. doi:10.4103/2229-516X.81980

Barua, A. (2009). Need for a realistic mental health programme in India. *Indian Journal of PsychologicalMedicine, 31*(1), 48–49. doi:10.4103/0253-7176.53316

Bertolote, J. M. (1995). Mental health legislation: A review of some international experiences. *Revista de Saúde Pública, 29*(2), 152–156.

Black, M. M., Sazawal, S., Black, R. E., Khosla, S., Kumar, J., & Menon, V. (2004). Cognitive and motor development among small-for-gestational-age infants: Impact of zinc supplementation, birth weight, and caregiving practices. *Pediatrics, 113*(5), 1297–1305.

Das, S. (2003). Holistic counseling for health and well-being. In H. L. Kaila & K. B. Kushal (Eds), *Towards development with young people*. Mumbai: Himalayan Publishing House.

Das, S., & Leibowitz, G. S. (2011). Mental health needs of people living with HIV/AIDS in India: A literature review. *AIDS Care, 23*(4), 417–425. doi:10.1080/09540121.2010.507752

Deivasigamani, T. R. (1990). Psychiatric morbidity in primary school children: An epidemiological study. *Indian Journal of Psychiatry, 32*(3), 235–240.

Drèze, J., Khera, R., & Narayanan, S. (2007). Early childhood in India: Facing the facts. *Indian Journal of Human Development, 1*(2), 377–388.

Ganesan. V. (2010). Yoga: Adaptive effects on brain biology. *Samatvam, 2*(5), 2. Retrieved from http://www.nimhans.kar.nic.in/yoga/samatvam2_5.pdf

Government of India. Department of Women and Child Development, Ministry of Human Resource Development. (2002). *The Indian child: A profile.* Retrieved from http://wcd.nic.in/indianchild/index.htm

Hackett, R., Hackett, L., Bhakta, P., & Gowers, S. (1999). The prevalence and association of psychiatric disorders in children in Kerala, South India. *Journal of Child Psychology and Psychiatry, 40*(5), 801–807. doi:10.1111/1469-7610.00495

Indian Council of Medical Research. (2001). *Epidemiological study of child and adolescent psychiatric disorders in urban and rural areas* [unpublished data]. New Delhi: Indian Council of Medical Research.

———. (2005). *Mental health research in India* (Technical Monograph on ICMR Mental Health Studies). Retrieved from http://www.icmr.nic.in/publ/Mental%20Helth%20.pdf

Isalkar, U. (2010, October 26). Funds squeeze derails mental health programme in civic schools. *The Times of India.* Retrieved from http://articles.timesofindia.indiatimes.com/2010-1026/pune/28219815_1_mental-health-programme-civic-schools-school-dropouts

Kapur, M. (2005). An integrated approach to the delivery of child mental health services. *Journal of Indian Association for Child and Adolescent Mental Health, 1*(1), 4.

Lal, N., & Sethi, B. B. (1977). Estimate of mental ill health in children of an urban community. *Indian Journal of Paediatrics, 44*(3), 55–64.

Math, S. B., & Nagaraja, D. (2008). Mental health legislation: An Indian perspective. In D. Nagaraja & P. Murthy (Eds), *Mental health care and human rights* (pp. 49–68). New Delhi: National Human Rights Commission.

Mental Health Policy Group. (2011). *About the mental health policy group.* Retrieved from http://mhpolicy.org/

Murthy, P. (2010) The Mental Health Act 1987: Quo Vadimus? *Indian Journal of Medical Ethics, 7*(3), 152–156.

Murthy, S. R. (2011). Mental health initiatives in India (1947–2010). *The National Medical Journal of India, 24*(2), 98–107.

National Health Policy. (2002). Ministry of Health and Family Welfare, Government of India. Available at http://www.mohfw.nic.in/NRHM/Documents/National_Health_policy_2002.pdf

National Institute of Health and Family Welfare. (2009). National mental health programme. Retrieved from http://www.nihfw.org/NDC/DocumentationServices/NationalHealthProgramme/NATIONALMENTALHEALTHPROGRAMME.html

Patel, V., Flisher A. J., Hetrick, S., & McGorry, P. (2007). Mental health of young people: A global public-health challenge. *Lancet, 369*(9569), 1302–1313. doi:10.1016/S0140-6736(07)60368-7

Raguram, R., Venkateswaran, A., Ramakrishna, J., & Weiss, M. G. (2002). Traditional community resources for mental health: A report of temple healing from India. *British Medical Journal, 325*(7354), 38–40. doi:10.1136/bmj.325.7354.38

Rose-Jacobs, R., Black, M. M., Casey, P. H., Cook, J. T., Cutts, D. B., Chilton, M., Heeren, T., & Frank, D. A. (2008). Household food insecurity: Associations with at-risk infant and toddler development. *Pediatrics, 121*(1), 65–72.

Save the Children. (2008). *The child development index: Holding governments to account for children's wellbeing.* Retrieved from http://www.savethechildren.org.uk/en/docs/child-development-index.pdf

Sekar, K. (2006). *Psychosocial support in Tsunami disaster—NIMHANS response in Tamil Nadu, Pondicherry and Andhra Pradesh.* Paper presented at the NIMHANS-WHO India Workshop on Psychosocial Support in Disaster, Bangalore, India.

Sen, A. (2003). Developing child and adolescent mental health services in India: Are we ready for it? *Indian Journal of Psychiatry, 45*(2), 3–4.

Shah, L. P., & Sheth, R. B. (1998, April). Development of child and adolescent mental health in India: The last 40 Years. In C. R. Pfeffer & J. Y. Hattab (Eds), *IACAPAP Bulletin*, 8. Retrieved from http://iacapap.org/bulletins

Shastri, P. C. (2009). Promotion and prevention in child mental health. *Indian Journal of Psychiatry, 51*(2), 88–95. doi:10.4103/0019-5545.49447

Sinha, H. (2009). UN Convention: Rights of persons with disabilities in context mental illness in India. Retrieved from http://www.globalmentalhealth.org/binary_data/393_harshit_sinha_unconvention_paperjan09.pdf

Substance Abuse Mental Health Services Administration. (2003). Fact sheet on school mental health services. Retrieved from http://www.bazelon.org/LinkClick.aspx?fileticket=bkausRzfY80%3D&tabid=134

Thara, R., & Patel, V. (2010). Role of non-governmental organizations in mental health in India. *Indian Journal of Psychiatry, 52* (Suppl 3), 389–395. doi:10.4103/0019-5545.69276

Tuli, K., & Alam, K. (2004). History of mental health sevices in India. *Journal of Personality and Clinical Studies, 20*, 171–180.

World Bank. (2010). *India country overview September 2010*. Retrieved from http://go.worldbank.org/ZUIBUQT360

World Health Organization. (2005). *Child and adolescent mental health policies and plans*. [WHO mental health policy and service guidance package—module 11]. Geneva: Author.

———. (2006). *WHO-AIMS Report on mental health system in Uttarkhand, India*, WHO and Ministry of Health, Dehradun, Uttarkhand, India.

About the Editor and Contributors

The Editor

Usha S. Nayar is Professor at the Tata Institute of Social Sciences in Mumbai, India. She has served as an expert for World Health Organization in the area of Mental Health and Social Change. Besides this, she has contributed to the formulation of many policies in India, such as the National Youth Policy, National Policy for Population and Family Welfare, and the National Child Labor Policy. Her website is www.usnayar.com and she can be contacted at usnayar@gmail.com.

The Contributors

Neli de Almeida, Faculty, The Federal Institute of Education, Science and Technology, Rio de Janeiro, Brazil.

Paula Bedregal, Departamento de Salud Publica (Department of Public Health), Facultad de Medicina (Faculty of Medicine), Pontificia Universidad Catolica de Chile, Chile.

Martín Benavides, Senior Researcher GRADE and Professor Pontificia Universidad Católica Del Perú, Lima, Perú.

Devi Bhuyan, Fellow, International Beliefs and Values Institute (IBAVI), Staunton, Virginia, USA.

Ragnhild Bjørnebekk, Researcher, Norwegian Police University College, Oslo, Norway.

Jorge Augusto Colombo, Professor, Unidad de Neurobiología Aplicada (The Applied Neurobiology Unit) (UNA, CEMIC-CONICET), Buenos Aires, Argentina.

Matthijs Cornelissen, Director, Indian Psychology Institute, Pondicherry, India.

Ajit K. Dalal, Professor, Department of Psychology, University of Allahabad, India.

Ashima Das, Consultant, Saptarishi Management and Research Foundation, Mumbai, India.

Shankar Das, Professor & Chair, Centre for Health Policy, Planning & Management, School of Health Systems Studies, Tata Institute of Social Sciences, Mumbai, India.

Maria Paz Guzman, Departamento de Salud Publica (Department of Public Health), Facultad de Medicina (Faculty of Medicine), Pontificia Universidad Catolica de Chile, Chile.

Ingunn Hagen, Professor, Department of Psychology, Norwegian University of Science and Technology (NTNU), Trondheim, Norway.

María Julia Hermida, Research Fellow, Unidad de Neurobiología Aplicada (UNA, CEMIC-CONICET), Buenos Aires, Argentina.

Dan Y. Jacobsen, Associate Professor, Department of Psychology, Norwegian University of Science and Technology (NTNU), Trondheim, Norway.

Martin Knapp, Professor of Social Policy and Director of the Personal Social Services Research Unit, London School of Economics and Political Science, UK.

Patricia L. Kohl, Assistant Professor, Washington University, St. Louis, Missouri, USA.

George Leibowitz, Assistant Professor, Department of Social Work, College of Education and Social Services, University of Vermont, Burlington, Vermont, USA.

Sebastián Javier Lipina, Professor, Unidad de Neurobiología Aplicada (The Applied Neurobiology Unit) (UNA, CEMIC CONICET), Buenos Aires, Argentina.

David McDaid, Senior Research Fellow, PSSRU and European Observatory on Health Systems and Policies, London School of Economics and Political Science, UK.

Manju Mehta, Professor, All India Institute of Medical Sciences, New Delhi, India.

Helia Molina, Professor, Departamento de Salud Publica (Department of Public Health), Facultad de Medicina (Faculty of Medicine), Pontificia Universidad Catolica de Chile, Chile.

Priya Nayar, Graduate Student, Department of Media Studies, School of Public Engagement, The New School University, New York, USA.

About the Editor and Contributors

Latha Nrugham, Researcher, National Centre for Suicide Research and Prevention, Institute of Clinical Medicine, Faculty of Medicine, University of Oslo, Norway.

Michael O'Loughlin, Professor, Derner Institute for Advanced Psychological Studies and School of Education, Adelphi University, New York, USA.

Beatriz Oré, Head, School of Psychology, Universidad Antonio Ruiz de Montoya, Lima, Perú.

Esha Patnaik, Counsellor, Indian Institute of Management, Ahmedabad, India.

Raman Deep Pattanayak, Senior Research Associate, All India Institute of Medical Sciences, New Delhi, India.

Vandana Verma Prakash, Head, Department of Psychology, Fortis International Hospital, Noida, Uttar Pradesh, India.

Irene Rizzini, Professor, Department of Social Work, Pontifical Catholic University of Rio de Janeiro (PUC-Rio), Rio de Janeiro, Brazil.

Jeanette Schmid, Research Fellow, Centre for Social Development in Africa, University of Johannesburg, South Africa.

María Soledad Segretin, Research Fellow, Unidad de Neurobiología Aplicada (UNA, CEMIC-CONICET), Buenos Aires, Argentina.

Mamta Sharma, Assistant Professor, Punjabi University, Patiala, India.

Vandana Sharma, Professor, Punjabi University, Patiala, India.

Craig N. Shealy, Professor of Graduate Psychology and Executive Director, International Beliefs and Values Institute (IBAVI), Staunton, Virginia, USA.

Lee G. Sternberger, Professor of Graduate Psychology and Executive Director, Office of International Programs James Madison University, Harrisonburg, Virginia, USA.

Shirley Telles, Director of Research, Patanjali Yogpeeth, Haridwar, Uttarakhand, India.

Maeve Thornton, Research Fellow, Economic and Social Research Institute, Dublin, Ireland.

Neharika Vohra, Professor, Indian Institute of Management, Ahmedabad, India.

Index

academic performance, poverty and, 142–144
    ability attribute, 148
    Dweck's seminal work, 143
    early intervention programs, 150–151
    effort attribute, 148
    learned resourcefulness model, 149
    parent involvement, effect of, 146
    planfulness attribute, 148
    policy and attitude level for enhancing academic performance, 151–152
    relation between motivation and achievement, 143
    resourcefulness approach, 151–152
    self-regulatory task-engagement behaviors, 148–149
    sense of self-efficacy in, 148–149
    Stipek and Ryan study, 143
academic resilience research, 145–146
academic stress, 227
    information age and, 230
    learning expectations at different grade levels, 229
    points, 229
    scale for measuring, 234–236
Active Parenting, 178
adolescence, psychosocial-biological stage of, 230
adolescents' IQ, impact of poverty on, 258–259
adrenocorticotrophic hormone (ACTH), 232, 236
adulthood economic consequences and childhood disorders, 4–5

ahata nada (perceivable sonic currents), 232
AIDS epidemic, 64
American Humane Association, 163
Analyst in the Inner City, The (Altman), 277
Anatomy of an Epidemic (Whitaker), 279
Anglo-American child protection system, 162, 165
Anglophone child welfare systems, 159–162
antecedents, behavior, and consequences (ABC) chart, 32
antisocial behavior
    among deliquents, 77–78
    definition, 76–77
    mitigating factors, 78–81
    relation with violence, 77–78
antisocial conduct on adult labor market, effects of, 5
anxiety disorders, 30, 35, 62, 78, 131, 249, 311
Argentina, developmental cognitive neuroscience in, 262–270
    cognitive exercising program, 260–266
    cognitive training, 267–270
    counseling for parents, teachers, and caregivers, 270
    nutritional supplementation program, 266, 270
    social and health counseling, 267
    teacher training program, 266
Ashtanga yoga program, 222
attention catcher, 235
attention deficit problems

attention deficit hyperactivity disorder (ADHD), 30, 78, 118, 261, 279
  employment rates and, 5
  medications for, 279–280
  prescription of SSRIs, 280
  yoga for, 223
attention, effects of socioeconomic disparities on, 259–261
Attention Network Test, 260
attribution theory, 147
auto-regulatory healing mechanism of body, 233

Be a Fit Kid program, 222
behavioral parent training (BPT), 174. *See also* disruptive behavior problems
  child welfare system in, 176
  coercive process, 177
  ecological-transactional model, 176–177
  evidence-based, 178
  interventions, 178–180
  maltreated parent-child dyads and, 180
  for maltreatment prevention, 181
  parent-child interaction and, 177
  theoretical perspectives on, 175–177
behavioral problems and later criminal activities, 5
beliefs, 242
Beliefs, Events, and Values Inventory (BEVI), 241, 243, 251
  factor analytic and correlation matrix of, 246
  formative variables of, 247–250
  intercorrelations with Needs Closure, 250
  interrelated components of, 244–246
  reliability of, 246
  validity of, 246
Biederman, Joseph, 279–280
Bisht Battery of Stress Scale, 234–235
brain development, 257–258
  effects of poverty on, 258–261
brain plasticity in humans, 257
Brazilian National Policy for People with Disability, 189

Broca's area in children, maturation of, 259
Browne, Richard, 231

California Evidence-Based Clearinghouse for Child Welfare, 179
Canadian child welfare system, 161
catecholamines, 232
Center for Epidemiological Studies Depression Scale (CES-D), 297
chakras of body, 231
Charles, Marilyn, 281
Child and Adolescent Psychiatric Assessment (CAPA), 34
childhood and adolescent depression
  case illustration, 28
  case of major depression, 22
  clinical evaluation, 30–34
  cognitive distortions, 24
  comorbid conditions, 30
  cross-cultural variations, 28–29
  developmental differences in clinical presentation, 27–28
  diagnosis of, 21–22
  diagnostic instruments and rating scales, 33–34
  differential diagnosis, 30
  Draw-a-Person (DAP) test, 32–33
  DSM-IV definition, 22
  epidemiology, 22–23
  ethnic differences, 23
  etiology, 24–26
  familial and social factors, 24–25
  gender differences, 23
  genetic factors, 26
  historical perspective, 21
  hypothalamo-pituitary-adrenal (HPA) axis abnormalities and, 26
  incidence rates, 22
  incompetence and lack of self-esteem in, 24
  interventions for, 34–35
  life events and stressors, 25–26
  neurobiological factors, 26

policies and programs, 35–36
prevalence rates, 22–23
projective tests, 32–33
psychological factors, 24
psychosocial factors, 29–30
repetitive transcranial magnetic stimulation (rTMS) for, 35
school factors, 25
selective serotonin reuptake inhibitors (SSRIs) for, 35
socioeconomic status, 23
somatic symptoms, 22
special treatment considerations, 35
subsyndromal symptoms, 22
Childhood Depression Inventory (CDI), 34
Childhood Depression Rating Scale (CDRS), 34
childhood victimization and disruptive behavior problems, 177
child mental health in Latin America
of 0–3-year-olds, 309–310
of 4–5-year-olds, 310
Chile Crece Contigo for children, 314
early childhood development, 313–314
epidemiological situation in, 309–313
implementation of new services, 317–318
JUNAEB's Student Health Program, 318
of school-age population, 310–313
Skills for Life program (SFL), 318–321
strategies for early development, 314–315
support program on biopsychosocial development, 315–317
vulnerable children and dysfunctional families, 317
child protection model in South Africa
Anglophone, 203–204
barriers to applying developmental principles, 210–211
collaborative participative approach, 208–210
developmental social welfare (DSW), 204–205
economic and social integration of social welfare, 205
family support services, 206
integrated developmental child welfare model, 204–208
integration of family group members' knowledge into child welfare services, 209–210
intra- and intersectoral collaboration to child welfare approach, 207–208
macro-approaches to social services, 206
micro-approaches to social services, 206
mobile services to child welfare approach, 208
operationalization of a developmental discourse, 210–211
socioeconomic integration of child welfare approach, 208
child protection system, 161
Maoris perception, 161
racial and cultural bias, 161
shortcomings of, 160
child-rearing practices, 28, 160
Children's Apperception Test (CAT), 32
Chile Crece Contigo (Chile Grows Along With You), 309, 316, 318
Civilization and its Discontents (Freud), 277
Civil Partnership and Certain Rights and Obligations of Cohabitants Act (2010), 292
coercion theory, 175, 177
cognitive behavioral therapy (CBT), 65
cognitive development, poverty and, 258–259
Coleman Report, 147–148
collaborative participative child welfare approach, 208–210
community-related factors for academic failure, 142
Computer Assisted Personal Interview (CAPI), 298
conduct disorders, 5, 9, 13, 30, 175, 177, 179, 281, 338, 343
coping of stress, 227–228
corpus callosum, 232
corticotrophin-releasing hormone (CRH), 232
cost-consequences analysis, 10

cost-effectiveness analysis (CEA), 3, 6–7, 9, 16
cost-utility analysis (CUA), 8, 11
cultural translator, 166
cultural unconscious, knowledge of, 284–285

decision making, family's style of, 166
developmental cognitive neuroscience, 261–262
   in Argentina, 262–270
developmental psychopathology, 242, 244, 248
developmental social welfare (DSW), 200,
   204–205, 208
Diagnostic Interview for Children and Adolescents
   (DICAs), 34
Dialectical Behavior Therapy (DBT), 49
diathesis, 46, 229
diathesis-stress model, 229
Disability Adjusted Life Year (DALY), 11
disadvantaged children
   development of resilient personality, 146
   early intervention programs, 150–151
   educational resourcefulness model for, 147–149
   learned helplessness of, 144
   negative outcomes, 145
   policy and attitude level for enhancing academic performance, 151–152
   poverty and academic performance, 142–144
   teachers' expectations from, 143–144
disruptive behavior problems, 174. *See also*
   behavioral parent training (BPT)
   among kindergarten-aged children, 175
   child neglect, 175
   cumulative risk factors, 176–177
   neglected school age children and, 175
   physical abuse and, 175
   risk factors, 177–178
   school aggression, 175
disruptive disorders, 30, 311
Dyadic Adjustment Scale (DAS), 297

early intervention program, for academic
   achievement, 150–151

ecological-transactional model of BPT, 176–177
economic evaluations
   cost-effectiveness study, 6–7
   cost measures, 8–9
   cost-utility analyses, 10–11
   effectiveness measurement, 9–10
   evidence base, 11–12
   health-related quality of life measures, 10
   monetary units, 11
   nature of trade-off, 10
   question and perspective to be addressed, 7–8
economic evidences, uses of
   in commissioning of therapies, 14–15
   in guideline development, 14
   for lobbyists and advocacy groups, 13
   in policy development and monitoring, 13–14
   for World Health Organization (WHO), 13–14
Edison, Thomas Alva, 145
educational resourcefulness model, for
   disadvantaged children, 147–149
EI Self, 243–245
EI theoretical framework, 241, 243
emotional attunement, 246–248, 251–252
Emotional Lives of Children and the Possibility of
   Classroom as Community, The, 282
endorphins, 232, 236
Epidemiology of Child and Adolescent Disorders
   study, 175
Equilintegration Theory (EI), 241, 243
   hypotheses and principles of, 243–244
ethanol and emotional health of individual, 232
EUROFIT battery of tests, 224
event related potential (ERP) techniques, 261
Eyberg, Sheila, 180

Families Act (1989), 162
Family Group Conferencing (FGC), 159
   abridged "partnership" models, 170
   in Anglo-American child protection context, 165
   authors of, 162
   children's mental health issues and, 167–169

coordinator, role of, 163, 165–166
cost factor, 169
countries implemented in, 162
date, selection of, 163
for developing countries, 169–170
diversity and, 165–167
family private time, 164–165
information-giving phase, 164
middle-class European values and, 161
Ontario program, 167
phases of, 163–165
preliminary processes, 164
preparation process, 163
and principle of inclusion, 166
principles of, 162–163
in promoting cultural sense of belonging, 167
role of family group in developing safety, 170–171
short-term plans, 165
Toronto model, 164
family group participation and conferencing experience, 170–171
family network, role in deciding child's future safety, 165
family private time, 164–165
First Nations children, 161
Forum BEVI Project, 241, 246, 251
Forum on Education Abroad, 246
Future of an Illusion, The (Freud), 277

globalization of Western medical models, of mental health, 277–280

hathayoga, 126
Head Start Program for Black children, 147
health-related quality of life measures, 10
HIV/AIDS counseling, 66
HIV/AIDS epidemic, 58
 and effectiveness of highly active antiretroviral therapy (HAART), 60
 mode of infection, 59
 mother-to-child transmission (MTCT) mode, 59
 National AIDS Control Organization (NACO) estimates, 60
 people living with HIV/AIDS (PLHA), 60
HIV/AIDS, impact on child and adolescent mental health
 community-based approaches, 67–68
 family-based approaches, 66–67
 household income and savings, impact on, 63
 Indian scenario, 58–60
 individual and school-based approaches, 65–66
 negative impact of life, 58
 policy and programs, 68–70
 psychosocial interventions, 65–70
 socioeconomic and psychological impacts, 60–65
Human Development Index (HDI), 58–59, 79

Ida Nadi, 231
inclusion, principle of, 166
Incredible Years, 178–180
India, mental health in contemporary
 of children and adolescents, 346–348
 hyperkinetic syndrome in children, 338
 Integrated Child Protection Scheme (ICPS), 344
 Juvenile Justice Act (2000), 346
 Juvenile Justice (Care and Protection of Children) Act (2000), 345
 Mental Health Act (1987), 345
 mental health legislation, 345–346
 mental health policy, 343–348
Muskaan, 339
 Narcotic Drugs & Psychotropic Substances Act (1985), 345
 National Institute of Mental Health and Neuro Sciences (NIMHANS), 340
 National Policy for Children, 344
 National Trust for Welfare of Persons with Autism, Cerebral Palsy, Mental Retardation and Multiple Disabilities Act (1999), 345
 NGOs, role in providing mental health services, 342–343

Persons with Disabilities (Equal Opportunities, Protection of Rights and Full Participation) Act (1995), 345
poverty, effect of, 337–338
prevalence rates of psychiatric disorders, 338
Protection of Women from Domestic Violence Act (2005), 345
PWD Act (1995), 346
Rehabilitation Council of India Act (1992), 345
School Health Annual Report Program (SHARP), 343
school, role in mental health needs of students, 340–341
status of mental health services, 339–340
traditional mental health resources, 341–342
Indian knowledge systems, 126–128
Indian school systems, 132–133
  effects of persistent malnutrition and under nourishment, 136–137
  experience of psychological vulnerability, 133–135
  and loss of childhood, 133–135
  trends of education, 133–135
information-giving phase of FGC, 164
integrated developmental child welfare model, 204–208
International Beliefs and Values Institute, 246
intra- and intersectoral collaboration to child welfare approach, 207–208
intrapsychic notion of clinical practice, 283–284
Ireland
  Article 41, 292
  divorce, prevalence of, 291
  family relationships, 294–295
  family structure, literature review, 292–293
  influence of Catholic Church on family life, 292
  National Longitudinal Study of Children, 295–304
  remarriage, prevalence of, 291–292
  socioeconomic factors of, 293
  traditional family unit in, 291–292

jnanayoga, 126

kapalabhati, 221
Kiddie Schedule of Affective Disorders and Schizophrenia for School-age Children-Present and Lifetime (K-SADS-PL), 33–34
Kleinian psychoanalytic theory, 281
komal (soft) notes, 321

Lacey, case study of, 241
learned resourcefulness model, 149
learning disabilities, 77
liberatory psychoanalysis, case for, 275–277
life transition of a child, 151
Lincoln, Abraham, 145
"lotus in the mud", 142, 145
low-socioeconomic status (SES) children
  academic performance of, 143–144
  selective attention task among, 261

macro-approaches to social services, 206
maltreatment, risk of, 176
mastery-oriented children, academic achievement of, 144
medial temporal/memory system, 260
media technologies and mediators for well-being
  children's changing media habits, 101
  children's participation and protection, 98–99
  from a child rights perspective, 100
  contextualization of, 99–100
  coping with Internet, 101–103
  development of digital media literacy, 107–108
  idea of privacy and personal information, 103
  Internet usage, 103–104
  media generation, 97–98
  and mental health, 104–105
  policies at national level for, 108
  reduction of risk among young media users, 106–108
  social networking sites, 105
  video games, 102
Medicina Musica, 231

mental disability, in context of Brazilian law, 189.
    See also Rio de Janeiro shelter system
    definition, 189
    expenditure of public resources for, 198
    measuring extent of disability, 189–190
    policies to promote family ties and return of
        children, 196–198
    psychological support, 198
    reliance on institutionalization needs, 197
    Statute on the Child and the Adolescent, 188,
        194, 197–198
mental health needs and FGC, 167–169
mental health, of school-going children
    child guidance clinics for, 139
    effects of persistent malnutrition and under
        nourishment, 136–137
    experience of psychological vulnerability,
        133–135
    familial relationship patterns, effect of, 131–132
    learner centered curricula for, 139
    media explosion, impact on, 137–138
    parent-child relationship and, 139
    psychopharmacological aid, 139
    suggestions for development and maintenance
        of, 138–140
mental health problems, economic implications
    adulthood economic implications, 4–5
    child and adolescent, 4
    commissioning of therapies, 14–15
    comparative costs and outcomes, 7–8
    cost-benefit analyses, of mental health care
        interventions, 11
    cost measurement associated with a disorder or
        its treatment, 8–9
    effectiveness measurement, 9–10
    efficiency and equity, 5–6
    evidence base, 11–12
    formulation and monitoring of policy, 13–14
    guideline development of cost-effectiveness of
        the intervention, 14
    impact of lobbyists and advocacy groups, 13
    resource distribution barrier, 15
    trade-off between better outcomes and higher
        costs, 10
    utility measures, 10–11
mental health systems, efficiency of, 6
micro-approaches to social services, 206
middle-class parenting failures, 160
Mindfulness Based Cognitive Therapy (MBCT),
    49
mood diary, 32
music therapy for stress, 231–237
    biochemical and electrical memory material,
        role of, 232
    Hindustani music, 231–232
    Indian, 230–232
    levels of adrenal corticosteroids post, 236–237
    physiological approach, 232
    popular Indian ragas, 231
    psychological approach, 232–233
    raga darbari kanada, 233–237
    raginis, 231
    therapeutic benefits of, 233

nada yoga, 233
National Coordinating Center for the Integration
    of People with Disability, 189
National Institute for Health and Clinical
    Excellence (NICE), 14
National Institute of Mental Health (NIMH), 34
    Diagnostic Interview Schedule for Children
        (DISC), 34
National Longitudinal Study of Children, Ireland,
    295–304
    family context variables, 298
    family environment, 303–304
    long parent families, 303
    methodology, 296–298
    parameters measured, 295–296
    reconstituted families, 302–303
    sample, 298–302
    scales used, 296–298
National Mental Health Strategy and Culture of
    Peace General Plan (2005–2010), 326

Needs Closure scale, 246–247, 251
  intercorrelations with BEVI, 250
  interrelationship with other scales, 248
neglected school age children and behavior problems, 175
neural language processing, role of poverty in, 259–260
neural plasticity in humans, 257
neuron endocrine system, 232
Nobody's Perfect program, 316
Norway, violence in, 76–77, 81–83
  factors contributing to, 81–82
  gang-problems, 82
  means of violence prevention, 81
  out of control youngsters, 83
  retrospective life-course study about youngsters out of control, 83–91
  treatment and social policy for youngsters out of control, 91–92
Nurturing Parenting, 176–178, 180

oppositional defiant disorder (ODD), 30, 249, 281, 310–311
orphanhood and HIV infection, 63

Parent–Child Interaction Therapy (PCIT), 178, 180
parent–child relationship, nature in Indian society, 139
Parents as Teachers, 178
personality disorders, 30, 47, 177, 346
Peru, approach to mental health
  childcare, 331
  domestic violence and, 332–335
  dynamic between care and violence in childcare, 331–332, 334
  ecological perspective, 334
  encounters of children, 328–331
  impact of poverty, 325–326
  objectives of study, 327
  protective factors, 333
Pianta Child–Parent Relationship Scale, 297

Pingala Nadi, 232
Positive Parenting Program (Triple P), 178–180
post-traumatic stress disorder (PTSD), 250
  and yoga, 224
poverty. *See also* academic performance, poverty and
  brain development and, 258–261
  cognitive development and, 258–259
  India, effect on mental health, 337–338
  neural language processing and, 259–260
  Peru, effect on mental health, 325–326
poverty-AIDS-crime complex, 203
pranic healing, 233
Preschool Age Psychiatric Assessment (PAPA), 33
pro-social behavior, 250–251, 296
psychic distress in children, 281–282

Quality Adjusted Life Year (QALY), 10–11, 14

Rabbit-proof Fence (film), 161
Radical Hope (Lear), 283
raga Darbari Kanada, effect on stress, 233–237
Ramsay, Carolyn, 285
rational disaster, 230
reactance theory, 144
Reactive Attachment Disorder (RAD), 249
relaxation therapy, 221
resiliency, concept of, 145
  community and social institutions, role of, 146
  and invulnerability, 146
resilient children, 145–146
  innate personal competencies associated with, 144
resource barriers, in mental health care, 15
retrospective life-course study about youngsters out of control, 83–91
  behavior and perpetrator pattern, 87–88
  family experiences, 88–89
  influence of media, 90–91
  vs ordinary youngsters, 84–87
  school experiences, 89–90
  sexual abuse, impact of, 89

social policy and treatment, 91–92
Rio de Janeiro shelter system, 188
    children in, 190–191
    children's connections to outside world, 195
    Continuous Cash Benefit Program, 194–195
    diagnosis of disabilities, 192–194
    family visits, 196
    Guardianship Councils, 192
    levels of functioning of children admitted, 192
    loss of family connections, 195–196
    mixed shelters, 192–194
    non-specified mental retardation, cases of, 194
    non-specified psychological development disorder, cases of, 194
    non-utilization of benefits by families, 194–195
    residency of children in, 194
    severe childhood encephalopathy, cases of, 193
    specialized shelters, 192–193, 196

Sanders, Matt, 179
saptak (seven chakras), 231
Schmid-Leiman transformation, 246
schooling, impact of
    authoritarian schooling, effective and viable alternatives to, 122–123
    communication, pragmatics of, 116
    competitive mentality, development of, 118–119
    education and scientific method of, 123–126
    from implicit curriculum, 116–122
    Indian knowledge systems, 126–128
    mental health of school-going children. *See* mental health, of school-going children
    motivation and will, corrupting influence of, 120–121
    standard classroom layout, problems with, 118–119
    standard school environment, 116–117
    traditional education system, negative effects of, 118–122
shahtriya ragas, 233

shuddha (pure) swaras, 231
Skills for Life program (SFL), 318–321
    future in Chile, 321
    objectives and beneficiaries, 319
    program management, 319–320
    structure of, 320–321
    validation of, 319
social services
    macro-approaches to, 206
    micro-approaches to, 206
socioeconomic integration, of child welfare approach, 208
socioemotional processes, role of, 250–251
South Africa
    AIDS epidemic, 203
    Anglophone child protection model, 203–204
    barriers to applying developmental principles, 210–211
    Black South Africans, living conditions, 203
    Children's Act (No. 38 of 2005), 204
    child welfare models, 200–203
    collaborative participative child welfare approach, 208–210
    developmental social welfare (DSW), 204–205
    economic and social integration of social welfare, 205
    family support services, 206
    integrated developmental child welfare model, 204–208
    intra- and intersectoral collaboration to child welfare approach, 207–208
    macro-approaches to social services, 206
    micro-approaches to social services, 206
    mobile services to child welfare approach, 208
    operationalization of a developmental discourse, 210–211
    poverty-AIDS-crime complex, 203
    problems with child protection system, 204
    service provision and social security net in, 203
    socioeconomic integration of child welfare approach, 208

Western model social work services, 203–204
spiritual hypnosis assisted therapy, 224
Strengths and Difficulties Questionnaire (SDQ), 296, 298, 302
stress
　academic, 229–231
　classical music therapy for, 231–237
　cognitive approach to, 228
　coping of, 227–228
　diathesis-stress model, 229
　hypothalamus activity during, 228
　psychological manifestations during, 228
　theoretical approaches, 228–229
substance abuse, 30
　disorders, 78
Suicidal Child (Pfeffer), 42
suicidality, among children and adolescents
　attempted suicide, 43
　Buddhist principles for, 49
　case study, 44–46
　Columbia Classification Algorithm of Suicide Assessment, 42
　coping skills, 47
　definitions of, 41–44
　effective therapy for, 48–49
　medical lethality, 43
　mood disorders, 46–47
　operationalized criteria of, 42
　parasuicide, 43
　presence of deep ambivalence, 44
　risk assessment, 48
　risk factors, 46–48
　suicidal intent, 43–44
　systematic review of, 39
　WHO/EURO study, 43
Systematic Training for Effective Parenting (STEP), 178

Taittreya Upanishad, 220
Tavistock Clinic, 281
tivra (fast) notes, 232

Tough Love, 178
Tower of London task, 221, 264
transcultural writings on trauma, 284

ubuntu, notion of, 209
unconscious knowledge, 284–285
Unsatisfied Basic Needs (UBN) homes, 262

Vidyasagar, Ishwar Chandra, 145
violence
　in Norwegian context, 76–77, 81–83
　WHO's definition, 76

Webster-Stratton, Carolyn, 180
Western medical models of mental health, globalization of, 277–280
Western model social work services, 203–204
Western psychiatric notion, 277–278
World Program of Action Concerning Disabled Persons, 189

yoga, 342
　beneficial effects, 224
　breathing practices, 220
　challenges to teaching and testing of effects, 224–225
　for childhood anxiety, 221
　for children, 219–224
　difficulties associated with research, 225
　as intervention for PTSD, 224
　for irritable bowel syndrome, 221
　kapalabhati, 221
　for memory improvement, 221
　mental benefits, 220–223
　nada, 233
　physical exercise and, 225
　prepubertal children and, 220
　psychological impact of, 222
　as stress coping strategy, 222
　understandability of, 225

Lightning Source UK Ltd.
Milton Keynes UK
UKHW032308171022
410613UK00011B/1472

9 789353 287313